W9-CJO-254

American Foreign Policy Since World War II

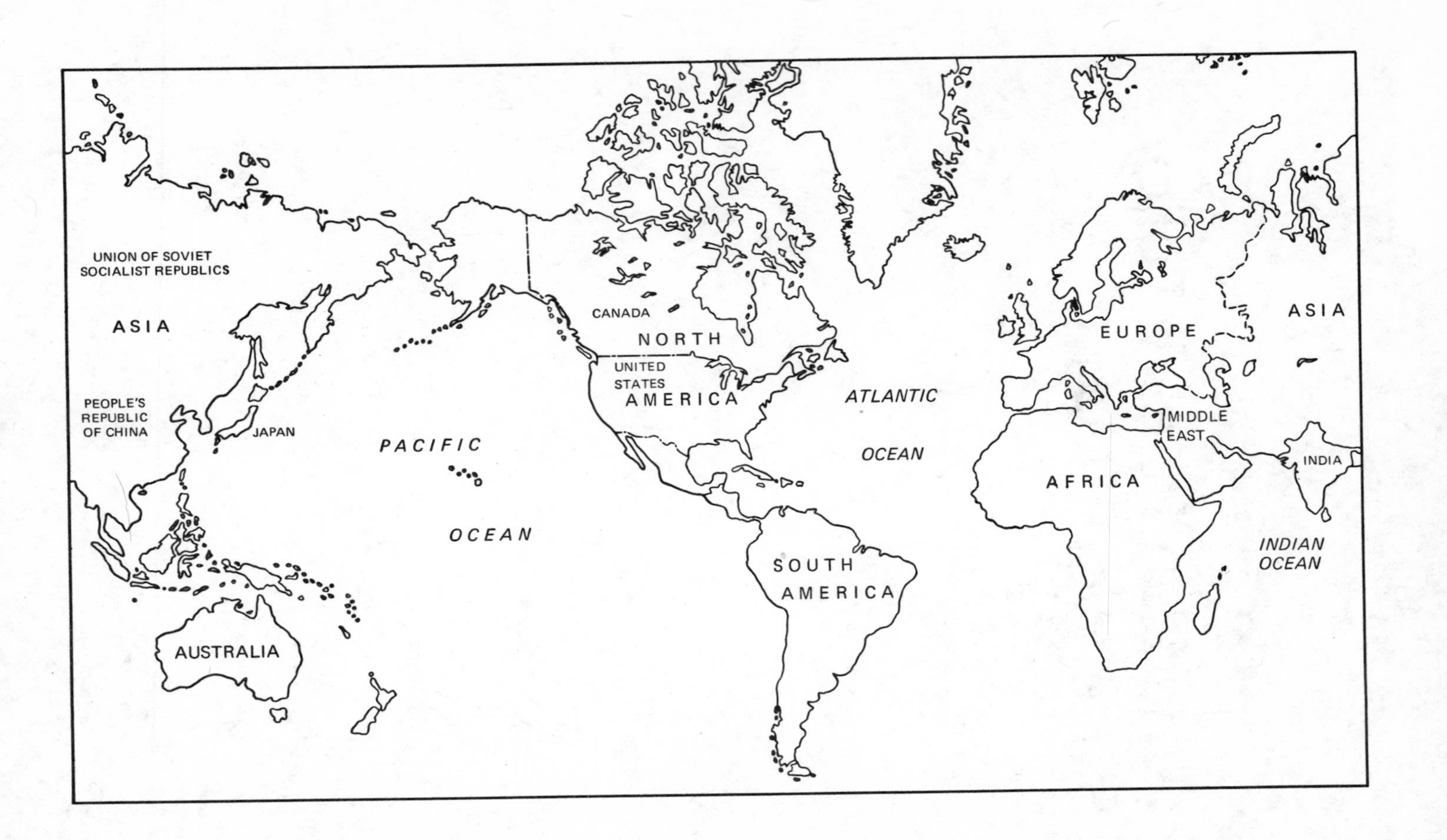
UNION OF SOVIET SOCIALIST REPUBLICS
ASIA
PEOPLE'S REPUBLIC OF CHINA
JAPAN
AUSTRALIA
PACIFIC
OCEAN
CANADA
NORTH
UNITED STATES
AMERICA
ATLANTIC
OCEAN
SOUTH
AMERICA
EUROPE
ASIA
MIDDLE EAST
INDIA
AFRICA
INDIAN OCEAN

American Foreign Policy Since World War II

Eighth Edition

John Spanier
University of Florida

Generously Donated to
The Frederick Douglass Institute
By Professor Jesse Moore
Fall 2000

HOLT, RINEHART AND WINSTON
New York Chicago San Francisco Dallas
Montreal Toronto London Sydney

Library of Congress Cataloging in Publication Data

Spanier, John W
American foreign policy since World War II.

Bibliography: p. 258
Includes index.
1. United States—Foreign relations—1945–
I. Title.
E744.S8 1980 327.73 79-20415
ISBN 0-03-054081-X

Copyright © 1960, 1962, 1965, 1968 by Frederick A. Praeger, Inc.
Copyright © 1971, 1973, 1977 by Praeger Publishers, Inc.
Copyright © 1980 by Holt, Rinehart and Winston
All rights reserved
Printed in the United States of America
0 1 2 3 059 9 8 7 6 5 4 3 2 1

Preface to the Eighth Edition

This edition appears as the Carter administration ends its first term of office. It is a time of widespread concern and uncertainty with American foreign policy. International events increasingly crowd in upon us and affect our everyday lives. Foreign affairs are no longer matters of concern just for the few (the policy makers who look after the nation's security) but for all of us because events beyond our boundaries are profoundly dislocating our economy, lifestyles, and standards of living. Americans, once confident about the future as they faced history, suddenly feel more and more uneasy as they look toward the future with foreboding. History no longer seems benign; indeed, it often appears hostile and America powerless to do much about it. In this context, the reexamination of the fundamental assumptions underlying the nation's foreign policy, which began during the Vietnam war, continues. It is the purpose of this book to provide the reader with both background and perspective on the role the United States has played in the world since the close of World War II so that he may judge for himself the current and past efforts of postwar administrations and evaluate what America's role should be today and in the future.

Two particular problems today confront the author of an analytical history of recent and contemporary events. One of these is how to convey to the reader, especially the younger reader who is likely to be a college student, an impression of the past without overwhelming him with a chronological recitation of all the events that together constitute the record of American foreign policy since World War II. The temptation is to concentrate on the more recent past and condense, if not eliminate, accounts of many past occurrences. After all, to most students born during the 1950s, much pre-Vietnam history might as well be ancient Greek history. Precisely because of that, I have made cuts for this edition, but only where I felt this could be done without seriously affecting the outlines of what did happen. Indeed, if the contemporary reader is to gain a perspective on the last three decades of America's active participation in world affairs, past events become more important, and too abbreviated an account of them can only produce a seriously distorted understanding of recent and contemporary events.

A knowledge of past events becomes all the more important because of the second problem confronting the political analyst: the continued attempts to view and seek to understand the cold war and *détente* through the prism of Vietnam. This approach suggests that, if the Vietnam war was the end product of our prior policy, the entire record of American foreign policy since 1945 stands condemned. For if Vietnam was allegedly the result of our great power and the instinct of the powerful to extend their control, could not this same "arrogance of power" have been a reason for the eruption of the cold war itself? Or, if Vietnam demonstrated that American capitalism, in its never-ending search for foreign markets and natural resources, would crush any national liberation movement that sought to throw off the imperialist (that is, American) economic chains, then could it not be equally true that this same capitalism after 1945 tried to roll back Russian power in Eastern Europe in order to capture new markets for American products? Indeed, had it not attempted during World War II and immediately thereafter to destroy the Soviet revolution, committed as the latter was to the destruction of world capitalism of which the United States later emerged as the leading exponent? Or, if Vietnam were said to be the product of American leaders' misperceptions of the nature of the Communist threat and the stakes at issue in the small Southeast Asian country, could it not be that a similarly distorted view of Stalin's Russia after 1945 led the American government to see a threat where none existed (or at least, to see a vastly exaggerated Soviet threat), and thus led Washington to overreact to Russia's essentially defensive moves in Eastern Europe by launching an anti-Communist crusade to ward off a presumed Communist world revolution? Or, lastly, if Vietnam reflected the result of President Johnson's hardline and aggressive attitudes, was the cold war perhaps not also the product of President Truman's personal anti-Communism and belief that the Soviets understand nothing but force and toughness?

These and other views, spelled out in greater detail, are part of the views of revisionist historians whose views, expressed largely during the Vietnam war, have affected post-Vietnam thinking and writing on American foreign policy. Essentially, their argument is twofold: One, the forces that precipitated the cold war and led to Vietnam exist *within* the United States; and two, but for America's expansionist and aggressive behavior, the world would be at peace. The "natural" harmony of interests among states and the "normal" condition of peaceful relationship among these states would, presumably, reemerge if men wedded to old myths were replaced with new men who recognize present realities or if fundamental structural changes, such as replacing capitalism with socialism, took place within the American system. In any event, the United States is at least as much to blame for the cold war as Russia, if not indeed far more so.

The framework within which we will recount and analyze postwar American foreign policy is quite different from this one, which focuses solely on internal American forces. We, too, will emphasize as one source of American foreign policy its domestic origin. This amalgam of American political values, experience, and history will be called national style. It is our contention that this style, which has shaped the way the nation and its leaders have seen the world and acted in it repeatedly in what can only be considered as characteristically American ways, has had a longer-range and profounder impact on the conduct of United States policy than the personalities and views of individual presidents. We shall also emphasize the nature of the international state system and suggest that the foreign policies of its members are greatly affected by the distribution of power within the state system. The security and independence of each member state are enhanced by a balance of power, whereas an imbalance in its distribution will grant one state a superiority of power that might tempt it to impose its will on a weaker opponent. Thus the balance, by seeking to prevent any state from gaining a predominant power position that enables it to subordinate other states to its control, is the principal "peace strategy" available for states, each of which must be its own protector. This means that a nation's foreign relations—certainly any Great Power's—are largely determined by the requirement of maintaining a balance of power; to neglect this essential task is to risk endangering its security. Since it is a nation's style which shapes how this world beyond its borders is perceived and the role a country defines for itself—including whether and how to play the historic balance of power game—it is the interplay and tension between style and the requirements of the system which is at the heart of our analysis.

The approach, then, to this analysis of American foreign policy is usually called "realist," although exactly what realism is and how it is to be used analytically remain a matter of debate. Other approaches exist, but by the very nature of this book and the attempt to keep it relatively short considering the time span it covers, these are not covered here. I have included short descriptions of at least the revisionist and more radical imperialist schools of thinking, as well as a longer one of the currently popular interdependence model. Students ought to be aware of other ways of interpreting American policy, but obviously I think the combination of national style and state system to be the most productive manner of understanding and analysis. Paperbacks featuring other approaches are available.

Because great stress has been placed in this book on the state system, and because the analysis suggests that the precipitation of the cold war and subsequent American and Soviet behavior were heavily influenced by the post-World War II emergence of a bipolar distribution of power, I have elaborated on this feature, especially in the section on the reexamination of containment in Chapter 8. To an extent, both of the superpowers were trapped by the system. Russia, as a state which has experienced repeated invasions and defeats, sought security by pushing out into Central and Eastern Europe to establish a protective perimeter; the United States, which had twice gone to war in this century to protect Western Europe, viewed Moscow's push toward Western Europe as a threat to its own security, especially when combined with Soviet moves in the area from Iran to Greece. The resulting conflict was the product of each nation's search for security in a basically insecure, if not hostile, systemic environment. Communist ideology and America's national style did exacerbate the conflict, to some extent increasing its scope and intensity. But the basic cause has to be found in the nature of the state system.

If this view of the critical nature of the external environment in which states must live is correct, then American postwar foreign policy can most fruitfully be evaluated by analyzing how well the United States, formerly an isolationist nation, adjusted to the changing distribution of power after the defeat of Germany and Japan. For there was simply no other nation at the time capable of establishing a balance of power in a new world characterized by the collapse of Europe, Soviet expansion, Chinese resurgence, and the birth of a multitude of new nations in the Third World between East and West. Given the United States' inexperience, the suddenness with which it was confronted by "reality," the scope and novelty of the challenges of nuclear technology, revolutionary Communism, the nationalist and social revolutions of the underdeveloped countries, and the increasing economic interdependence of the world after 1973, the American response to its new role in the world needs to be judged in a broader perspective than that of Vietnam alone, although this is not to deny the significance of Vietnam.

In the final analysis, the reader must, of course, judge for himself how he would evaluate the overall record of American foreign policy. Such an evaluation should help shape his own views toward current issues confronting the nation and the positions he feels the United States should adopt toward these problems in this more complex and often bewildering and frustrating contemporary world. The purpose of this book is to provide him with an analytical framework for making such judgments.

Gainesville, Florida
Winter 1979

Contents

chapter 1

the american approach to foreign policy

THE STATE SYSTEM

American foreign policy since World War II is the story of the interaction between the state system and the American style of conducting foreign policy. In this state system, each member—especially the Great Powers, its principal actors—tends to feel a high degree of insecurity. In the absence of a world government which could govern and safeguard it, each state knows that it can depend on no one but itself for its own preservation and safety. Self-protection is the only protection in an essentially anarchical system; understandably, states tend to regard one another as potential adversaries, menaces to each other's territorial integrity and political independence. In short, the very nature of the state system breeds feelings of insecurity, distrust, suspicion, and fear.

It is this atmosphere that produces a constant scramble for power. Enhancing one's power relative to that of a possible foe becomes a principal means of reducing one's own insecurity. When a state perceives its neighbor as a potential enemy, it will try to deter a possible attack by becoming a little stronger than its neighbor; the latter, in its turn, will also fear an attack and, therefore, will perceive its own best interest to lie in sufficient strength to forestall such a contingency, or, failing that, to win the resulting war. Thus, it is not man's alleged aggressive instinct as a "naked ape" or man's presumed desire for acquiring ever greater power that accounts for what is popularly called "power politics"; rather, power politics stems from each state's continuous concern with its security. Because the external environment is perceived by states as menacing to their security—the prerequisite for the enjoyment by each one of them of its particular way of life—they are naturally prone to react fearfully against what they believe to be threats. And in such a context it does not take much to arouse and confirm another state's apprehensions and thereby stimulate reciprocal images of hostility, which each state will find it easy to substantiate by the opponent's behavior. Indeed, this enmity will in most instances be maintained despite contradictory evidence and even avowedly friendly acts. Conciliatory behavior is likely to be dismissed as an indicator of weakness or as a trick to relax one's guard and, therefore, not to be accepted at face value but exploited or guarded against.

In any event, it is easy to understand why in these circumstances states pursue a "balance of power" policy. A balance or equilibrium would make victory in a war less probable for an opponent and certainly very costly in comparison to any possible gains. Logically, therefore, a balance is presumed to be that distribution of power most likely to deter an attack. By contrast, possession of disproportionate power might tempt a state to undertake aggression by making it far less costly to gain a predominant position and impose its will upon other states. In other words, the fundamental assumption underlying the state system is that its members cannot be trusted with power, since they will be tempted to abuse it. Unrestrained power in the system constitutes a threat to all states; power is, therefore, the best antidote to power. As one close observer of international politics, Arnold Wolfers, has noted:

> Under these conditions of anarchy the expectation of violence and even of annihilation is ever-present. To forget this and thus fail in the concern for enhanced power spells the doom of a state. This does not mean open constant warfare; expansion of power at the expense of others will not take place if there is enough counterpower to deter or to stop states from undertaking it. Although no state is interested in a mere balance of power, the efforts of all states to maximize power may lead to equilibrium. If and when that happens, there is "peace" or, more exactly, a condition of stalemate or truce. Under the conditions described here, this balancing of power process is the only available "peace" strategy.

Power thus elicits countervailing power. The basic rule of the "international game" is to resist attempts by any state to expand and seek a predominant position in the international system. Therefore, when the balance is disturbed, equilibrium will tend to be restored by the emergence of counterpower. States ignore at their peril this rule to maintain a balance of power; policy-makers need to be equally careful that they judge correctly the necessary countervailing power.

What all this means is that we can to a very significant degree explain any state's behavior in terms of the ever changing distribution of power. As that distribution changes, so does a state's foreign policy. For example, the impact of a shift in the distribution of power is evident in America's involvements in the two world wars of this century. During most of the nineteenth century and early twentieth century the United States was able to preserve its historical isolation from "power politics" thanks to the balance of power on the European continent maintained by Britain to protect its own security. No one state or coalition of states was able to conquer most of Europe, organize its vast resources in manpower and industrial strength, and then use these to menace the United States. England's opposition to any state's seeking such hegemony therefore made it possible for the United States to remain what today is called "nonaligned."

However, after 1870, when Germany was unified and launched a massive program of industrialization, British power declined relative to Germany's growing capability. The early years of World War I showed clearly that even British and French power together could not contain Germany. With the collapse of Tsarist Russia in the East and the transfer of almost 2 million German soldiers to the Western Front, a German victory became a distinct possibility. It was at that point that Germany's unrestricted submarine warfare, which included attacks on American shipping, precipitated U.S. intervention, and this was what made it possible to contain the German spring offensive of 1918 and led to Germany's defeat.

After victory America retreated into isolationism again, only to be compelled just over two decades later once more to concern itself with the European balance of power. The unexpected German defeat of France in 1940 again confronted the United States with the specter of an invasion and defeat of England. President Franklin D. Roosevelt therefore undertook a number of measures to strengthen Britain to withstand any Nazi assault. He sent fifty old destroyers to help defend the English Channel, and he set up the Lend-Lease program, which made the United States the "arsenal of democracy." The balance of power had made this increasing commitment to Britain necessary, even though such actions increased the risk of war with Germany. In fact, by the time of Pearl Harbor, the United States was already engaged in an undeclared naval war with Germany in the Atlantic, and full-scale war with Germany was merely a matter of time: German submarines would, sooner or later, start sinking American ships carrying war supplies for Britain in order to compel its surrender. The German invasion of Russia in 1941 briefly postponed the Battle of the Atlantic, and when it did take place the United States was already at war. But had Hitler, in 1940–1941, given the order to sink all ships bound for England, President Roosevelt, like President Wilson before him, would have had to ask Congress for a declaration of war.

One further point is worth noting about these two examples, namely, that the issue in neither case was whether the American people wished to go to war against Germany. The isolationist mood was still far too strong. Nevertheless, the United States did intervene in both cases; in neither instance, furthermore, was there any existing commitment, legal or moral, which obligated the nation to intervene. The issue in 1917 and in 1941 was not whether the nation preferred peace and domestic preoccupation to foreign involvement, but what self-preservation obliged it to do. The shifting balance of power left the country little choice if it wished to preserve its security. To sum up: the strategy of any nation in the state system is—or should be—to oppose any state which seeks predominance since this would constitute a threat to its security and national independence. Power is the best antidote to power and a balance of power in the state system provides the best protection for all of its members.

THE AMERICAN NATIONAL STYLE

The particular style which characterized the American approach to World War II and later the Cold War—that is, the distinctive set of national perceptions and repetitive patterns of behavior—was the product of domestic experiences. The priority of internal political and economic tasks, all of which were reinforced by the opening of the West and the subsequent transcontinental drive to the Pacific, led to the depreciation of the importance of foreign policy and the role that power plays in protecting the nation's interests. The ability of the United States to live in isolation during the nineteenth century and a good part of the twentieth century was attributed not to the nation's geographic distance from Europe or to the Royal Navy as the protector of the *Pax Britannica,* but to the nature of democracy. The United States was more than just the world's first "new nation"; it was also the world's first democracy and, as such, the first country in history that would devote itself to improving the lot of the common man, granting each individual the opportunity to enrich and ennoble his life. ("Give me your tired, your poor, your huddled masses yearning to breathe free," reads the inscription on the Statue of Liberty.) The more perfect union was to be an egalitarian society. European concepts of social hierarchy, nobility and titles, and bitter class struggles were not to be planted in its democratic soil. "Here the free spirit of mankind, at length, throws its last fetters off," exclaimed one writer. America was to be a "beacon lighting for all the world the paths of human destiny," wrote Emerson. From the very beginning of their national life, Americans believed strongly in their destiny—to spread, *by example,* freedom and social justice to all men and to lead mankind away from its wicked ways to the New Jerusalem on earth. The massive immigration of the nineteenth century—particularly after 1865—was to reinforce this sense of destiny. "Repudiation of

Europe," as John Dos Passos once said, "is, after all, America's main excuse for being." Europe stood for war, poverty, and exploitation; America, for peace, opportunity, and democracy. But the United States was not merely to be a beacon of a superior democratic domestic way of life. It was also to be an example of a morally superior democratic pattern of international behavior. The United States would voluntarily reject power politics as unfit for the conduct of its foreign policy. Democratic theory posits that man is a rational and moral creature, and that differences among men can be settled by rational persuasion and moral exhortation. Indeed, granted this assumption about man, the only differences that could arise would simply be misunderstandings, and, since man is endowed with reason and a moral sense, what quarrels could not be settled, given the necessary good will? Peace—the result of harmony among men—was thus considered the natural or normal state.

Conversely, conflict was considered a deviation from this norm, caused primarily by wicked statesmen whose morality and reason had been corrupted by the exercise of uncontrolled authority. Power politics was an instrument of selfish and autocratic rulers—that is, men unrestrained by democratic public opinion—who loved to wield it for their own personal advantage. To them, war was a grand game. They could remain in their palatial homes, continuing to eat well and to enjoy the luxuries of life. They suffered none of the hardships of war. These hardships fell upon the ordinary people; it was they who had to leave their families to fight, to endure the higher taxes made necessary by the costs of war, possibly to see their homes destroyed and their loved ones maimed or killed. It was only the despot who thought of war as a sport, as a sort of "bully" fox hunt; the common man, who had to endure all the cruelties of war, was therefore by his very nature peaceful. The conclusion was clear: Undemocratic states were inherently warlike and evil; democratic nations, in which the people controlled and regularly changed their leaders, were peaceful and moral.

American experience seemed to support this conclusion. The United States was a democracy, and it was at peace. Furthermore, peace seemed to be the normal state of affairs. It was therefore logical that democracy and peaceful behavior and intentions should be thought of as synonymous. Americans never asked themselves whether democracy was really responsible for the peace they enjoyed, or whether this peace they assumed to be a natural condition was the product of other forces. The constant wars of Europe appeared to provide the answer: European politics was power politics, and this was because of the undemocratic nature of European regimes. Americans were therefore relieved that they had long ago, at the time of the Revolutionary War, cut themselves off from Europe and its class conflicts and power politics. America had to guard its democratic purity and abstain from any involvement in the affairs of Europe lest it be soiled and corrupted. Nonalignment was therefore the morally correct policy which allowed the United States to quarantine itself from contact with Europe's hierarchical social structures and immoral international habits. At the same time, by confusing the results of geography and international politics with the supposed consequences of democracy, Americans could smugly enjoy their self-conferred moral superiority as the world's first democracy. It was the Monroe Doctrine, proclaimed in 1823, that first stressed, officially and explicitly, this ideological difference between the New and Old Worlds. It declared specifically that the American political system was "essentially different" from that of Europe, whose nations were constantly engaged in warfare. The implication was very clear: Democratic government equals peace, and aristocratic government—which was identified with despotism—means war.

But this association of peace with democracy was not the only reason for the American depreciation of power politics. Another was that the United States was an overwhelmingly one-class society—one in which most shared a common set of middle-class, capitalistic, and democratic values or beliefs. America was unique among nations in this respect. The European countries were, by contrast, three-class societies. In addition to the middle class, they contained in their bodies politic an aristocratic class, whose energies were devoted either to maintaining itself in power or to recapturing power in order to return to the glorious days of a feudal past. Moreover, European urbanization and industrialization during the nineteenth century gave birth to a proletariat, which, because it felt it did not receive a fair share of the national income, became a revolutionary class. The nations of the Old World were, in short, a composite of three elements: a reactionary aristocracy, a democratic middle class, and a revolutionary proletariat. Or, to put it another way, these nations had, in an intellectual as well as a political sense, a right, a center, and a left. The United States had only a center, both intellectually and politically. It had never experienced a feudal past and therefore possessed no large and powerful aristocratic class on the right; and because it was, by and large, an egalitarian society, it also lacked a genuine left-wing movement of protest, such as socialism or communism. America was, as Tocqueville had said, "born free" as a middle-class, individualistic, capitalistic, and democratic society. It was not divided by the kind of deep ideological conflicts that in France, for instance, set one class of Frenchmen against another. No one class was ever so afraid of another that it preferred national defeat to domestic revolution —as in France in the late 1930s, when the *haute bourgeoisie* was so apprehensive of a proletarian upheaval that its slogan became "Better Hitler than Blum [the French Socialist leader]."

Americans in the past have been so in accord on basic values that whenever the nation has been threatened externally the public has become fearful of internal disloyalty. It is one of the great ironies of American society that, while Americans possessed this unity of shared beliefs to a greater degree than any other people, their apprehension of external danger led them, first, to insist upon a general and somewhat dogmatic reaffirmation of loyalty to the "American way of life," and then to hunt for internal groups that might betray this way of life. Disagreement tended to become suspect as disloyalty; men were accused of "un-American" thinking and behavior, and labeled "loyalty or security risks." Perhaps only a society so overwhelmingly committed to one set of values could have been so sensitive to internal subversion and so fearful of internal betrayal; perhaps only a society in which two or more ideologies have long since learned to live together can genuinely tolerate diverse opinions. Who has ever heard of "un-British" or "un-French" activities? The United States has often been called a "melting pot" because of the many different nationality groups it comprises, but, before each generation of immigrants has been fully accepted into American society, it has had to be "Americanized." Few Americans have ever accepted diversity as a value. American society has, in fact, taken great pride in destroying diversity through assimilation.

It was precisely this overwhelming agreement on the fundamental values of American society and Europe's intense class struggles that reinforced the American misunderstanding of the nature and functions of power on the international scene. Dissatisfied groups never developed a revolutionary ideology because the growing prosperity spread to them before they could translate their grievances against the capitalist system into political action. (The black American, of course, represents a clear and important exception.) With the exception of the Civil War, America—politically secure, socially cohesive, and economically prosperous—was able, therefore, to resolve most of its differences peacefully. Living in isolation, this country could therefore believe in an evolutionary, democratic, economically prosperous, historical process; revolution and radicalism were considered bad. In sharp contrast, because of their internal class struggles and external conflicts among themselves, the nations of Europe fully appreciated the role of power politics.

Politics did not, in any event, seem very important to Americans. The United States matured during the nineteenth century, the era of *laissez-faire* capitalism whose basic assumption was that man was economically motivated. It was self-interest that governed the behavior of man; It might be referred to as "enlightened self-interest," but it was nevertheless self-interest. Each individual, seeking to maximize his wealth, responded to the demand of the free market. In an effort to increase his profit, he supplied the product the consumers wanted. The laws of supply and demand therefore transformed each person's economic selfishness into socially beneficial results. The entire society would prosper. The free market was thus considered the central institution that provided "the greatest good for the greatest number." Politics mattered little in this self-adjusting economic system based upon individuals whose combined efforts resulted in the general welfare. The best government was the government that governed least. Arbitrary political interference with the economic laws of the market would only upset the results these laws were intended to produce. Private property, profit, and the free market were thus the keys to ensuring the happiness of man by providing him with abundance. Capitalism, in short, reflected the materialism of the age of industrialization.

To state the issue even more bluntly: Economics was good, politics was bad. This simple dichotomy came naturally to the capitalist middle class. Were the benefits of economic freedom not as "self-evident" as the truths stated in the Declaration of Independence? And had this economic freedom not been gained only by a long and bitter struggle of the European middle class to cut down the authority of the powerful monarchical state, and finally to overthrow it by revolution in France? The middle class, as it had grown more prosperous and numerous, had become increasingly resentful of paying taxes from which the aristocracy was usually exempt, of the restrictions placed upon trade and industry, of the absence of institutions in which middle-class economic and political interests were represented, of the class barriers to the social status that came with careers in the army and in the bureaucracy, and of the general lack of freedom of thought and expression. Since the middle class identified the power of the state with its own lack of freedom, its aim was to restrict this power. Only by placing restraints upon the authority of the state could it gain the individual liberty and, above all, the right to private enterprise it sought. Democratic philosophy stated these claims in terms of the individual's "natural rights" against the state. The exercise of political authority was thus equated with the abuse of that authority and the suppression of personal freedoms. The power of the state had therefore to be restricted to the minimum to ensure the individual's maximum political and economic liberties. It was with this purpose in mind that the American Constitution divided authority between the states and the federal government, and, within the latter, among the executive, legislative, and judicial branches. Federalism and the separation of powers were deliberately designed to keep all governments—and especially the national government—weak. Man's secular problems would be resolved not by the state's political actions but by the individual's own economic actions in society.

Again, both man's economic motivation and the benefits of a government that acts least were considered to be reflected in the American experience. Millions came to the United States from other lands to seek a better way of life. America was the earthly paradise where all men, no matter how poor or humble they had been in the old country, could earn a respectable living. A virgin and underdeveloped land, America presented magnificent opportunities for individual enterprise. First, there was the Western frontier with its rich soil; later, during the Industrial Revolution, the country's bountiful natural resources were exploited. The environment, technology, individual enterprise, and helpful governmental policies enabled the American people to become the "people of plenty." But to earn money was not only economically necessary in order to attain a comfortable standard of living; it was also psychologically necessary in order to gain social status and to earn the respect of one's fellow citizens.

It follows logically that, if material gain confers social respect and position upon men, everyone will preoccupy himself with the pursuit and accumulation of the "almighty dollar." If men in an egalitarian society are judged primarily by their economic achievements, they will concentrate on "getting ahead." It is not surprising, therefore, that money comes closer to being the common standard of value in the United States than in any other country. For money is the symbol of power and prestige; it is the sign of success, just as failure to earn enough money is a token of personal failure. It has been said, not without some justice, that the American prefers two cars to two mistresses.

It was hardly surprising that in these circumstances the solution to international problems should be thought of in economic terms. Economics was identified with social harmony and the welfare of all men; politics was equated with conflict and war and death. Just as the "good society" was to be the product of free competition, so the peaceful international society would be created by free trade. An international *laissez-faire* policy would benefit all states just as a national *laissez-faire* policy benefited each individual within these states. Consequently, people all over the world had a vested interest in peace in order to carry on their economic relations. Trade and war were incompatible. Trade depended upon mutual prosperity (the poor do not buy much from one another). War impoverishes and destroys and creates ill will among nations. Commerce benefits all the participating states; the more trade, the greater the number of individual interests involved. Commerce was consequently nationally and individually profitable and created a vested interest in peace. War, by contrast, was economically unprofitable and therefore obsolete. Free trade and peace, in short, were one and the same cause.

One result of this American depreciation of power was that the United States had historically drawn a clear-cut distinction between war and peace in its approach to foreign policy. Peace was characterized by a state of harmony among nations; power politics, on the other hand, was considered abnormal and war a crime. In peacetime, one needed to pay little or no attention to foreign problems; indeed, to do so would have diverted men from their individual, materialistic concerns and upset the whole scale of social values. The effect of this attitude was clear: Americans turned their attention toward the outside world with reluctance and usually only when they felt provoked—that is, when the foreign menace had become so clear that it could no longer be ignored. Or, to state it somewhat differently, the United States rarely initiated policy; the stimuli that were responsible for the formulation of American foreign policy came from beyond America's frontiers.

Once Americans were provoked, however, and the United States had to resort to force, the employment of this force was justified in terms of the universal moral principles with which the United States, as a democratic country, identified itself. Resort to the evil instrument of war could be justified only by presuming noble purposes and completely destroying the immoral enemy who threatened the integrity, if not the existence, of these principles. American power had to be "righteous" power; only its full exercise could ensure salvation or the absolution of sin. A second result of the depreciation of power was, therefore, that the national aversion to violence became transformed into a national glorification of violence, and wars became ideological crusades to make the world safe for democracy—by democratizing it or by converting the authoritarian or totalitarian states into peaceful, democratic states and thereby banishing power politics for all time. Once that aim had been achieved, the United States could again withdraw into itself, secure in the knowledge that American works had again proved to be "good works." In this context, foreign affairs were an annoying diversion from more important domestic matters. But such diversions were only temporary, since maximum force was applied to the aggressor or warmonger to punish him for his provocation and to teach him that aggression was immoral and would not be rewarded. As a result, American wars were total wars—that is, wars aimed at the total destruction of the enemy.

Third, not only did the American approach to international politics consider peace and war as two mutually exclusive states of affairs; it also divorced force from diplomacy. In peacetime, diplomacy unsupported by force was supposed to preserve the harmony among states. But, in wartime, political considerations were subordinated to force. Once the diplomats had failed to keep the peace with appeals to morality and reason, military considerations became primary. During war, the soldier was placed in charge. Just as the professional medical man had the responsibility for curing his patients of their several maladies, so the military "doctor" had to control the curative treatment of the international society when it was infected with the disease of power politics.

The United States, then, had traditionally rejected the concept of war as a political instrument and the Clausewitzian definition of war as the continuation of politics by other means. Instead, it had regarded war as a politically neutral operation which should be guided by its own professional rules and imperatives. The military officer was a nonpolitical man who conducted his campaign in a strictly military, technically efficient manner. And war was a purely military instrument whose sole aim was the destruction of the enemy's forces and of his despotic regime so that his people could be democratized.

War was thus a means employed to abolish power politics; war was conducted to end all wars. This same moralistic attitude, which was responsible for the Americans' all-or-nothing approach to war—either to abstain from the dirty game of power politics or to crusade for its complete elimination—also militated against the use of diplomacy in its classical sense: to compromise interests, to conciliate differences, and to moderate and isolate conflicts. While, on the one hand, Americans regarded diplomacy as a rational process for straightening out misunderstandings between nations, they were, on the other hand, extremely suspicious of diplomacy. If the United States is by definition moral, it obviously could not compromise; for a nation endowed with a moral mission could hardly violate its own principles. That constituted appeasement and national humiliation. The nation's principles would be transgressed, the nation's interests improperly defended, the national honor stained. For to compromise with the immoral enemy was to be contaminated with evil. Moreover, to reach a settlement with him, rather than wiping him out in order to safeguard those principles, would be to acknowledge American weakness. This attitude toward diplomacy, which, in effect, made its use as an instrument of compromise difficult, thus reinforced the predilection for violence as a means of settling international problems. For war allowed the nation to destroy its evil opponent, while permitting it to keep its moral mission intact and unsullied by any compromises which might infect its purity.

THE CONTRAST BETWEEN SYSTEMIC AND NATIONAL BEHAVIOR

Thus, on the eve of the eruption of the cold war, the American approach to foreign policy contrasted sharply in a number of important respects with the conduct required by the state system. For example, having historically given precedence to domestic affairs, the United States, not surprisingly, has found it difficult to attain and maintain a balance between foreign and domestic priorities. On the whole, American foreign policy has tended to swing from an isolationist position in which the country served as an example of democratic brotherhood and social justice on earth to a posture of massive and violent intervention once provoked. Level-headed, consistent participation in the international system has been difficult; all-or-nothing swings have been the more common pattern.

Furthermore, the American perception of an international harmony of interests stood in stark contrast to the state system's emphasis on the inevitability of conflict and differences of interests among states. The former view regarded conflict as an abnormal condition, the latter perceived harmony as an illusion. The United States, long isolated from Europe and therefore not socialized into the state system, did not accept the reality and permanence of conflicts among its members. Differences between states were not considered natural, and certainly not deep and long-range; rather, they were attributed to wicked leaders (who could be eliminated), authoritarian political systems (which could be reformed), or misunderstandings (which could be straightened out if the adversaries approached each other with sincerity and empathy). Once these obstacles had been removed, peace, harmony, and goodwill would reign supreme.

Above all, America had always considered itself a morally and politically superior society due to its democratic culture. This meant that its attitude toward the use of power internationally had been dominated by the belief that the struggle for power did not exist or could be avoided by isolating oneself from it or could be eliminated by crusading against those countries indulging in power politics. Moralism in foreign policy proscribed the use of power in peacetime lest one became tainted; it could be employed only in confrontations with unambiguous aggression, transformed then into an obligation to fight on behalf of righteous causes. In short, power, internationally just as domestically, could be legitimated only by democratic purposes; otherwise, its exercise would be evil and would necessarily arouse guilt feelings.

The great American compulsion to feel moral about the nation's behavior reinforced the cyclical swings from isolationism to crusading and back again. The perception of power as simply the raw material of international politics —its use as an instrument of compromise, conciliation, and moderation of interstate politics, its discriminating application toward achievement of specific and less-than-total objectives—was clearly antithetical to the American understanding of power. The term "power politics" was itself kind of "dirty," an anathema, a reminder of a way of doing things that the New World had hopefully left behind, and a potential threat to its virtue if the nation were to indulge in that kind of immoral Old World behavior.

One of the most telling symptoms of America's national style in conducting foreign policy is that after every major war the reasons for the country's participation in struggle and bloodshed have been reinterpreted. These revisionist histories have certain common themes: the conflicts in which the nation had become entangled did not in fact threaten its security interests; it became involved because the politicians saw a menace where none existed, and this illusion had been promoted by propagandists who aroused and manipulated public opinion, by soldiers with bureaucratic motives, and, above all else, by bankers and industrialists—the "merchants of death" of the 1930s, the "military industrial complex" of the 1960s—whose economic interests benefited from the struggle. America's engagements in the two world wars of this century (as in the cold war later) were mistakes; they were really unnecessary or immoral, if not both. The evil enemy yesterday identified as the aggressor and *provocateur* thus apparently did not represent a threat to American security at all; to the contrary, the threat turns out to have come from within, not from without. But for certain *domestic forces,* the United States could have continued to isolate itself from international politics; note also that these internal groups propelling the nation into war were in characteristic American fashion, said to be motivated by profit.

The fundamental revisionist assumption, then, has been that the nation had a choice whether it wanted to employ "power politics." Conversely, revisionism rejected the idea that the distribution of power in the state system left the United States—or any other country, for that matter—with a choice only of whether it would help maintain the balance of power or not. Power was equated with its abuse. Abstention from its use and creating a truly just society at home were considered wiser and more moral policies. Crusading, allegedly for the reform of the world, risked corrupting America's very soul, since it diverted attention and resources from reform at home to military preparation and war. Revisionism, then, was essentially an argument for continued isolation from world politics.

But if one could no longer avoid power politics or crusade against it in order to abolish it, there was yet another solution: to escape from it, to flee the troublesome and divisive world of power into the more peaceful and united world of economics. The belief that political conflict among states could be transformed into cooperation among nations when they focused on what was truly important—the improvement of man's material and social life—was another major characteristic of American style. Whereas power was rather negatively associated with strife, destruction, and loss of life, economics was by contrast positively viewed because it was concerned with creating prosperity and improving man's welfare. Politics was bad and economics good, it is worth repeating, because by the logic of the free market international trade would benefit all states and this, in turn, would give each of them a vested interest in peace. If power politics and concern for security led to conflict and war, economics with its concern for raising everyone's standard of living bound all men, regardless of nationality or race, together. They had to cooperate for the common good in which they all shared. The post-Vietnam revulsion against the balance of power and emphasis on "interdependence" was hardly novel. Even while the Republic was still young there were already those who felt that

> The [national political] barriers that existed seemed artificial and ephemeral in comparison with the fine net by which the merchants tied the individuals of the different nations together like "threads of silk." . . . [T]he merchants—whether they are English, Dutch, Russian, or Chinese—do not serve a single nation; they serve everyone and are citizens of the whole world. Commerce was believed to bind the nations together and to create not only a community of interests but also a distribution of labor among them—a new comprehensive principle placing the isolated sovereign nations in a higher political unit. In the eighteenth century, writers were likely to say that the various nations belonged to "one society"; it was stated that all states together formed "a family of nations," and the whole globe a "general and unbreakable confederation."*

The United States after World War II, therefore, confronted a world with attitudes and behavior patterns inherited from its long period of isolationism from Europe. But the situation that faced the United States in 1945 no longer allowed it to abstain from this political struggle. The need to contain the Soviet Union by establishing and maintaining the balance of power required long-range policies that would effectively combine the political, military, and economic components of power. American security interests demanded no

*Felix Gilbert, *To The Farewell Address* (Princeton, N.J.: Princeton University Press, 1961), p. 57.

less. It remained to be seen whether a nation, inwardly oriented and temperamentally impatient, with little experience in international politics, could adjust to the sudden demands of "power politics," switching quickly from isolationism to involvement first in the eastern Mediterranean, then Western Europe, and shortly after that, Asia.

chapter **2**

the beginning of the cold war

AMERICAN WARTIME ILLUSIONS

Before one of the wartime conferences between Prime Minister Winston Churchill and President Franklin Roosevelt, an American intelligence forecast of Russia's postwar position in Europe concluded that the Soviet Union would be the dominant power on the continent of Europe: "With Germany crushed, there is no power in Europe to oppose her tremendous military forces. . . . The conclusions from the foregoing are obvious. Since Russia is the decisive factor in the war, she must be given every assistance, and every effort must be made to obtain her friendship. Likewise, since without question she will dominate Europe on the defeat of the Axis, it is even more essential to develop and maintain the most friendly relations with Russia."

The importance of this estimate lies less in its prediction of the Soviet Union's postwar position—which was, after all, fairly obvious—than in its reflection of American expectations about future Russo-American relations. American policymakers were apparently unable to conceive of the Soviet Union, the acknowledged new dominant power in Europe, replacing Nazi Germany as a grave threat to the European and global balance of power. Yet the United States had already twice in this century been propelled into Europe's wars at exactly those moments when Germany became so powerful that it menaced—indeed, almost destroyed—this balance. The lessons of history—specifically, the impact of any nation's domination of Europe upon

American security—had not yet been absorbed. President Roosevelt and the American government did not aim at reestablishing a balance of power in Europe to safeguard the United States; they expected this security to stem from mutual Russo-American goodwill, unsupported by any power considerations. This reliance upon mere goodwill and mutual esteem was to prove foolish at best and, at worst, might have been fatal.

Indeed, the expectation of a postwar "era of good feeling" between the Soviet Union and the United States was characteristic of the unsuspecting and utopian nature of American wartime thinking, which held that war was an interruption of the normal state of harmony among nations, that military force was an instrument for punishing the aggressor or war criminals, that those who cooperated with their country in its ideological crusade were equally moral and selfless, and that, once the war was finished, the natural harmony would be restored and the struggle for power ended. The implication was clear: The United States need take no precautionary steps against its noble wartime allies in anticipation of a possible disintegration of the alliance and potential hostility among its partners. Instead, it was hoped that the friendly relations and mutual respect which American leaders believed had matured during the war would preserve the common outlook and purposes and guarantee an enduring peace.

These optimistic expectations of future Russo-American relations made it necessary, however, to explain away continuing signs of Soviet hostility and suspicion. Throughout the war, the Russians constantly suspected the United States and Britain of devious intentions. This was particularly true with regard to the Western delay in opening up a second front. When the front was postponed from 1942 to 1943 to 1944, Stalin, Russia's dictator, became very bitter. He brusquely rejected Allied explanations that sufficient invasion barges for such an enormous undertaking were not available, and he especially denounced Prime Minister Churchill for declaring that there would be no invasion until the Germans were so weakened that Allied forces would not have to suffer forbiddingly high losses. To Stalin, this was no explanation, for the Russians accepted huge losses of men as a matter of course. "When we come to a minefield," Marshall Zhukov explained to General Eisenhower after the war, "our infantry attacks exactly as if it were not there. The losses we get from personnel mines we consider only equal to those we would have gotten from machine guns and artillery if the Germans had chosen to defend that particular area with strong bodies of troops instead of with minefields." It was no wonder, then, that the Russians should dismiss these Allied explanations and fasten instead upon a more reasonable interpretation which, to them, would account for American and British behavior. From the Marxist viewpoint, the Allies were doing exactly what they should be doing—namely, postponing the second front until the Soviet Union and Germany had exhausted each other. Then the two Western powers could land in France, march bloodlessly into Germany, and dictate the peace to both Germany and Russia. The Western delay was, in short, apparently seen as a deliberate attempt by the world's two leading capitalist powers to destroy both of their two major ideological opponents at one and the same time. Throughout the war, the Russians displayed again and again this almost paranoid fear of hostile Western intentions.

American leaders found a ready explanation for these repeated indications of Soviet suspicion. They thought of Soviet foreign policy not in terms of the internal dynamics of the regime and its enmity toward all non-Communist nations, but solely in terms of Russian reactions to Western policies. The Soviet attitude was viewed against the pattern of prewar anti-Soviet Western acts: the Allied intervention in Russia at the end of World War I in order to overthrow the Soviet regime and, after the failure of that attempt, the establishment by France of the *cordon sanitaire* in Eastern Europe to keep the Soviet virus from infecting Europe; the West's rejection of Soviet efforts in the mid- and late 1930s to build an alliance against Hitler; and especially, the Munich agreement in 1938, which, by destroying Czechoslovakia, in effect opened Hitler's gateway to the East. In short, Western efforts to ostracize and ultimately destroy the Soviet Union, as well as attempts to turn the Hitlerian threat away from the West and toward Russia, were considered the primary reasons for the existence of Soviet hostility. To overcome this attitude, the West had only to demonstrate its good intentions and prove its friendliness. The question was not *whether* Soviet cooperation could be won for the postwar world, only *how* it could be gained. And if Western efforts did bear fruit and create goodwill, what conflicts of interest could not be settled peacefully in the future? Various Soviet policies and acts during the war—the disbanding of the Comintern (the instrument of international Communism), the toning down of Communist ideology and new emphasis placed on Russian nationalism, the relaxation of restrictions upon the Church, the praise of the United States and Britain for also being democratic, and, above all, the statement of Russian war aims in the same language of peace, democracy, and freedom used by the West—all seemed to prove that if the Western powers demonstrated their friendship they could convert the Russians into friends.

President Roosevelt and his advisors certainly believed that they had firmly established such amicable relations with the Soviet Union at the Yalta Conference in February 1945. Stalin had made concessions on a number of vital issues and promised goodwill for the future. He had accepted the United Nations on the basis of the American formula that the veto in the Security Council should be applied only to enforcement action, and not to peaceful attempts at the settlement of disputes. Moreover, in the "Declaration on Liberated Europe," he had promised to support self-government and allow free elections in Eastern Europe. And regarding the Far East, he had responded to the wishes of the American military and promised to enter the war against Japan. Finally, he had repeatedly expressed his hope for fifty years of peace and "big power" cooperation.

It is little wonder that at the end of the conference the American delegation felt a mood of "supreme exultation." The new era of goodwill was to be embodied in the United Nations. Here the peoples of the world could exercise vigilance over the statesmen in their dealings with one another and prevent them from striking any wicked bargains that might erupt into another global war. The United Nations was regarded as an example of democracy on an international scale: Just as the people within democratic states could constantly watch their representatives and prevent them from effecting compromises injurious to their interests, so the people of all countries would now be able to keep an eye on their statesmen, making it impossible for them to arrange any secret deals which would betray the people's interests and shatter the peace of the world. Peace-loving world public opinion, expressing itself across national boundaries, would maintain a constant guard over the diplomats and hold them accountable. Covenants were to be open, and "openly arrived at," as President Wilson had once expressed it. Power politics would then be banned once and for all. In the words of Secretary of State Cordell Hull: "There will no longer be need for spheres of influence, for alliances, balance of power, or any other of the special arrangements through which, in the unhappy past, the nations strove to safeguard their security or promote their interests." Reliance would instead be placed upon sound principles and good fellowship. Again, in Hull's words: "All these principles and policies [of international cooperation] are so beneficial and appealing to the sense of justice, of right and of the well-being of free peoples everywhere that in the course of a few years the entire international machinery should be working fairly satisfactorily." The Advisory Commission on Postwar Foreign Policy had been even more emphatic in its stress on the subordination of power politics to principles: "International security was regarded as the supreme objective, but at the same time the subcommittee held that the attainment of security must square with principles of justice in order to be actual and enduring . . . the vital interests of the United States lay in following a 'diplomacy of principle'—of moral disinterestedness instead of power politics." No comment could more aptly have summed up the American habit of viewing international politics in terms of abstract moral principles instead of clashes of interest and power.

SOVIET POSTWAR EXPANSION

The American dream of postwar peace and Big Three cooperation was to be shattered as the Soviet Union expanded into Eastern and Central Europe, imposing its control upon Poland, Hungary, Bulgaria, Romania, and Albania. (Yugoslavia was already under the Communist control of Marshal Tito, and Czechoslovakia was living under the shadow of the Red Army.) In each of these nations of Eastern Europe where the Russians had their troops, they unilaterally established pro-Soviet coalition governments. The key post in these regimes—the ministry of the interior, which usually controlled the police—was in the hands of the Communists. With this decisive lever of power in their grasp, it was an easy matter to extend their domination and subvert the independence of these countries. Thus, as the war drew to a close, it became clear that the words of the Yalta Declaration, in which the Russians had committed themselves to free elections and democratic governments in Eastern Europe, meant quite different things to the Russians and to Americans. For the Soviet Union, control of Eastern Europe, and especially Poland, was essential. This area constituted a vital link in its security belt. After two German invasions in less than thirty years, it was perhaps inevitable that Russia would try to establish "friendly" governments throughout the area. To the Russians, "democratic governments" meant Communist governments, and "free elections" meant elections from which parties not favorable to the Communists were barred. The peace treaties with the former German satellite states (Hungary, Bulgaria, Romania), which were painfully negotiated by the victors in a series of foreign ministers' conferences during 1945 and 1946, could not therefore loosen the tight Soviet grip on what were by now Russian satellite states.

In terms of the state system, this Soviet behavior is understandable. Each state must act as its own guardian against potential adversaries in a system characterized by conflict among states and a sense of insecurity and fear on the part of its members. Thus, as the alliance against the common enemy came to an end, Soviet Russia would predictably strengthen itself against the power most likely to be its new opponent. As Russia, with a long history of invasions from the West, it had learned the basic rules of the international game through bitter experience; as *Soviet* Russia, its sense of peril had been intensified by an ideology that posited capitalist states as implacable enemies, merely waiting for the opportunity to strike. Hence, the establishment of anti-Communist regimes in Eastern Europe would have been intolerable, and the American insistence upon free elections was seen as an attempt to push the Soviet Union out of Europe. As a state that had no natural protective barriers, such as the English Channel or the Atlantic Ocean, the Soviet Union not unnaturally pushed outward to keep enemies as far away as possible; "defensive expansionism," as it has been called, became mingled with expansionism for offensive motives, such as extending the sphere of Communist control.

President Roosevelt during the war had been all too aware of the consequences of a possible Russian-American clash in the wake of Germany's defeat. As the leader of a nation that had *not* been socialized by the state system, he accurately represented American attitudes and expectations when he so single-mindedly pursued his policy of friendship toward the Soviet Union to reduce its suspicions of the West and lay a foundation of mutual trust and goodwill upon which the postwar peace could be built. Roosevelt, as we have seen, explained Soviet behavior almost exclusively as a reaction to such interwar Western steps as the establishment of the *cordon sanitaire* in Eastern Europe. Thus, he did not view free elections in that area in terms of the creation of a new anti-Soviet belt. For him, free elections, non-Communist coalition governments in which Communists might participate if they gained a sizable vote, and a friendly attitude toward both the West *and* the East were quite compatible. The model he had in mind was Czechoslovakia, a democracy that had ties to the West but had become friendly to Russia, especially in view of the West's failure to come to its rescue before Munich. But this model was not feasible, if only because the Soviet Union was unwilling to tolerate even an independent Czechoslovakia in which the Communist Party received the largest vote of any party in a postwar free election and thus held key posts in the government. To share power in a coalition government was to share power with class enemies. A "friendly" state, to the Soviets, was a completely Communist state, and a Communist state could not be friendly to the capitalist enemy.

The power vacuum created by Germany's defeat, which permitted Russian power to extend into the center of Europe and which precipitated the cold war, was almost exactly a replay of the struggle that erupted after the end of the war against Napoleon. The tsar's troops on that occasion entered Paris; his alliance with Prussia and his control over what then constituted Poland presented Russia's allies—Austria-Hungary and England—with the possibility of Russian Continental hegemony. These two states plus the former enemy, France, therefore signed a secret alliance threatening to go to war with Russia if the tsar remained adamantly opposed to a peace treaty that distributed power in such a manner that all the principal states could feel reasonably secure. When the news of this secret arrangement was leaked, the tsar became more compliant. In brief, *the post–World War II conflict*—with Stalin taking Tsar Alexander's place and the United States playing the role of England in rearranging the new balance of power—*was not fundamentally due to the personalities of leaders or to the principal contestants' domestic political or economic systems; it was essentially due to the nature of the state system and the emergent bipolar distribution of power, which led each state to see the other as the principal threat to its security and to take appropriate steps which each deemed essentially defensive but was seen by the other as offensive, expansionist, and aggressive.* In a real sense, the cold war was structurally or systemically determined and its unfolding contained elements of a Greek tragedy. There was one further element of continuity. As in the two world wars, in which England had led the effort to contain Germany, London—not Washington—took the first steps in opposing Russia after 1945. Indeed, the United States attempted initially to play the role of mediator between Russia and England! Only as English power proved to be insufficient did the United States, as before but more quickly, take over the task of balancing Russian power.

American initiative came about gradually in the 1946–1947 period and was precipitated mainly when Stalin turned from consolidating his grip in Eastern Europe to seeking to extend Soviet influence beyond the lines drawn by allied armies during the war. The United States had accommodated itself to Russian control over Eastern Europe, especially Poland, the corridor through which German armies had marched on Russia twice in a quarter-century. Moscow's security interests were understandable, and Washington, despite its disappointments over the Soviet nonfulfillment of its Yalta obligations in Poland, quickly recognized the new Polish government. Only when the Russians attempted to effect a major breakthrough into the Middle East did American opposition become genuinely aroused. Greece, Turkey, and Iran were the first states beyond the confines of the Red Army to feel the pressure of the Soviet Union.

The pressure on Iran began in early 1946, when the Russians refused to withdraw their troops from that country. These troops had been there since late 1941, when Russia and Britain had invaded Iran in order to forestall increased Nazi influence and to use Iran as a corridor for the transportation of military aid shipped by the West to the Persian Gulf for transit to Russia. The Russians had occupied northern Iran, the British the central and southern sections. When the latter withdrew their troops after the war, the Soviets sought to convert Iran into a Soviet satellite. Oil concessions offered in return for Soviet permission to let Iran exercise its sovereign authority over northern Iran were rejected.

During this period, the Soviet Union also put pressure on Turkey. Indeed, the Russians had begun to do this as early as June 1945, when they suddenly demanded the cession of several Turkish districts lying on the Turkish–Russian frontier, the revision of the Montreux Convention governing the Dardenelles Straits in favor of a joint Russo-Turkish administration, Turkey's severance of ties with Britain and the conclusion of a treaty with the Soviet Union similar to those which Russia had concluded with its Balkan satellites, and finally, the leasing to the Soviet Union of bases for naval and land forces in the Dardenelles for its "joint defense." This time Moscow rejected a compromise proposal that would have given Russia a veto over any non-Black Sea powers' warships seeking passage through the straits. In August 1946, the Soviet Union renewed its demand, in a note to the United States and Britain, for a new administration of the straits. In effect, this would have turned Turkey into a Soviet satellite.

In Greece, too, Communist pressure was exerted on the government through wide-scale guerrilla warfare, which began in the fall of 1946. Civil war in Greece was actually nothing new. During the war, the Communist and anti-Communist guerrillas fighting the Germans had spent much of their energy battling each other. When the British landed in Greece and the Germans withdrew from the country, the Communists had attempted to take over the capital city of Athens. Only after several weeks of bitter street fighting and the landing of British reinforcements was the Communist control of Athens dislodged and a truce signed in January 1945. Just over a year later —in March 1946—the Greeks held a general election in which right-wing forces captured the majority of votes.

The Greek situation did not improve, however. The country was exhausted from the Italian and German invasions, the four years of occupation, and the Germans' scorched-earth policy as they retreated. Moreover, Greece had always been dependent upon imports that were paid for by exports, but its traditional market in Central Europe was now closed. While the masses lived at a bare subsistence level, the black market flourished. The inability of any government to deal with this situation aroused a good deal of social discontent. And the large, 100,000-man army which Greece needed to protect itself from its Communist neighbors (Albania, Yugoslavia, and Bulgaria) had brought the country to near-bankruptcy. If Britain had not helped finance—as well as train and equip—the army and kept troops in the country to stabilize the situation, Greece would in all probability have collapsed. It was in these circumstances that in August 1946, the Communist forces began to squeeze Greece by renewing the guerrilla warfare in the north, where the guerrillas could be kept well supplied by Greece's Communist neighbors.

In all these situations, the American government was suddenly confronted with the need for action to support Britain, the traditional guardian of this area against encroachment. In the case of Iran, the United States and Britain delivered firm statements which strongly implied that the two countries would use force to defend Iran. The Soviet response in late March 1946 was the announcement that the Red Army would be withdrawn during the next five to six weeks. In the Turkish case, the United States sent a naval task force into the Mediterranean immediately after the receipt of the Soviet note on August 7. Twelve days later, the United States replied to the note by rejecting the Russian demand to share exclusive responsibility for the defense of the straits with Turkey. Britain sent a similar reply. The Greek situation had not yet come to a head, and the need for American action could be postponed for a while longer. But it should be pointed out that the Truman administration's actions in Iran and Turkey were merely swift reactions to immediate crises. They were not the product of an overall American strategy. Such a coherent strategy came only after a new assessment of Soviet foreign policy had occurred.

THE STRATEGY OF CONTAINMENT

A period of 18 months passed before the United States undertook that reassessment—from the surrender of Japan on September 2, 1945, until the announcement of the Truman Doctrine on March 12, 1947. Perhaps such a reevaluation could not have been made any more quickly. Public opinion in a democratic country does not normally shift drastically overnight. It would have been too much to expect the American public to change suddenly from an attitude of friendliness toward the Soviet Union—inspired largely by the picture of Russian wartime bravery and endurance and by hopes for peaceful postwar cooperation—to a hostile mood. The United States wished only to be left alone to preoccupy itself once more with domestic affairs. The end of the war signaled the end of power politics and the restoration of normal peacetime harmony among nations. In response to this expectation, the public demanded a speedy demobilization. In May 1945, at the end of the war with Germany, the United States had an army of 3.5 million men organized into 68 divisions in Europe, supported by 149 air groups. By March 1946, only ten months later, the United States had only 400,000 troops left, mainly new recruits; the homeland reserve was six battalions. Further reductions in army strength followed. Air force and navy cuts duplicated this same pattern.

This deliberate reduction of military strength, as a symptom of America's psychological demobilization could not have failed to encourage Russian intransigence in Europe and increased Soviet pressure in southeastern Europe and the Middle East. As this pressure increased in intensity and scope, however, American policy toward the Soviet Union began to be reevaluated.

Three positions became clear during this period. At one extreme stood that old realist Winston Churchill. At the end of the European war, he had counseled against the withdrawal of American troops. He had insisted that they stay, together with British troops, in order to force the Soviet Union to live up to its Yalta obligations regarding free elections in Eastern Europe and the withdrawal of the Red Army from eastern Germany. The United States had rejected Churchill's plea. In early 1946, at Fulton, Missouri, Churchill took his case directly to the American public. The Soviet Union, he asserted, was an expansionist state. "From Stettin in the Baltic to Trieste in the Adriatic, an iron curtain has descended across the continent. Behind that line lie all the capitals of the ancient states of Central and Eastern Europe. Warsaw, Berlin, Prague, Vienna, Budapest, Belgrade, Bucharest, and Sofia, all the famous cities and populations around them lie in the Soviet sphere and all are subject in one form or another, not only to Soviet influence but to a very high and increasing measure of control from Moscow." Churchill did not believe that the Russians wanted war: "What they desire is the fruits of war and the indefinite expansion of their power and doctrines." This could be prevented only by the opposing power of the British Commonwealth and the United States. Churchill, in short, said bluntly that the cold war had begun, that Americans must recognize this fact and give up their dreams of Big Three unity in the United Nations. International organization was no substitute for the balance of power. "Our difficulties and dangers will not be removed by closing our eyes to them. They will not be removed by mere waiting to see what happens; nor will they be relieved by a policy of appeasement." An alliance of the English-speaking peoples was the prerequisite for American and British security and world peace.

At the other extreme stood Secretary of Commerce Henry Wallace, who felt it was precisely the kind of aggressive attitude expressed by Churchill that was to blame for Soviet hostility. The United States and Britain had no more business in Eastern Europe than had the Soviet Union in Latin America; to each, the respective area was vital for national security. Western interference in nations bordering on Russia was bound to arouse Soviet suspicion, just as Soviet intervention in countries neighboring on the United States would. "We may not like what Russia does in Eastern Europe," said Wallace. "Her type of land reform, industrial expropriation, and suspension of basic liberties offends the great majority of the people of the United States. But whether we like it or not, the Russians will try to socialize their sphere of influence just as we try to democratize our sphere of influence (including Japan and Western Germany)." The tough attitude that Churchill and other "reactionaries" at home and abroad demanded was precisely the wrong policy; it would only increase international tension. "We must not let British balance-of-power manipulations determine whether and when the United States gets into a war . . . 'getting tough' never bought anything real and lasting—whether for schoolyard bullies or world powers. The tougher we get, the tougher the Russians will get." Only mutual trust would allow the United States and Russia to live together peacefully, and such trust could not be created by an unfriendly American attitude and policy.

The American government and public wavered between these two positions. The administration recognized that Big Three cooperation had ended, and it realized that the time when the United States needed to demonstrate goodwill toward the Soviet Union in order to overcome the latter's suspicions had passed. No further concessions would be made to preserve the surface friendship with the Soviet Union. America had tried to gain Russia's amity by being a friend; it was now up to its leaders to demonstrate a similarly friendly attitude toward America as well. Paper agreements, written in such general terms that they actually hid divergent purposes, were no longer regarded as demonstrating such friendship. Something more than paper agreements was needed: Russian words would have to be matched by Russian deeds.

The American secretary of state, James Byrnes, called this new line the "policy of firmness and patience." This phrase meant that the United States would take a firm position whenever the Soviet Union became intransigent, and that it would not compromise simply in order to reach a quick agreement. This change in official American attitude toward the Soviet Union was not, however, a fundamental one. A firm line was to be followed only on concrete issues. The assumption was that if the United States took a tougher bargaining position and no longer seemed in a hurry to resolve particular points of tension, the Soviet rulers would see the pointlessness of their obduracy and agree to fair compromise solutions of their differences with the United States and the West. In short, American firmness would make the Russians "reasonable." For they were regarded as "unreasonable" merely on particular issues. The new American position, as one political analyst has aptly summed it up, "meant to most of its exponents that the Soviet Union had to be induced by firmness to play the game in the American way. There was no consistent official suggestion that the United States should begin to play a different game." The prerequisite for such a suggestion was that American policymakers recognize the revolutionary nature of the Soviet regime.

This recognition came with increasing speed as the Greek crisis reached a peak. By early 1947, it was obvious that the United States would have to play a different game. It was George Kennan, the Foreign Service's foremost expert on the Soviet Union, who first presented the basis of what was to be a new American policy. Kennan's analysis focused on the Communist outlook on world affairs. In the Soviet leaders' pattern of thought, he said, Russia had no community of interest with the capitalist states; indeed, they saw their relationship with the Western powers in terms of an innate antagonism. Communist ideology had taught them "that the outside world was hostile and that it was their duty eventually to overthrow the political forces beyond their borders. The powerful hands of Russian history and tradition reached up to sustain them in this feeling. Finally, their own aggressive intransigence with respect to the outside world began to find its own reaction. . . . It is an undeniable privilege for every man to prove himself right in the thesis that the world is his enemy; for if he reiterates it frequently enough and makes it the background for his conduct, he is bound to be right." According to Kennan, this Soviet hostility was a constant factor; it would continue until the capitalist world had been destroyed: "Basically, the antagonism remains. It is postulated. And from it flow many of the phenomena which we find disturbing in the Kremlin's conduct of foreign policy: the secretiveness, the lack of frankness, the duplicity, the war suspiciousness, and the basic unfriendliness of purpose. . . . These characteristics of the Soviet policy, like the postulates from which they flow, are basic to the *internal* nature of Soviet power, and will be with us . . . until the nature of Soviet power is changed [italics added]." Until that moment, he said, Soviet strategy and objectives would remain the same.

The struggle would thus be a long one. Kennan stressed that Soviet hostility did not mean the Russians would embark upon a do-or-die program to overthrow capitalism by a fixed date. They had no timetable for conquest. In a brilliant passage, Kennan outlined the Soviet concept of the struggle:

> The Kremlin is under no ideological compulsion to accomplish its purposes in a hurry. Like the Church, it is dealing in ideological concepts which are of a long-term validity, and it can afford to be patient. It has no right to risk the existing achievements of the revolution for the sake of vain baubles of the future.

> The very teachings of Lenin himself require great caution and flexibility in the pursuit of Communist purposes. Again, these precepts are fortified by the lessons of Russian history: of centuries of obscure battles between nomadic forces over the stretches of a vast unfortified plain. Here caution, circumspection, flexibility, and deception are the valuable qualities; and their value finds natural appreciation in the Russian, or the Oriental mind. Thus the Kremlin has no compunction about retreating in the face of superior force. And being under the compulsion of no timetable, it does not get panicky under the necessity of such a retreat. Its political action is a fluid stream which moves constantly, wherever it is permitted to move, toward a given goal. Its main concern is to make sure that it has filled every nook and cranny available to it in the basin of world power. But if it finds unassailable barriers in its path, it accepts these philosophically and accommodates itself to them. The main thing is that there should always be pressure, increasing constant pressure, toward the desired goal. There is no trace of any feeling in Soviet psychology that the goal must be reached at any given time.

How could the United States counter such a policy—a policy that was always pushing, seeking weak spots, attempting to fill power vacuums? Kennan's answer was that American policy would have to be one of "long-term, patient, but firm and vigilant containment." The United States would find Soviet diplomacy both easier and more difficult to deal with than that of dictators such as Napoleon or Hitler. "On the one hand, it [Soviet policy] is more sensitive to contrary force, more ready to yield on individual sectors of the diplomatic front when that force is felt to be too strong, and thus more rational in the logic and rhetoric of power. On the other hand, it cannot be easily defeated or discouraged by a single victory on the part of its opponents. And the patient persistence by which it is animated means that it can be effectively countered not by sporadic acts which represent the momentary whims of democratic opinion, but only by intelligent long-range policies on the part of Russia's adversaries—policies no less steady in their purpose, and no less variegated and resourceful in their application, than those of the Soviet Union itself." Hence, George Kennan was envisaging containment as a test of American democracy to conduct an effective and responsible foreign policy *and* contribute to changes within the Soviet Union which might bring about a moderation of its revolutionary aims. The United States, he emphasized, "has it in its power to increase enormously the strains under which Soviet policy must operate, to force upon the Kremlin a far greater degree of moderation and circumspection than it has had to observe in recent years, and in this way to promote tendencies which must eventually find their outlet in either the breakup or the gradual mellowing of Soviet power. For no mystical, messianic movement—and particularly not that of the Kremlin—can face frustration indefinitely without eventually adjusting itself in one way or another to the logic of that state of affairs."

Kennan was, in effect, asserting the thesis that within an authoritarian or totalitarian society there are certain strains and stresses, and that these give rise to frustrations which can only be relieved by being channeled into an aggressive and expansionist foreign policy. Kennan's remedy was to prevent this expansion, thereby aggravating the internal tensions in such a way that they would either distroy the Soviet system or force the Soviet leaders to placate the domestic dissatisfaction. Assuming that the Soviet leaders preferred to remain in power and that they would therefore be compelled to adopt the second course, they would have no alternative but to moderate their foreign policy. For a relaxation of international tensions was the prerequisite for coping with their domestic problems. Thus, the Kremlin would have no choice but to surrender its revolutionary aims and arrange a *modus vivendi* with the Western powers—above all, with the United States.

THE TRUMAN DOCTRINE

Whether the United States could meet this Soviet challenge became a pressing question when, on the afternoon of February 21, 1947, the First Secretary of the British Embassy in Washington visited the State Department and handed American officials two notes from His Majesty's government. One concerned Greece, the other Turkey. In effect, they both stated the same thing: that Britain could no longer meet its traditional responsibilities in those two countries. Since both were on the verge of collapse, the import of the British notes was clear: that a Russian breakthrough could be prevented only by an all-out American commitment.

February 21 was thus a historic day. On that day, Great Britain, the only remaining power in Europe, acknowledged its exhaustion. It had fought Philip II of Spain, Louis XIV and Napoleon of France, Kaiser Wilhelm II and Adolf Hitler of Germany. It had preserved the balance of power which protected the United States for so long that it seemed almost natural for it to continue to do so. But its ability to protect that balance had steadily declined in the twentieth century. Twice it had needed American help. Each time, however, it had fought the longer battle; on neither occasion had the United States entered the war until it became clear that Germany and its allies were too strong for Great Britain and that America would have to help in safeguarding its own security. Now, all of a sudden, there was no power to protect the United States but the United States itself; no one stood between that country and the present threat to its security. All the other major powers of the world had collapsed—except the Soviet Union. A bipolar world suddenly faced the United States.

The immediate crisis suddenly confronting the United States had its locale in the eastern Mediterranean. Direct Soviet pressure on Iran and Turkey had temporarily been successfully resisted. The Russians had now turned to outflanking these two nations by concentrating their attention on Greece. If Greece collapsed—and all reports from that hapless country indicated that it would fall within a few weeks—it was thought in Washington that it would only be a question of time until Turkey and Iran would crumble before Soviet power. But the fall of Greece would not only affect its neighbors to the east; it would also lead to an increase of Communist pressure on Italy. Italy would then be faced with two Communist states to its east—Yugoslavia and Greece—and with the largest Communist party in Western Europe in its own midst. And to the northwest of Italy lay France, with the second largest Communist party in the West. Thus, the security of all of Western Europe would be endangered as well.

Consequently, the United States felt it had no choice but to act in this situation. On March 12, 1947, President Truman went before a joint session of Congress to deliver a speech that must rank as one of the most important in American history. After outlining the situation in Greece, he spelled out what was to become known as the Truman Doctrine. The United States, he emphasized, could survive only in a world in which freedom flourished. And it would not realize this objective

> ... unless we are willing to help free peoples to maintain their institutions and their national integrity against aggressive movements that seek to impose upon them totalitarian regimes. *This is no more than a frank recognition that totalitarian regimes imposed on free peoples, by direct or indirect aggression, undermine the foundations of international peace and hence the security of the United States* [italics added].
>
> The peoples of a number of countries of the world have recently had totalitarian regimes forced upon them against their will. The Government of the United States has made frequent protests against coercion and intimidation, in violation of the Yalta agreement, in Poland, Romania, and Bulgaria. I must also state that in a number of other countries there have been similar developments.
>
> At the present moment in world history nearly every nation must choose between alternative ways of life. The choice is often not a free one.
>
> One way of life is based upon the will of the majority, and is distinguished by free institutions, representative government, free elections, guarantees of individual liberty, freedom of speech and religion, and freedom from political oppression.
>
> The second way of life is based upon the will of a minority forcibly imposed upon the majority. It relies upon terror and oppression, a controlled press and radio, fixed elections, and the suppression of personal freedoms.
>
> I believe it must be the policy of the United States to support free peoples who are resisting attempted subjugations by armed minorities or by outside pressure.
>
> I believe that we must assist free peoples to work out their own destinies in their own way.
>
> I believe that our help should be primarily through economic and financial aid which is essential to economic stability and orderly political processes.

Stressing the impact of Greece's collapse upon Turkey and the Middle East, as well as upon Europe, the president asked Congress to appropriate $400 million for economic aid and military supplies for both countries and to authorize the dispatch of American civilian and military personnel in order to help the two nations in their tasks of reconstruction and provide their armies with appropriate instruction and training.

Thus the United States began the policy of containment. A number of points about this initial commitment need special emphasis. First, the Soviet threat to the balance of power left the United States no choice but to adopt a countervailing policy. With the war over, the United States would have much preferred to concentrate on domestic affairs; the massive postwar demobilization clearly demonstrated this preference. But the external environment intervened: the bipolar distribution of power molded the nation's policy course. Such a distribution of power is the most sensitive of all because the two states are bound to be alert to the slightest shift in the balance lest one adversary gain the power he needs to assert and impose his will upon the other. For a gain of power and security by one tends to be seen as a loss of power and security for the other. A bipolar balance is therefore very dangerous, for it produces, among its effects, constant confrontations and crises which could spark a military clash. Yet they are also an indication that the balance is being kept. As one side pushes, his opponent pushes him back.

The second point to stress is that anti-Communism was not the major ingredient of American policy during and immediately after World War II. During the war, the United States had constantly sought to overcome the Kremlin's suspicions of the West in order to lay the foundation for postwar harmony and peace. And as the war drew to its conclusion, the principal concern of American policy-makers was not to eliminate the self-proclaimed bastion of world revolution and enemy of Western capitalism, nor to push Russia out of Eastern Europe and convert that area into a market for American corporations (even had that desire existed, poverty-stricken Eastern Europe would not have been a very profitable market for American goods), but to forestall a complete return to the historic position of isolationism. The public mood was all too evident in the hasty military demobilizaiton, the riots of some overseas units that felt that their demobilization was not rapid enough, and the cries of America's children heard both in Congress and the White House: "We want our daddies." For the United States to have pursued the assertive foreign policy complete with atomic threats that the revisionists have claimed it did, would have required a dictatorial disregard for the widespread demands of public opinion.

It was not until a year and a half after World War II ended that the Truman Doctrine was enunciated. Only after further attempts to reconcile differences with Moscow, after continued Soviet pressure, denunciations, and vilifications, was containment launched. Hostile Soviet behavior was the reason for the gradual shift of American policy and public opinion from amity to enmity; American policy was not the product of a virulent and preexisting anti-Communist ideology. Rather, it was activated by the same concern for preventing a major nation from achieving dominance in Europe that had already twice in this century led the United States into war. Thus, post-1945 American policy was consistent with United States behavior in 1917 and 1940-1941; in both cases, the nation had gone to war to prevent such an outcome. This was not fundamentally an ideological issue. In World Wars I and II, the enemy was Germany; in the initial engagement, it was led by a conservative monarchy, in the second, by an extreme right-wing fascist regime. In the cold war, the adversary was Soviet Russia, a radical left-wing regime. American action, however, remained the same, regardless of the ideological nature of the opponent.

Third, the role of anti-Communism in American policy was essentially to mobilize Congressional and public support for the policy once it had been decided upon. A nation that had historically condemned power politics as immoral and as a corruption of the democratic ideal needed a moral basis for its new use of power. Anti-Communism fitted into the familiar dichotomy of a peaceful and democratic New World confronted by a warlike and dictatorial Old Europe. For a people weary after four years of war, who identified the termination of war with the end of power politics, who were used to isolation from Europe's wicked affairs, and who were preoccupied with the pursuit of happiness, success, and the dollar at home, anti-Communism was like the cavalry's bugle call to charge; it fitted neatly into the traditional American dichotomy of the world into extremes of evil and morality, thereby arousing the nation for yet another foreign policy mission. Until Vietnam, anti-Communism served the policy-makers' purposes; the policy of containment received long and widespread public and Congressional support from both Democrats and Republicans. (Asian policy was to be the major exception to this rule, as we shall see.)

The fourth point worth noting is that, despite the universalism of the Truman Doctrine, its application was intended to be specific and limited, not global. American policy-makers were well aware that the United States, though a Great Power, was not omnipotent; therefore, national priorities—which interests were vital and which were not—had to be decided carefully and power applied discriminately. American responses would depend, then, both on where the external challenges occurred and on how Washington defined the relationship of such challenges to the nation's security. Under the guise of a crusading rhetoric, containment was to be implemented only where the Russian state appeared to be seeking to expand its power. The priority given to balance of power considerations was evident from the very beginning since, despite the declared democratic purposes stated by the Truman Doctrine, the first application of the Doctrine was to Greece and Turkey, neither of whom were democratic.

Their strategic location was given precedence of their domestic nature. In Western Europe, of course, America's strategic and power considerations were compatible with its democratic values. The containment of Russia could be equated with the defense of democracy. But outside of Western Europe, strategy and values were often incompatible with one another, thus confronting the United States with a classic dilemma: to protect strategically located undemocratic regimes might fortify containment (in the short-run, at least) but stain America's reputation and weaken the justification for United States policy; on the other hand, to align herself only with democratic states, of whom there were all too few, might make it impossible to carry out the containment policy. The cause might thus be kept pure, but the security of democracy would be weakened. This dilemma was to plague this nation's policy in subsequent years and often make the declared aim that the United States was seeking to protect the democratic way of life appear as hypocritical.

chapter 3

containment in europe

THE MARSHALL PLAN

The commitment to Greece and Turkey was only the first act under the new American policy of containing Soviet expansion. Britain's state of near-collapse was symptomatic of all of Europe's collapse. Basically, her crisis was an economic one. As an island-nation, it was dependent for its livelihood upon international trade. It had to export or die, for the Industrial Revolution it had undergone during the nineteenth century had almost completely urbanized it. Less than 5 percent of Britain's population was engaged in agriculture. This meant that it had to import much of its food: meat, wheat, butter, tea, cocoa, coffee, and sugar. Except for coal, Britain also had to import most of the raw materials needed by its industries: cotton, rubber, wool, iron ore, timber, and oil.

Before 1939, Britain had paid for these foods and raw materials by one of three means: services such as shipping, income from foreign investments, and manufactured exports. But the war had crippled its merchant marine, liquidated most of its investments, and destroyed many of its factories. With the first two means of financing its imports all but gone, it had to increase its export drive. Just to maintain the 1939 standard of living, it had to raise its exports by 75 percent. By December 1946, despite an American loan and a severe austerity program which included the rationing of bread, Britain had only reached its prewar level of production. It was in these circumstances that nature delivered what almost proved to be a knockout blow. In the winter of 1946–1947, Europe suffered one of its severest cold periods in history; temperatures went below zero. In Britain, the transportation system came to a virtual standstill. Industries could not be supplied with the fuel to keep them running, and factories were closed. By February 1947, more than half of Britain's factories lay idle. Coal was not even mined, and gas and electricity were in short supply. When the thaw finally arrived, Britain was beset by floods.

The export drive thus completely collapsed, and Britain had come to the end of its rope. The financial editor of Reuter's saw the true measure of the winter disaster: "The biggest crash since the fall of Constantinople—the collapse of the heart of an Empire—impends. This is not the story of a couple of snowstorms. It is the story of the awful debility in which a couple of snowstorms could have such effects." The future looked bleak and ominous: millions of Britons were unemployed, cold and hungry, worn out by the long years of war and the determined postwar efforts to recover. Despite all the personal and uncomplaining sacrifices they had made, their efforts had come to nothing. Britain's fate could have been worse only if it had lost the war.

In Germany, postwar conditions were truly horrible. The war had been carried into the heart of Germany. Few German cities or towns had escaped Allied bombing, street fighting, or willful destruction by the Nazis themselves as they retreated. To aggravate this situation, 10 million additional Germans came into these ruins from former German territory annexed by Poland. There was only one word to describe Germany in 1945—chaos. Millions of people were faced with the basic necessity of finding food, shelter, and work.

The measure of Germany's collapse was indicated by the fact that the cigarette had replaced money as the prevailing unit of exchange. Cigarettes could buy almost anything. The black market flourished. Even as late as 1947, a package of cigarettes was equivalent to a working man's entire wages for a month. The Allied target ration of 1550 calories per day, which was hardly sufficient to sustain a healthy human being, was rarely reached. Everywhere people were hungry. It was a desperate situation. Respectable girls sold their bodies for one or two cigarettes, a pair of nylons, or an army ration; dishonor was preferable to death. Juvenile delinquency increased and stealing became as respectable a way of earning a living for boys as did prostitution for girls. Along with this economic, social, political, and moral breakdown came the cold weather. There was no fuel for heating. During the severe winter of 1946–1947, 200 people froze to death in Berlin alone. Three-quarters of the factories still standing in the American and British zones of occupation were closed. In January 1947, production fell to 31 per cent of the 1936 level, Germany's best year; by February, it had declined to 29 percent. Even before this industrial shutdown German steel production during 1946 had reached only 2 million tons—approximately only one-third of Allied authorization.

Allied policy was not designed to alleviate this situation. The Allies were still primarily engaged with Germany's disarmament and demilitarization, and with the elimination of all industries whose output could be used for military production. America and Britain were not particularly anxious to rebuild Germany's industrial power. They recalled only too vividly that it had taken the combined efforts of three world powers to bring the Nazi war machine to a halt and defeat it. Nor were the Allies especially concerned with the lot of the German people during the immediate postwar days. After six years of war, such concern could hardly have been expected. The memories of Nazi atrocities and crimes, of wanton destruction, and of millions of innocent people slaughtered in concentration camps were still very much alive. The hatred the Nazis had engendered could not be erased overnight. After six years of brutal warfare, the Allies were unlikely to display much forgiveness and chivalry toward the Germans.

The French, above all others, were not likely to forget the Nazis. Though their economy had been badly damaged during the war, by late 1946 the French had made a remarkable recovery. But iron and steel production had reached only half the prewar total. Here, too, coal was the key factor, since the iron and steel industry was dependent upon imported coal. But European coal production was still well below the pre-1939 annual average. German production was low, and Britain needed for itself all the coal it mined. Therefore, scarce dollars had to be spent for the purchase of high-cost American coal. The result was a vivid demonstration of the division of labor in the modern economy. France's industry was unable to produce sufficient goods to exchange for food. The farmer thereupon withdrew fields from crop cultivation and used them for grazing. He kept more food for himself and his family, and also fed his livestock more grain. Meanwhile, the urban population was short of food, and the government had to spend its few remaining dollars—which it needed for reconstruction—to buy food from abroad. The winter of 1946–1947 aggravated this situation even further by destroying an estimated 3 to 4 million acres of wheat.

This situation was made to order for the large and well-organized French Communist Party. One-quarter of France's electorate—practically the entire working class—voted for the Party. (In Italy, the figure was one-third of the electorate.) The reason for this was simple: Capitalism had alienated these people. The workers were, in effect, internal *émigrés* who voted Communist in protest against a system they felt had long mistreated them; unlike workers in Britain and in the United States, they had suffered all the hardships of capitalism while enjoying few of its benefits, such as good wages and social opportunities. As a result, the Communist Party in France was placed in a powerful position in political and trade union life. The Party was the largest in France and could prevent any reforms from being adopted, thereby preserving its *raison d'être*. The Party also controlled the largest French trade union, which had a membership of 80 percent of the workers in the immediate postwar years. In 1947, as United States–Soviet tensions increased, the Party used this control to initiate or exploit strikes in order to paralyze the entire economy and bring the Republic to its knees.

With Europe on the verge of collapse, everything seemed to force it into dependence upon America. Most of the items needed for reconstruction—wheat, cotton, sulphur, sugar, machinery, trucks, and coal—could be obtained in sufficient quantities only from the United States. Yet, Europe, with a stagnating economy, was in no position to earn the dollars needed to pay for these goods. Moreover, the United States was so well supplied with everything that it did not have to buy much from abroad. Thus, the European countries were unable to obtain enough dollars for the purchase of the commodities required for their recovery. The result was the ominous "dollar gap"—a term that frightened the Europeans as much as the "cold war."

Europe's collapse thus posed a fundamental question to the United States: Is Europe vital to American security? The answer was never in doubt: American independence and security required that the United States establish a balance of power in the interior of Europe. This was necessary to check any nation with designs on the sea-bordering states as a prerequisite to the elimination of England and eventual world conquest. During most of the nineteenth century, this balance had been maintained by the English navy. Now that Britain's power had declined drastically, the United States would have to carry out the task alone. Western Europe possessed the largest aggregation of skilled workers, technicians, and managers outside the United States. It maintained the second greatest concentration of industrial power in the world. A healthy and strong Europe could help shore up the balance of power.

The role of the United States toward Europe, therefore, had to be that of a doctor toward an ill patient—and the prescribed cure was a massive injection of dollars. A large-scale program of economic aid was to be administered in the form of grants rather than loans, which would only intensify Europe's dollar problems. Only such a program could restore and surpass Europe's prewar agricultural and industrial production, close the dollar gap, and lead Europe to the recovery of its *élan vital*, political stability, and economic prosperity, thereby possibly allowing France and Italy to reintegrate their working classes into their bodies politic.

American aid was made conditional, however, upon economic cooperation among the European states. In this respect, the United States clearly held itself up as a model for the Europeans. The Economic Cooperation Act of 1948 called specifically for European economic integration. America, it stated, was "mindful of the advantage which the United States has enjoyed through the existence of a large-scale domestic market with no internal trade barriers and [believed] that similar advantages can accrue to the countries of Europe." Thus, in official American opinion, European integration became both the

prerequisite for Europe's recovery and the necessary basis for Europe's long-range prosperity. It is not difficult to see why American policy-makers, with their belief in low-cost mass production, should have felt that Europe's economic recovery and health were dependent upon the creation of a mass market. For decades, the European nations living together on a continent one-fourth the size of the United States had shut their markets off from one another with tariff walls, quota systems, and import and export licenses. By this means, national manufacturers assured themselves of the lion's share of their national markets. Sheltered from external competition, they had little incentive to modernize their equipment or techniques, for they minimized domestic competition by dividing their relatively small domestic markets among themselves. The American aim was to modernize this machinery, to overcome the cartelization of industry and the inefficiency of small family enterprises (as in France), and to destroy the artificial national divisions. Europe's industries were to be compelled to become large-scale and competitive by the creation of a "united states" of Europe.

The economic cooperation required by the United States was first stressed by Secretary of State George C. Marshall's call upon the European states to present his country with a plan for their *common* needs and *common* recovery. The result was the Organization for European Economic Cooperation, whose seventeen members pledged themselves to "cooperate with one another and with other like-minded countries in reducing tariffs and other barriers to trade" and "to promote with vigor the development of productivity through [the] efficient use of the resources at their command." The OEEC's estimate of the cost of Europe's recovery over a four-year period was $22 billion. Congress was to cut this figure down to $17 billion, and the amount actually used by the Economic Cooperation Administration (ECA) between 1948 and 1952 was just over $12 billion. Britain, France, and West Germany received more than half of this amount.

The original invitation by the United States to the nations of Europe to plan their joint recovery was deliberately extended to *all* European countries, including the Soviet Union and the nations of Eastern Europe. If the United States had invited only the nations of Western Europe, it would have placed itself in a politically disadvantageous position in which it would have been blamed for the division of Europe and the intensification of the cold war. Actually, if the Russians had participated, it seems unlikely that Congress would have supported the Marshall Plan: first, because the costs of the plan would have risen astronomically as a result of the very heavy and extensive damage suffered by Russia during the war; and second, because of the growing anti-Soviet feeling which the Soviet Union had engendered. The risk had to be accepted, however; it had to be the Russians who, by their rejection of Marshall Plan aid, would be responsible for the division of Europe. And the chances that the Russians would do precisely that were very good. For European cooperation would mean that Russia would have to disclose full information about its economy and allow the United States to have some control in its economic planning, as well as in that of its satellites. This was unthinkable to a totalitarian state; a Communist state could hardly permit capitalists to have a voice in its economic development. Soviet participation would also require the Soviet Union and its satellites to contribute toward Europe's recovery with food and raw materials, in return for the help they were receiving form the United States. Thus, the Russians would actually be helping to stabilize the European situation. But if they did not participate—preferring to exploit Europe's misery—they would be blamed for continuing and aggravating the cold war. In either case, the United States could not lose by invoking Marx's slogan, "From each according to his ability, to each according to his need." Actually, Soviet Foreign Minister Molotov did arrive in Paris with a large delegation of experts, and he gave American policy-makers a scare. But only for a moment. Molotov soon denounced the plan as an attempt to interfere with Soviet sovereignty and withdrew. Western Europe could now plan the use of America's dollars for its recovery.

Was the Marshall Plan a success? The results tell their own story. By 1950—when the Korean War broke out—Europe was already exceeding its prewar production by 25 percent; two years later, this figure was 200 percent higher. English exports were doing well, the French inflation was being slowed down, and German production had reached Germany's 1936 level. The dollar gap had been reduced from $12 billion to $2 billion. The Marshall Plan had been a massive success, and at a cost that represented only a tiny fraction of the U.S. national income over the same four-year period; it was, indeed, smaller than America's liquor bill for these same years!

THE NORTH ATLANTIC TREATY ORGANIZATION

Soon after the Marshall Plan was launched, however, it became clear that the plan by itself would not suffice. For in February 1948, the Russians engineered a *coup d'état* in Prague, and—ten years after Munich and Hitler's subsequent seizure of that hapless nation—Czechoslovakia disappeared behind the iron curtain. A few months later, in June, the Russians imposed a blockade on Berlin in an effort to dislodge the Western powers from that city. It is hardly surprising that the Europeans, who lived closer to these events than Americans, felt extremely jittery at these overt signs of Russian hostility and aggressive intent. In this atmosphere of tension and insecurity, in which comparisons of Stalin's Russia with Hitler's Germany seemed all too valid, it became obvious that Europe's economic recovery was impossible; people do not make the necessary sacrifices and work hard to recuperate today if they feel that tomorrow they will be conquered and that their efforts will all have been in vain. In short, it suddenly became crystal clear that a prerequisite for Europe's recovery was military security.

The Europeans had already made some moves in this direction. In March 1947, France and England had signed the Treaty of Dunkirk to provide for their mutual defense against a threat to their security. Exactly a year later, in March 1948, Great Britain, France, the Netherlands, Belgium, and Luxembourg signed the Brussels Pact of collective self-defense. This Brussels Pact was established as a military counterpart to OEEC. Just as OEEC represented an organization dedicated to economic cooperation, the Brussels Pact represented one dedicated to military cooperation. And just as the vitality of OEEC had depended upon American capital for its success, the Brussels Pact members expected their alliance to attract American military support.

They were not to be disappointed. In April 1949, Belgium, Canada, Denmark, France, Great Britain, Iceland, Italy, Luxembourg, the Netherlands,

Norway, Portugal, and the United States signed the North Atlantic Treaty. The U.S. Senate ratified the treaty in July after extended hearings and debates, and the other ratifications were completed by August 1949. For the United States, this NATO commitment set a precedent: For the first time in its history, the country had committed itself to an alliance in peacetime. Europe had become "our first line of defense." It was precisely this knowledge that the United States would fight to preserve Europe's freedom that was supposed to prevent a Soviet attack. Two world wars had proved Europe's vital importance to American security. Instead of again allowing the balance of power to be upset and thereby once more becoming drawn into war, the United States now expected to eliminate this contingency by committing itself to the preservation of the European balance in peacetime—that is, *before* the enemy attack took place. The presumption was that the fear of meeting American resistance and fighting an all-out war with the United States would deter the potential aggressor from launching his attack.

This strategy of deterrence relied almost exclusively upon American strategic air power—that is, upon the ability of the Strategic Air Command (SAC) to destroy completely the Soviet Union with atomic bombs. This strategy was based upon two assumptions: first, that the only form of future war would be a total war, which would be precipitated by a direct Soviet attack upon the United States or Western Europe, and second, that deterrence could be achieved by air power and its ability to inflict such heavy damage upon an enemy that he would, in effect, be committing suicide if he launched an attack.

Two events were to change this reliance upon air power alone to deter or destroy the enemy. The first was the explosion of the first Soviet atomic bomb in late 1949. This foreshadowed a time when the Soviet Union, too, would possess an atomic stockpile; in short, it portended a significant increase in Soviet capability. The second event was the North Korean attack upon South Korea in June 1950. Since it was presumed that this attack could not have occurred without Soviet permission, the North Korean aggression suggested a change in Soviet intentions. And this possibility was strengthened in Washington's view by Communist China's intervention in North Korea in late November. The Western response was large-scale rearmament.

This involved three tasks for NATO: the establishment of a command structure, the formulation of a strategy by which to defend Europe on the ground, and the rebuilding of its ground forces. These efforts received their initial impetus when, in the dark days after Communist China's entry into the Korean War, President Truman appointed General Eisenhower to serve as Supreme Allied Commander in Europe. Eisenhower, in turn, strove to make his command operational. His first move was to establish three commands under him: a Central Europe Command, a Northern Europe Command, and a Southern Europe Command. The first of these commands presided over the most important front—militarily because here was the plane upon which the Red Army could apply its full force and be met with full counterforce, and politically because Germany, France, and Great Britain lay on this axis.

The strategy NATO adopted was known as the "forward strategy"—that is, a defense at the Elbe. Politically, the Europeans wanted no part of a strategy that called for a withdrawal and would bring the Red Army to their borders, and most probably into their countries. They had no desire to provide battlefields again; they wanted the Red Army to be kept far from their frontiers. And liberation in a war in which atomic bombs would be dropped was no liberation at all: One could not liberate a corpse. Indeed, if the first Soviet onslaught were to drive the Allies completely out of Europe, the continent would fall permanently under Soviet control. The atomic bomb forbade a Normandy-type landing. Thus, from a political standpoint, Allied forces could not retreat. Europe would have to be defended as far east in Western Germany as possible.

Such a defense required troops and proper logistical support. When Eisenhower arrived in Europe, he found only twelve divisions—including the American ones—none of which was at full strength, properly trained, or fully equipped with the latest weapons. Nor were there any effective reserves to back them up. Perhaps neither of these facts was surprising: The European powers had greater needs and more important things to do in the immediate postwar days than to maintain or rebuild sizable military forces. In addition, because of America's atomic monopoly, it had seemed quite safe to rely solely upon SAC for deterrence and to use the troops in Germany solely for occupation duties.

But Eisenhower needed more ground forces for two purposes: The first would be to act as a "tripwire." In case the Russians had any delusion that the United States would not go to war to defend Europe, the tripwire troops were to remove this belief. An attack by the Red Army would be bound to run into American troops, some of whom would obviously be killed. This would ensure American retaliation against the Soviet Union. The second function of the NATO army was to act as a "shield" by holding the Red Army at the point of attack, the Elbe River, while SAC laid waste the Soviet Union. Military planners believed that such shield forces would have to be quite large because of the size of the Red Army.

But the need for an ample number of divisions faced the European states with a dreadful dilemma. They were unable and unwilling to mobilize the necessary troops. They were still in the midst of economic recovery and unprepared to make the necessary sacrifices to raise large national armies. Unlike the United States, which was rich enough to produce both guns and butter, the Europeans had to choose guns or butter. While the Soviet threat made it necessary to have a minimal military protection, the task of economic reconstruction made it undesirable to devote too large a share of national budgets to rearmament. The American answer was the rearmament of Germany. If France and Britain could not supply the necessary troops, Germany would serve to supply them. Moreover, this decision seemed an eminently correct one. For the forward strategy meant that NATO would try to hold West Germany. It was only fitting that the Germans, should contribute to their own defense. In turn, of course, German rearmament reinforced the need for a forward strategy. For the West Germans could hardly be persuaded to rearm if they could not be assured that West Germany would not be turned into a battlefield and that German troops would not be used merely for the defense of France and England. Thus, the German question once more raised its head. It was not a new question—but this time it received new answers.

GERMAN RECOVERY AND REARMAMENT

Ever since the middle of the nineteenth century—if not since the Congress of Vienna in 1815—Germany has held the key to the European balance of power. This was true of Germany even in defeat in 1945. Almost from the cessation of hostilities, the Soviet Union and the United States began their contest over Germany. East Germany had fallen into Russian hands; West Germany was occupied by the Western powers. Actually, the Allies were lucky, for West Germany contained the great majority of Germany's population and held the heart of its industrial power. West Germany, in short, was the chief prize in Europe.

During the war, Stalin, Churchill, and Roosevelt had decided to govern Germany through a four-power Allied Control Commission (with France as the fourth power), which would administer the entire country as a single economic unit. In practice, this task proved impossible. The Russians, the British, and the French, as well as the smaller European nations, had been promised reparations payments in compensation for the widespread destruction the Germans had caused in their countries. The Russian sum was to consist of all the industrial equipment in the Soviet zone, plus one-quarter of the far greater industrial complex in West Germany (it was assumed during the war that Germany's industrial power would be intact at the end of the war). But—and these were to be the decisive points—the United States and Great Britain had insisted upon two restrictions on these reparations payments. First, Germany was to be left enough of its nonmilitary industries to maintain its standard of living at the same level as the rest of Europe (but definitely not higher); and second, no reparations were to be paid out of current production until Germany had earned enough money with its exports to pay for the imports it needed. Germany was to support itself. The Allies had no desire—to put it mildly—to spend their money supporting their former enemy.

The Russians quickly began demolishing the industry in their zone with great gusto—never, of course, informing the Western powers how much they were taking. The Russians also cut off the regular food supply from East Germany, which had traditionally been Germany's breadbasket; under the original agreement, they were to furnish this food in return for the three-fifths of capital equipment they were allowed to remove from the Western zones. These Soviet actions were bound to lead to trouble, and they did. Almost exactly a year after V-E Day, the United States announced that it was suspending all further West German reparations payments to the Soviet Union. They were not to be resumed until the Soviet Union operated its zone as part of Germany under the original terms of agreement. The reason for this American action was clear: If East Germany no longer furnished the supplies of food which West Germany needed, West Germany would have to increase its exports to buy food from abroad; and if it had to increase exports, it had to increase production. The British agreed; they were unwilling to spend their few remaining dollars buying food for the Germans. Thus, the wartime agreement to hold German industrial production down for fear that Germany would again use its heavy industry in a secret rearmament program—as it had during the years between the two world wars—collapsed. The American and British purpose was to make Germany pay for its own needs.

But the two powers also had another and more important aim in mind: As Europe's economic collapse became clearer and the cold war intensified, it became necessary to lift Germany out of its economic stagnation and make its industry contribute to the general economic recovery of Europe. In July 1946, the United States offered to merge its zone with those of Britain and France; Germany was to be decompartmentalized in order to speed up its industrial recovery. The French, fearing Germany's reviving strength, refused to participate. The result was that in January 1947, an embryonic German state known as Bizonia (France was to join later) formally emerged. But this fusion would not by itself suffice to achieve Germany's economic recovery. The willing cooperation of the Germans themselves was needed. America and Britain therefore decided to let the Germans begin to take a more active part in running their own country; this, in effect, foreshadowed the eventual establishment of a West German government. Lastly, Germany needed a sound currency; without it, its economy could not recover. The subsequent currency reform carried out by the U.S. military government became the basis of West Germany's amazing economic recovery.

The Russians reacted by blockading Berlin. The issue at stake was more than just Berlin: It was Germany itself. Berlin, as the old capital of Germany, was the symbol of the conflict over Germany. The Russians certainly did not want to see West Germany become a partner of the West. Germany and Russia had fought two wars in forty years. Germany had beaten Russia the first time and almost defeated it again on the second occasion. Moreover, Germany was not a *status quo* power but a revisionist state eyeing territory now controlled by the Soviet Union and Poland. Whether these defensive reasons, springing from Russia's fear of Germany, were primary in precipitating the Berlin crisis, however, is rather doubtful. For if Russia's fear of Germany was so deep, it is difficult to understand why the Russians did not accept the American proposal, offered them by Secretary Byrnes, of an alliance of twenty-five or even forty years to neutralize Germany. In any case, whereas Russia had been much weaker than Germany before World War II, it emerged from that conflict far stronger—a superpower, in fact—while Germany, in spite of its potential strength, was now only a second-class power. The Russo-German balance of power had decisively changed in Russia's favor, and an independent German attack upon Russia was unlikely in these circumstances. For in any war, whether it acted unilaterally or as an ally of the United States, Germany would be the battlefield and therefore the first country to be destroyed. Fear of this consequence was a sufficient deterrent. The real danger to the Soviet Union of a revived Germany came from the fact that, once Germany's power had been added to that of the United States and its allies, the American position in Europe would obviously be greatly consolidated. This, in turn, stood in the way of two Russian objectives: one, the withdrawal of American forces and the liquidation of American bases on the Continent; and two, the long-term aim of winning Germany's participation in a subservient partnership. Germany's recovery, in short, would block Russia's expansionist purposes in Europe.

In order to forestall Germany's revival, therefore, the Russians resorted to a test of strength. If the Allies could be forced out of Berlin, German confidence in American strength would be undermined. The Germans would hardly attach themselves to a friend too weak to protect them. Indeed, if American will power would crumble under Soviet pressure, France and Britain also might reconsider their adherence to NATO. The Berlin crisis, then, if it were not met, would disintegrate the entire American position in Europe and nullify America's postwar efforts to rebuild Europe as a partner in the struggle against the Soviet Union.

The method of conflict was decided at the outset by the unwillingness of either the United States or the Soviet Union to risk a total war. Thus, the Western powers ruled out almost at the start an attempt to reopen the corridor to Berlin by sending troops and tanks to challenge the Red Army. Instead, they limited themselves to an airlift to supply the city with all its needs. The Russians did not challenge this effort, for they were aware that in doing so they would leave the West no alternative but to fight a total war. Instead, they decided to wait and see whether the Western powers could take care of the needs of Berlin's 2.5 million citizens. It would take a minimum of 4000 tons of food and fuel daily—an enormous amount of tonnage to ship in by air. After 324 days of waiting, the Russians were convinced that the Americans and the British were more than equal to the task. While the total supplies did not immediately attain the 4000-ton target, Allied planes were eventually to fly in as much as 13,000 tons daily. Planes landing at three-minute intervals flew in 60 per cent more than the 8000 tons that had previously been sent each day by ground transport. By the spring of 1949, West Berliners were eating more than at the beginning of the blockade—and considerably more than the East Berliners! Faced with this colossal Allied achievement, the Russians called off the blockade in May.

America's determination to hold Europe and not to allow further Soviet expansion had been demonstrated. The West Germans clearly saw that they could count on America to protect them. Just as NATO had been the prerequisite for Europe's economic recovery, the Berlin airlift was the final American act which led to Germany's resurgence. America had laid the basis for Germany's economic recovery through Marshall Plan funds and the currency reforms; and now, it had given Germany the sense of military security without which its economic reconstruction could not have been completed.

EUROPEAN INTEGRATION

Ironically, it was the fear of Germany's rising strength that was now, in turn, to stimulate further efforts toward European integration. The specter of a fully revived Germany struck fear into most of Germany's neighbors. The French, with their memories of 1870, 1914, and 1940, were particularly alarmed. Germany's recovery—stimulated by America's response to the cold war—thus posed a serious problem for Germany's partners: How could they hold Germany, potentially the strongest nation in Europe outside of Russia, in check? Ever since Germany's unification in the late nineteenth century, France had attempted to deal with the inherently greater strength of its aggressive and militaristic neighbor by forming alliances which could balance Germany's power. Since Britain had usually preferred to retain a free hand, and since its interests were also at times opposed to those of France, the French had relied primarily upon Continental allies. Before World War I, they discovered such an ally in Russia, and between the two wars they found partners in Poland, Czechoslovakia, Romania, and Yugoslavia. None of these alliances had saved France, however; in both wars, British power and especially American power had been the decisive factors in defeating Germany (aided by Russian power, of course, in World War II). But once saved, the French again responded in terms of their traditional reflex—despite the extension of Soviet power into the heart of Europe. For France, Germany was still *the* enemy, and in December 1944, the French signed a Treaty of Mutual Assistance with the Russians, thus making an alliance which they considered necessary for their security. Soviet hostility soon disillusioned the French and deprived the treaty of any meaning, however, and in fact made it necessary to add Germany's power to that of the West.

The failure of the traditional balance-of-power technique, by which an inferior power had always sought to balance a stronger nation, led France to seek a new way of exerting some control over Germany's growing power.

French statesmen found an imaginative means in European integration. It was through the creation of a supranational community, to which Germany could transfer certain sovereign rights, that German power could be controlled. Only in this manner could German strength be prevented from again causing harm to all of Europe, and at the same time be employed instead for Europe's welfare and security.

France made its first move in this direction of a united Europe in May 1950, when Foreign Minister Robert Schuman proposed the plan that has since borne his name: a European Coal and Steel Community (ECSC) composed of "Little Europe" (France, Germany, Italy, and the Benelux countries of Belgium, the Netherlands, and Luxembourg). The Schuman Plan was to interweave German and French heavy industry to such an extent that it would become impossible ever to separate them again. Germany would never again be able to use its coal and steel industries for nationalistic and militaristic purposes. The political and military power of the Ruhr, for purely German purposes, was to be destroyed for all time. War between Germany and France would become not only unthinkable but impossible under these circumstances.

But the new French technique of restraining Germany did not consist merely of fusing Germany's superior strength with France's own lesser strength and thereby subjecting Germany's power to a certain degree of French control. "Europeanization" was also a means for France to achieve a balance with Germany. The combination of the French and German coal and steel industries would strengthen French heavy industry and create a Franco-German equilibrium with ECSC. Economic integration would thus allow France to overcome its inferior industrial strength, which had been imposed upon it in large part by the division of Europe into separate national markets. One of the main reasons for France's industrial lag has been its lack of energy sources. It possessed Europe's largest iron ore deposits, in Lorraine—resources which during Germany's annexation of Alsace-Lorraine from 1871 to 1918 had added in considerable measure to making Germany the second greatest industrial power in the world before 1914. But even when it had regained Alsace-Lorraine after World War I, France still lacked the coal to heat the furnaces. Europe's largest coal deposits lay in the Ruhr, and to a lesser extent in the Saar—that is, in Germany. The Schuman Plan now, in effect, held out a bargain to West Germany. France was to receive coal from Germany at the same price paid by German manufacturers—and not at the previously much higher prices that made French products more expensive than German ones. In return, France was to abandon its opposition to raising German production, and prevail upon Britain and the United States to lift *all* controls from Germany's heavy industry—which would mean that Germany could once more compete on the international market. Even more important for Germany, entry into ECSC would be the first step toward regaining equal status with its former Western enemies, recovering its sovereignty, and strengthening its ties with the Western powers so that they would eventually include Germany in NATO. Thus, the Schuman Plan had both an economic and a political appeal for the Germans as well as the French.

The French plan was not, however, devised only to control Germany's resurgent power or to give France a strength equal to that of Germany. It had a third and more ambitious goal in mind: a united Europe under French leadership. For only by creating Little Europe could France again play a major role in world affairs. France alone was too weak to pursue an active part in a world dominated by two superpowers. Even in the Western coalition, the most influential European nation was Britain, not France; and, with Germany's recovery, it was very likely that Bonn's voice and opinions would also out-weigh those of Paris in Washington. By itself, France would remain dependent upon its American protector, powerless to affect major Western policy decisions. A united Europe, with Franco-German unity at its core, was therefore France's alternative to remaining subservient to the United States and without influence either in NATO or on the world stage. Only through a united Europe could France gain an equal voice with what De Gaulle was later to call the "Anglo-Saxons" in NATO, and possibly even exert independent pressure upon the Soviet Union.

These, then, were the benefits the French expected to gain from the Schuman Plan, and their approach was a highly realistic one. For they clearly saw that the nucleus of a united Europe would have to be a Franco-German union. The antagonism between these two states, born of their traditional enmity, would first have to be healed. Moreover, the French scheme did more than just evoke the dream of a united Europe, hoping that its vision would so fire people's imagination that they would suddenly discard their narrow nationalistic loyalties for a wider European allegiance. Europe could not be created by sentiment alone. The French determined to erect the new Europe upon a solid foundation, building from the bottom upward. Europe, they knew, could be forged only by tying together the interests of politically powerful and economically important groups in the various nations *across* national boundaries. For instance, the removal of all trade barriers in the coal and steel sector of the economy would encourage the modernization of mines and plants, as well as the elimination of those mines and plants that continued to operate inefficiently. And once the efficient producers had adjusted to the wider market and witnessed its opportunities, they would want to remove national barriers in other areas. Further, as production increased, Europe's standard of living would rise, and as French and Italian workers received more of what they believed to be their share, labor would see that its goal of a welfare state could be achieved only at the European level.

The French showed great political astuteness in their selection of heavy industry as the first to be integrated. Coal and steel form the basis of the entire industrial structure—they represent a sector that cannot possibly be separated from the overall economy. Since the separation created by ECSC was to be an artificial one to begin with, this would create a "spillover" effect. Or to put it another way: This would exert pressure on the unintegrated sectors of the economy; and as the benefits of the pooling of heavy industry became clearly observable, these sectors would follow suit. The Coal and Steel Community was thus seen as the first stage of an attempt to create a wider market in one particular area of the economy; and it was expected that this approach would be gradually extended to other areas of the economy, such as agriculture, transportation, and electricity, eventually leading to the creation of a "united states" of Europe with a huge market and a mass-production system. In brief, this functional approach stressed supranational cooperation and institutions within a limited functional sphere and the creation of common interests within that particular area of activity before extending it to other fields.

The ECSC institutions, then, were the embryo of a united Europe. They were soon to be applied to an area that their initial planners had not expected to include—the military forces of the different nationalities. The French originated this idea, too. American insistence on German rearmament made it unavoidable. To the French, the rearmament of their old enemy was both distasteful and dangerous. But France was faced with the inevitable, since German rearmament was made necessary primarily by France's own inability to supply more troops itself. Yet the French remained determined that the world would never see another *German* army, *German* general staff, *German* war ministry, or *German* ministry of armaments. The solution they proposed was the formation of a European Defense Community. Just as the French had conceived of ECSC as a means for controlling Germany's growing economic strength and harnessing it to Europe's welfare, so they now proposed a European army, composed of army corps in which no more than two divisions could be of one nationality, as an instrument for checking Germany's rising military power and using it for Europe's defense. The EDC Treaty was signed in May 1952. NATO, of course, remained the supreme command. EDC and NATO were, however, formally linked. Since all EDC members except Germany were members of NATO, this link ensured that Germany was obligated to come to NATO's defense and vice versa.

For Germany, entry into EDC was another step toward regaining full equality with the other Western powers and asserting its political prestige. Most important, in return for providing EDC with 500,000 men organized into twelve divisions, Germany would recover its sovereignty, with certain limitations. The Allies would reserve their authority to take the necessary measures to protect the security of their forces in Germany (not only against external aggression, but also against possible attempts by the extreme left or right to subvert West Germany from within), to continue governing Berlin, and—in order to prevent any Russo-German deal—to preserve their exclusive right to negotiate with the Soviet Union on the question of German reunification. The kind of Germany they would seek—the United States, Britain, and

France declared—would be "a unified Germany enjoying a liberal-democratic constitution, like that of the Federal Republic, and integrated within the European community."

The likelihood of attaining this objective was very small indeed. Western proposals to unite Germany constantly included terms which the Soviet Union could not possibly accept. These terms included reunification via free elections in both halves of Germany and insistence upon allowing the government of this reunified Germany freedom to conduct its own foreign policy. The former would have meant the end of the Soviet-imposed Communist regime in East Germany; and the latter condition would have allied a unified Germany, probably headed by the pro-Western government of Konrad Adenauer, with the West. NATO would thus be extended to the Polish frontier and the Eastern satellite belt. The Russians were hardly likely to accept such a restriction of their sphere of influence or permit willingly such an advance of Western power. Allied terms thus ensured a continuation of a divided Germany—which was precisely what they wanted. France did not wish to integrate with a united Germany—only with a split Germany. A reunited Germany would tend to dominate Little Europe, for it would certainly be more powerful than France or Italy. These nations were therefore opposed to Germany's reunification; and they, together with the United States, paid verbal allegiance to this goal only to keep the West German government of Chancellor Adenauer in power. For the German people, reunification was of course a vital concern, and Adenauer's claim was that through the alliance with America, Britain, and France, West Germany and the Western powers would be placed in such a strong position that one day they could negotiate Russia's exit from East Germany. Yet it must also be noted that the Federal Republic between the Elbe and the Rhine is a Germany without Prussia, that South Germany has long been hostile to Protestant Prussia, and the Rhineland has been much influenced by Western (especially French) democratic thought. A reunified Germany would undoubtedly stimulate a movement to resurrect Prussia. It might therefore be said that, if Germany had to be divided, the present division which cuts Prussia off from the Western part of Germany could not have been more aptly drawn. It is this latter half which is integrating with the West in defense against the Soviet pressure from the East.

THE SOVIET SHIFT TO ASIA

It seems a cruel twist of fate that this very success of American foreign policy in Europe should have brought about a shift in the focus of Soviet pressure from Europe to Asia—a shift which in June 1950, led to the outbreak of the Korean War. The Truman Doctrine had prevented a Russian breakthrough into Southeast Europe and the Middle East and established Western

Europe's flank in the eastern Mediterranean. The Marshall Plan had set Europe on the path to economic recovery and health. NATO had guaranteed Europe its security. The lessons of two world wars had been absorbed, and the NATO commitment was the proof of this.

The United States had transformed a position of great weakness and vulnerability into one of relative strength. It had drawn a clear line between the American and Russian spheres of influence and had demonstrated, in both Greece and Berlin, that it was in Europe to stay. (The Greek crisis had passed when Yugoslavia was ejected from the Soviet bloc in 1948; the Yugoslavs no longer provided aid to the Greek guerrillas.) What all this meant was that Europe was no longer a profitable field for guerrilla warfare, *coups d'état,* or subversive attempts.

Opportunities for immediate expansion had disappeared. To cross the line drawn by the United States was to risk total war, and this risk was hardly one the Soviet Union was willing to assume during a period in which the United States held atomic superiority. The Russian leaders, as George Kennan had said, did not believe in pursuing an "adventuristic" policy which gambled with the very existence of the Soviet state.

So they turned their attention to the Far East. Here was a much more attractive field for political and military exploitation. Most countries in this area had only recently emerged from Western colonialism, and their nationalistic and anti-Western feelings were very strong. Nationalist China's collapse and the establishment of a Communist government on the mainland in late 1949 had even further weakened the Western position in Asia, for it had gravely shifted the balance of power in the Far East against the United States. The United States no longer confronted only Russia; it was now faced with the challenge of the combined power of the Sino-Soviet bloc. Moreover, whereas pressure in Europe united the Western powers, pressure in Asia divided them, because they were fundamentally split over the character and nature of the new Chinese regime. And finally, no expansionist move in the Far East would entail the risk of total war. In the American pattern of defense, Europe held strategic priority; Asia was of secondary interest. Europe was so vital to American defense that any Soviet move in Western Europe entailed the risk of an all-out clash with the United States; no single area in Asia was so immediately vital to American security that it was worth the cost of total war. The recovery of Europe and China's collapse, then, created a vacuum in the East and turned Russian pressure toward Asia. It was here that the dramatic clashes of the cold war were to occur during the next four years. And it was these clashes that were to lead to a reaction within the United States itself against American foreign policy.

chapter 4

containment in the far east

THE FALL OF CHINA

During World War II, the United States had a twofold purpose in the Pacific: to defeat Japan and to create a powerful and friendly China in its place. It was hoped that a strong and democratic China would play a leading role in protecting the postwar peace in the Far East. The United States took several actions to confer upon China the status of a great power. It renounced its extraterritorial rights in China, repealed the Chinese exclusion laws, established an annual Chinese immigration quota, and made it possible for legally admitted Chinese to become American citizens. At Cairo in 1943, together with Great Britain, the United States promised to return "all the territories Japan had stolen from the Chinese, such as Manchuria, Formosa, and the Pescadores." It also awarded to China one of the five permanent seats on the United Nations Security Council; China was thus granted equal status with the Soviet Union, Great Britain, France, and the United States.

The belief of American statesmen that the mere pronouncement of China as a Great Power could actually convert it into one was typically American: One need only believe strongly enough in the desirability of an event for it to happen. Perhaps American policy-makers also hoped that if China were admitted into the Great-Power club, it would behave like one. But American faith without Chinese works was insufficient to accomplish the task. It would have taken a miracle to do that; and while statesmen at times delude themselves into thinking that they can perform miracles, such things happen only in storybooks.

The first obstacle to creating a strong China was the sharp division within the country. Quite apart from the Japanese occupation of large areas of the country during the war, the Chinese were deeply split among themselves. There was not one China; there were two—a Communist China and a Nationalist China. The Communists were not scattered throughout the whole population, as in Europe; already in control of large segments of northwest China, they extended their sphere during the war by infiltrating into north-central China. In this area, the Japanese held the cities and the major lines of communication, while the Communists organized the countryside. By 1945, they controlled 116 million people, one-fourth of China's entire population, within an area that constituted 15 percent of China's territory, exclusive of Manchuria. Communist China was, in short, a nation within a nation.

Thus, if the United States wanted to create a united China, it would have to end this internal split. The American aim was to achieve this objective by establishing a coalition government in which all parties would be represented. The desirability of such a government was not questioned. What possible harm could there be in uniting the Nationalists and the Communists? The United States and the Soviet Union were cooperating against the common enemy, and most leaders and officials of the American government looked forward to friendly postwar relations. If these two nations, each representing a totally different way of life, could overcome past differences and get along together, why should the two Chinese parties not be able to settle their conflict? There was also another and more immediate reason why the United States wished to end China's division as quickly as possible. A China torn apart by internal strife could not make an effective contribution to the winning of the war. Both the Nationalists and the Communists were concerned more with fighting each other than with fighting the Japanese. But the American attitude is that once war breaks out, the total effort must be directed toward the single goal of military victory; any diversion of strength—particularly for "extraneous" political purposes—is considered unjustifiable. The war had to be won in the quickest possible time and with the minimum number of casualties. This attitude, then, reinforced the American desire to establish a coalition government in China.

All efforts aimed at achieving this goal, both during the war and afterward, were, however, in vain. Neither the Nationalists nor the Communists trusted one another. Both sought a monopoly of power, and both were constantly aware of the important rôle their armies played in the struggle for power: The Nationalists recognized that they would have to deprive their enemy of his army in order to ensure their own survival; and the Communists were realists enough to know that they needed their army to defeat Chiang. At the end of the war, both parties—and particularly the Nationalists—believed that they had the capabilities to defeat their opponent; compromise was therefore unnecessary.

China was not, however, divided only between two irreconcilable parties. Its pro-American Nationalist government was losing popular support and disintegrating. Perhaps the Nationalists were merely the victims of fate. Except for the two years from 1929 to 1931, the government was constantly engaged in fighting for its very survival—against the Japanese (who attacked Manchuria in 1931, Shanghai in 1932, and China itself in 1937), as well as the Communists. Faced with both external and internal danger, Chiang Kai-shek had neither the time nor the resources to concern himself with formulating and implementing the political, social, and economic reforms China needed. His principal concern was military: to stem the Japanese advance and maintain himself in power. The problem of modernizing China—above all, of meeting peasant aspirations—was strictly a subsidiary problem. Moreover, Japanese successes during the war changed the basis of Chiang's support and thereby rendered any agrarian reform impossible. By 1939, the Japanese had occupied the entire coastal area of China and had driven the Nationalists inland. This meant that Chiang's Kuomintang Party, which controlled the government, had lost the main pillar of its support, the progressive commercial and financial interests in the coastal cities. Instead, it was forced to rely upon the conservative landlord class.

No government ever likes to commit suicide, and the Nationalist government proved no exception. A government whose principal social and economic support came from the landlords was unlikely to carry out any land reforms. Probably a majority of peasants were independent landowners, but many of China's peasants were tenants. Both groups were, at any rate, profoundly dissatisfied. Those who rented their land had to pay excessive sums; after the war, these sometimes amounted to 50 to 90 percent of the peasant's crops. Those who owned their own land were handicapped by the small size of their holding and the lack of capital. The government's taxation policies further impoverished the peasant, who bore the main burden of the taxes. Since the peasant's crops were visible and easily appraisable, corrupt officials usually took more of the crops than the peasant could afford to spare. The result was that the peasant lived in a constant state of impoverishment and indebtedness. In order to survive, he had to seek funds from a money-lender, usually the local landlord, who charged him an extremely high rate of interest, often from 20 to 30 percent. Consequently, the peasant got himself deeper and deeper into debt.

The fact that the peasants constituted four-fifths of China's population also meant that they had to provide most of the conscripts for the Nationalist army. But the able-bodied and eligible sons of the rich avoided military service; there were always enough corrupt officials who could be bribed. In the same way, the rich tended to avoid paying taxes. Chiang, in short, seemed to be doing his best to earn the peasants' hatred.

After the war, the Nationalists even managed to alienate the business circles which had formerly supported them. As the Nationalists returned to the coastal cities, they took over all Japanese-owned industries and ran them as state enterprises. This incensed the business community. Some of the Japanese property had formerly belonged to the Chinese, but the government simply neglected to return such property to its owners. Even worse was the fact that private enterprise now found itself faced with the powerful competition of state industries, which were controlled by relatives and close friends of Chiang. Naturally, the American aid funds with which the government supported its enterprises provided great profits for these people. As the American commander in China during the war, General Wedemeyer, observed in 1947 upon his return on a fact-finding mission for the American government: "Certain rich families, some of whom have relatives in high positions of the Government, have been greatly increasing their fortunes. Nepotism is rife . . . sons, nephews, and brothers of government officials have been put into positions within the government-sponsored firms or in private firms to enable them to make huge profits at the expense of their government and their people."

The Nationalist position deteriorated even further because of China's unchecked inflation. The government had no fixed budget, and its accounting system did not function. When the government needed money, it simply printed it, thereby further inflating the currency. Prices doubled 67 times in the two and a half years from early 1946 to late 1948. No one seemed willing or able to control this spiral. The most devastating impact of this hyperinflation was upon government officials at the lower level; it provided them with a massive incentive for corruption. Their salaries were wholly inadequate, and they had to find means of supplementing their meager incomes. Honesty in these circumstances simply did not pay. Corruption became rife throughout the government.

As Chiang's government lost popularity, it began to resort increasingly to force to hold its position. The resulting police and military measures only further alienated the people. Wedemeyer found this situation: "Secret police operate widely, very much as they do in Russia and as they did in Germany. People disappear. . . . No trials and no sentences. . . . Everyone lives with a feeling of fear and loses confidence in the government." This was particularly true of the intellectuals, who, together with the peasantry, have been the traditional supporters of China's governments. Professors were dismissed, even arrested, when they began to criticize the government for its policies. Students similarly inclined were also thrown into jail.

The behavior of the army also spread hatred of the government. The Manchurian episode was typical. In Manchuria, according to Wedemeyer,

> the Central Government armies were [at the end of the war with Japan] welcomed enthusiastically by the people as deliverers from Japanese oppression.

> Today, after several months of experience with the Central Government armies, the people experience a feeling of hatred and distrust because the officers and enlisted men were arrogant and rude. Also, they stole and looted freely; their general attitude was that of conquerors instead of liberators.

To sum up the position of the Nationalists: The government had alienated important segments of the politically articulate minority, especially the businessmen and intellectuals. The more inarticulate and passive peasants were tired of the constant fighting, the high rents and taxes. All three groups had either lost confidence in the ability of the government to take care of the problems of postwar China, or felt that the government was not interested in their welfare. But only minorities in each group turned to the Communists. The majority simply disengaged themselves from the Nationalists and became indifferent to the outcome of the civil war. They did not rise up against the government in a "popular revolution." If the Communists won the civil war—and the military conflict would play the decisive role in determining this issue—they did so because most Chinese were willing to give the Communists the benefit of the doubt and allow them to demonstrate that they could give China a more effective government.

One reason for this lack of popular hostility and suspicion toward the Communists was, of course, the reverse side of the widespread anti-Nationalist sentiment. But another was the favorable picture the Communists presented of themselves to the Chinese population. The policies they pursued in the areas under their control were responsible for this. They did not destroy the traditional tenure system and expropriate or eliminate the landlords and money-lenders. They only reduced the rents to a fixed maximum and lowered the interest rates that could be charged on borrowed money. They permitted private enterprise and allowed all factions to participate in local government. Though they did assure Communist control by retaining the power to approve all candidates, their activities nevertheless seemed to support their claim that they stood for democracy, freedom, and individual liberty. Certainly, their economic and political practices demonstrated little Marxist bias. They appeared, instead, in the guise of genuine democrats; and their pose as agrarian reformers was widely accepted—precisely because, as an agrarian-based party, they actually did act as agrarian reformers.

If the Communists acted as if their only wish was to reform China along democratic and capitalistic lines, this was, of course, a tactical device. But the point remains that it was effective and achieved its purposes: It attracted minority support among the various strata of China's population disaffected by Nationalist policies, and it gained extensive acquiescence among the rest of the population. Chiang had alienated most of his popular support. The Communists, by cleverly hiding their real intentions, exploited this feeling of neutrality. For their purposes, a large neutral public was almost as beneficial as positive majority support; the only thing that really mattered was that this support had been withdrawn from Chiang.

The Communist position for the final military struggle was further strengthened when, near the end of the Pacific war, the Russian army marched into Manchuria. Once established, the Russians did two things that badly hurt China. First, they dismantled Manchuria's industry and transported the machinery back to Russia to help restore their own badly destroyed industry; as a result, Manchuria, China's industrial heartland, was unable to contribute to the country's economic recovery. Second, the Russians allowed the Chinese Communists to infiltrate the countryside and handed them large stocks of Japanese arms and ammunition. Conversely, the Russians delayed the return of Nationalist troops, who had to launch a major offensive to establish their control over Manchuria. The government forces did capture the cities, but the Communists remained in control of the countryside. The Soviet invasion of Manchuria thus was a serious blow to the Nationalists.

The blame for these events has often been attributed to President Roosevelt and the Yalta "betrayal," which granted Russia, among other things, a restoration of the rights Russia had held in Manchuria before its defeat by Japan in 1904–1905: the lease of Port Arthur as a Soviet naval base; the internationalization of the commercial port Dairen, which, unlike Russia's own Siberian port of Vladivostok, was not icebound part of the year; and the joint Sino-Soviet operation of the Chinese–Eastern and South Manchurian Railroads, which served these three cities. To take this charge seriously, though, one has to deny certain clear facts of wartime military strategy: namely, that American military men were unsure that the atomic bomb would be a success; that they believed an invasion of Japan would be necessary to bring about Japan's surrender; that they expected to suffer at least 1 million casualties, and feared even more if the Japanese reinforced the home-island garrison with troops from Manchuria and northern China; and that they therefore wanted the Red Army to tackle these mainland forces before their invasion. The American government was willing to pay the Russians the price they demanded if this would help save the lives of American soldiers, and this willingness was further increased by its suspicion that the Russians planned to restore their tsarist position in Manchuria by declaring war on Japan at the moment when the United States seemed on the verge of victory. The Russian takeover would then be a practically bloodless operation, with a minimal contribution to Japan's defeat. American officials wanted Russia to pay some kind of price, at least, for what it could actually take for nothing. Finally, they wanted to secure a promise from the Russians that they would sign a treaty of alliance and friendship with the Nationalist government. The purpose of this treaty was to secure the Soviet Union's support for Chiang Kai-shek and to isolate his Communist opponents; this would enable Chiang to consolidate his grip on China and perhaps allow him to defeat his domestic enemy. The Russians did, in fact, sign such a treaty, but then proceeded to violate it by aiding their Chinese comrades. However, Stalin apparently did not believe that this help strengthened the Chinese Communists sufficiently to defeat the Nationalists. He is reported to have counseled Mao Tse-tung to join Chiang in a coalition government and accept Chiang's supremacy; in this respect, Stalin's policy seemed to have been the same as Truman's. Mao is said to have nodded his assent to Stalin's advice and then disregarded it; he was more confident than Stalin in a final victory.

So was Chiang, as the decisive stage of the civil war began in 1947. The Nationalist army had a strength of approximately 2.7 million troops, while the Communists had 1.1 million men, including 400,000 guerrillas; the Nationalists held a superiority of rifle firepower of more than three to one. However, the Nationalists should not have been so confident. In the first place, Chiang tended to choose his top generals for their personal loyalty rather than their ability. He constantly interfered in the chain of command. He would send orders to officers in the field countermanding those of the local commanders, or change generals in the middle of a battle or campaign. This lack of continuity in the field command and Chiang's own interventions caused uncertainty, confusion, and resentment. In the second place, Nationalist strategy was unsound and could not have been better selected to ensure defeat. Chiang and his commanders were imbued with the "wall" psychology: Their military strategy was to employ their forces only to capture cities and then to hold these cities. Instead of conducting a war of maneuver in order to find the Communist armies and destroy them in battle, the Nationalist forces immobilized their strength by walling themselves up in the cities. Consequently, they failed either to hurt the Communists' strength or to weaken their hold on the countryside. At the same time, however, their armies in the cities degenerated from the status of field armies capable of offensive operations to that of garrison troops; this sapped them of any aggressive spirit.

Throughout 1946 and 1947, the Communists limited their operations largely to raiding supply depots and communication lines, ambushing Nationalist forces, engaging in skirmishes, and attacking isolated garrisons. These local tactical successes heightened the Communist forces' confidence and morale just as they added to their opponents' demoralization. By 1948, the Communists had so increased the strength of their forces and firepower that they no longer had to rely solely upon hit-and-run tactics; they now sought out the Nationalist forces in order to completely annihilate them by concentrating superior masses of troops against them and attacking without respite. Throughout the whole campaign, the Communists kept the initiative; it was they who constantly chose the time and place of attack. By February 1, 1949, they controlled Manchuria. Nationalist strength had by then declined to 1.5 million men, including 500,000 service troops. Up until mid-September

1948, the Nationalists had been able to replace their combat losses and thereby maintain their army at a strength of 2.7 million men. In other words, in only four and a half months, the Nationalists had lost 45 percent of their troops. Meanwhile, Communist strength had risen to 1.6 million regular troops—partly as the result of defections from the Nationalist armies. Eighty percent of the American equipment furnished to the government forces during and after the war had been lost, with an estimated 75 percent of it falling into the Communists' hands. General Barr, the head of the American military mission in China, summed up the situation succinctly: "No battle has been lost since my arrival due to lack of ammunition or equipment. Their [the Nationalists'] military debacle, in my opinion, can all be attributed to the world's worst leadership and many other morale-destroying factors that led to a complete loss of the will to fight." Nowhere was this more clearly demonstrated than in Chiang's failure, after his loss of northern China, even to attempt a defense of south China by making a stand along the Yangtze River. Chiang thereby forfeited the mainland, and he withdrew to Formosa, an island lying 100 miles off the mainland coast. In the fall of 1949, Mao Tse-tung proclaimed the People's Republic of China.

One question about Nationalist China's defeat remains: Could the United States have prevented it? The answer is "Probably"—*if* American officers had taken over the command of the Nationalist armies; *if* the United States had been willing to commit large-scale land, air, and sea forces to fight in China; and *if* the United States had been willing to commit even greater financial aid than the approximately $2 billion it had already given in grants and credits since V-J Day. But these conditions could not have been met. America's helterskelter demobilization left it with insufficient forces either for supplying the officers for the direction of the Nationalist forces or for intervention in China. The United States had only one and one-third divisions at home. Nor did the American people seem to be in any mood to rearm in 1947–1948, particularly to fight a war in China.

The problem of extending further economic aid to Chiang was equally vexing. His corrupt, inefficient, and reactionary government did not provide a politically effective instrument through which to carry out the social and economic reforms China needed. Aiding Chiang seemed to be "pouring money down the drain." In contrast, U.S. economic aid to Europe, which the Administration considered the area most vital to American security, had a good chance of achieving its objective—political and economic recovery for Britain and the Continent. It would probably have been unwise in these circumstances to divert a very large slice of the government's not unlimited funds to attempt to restore a government that had lost the confidence of its own people. The power of the United States was, after all, not infinite; it would have to be applied selectively. Hence, those areas of vital interest in which its use would be most effective were to be the prime focus. As Secretary Acheson stated it: "Nothing that this country did or could have done within the reasonable limits of its capabilities could have changed that result; nothing that was left undone by this country has contributed to it. It was the product of internal Chinese forces, forces which this country tried to influence but could not. A decision was arrived at within China, if only a decision by default."

REEVALUATION OF AMERICAN FAR EASTERN POLICY

Despite Chiang's debacle and the disintegration of the Far Eastern balance of power, the U.S. government took an optimistic view of developments. Shortly after the Nationalist collapse, Secretary Acheson expressed his belief that despite the common ideological points of view of the Chinese and Russian regimes, they would eventually clash with one another. Acheson predicted that Russia's appetite for a sphere of influence in Manchuria and northern China would alienate Chinese nationalism. The implications of this point of view are clear. The first is that if the Chinese Communists were genuinely concerned with the preservation of China's national interest, they would resist Soviet penetration. Mao Tse-tung might, therefore, be a potential Tito. On the other hand, if Mao proved himself to be subservient to Russia, he would lose the support of the Chinese people. Since he would have shown that he served not the interests of China but those of another power, his regime would be identified with foreign rule. Given time, Acheson declared, the Chinese people would throw off this "foreign yoke." Thus, whichever of these two developments occurred, the United States could only gain from the antithesis between Communism and Chinese nationalism.

This analysis of Sino-Soviet relations indicated that the United States must first disentangle itself from Chiang Kai-shek. Until this disassociation had been completed, the United States would remain identified with the government rejected by the Chinese people. This could only foster the growth of anti-American sentiment in China. It was precisely this that had to be avoided, for the attention of the Chinese people should not be diverted from the Soviet Union's actions. Under no circumstances, Acheson emphasized, must America "seize the unenviable position which the Russians have carved out for themselves. We must not undertake to deflect from the Russians to ourselves the righteous anger, and the wrath, and the hatred of the Chinese people which must develop." Only by disengaging itself from Chiang Kai-shek could the United States exploit the alleged clash of interests between China and Russia.

The first step taken by the Truman administration to implement this policy was the release of a White Paper which argued that the Nationalists had lost control of the mainland despite adequate American economic and military aid. The clear implication was that Chiang was no longer worthy of American support; hence, American recognition of Chiang's government as the official government of China should be withdrawn. Conversely, it was suggested that the Communists should be recognized as the official government of China, both as a matter of fact and as a gesture of friendship. A second act was an announcement that American forces would not be used to defend Formosa, and that the administration would no longer provide the Nationalists with military aid or advice: "The United States Government will not pursue a course which will lead to involvement in the civil conflict in China." This opened the way for the Chinese Communists to take Formosa—an event that was expected before the end of 1950. The Communist government would then be the only claimant to represent China, and the United States could extend it recognition. Chiang, through whom containment had been impossible because he had been not a container but a sieve, would have been eliminated; containment of Russia could then be implemented through "Mao Tse-tito." But before this could happen, war had broken out in another area in the Far East—Korea.

THE KOREAN WAR AND THE TRUMAN–MACARTHUR CONTROVERSY

Korea had been a divided nation since 1945. Soviet forces had entered Korea two days after Japan surrendered. The nearest American troops at the time were in Okinawa, 600 miles away, and in the Philippines, 1500 to 2000 miles away. Consequently, the two powers decided to divide the country temporarily at the thirty-eighth parallel; the Russians would disarm the Japanese above the parallel, the United States below. With the beginning of the cold war, this division became permanent. All American attempts to negotiate an end to the division and establish a democratic and united Korea failed.

As a result, the United States took the problem to the United Nations in late 1947 and called upon that organization to sponsor a free election throughout all of Korea. The General Assembly thereupon established a temporary commission in Korea and charged it with the responsibility of holding and supervising such an election. The Russians, however, refused to grant the Commission access to North Korea, and the election was thus limited to South Korea. Afterward, the United States recognized South Korea as the official republic and the government of Syngman Rhee as its legitimate representative. The American government also extended to Rhee economic, technical, and military aid to bolster his non-Communist government and help Korea establish a democratic society. Thus, while South Korea was not an ally of the United States, there could be little doubt that the young republic was America's protégé.

It was this country which the North Korean Communists attacked in late June 1950. The Communist aggression took the American government by complete surprise. American policy-makers had believed that the Soviet leaders, like themselves, thought only in terms of all-out war. It was precisely this single-minded American preoccupation with total war that had accounted for Korea's being left outside the American Pacific defense perimeter, which ran from the Aleutians to Japan, through the Ryukyus (Okinawa) to the Philippines. This made Korea militarily dispensable within the pattern of American security, for in a global war its fate would be decided in other theaters of war. A Soviet occupation of Korea would not raise Korea's strategic significance, since the peninsula could be neutralized by American air and sea power. American troops had therefore been withdrawn from Korea, because in a major war they would be vulnerable to Russian land power and would probably be trapped. The resulting absence of pledged American military support to resist North Korean aggression rendered South Korea highly vulnerable; indeed, it left South Korea as an attractive vacuum inviting Communist expansion. On June 25, the North Korean Army struck.

Overnight, the survival of South Korea became identified with the survival of the United States itself. For North Korea's aggression, which in Washington's opinion could hardly have been launched without Soviet encouragement and support, altered the basis upon which Korea's strategic significance had been calculated. Korea's value could no longer be assessed in terms of its relative importance during a total war. The cold war focused attention upon the wider political and military implications of a Communist occupation of South Korea and upon the threat such an occupation would pose for the entire containment policy. If the principal purpose of containment was to prevent further Soviet expansion, American inaction in the face of Soviet aggression could only encourage further aggressive acts in the future. The appetites of dictators were believed to be insatiable. And if containment was possible only through an alignment of the United States' power with that of its allies, then failure to respond to South Korea's pleas for help must result in the disintegration of the alliance system and the isolation of the United States. If the United Sates merely stood by while South Korea fell, it would demonstrate to the world that it was either afraid of Russian power or unconcerned with the safety of its allies. American guarantees to help preserve their national integrity and political independence would thereafter be regarded as valueless; and this would leave nations whose security depended upon U.S. willingness to live up to its commitments with no alternative but to turn to neutralism for protection—a state in which they would be subject to increasing Soviet pressure and possibly eventual domination.

This reasoning applied particularly to Japan. With the demise of Nationalist China and the disintegration of the Far Eastern balance of power, the United States was about to turn Japan into an ally and rearm it in an effort to recreate some semblance of strength in the Pacific. The same rationale applied equally to the NATO countries in Europe. If NATO collapsed, the balance of power would shift drastically in favor of Russia. In these circumstances, the consequences of American inaction would be extremely grave. In fact, the United States had no choice in a bipolar world but to oppose force with force—if it wished to prevent an upset of the global balance of power and its own strategic isolation.

Nevertheless, the limited Soviet aggression did not fit American strategic doctrine, based on a one-sided concentration upon air-atomic striking power. The Russians had cleverly faced the United States with the dilemma of either risking a total war for a limited objective or taking no action at all and thus surrendering South Korea. American policy was prepared to deal only with an all-out Soviet surprise attack upon the United States or Western Europe; such an attack would be met by the power of SAC. But American strategy was completely unprepared to deal with the kind of less than total challenge which the Russians had now posed in Asia. The North Korean aggression, in effect, meant that massive retaliation outside of Europe was not an effective policy. For the deterrent effect of U.S. retaliatory power depended upon whether an enemy believed that the country would actually "unleash" this power if he committed aggression. The limited attack in Korea clearly demonstrated that the Soviet leaders were not deterred by the policy of massive retaliation, despite America's far greater atomic stockpile and ability to deliver it. They did not believe that the United States would risk all-out war to save Korea. For the Korean type of challenge could be met only by local response and primarily through the commitment of American ground forces. Containment depended not just upon the capacity to deter total war with strategic air power; it required, in addition, an army to meet precisely this kind of limited incursion.

But it was the army forces that the administration had been cutting since the end of World War II. General Marshall recalled in 1951 that the army had been so small in the years preceding the Korean War that there had been only one and one-third divisions in the United States. The Chiefs of Staff had had so few troops at their command that they had even been worried about obtaining enough men to guard airstrips at Fairbanks, Alaska. According to Marshall, "We had literally almost no military forces outside of our Navy and outside of an effective but not too large Air Force, except the occupation garrisons, and ... even in Japan they were only at about 60 percent strength."

Yet, if the United States was to escape the dilemma of total war or surrender, the Japanese-occupation divisions—undermanned and undertrained but luckily near the scene of battle—had to be committed. For two days, on June 27 and 28, the United States tried to stem the North Korean advance with air and sea forces alone. But on June 29, General MacArthur, the commander-in-chief in the Far East, reported that Korea would be lost unless ground forces were employed to halt the enemy army. These forces were then sent in under the aegis of the United Nations. This was done for two reasons. First, because by virtue of the free election it had sponsored in South Korea, the United Nations had been intimately concerned with the birth of the young state.

Second, one of the aims of American foreign policy was to associate its cold war policies with the symbolic, humanitarian values of the United Nations. Though it is traditional for nations to attempt to justify their policies in such a manner, the United States has shown a marked propensity for doing so. American depreciation of power and reluctance to recognize it as a factor in human affairs makes it psychologically necessary to rationalize actions in the international arena in terms of ideological objectives and universal moral principles. American power must be "righteous" power used not for purposes of power politics and selfish national advantage but for the peace and welfare of all mankind. Inherent in this public self-image of the United States as a noble and unselfish crusader on behalf of moral principles was an extreme danger, however—namely, that if the enemy were not properly punished through total defeat, the reaction to the war would be one of frustration and disillusionment, which could only jeopardize the containment policy itself.

This was precisely what was to happen, although, after initial setbacks, the war went well for a while. In a daring operation on September 15, General MacArthur, now U.N. Supreme Commander, landed an army at the west coast port of Inchon, 150 miles behind the North Korean lines. These forces then drove northward, thereby trapping more than half the enemy army. The rest of the shattered Communist army was in flight. On September 30, the U.N. forces reached the thirty-eighth parallel.

The question now confronting the United States was whether to cross the parallel. The war had been fought to restore South Korea; this implied a negotiated settlement on the parallel. This goal was now abandoned. The military situation favored the fulfillment of an American goal of several years' standing: the unification of the whole of Korea. The U.S. government therefore shifted its emphasis from containing the expansion of Soviet power to the forceful liberation of a Soviet satellite. Inchon, in short, transformed the whole character of the war—from a defensive action seeking only to reestablish the *status quo,* to an offensive one designed to effect a permanent change in the *status quo.*

The U.S. government believed that it was politically safe to attempt this. The administration did not believe that the Chinese Communist leaders would consider the U.N. advance a threat to their security, because they were Chinese first and Communists second. Mao and his colleagues were already thought to be so involved in their struggle with the Soviet Union over the detachment of northern China, Manchuria, and Sinkiang that their eyes were fixed on their own northern provinces rather than on North Korea. In short, there was nothing to fear. The new objective of a militarily unified Korea was sanctioned by a U.N. resolution on October 7.

But American policy-makers miscalculated. The Chinese did view the American march to their border as threatening, just as Washington had perceived the North Korean march southward toward Japan as threatening. So Peking sent its armies into North Korea under the guise of "volunteers," and in late November it launched a major offensive which drove the U.N. forces back below the thirty-eighth parallel. Throughout December 1950, and early January 1951, there was no certainty that U.N. troops could hold the peninsula; but the tired, defeated, and outnumbered troops managed to rally and stem the Chinese offensives. By March, they had once more advanced to the thirty-eighth parallel. The administration was again faced with a decision: whether to seek a militarily unified Korea or to accept a divided Korea.

There was no doubt about what the American field commander wanted to do. MacArthur insisted that the political aim of the war was the establishment of a unified Korea. He maintained that failure to prosecute the military campaign with the vigor necessary to achieve this objective would constitute rank appeasement. Above all, MacArthur felt that the United States should take advantage of China's intervention to weaken her before she became too strong. He wished to "severely cripple and largely neutralize China's capability to wage aggressive war and thus save Asia from the engulfment otherwise facing it." This purpose, MacArthur felt, could be achieved with minimum risk, since the Soviet Union would not dare to resort to war until its atomic and industrial power more nearly matched that of the United States. MacArthur's aim, in short, was not only to unify Korea but to change the entire strategic picture in the Far East.

The strategy with which MacArthur expected to accomplish these objectives consisted of a naval blockade of the Chinese coast; air bombardment of China's industrial complex, communication network, supply depots, and troop assembly points; reinforcement of his forces with Chinese Nationalist troops; and "diversionary action possibly leading to counter-invasion" by Chiang against the mainland.

The Truman administration, however, rejected MacArthur's proposals because they were considered too risky. It was feared that bombing China and inflicting a defeat upon Russia's principal ally would probably precipitate World War III. The Sino-Soviet Treaty of February 1950 bound the Soviet Union to come to the aid of China if the latter were attacked by Japan "or any other state which should unite with Japan" (an obvious reference to the United States). But even without this treaty, China was the Soviet Union's largest and most important ally. Russian self-interest in the Far East and the necessity of maintaining Russian prestige in the Communist sphere would make it difficult for the Soviet Union to ignore a direct attack upon the Chinese mainland.

But even if the Soviet Union remained a spectator, the United States could not extend the war. A "war of attrition" waged by Chinese manpower in Korea would "bleed us dry" and make it impossible to build a strong military defense in Europe. A large-scale diversion of American power to Asia would expose Europe to Soviet armies and might very well incite an attack at a moment of maximum American weakness on the Continent. The United States had to conserve its strength to check its principal enemy, the Soviet

Union; the country could not afford to dissipate its power in a peripheral area against a secondary enemy. MacArthur's strategy, in the opinion of General Bradley, Chairman of the Joint Chiefs of Staff, would therefore involve the United States in the wrong war, at the wrong place, at the wrong time, and with the wrong enemy.

This view was shared by Britain and France. America's chief allies were naturally reluctant to see American power diverted to the Far East before Europe was secure against Russian attack; and they had no desire to risk such an early outbreak of World War III for an area that was of minor strategic significance to them. Thus, if the United States decided to carry the war to China, it would have to act unilaterally. But the objective of balancing Soviet might or winning a total war was predicated on NATO's unity and combined strength.

Finally, the Joint Chiefs of Staff rejected MacArthur's proposals because they were judged militarily ineffective. A naval blockade would be of very limited use for two reasons: first, because China was so lacking in industrialization that a blockade would not have sufficient immediate impact; and second, because China's essential supplies came overland from Russia. Air bombardment of China's population and industrial centers would have an equally limited effect, for Communist China's arsenal lay in the Soviet Union. Even with the complete destruction of China's industrial heartland in Manchuria, Russia would still be in a position to supply China with the military equipment and ammunition it required. It was therefore decided to concentrate U.S. air power upon the 200 miles of supply line in North Korea in order to interdict the Chinese logistical system. The employment of Nationalist troops was rejected because they had already demonstrated their ineffectiveness in China. Moreover, the Chinese people were hardly likely to welcome Chiang back.

Inherent in the administration's rejection of MacArthur's recommendations was the reversal of its position of October 7, that its objective was a militarily unified Korea, and a reassertion of its original attitude that the aim of the war was to restore the *status quo.* The Communists had attempted to erase the thirty-eighth parallel and incorporate South Korea into the Communist bloc; neither the North Koreans nor the Chinese Communists had succeeded in achieving this objective. The Communists had also hoped to destroy the Western alliance and isolate the United States; in this, too, they had failed. NATO had been preserved and greatly strengthened by its rearmament program and the stationing of four new American divisions in Europe. And the primary purpose of U.N. action in Korea, to put the Communists on notice that the Western powers would not tolerate Communist expansion by force, had been achieved. Thus, the wisest course seemed to be to attempt to end the war where it had begun.

However, MacArthur refused to accept this dismissal of his strategy and limitation of the war to the Korean peninsula. He maintained that his strategy was both feasible and without great risk. He therefore continued to urge the president and the Joint Chiefs of Staff to lift the restrictions they had imposed upon him; and when they refused, he attempted to force their hand by taking his case into the public arena and appealing over their heads to the opposition party in Congress and to the American people themselves. This produced an intolerable situation. The president is responsible for the formulation of foreign policy; he is the nation's chief diplomat and commander-in-chief. No government can allow a field commander to challenge its policies, to appeal to the public and the opposition for a change in these policies, thus undermining its control over the military. The soldier is expected to obey his orders. He is judged not by the nature of the policy he executes—only by how well he executes it. If he cannot accept this policy, he must resign; otherwise, he must be dismissed. In early April, President Truman did precisely that. The resulting furor brought to the surface the public's disillusionment with containment.

THE REACTION TO CONTAINMENT

MacArthur's dismissal was met with a storm of disapproval throughout the United States. The president received a flood of vituperous telegrams and letters informing him in no uncertain terms that his decision had been a mistake. In his first public appearance after MacArthur's dismissal, when President Truman attended the first baseball game of the season to throw out the opening ball, he was booed. Several state legislatures condemned him for his "irresponsible and capricious action." Republicans in Congress announced their intention of initiating impeachment proceedings against him and Secretary Acheson. Both Truman and Acheson were burned in effigy in many communities throughout the land. In contrast, MacArthur was received everywhere not as a man who had openly attempted to undermine the cherished American principle of civilian supremacy over the military, but as a great returning hero. In each of the cities he visited—San Francisco, Washington, Chicago, Boston—millions turned out to cheer him. In New York City alone, an estimated 7.5 million people lined the streets to see him—twice the number that had witnessed General Eisenhower's triumphal return from Europe in 1945; 2850 tons of ticker tape, confetti, and streamers were showered upon MacArthur; New York looked as if it had been hit by a snowstorm in April.

This almost hysterical reception was primarily the result of the nation's frustration with the containment policy, which was psychologically and emotionally in contradiction with American values and experience in foreign affairs. Traditionally, the United States had abstained from involvement in foreign affairs. Attention had, instead, been focused on domestic development. The business of America had been America—not foreign countries.

When foreign affairs had occasionally interrupted this preoccupation with domestic concerns, such matters had been quickly settled: If a Latin American state "misbehaved," a few thousand marines soon "corrected" the misdeeds of the offender; or if—as did happen twice in this century—Germany set out to conquer continental Europe, the United States harnessed all its resources, maximized its military strength, and crushed the enemy in the shortest possible time. Whatever the technique employed, the main point was that the conflict was settled quickly and completely. Only if the external crisis were solved immediately and totally could the American people return to their more important tasks—the internal development of their country and earning their living. In this context, foreign affairs were merely an annoying but temporary diversion.

Containment ran directly contrary to this experience. The cold war did not draw a clear-cut line between peace and war. It allowed the United States neither to abstain from foreign entanglement nor to harness its giant strength for one quick and all-out military effort to "punish" the enemy who had forced it to divert its attention from more pressing domestic matters. The administration's aim was not the destruction of Russia and its satellites, but only the creation of a balance of power to effect the "containment" of further Soviet attempts to expand. The objective of the government was not to erase the Soviet Union with a swift blow, but to accept the basic fact of coexistence. Truman and Acheson sought only to strengthen the United States and its allies in order to improve the terms of coexistence and the possibility of survival, not to end the Soviet threat once and for all.

The frustrations of such a continued defensive and negative policy, which left the initiative to the Soviet Union, were bad enough; failures made it intolerable. This was especially the case with China. Americans had long regarded China as their special ward. Whereas American foreign policy toward Europe during the last fifty years had been limited to two short but decisive military interventions occasioned by Germany's threats to the European balance of power, American involvement in the Far East, and particularly in China, had been active since the turn of the century. The original interest in China had not been political but commercial: China was potentially a huge market for American products. But U.S. policy toward China had contained some elements of altruistic intent as well—a genuine interest in the welfare and Christian salvation of the Chinese people. In fact, the United States had long regarded itself as the protector of China from foreign exploitation and invasion. Through the Open-Door policy—aimed at preventing Great Britain, France, Russia, Germany, and Japan from shutting American commerce out of China and at obtaining an equal opportunity to sell on the Chinese market—the United States had become politically committed to preserve the territorial integrity and political independence of China. Since the American people had never been prepared to fight for this objective, however, the United States had failed to protect China from external pressures and invasions: The Russians had established a sphere of influence in Manchuria about 1900, and the Japanese had replaced the Russians as the actual rulers of this strategic area after the Russo-Japanese War. During and after World War I, Japan had expanded its influence and control over China, and in 1931 Japan had initiated the Sino-Japanese War to consummate its ambition to turn China into a Japanese vassal or colony. The Open-Door policy, then, had been largely a verbal one. Indeed, the United States had never been prepared to support this policy militarily; it was one in which diplomacy was divorced from force, and what it meant was that the United States usually disregarded its commitment whenever Russia or Japan challenged it. But Americans, even in those days, believed that words were a substitute for an effective policy; out of this arose the illusion that the United States had long been China's protector and friend, extending to the Chinese people the bountiful benefits of Western Christianity, political ideals, science, and medicine.

Americans were, therefore, shocked by Chiang Kai-shek's collapse in 1949 and the establishment of Communist control of the Chinese mainland. Certainly, they were totally unprepared for, and deeply resentful of, the propaganda emanating from Peking accusing the United States of being "the Chinese people's implacable enemy ... a corrupt imperialistic nation, the world center of reaction and decadence ... a paper tiger and entirely vulnerable to defeat." They had expected that a "loyal" and fundamentally democratic China, grateful to America for past protection and help, would emerge from World War II as a strong friend of this country and as a powerful and reliable ally in the Far East. The failure of these expectations in late 1949 came as a blow to the American public. Suddenly, the relative security founded on the successful application of containment policies in Europe—the Truman Doctrine, the Marshall Plan, the Berlin airlift, and NATO—seemed to have disintegrated. It appeared that the United States had stemmed the Communist menace in Europe only to allow it to achieve a breakthrough in Asia. The resulting insecurity and anxiety were further heightened by two other events about the same time: the news that Russia had exploded its first atomic bomb and thereby shattered the American monopoly of the weapon widely regarded as the principal deterrent to a Soviet attack, and the conviction in early 1950 of Alger Hiss, followed shortly by the trial of Judith Coplon and the confession of Klaus Fuchs—which suggested continued Soviet espionage in high places. The outbreak of the Korean War and Communist China's subsequent intervention added more fuel to the fires of discontent.

The public did not understand the causes of its frustration; it could not comprehend the reasons for these alleged failures of American foreign policy. Whenever the United States had been drawn into the international arena in the past, its actions had met with quick success. It had beaten the British, the Mexicans, the Spaniards, the Germans, and the Japanese. America had never been invaded, defeated, or occupied as most other nations had been; it had, to be sure, committed mistakes, but with its great power it had always been able to rectify these. To a nation in which one popular slogan expressed confidence in doing "the difficult today, the impossible tomorrow," failure was a new experience. America's history had been a witness to victories only; its unbroken string of successes seemed evidence of national omnipotence.

It was this unquestioned assumption that the United States was omnipotent that suggested the reason for America's political and military failures: treason within its own government! For if America was all-powerful, it could not be its lack of strength that accounted for its defeats. It could not be that there was a limit to its ability to influence events abroad, far away from its shores. America's setbacks must have been the result of its own policies. Ostensibly, the reason China fell was that the "pro-Communist" administrations of Franklin Roosevelt and Harry Truman had either deliberately or unwittingly "sold China down the river." This charge—made primarily by the dominant conservative wing of the Republican Party, and particularly by Senators Taft, Joseph R. McCarthy, and Nixon—was simplicity itself: America's China policy had ended in Communist control of the mainland; the administration leaders and the State Department were responsible for the formulation and execution of foreign policy; thus, the government must be filled with Communists and Communist sympathizers who "tailored" American policy to advance the global aims of the Soviet Union. In short, disloyal or grossly incompetent American statesmen were responsible for the "loss" of China; it was to them, not to China, that the collapse of Nationalist China was due. Low Nationalist morale, administrative and military ineptness, and repressive policies that had alienated mass support had nothing to do with it; nor did the superior Communist organization, direction, morale, and ability to identify with popular aspirations.

This conspiratorial interpretation thus bridged the gap between the public's illusion of American omnipotence and the limits of America's power. The belief that Communist victories were caused by the treachery or stupidity of American policy-makers made it unnecessary both to recognize this fact and to reevaluate the traditional American approach to foreign policy. It was also highly flattering to the Americans' chauvinistic sense of pride, for it permitted the public to continue to believe in America's omnipotence—and in its opponent's inferiority. Secretary Acheson had once said: "Our name for problems is significant. We call them headaches. You can take a powder, and they are gone. These pains [brought on by the world situation] are not like that. They . . . will stay with us until death. We have got to understand that all our lives danger, the uncertainty, the need for alertness, for efforts, for discipline will be upon us. This is new to us. It will be hard for us." MacArthur's return demonstrated that it was still very hard for us. The American people were still looking for the aspirin that would dissolve all their foreign-policy problems.

It was precisely because MacArthur identified himself with this illusion of omnipotence that he received such a tumultuous welcome upon his return to the United States. He understood the public's frustration, and he gave voice to it in familiar—one might even say, in "American"—words, words of victory holding forth a view of a quick and successful end to the bloodshed on the battlefield, words of confidence and praise for an America strong enough to accomplish anything it had the mind to do in this world, and words of condemnation for those who, driven by fear of Russia and troublesome allies, chained the proud and invincible American giant to the rock of "weakness" and "appeasement." War, he said, indicated that "you have exhausted all other potentialities of bringing the disagreements to an end," and once engaged, "there is no alternative than to apply every available means to bring it to a swift end. War's very objective is victory—not prolonged indecision. In war there is no substitute for victory." The very term "resisting aggression" indicated "that you can destroy the potentialities of the aggressor to continually hit you" and not "go on indefinitely, neither to win or lose." One cannot fight a "half war." The administration's policy was based upon the assumption that "when you use force, you can limit that force." This introduced "a new concept into military operations—the concept of appeasement."

Here was the kind of language the public could understand. Once the diplomats had failed to keep the peace and war had erupted, the military expert took over and fought a technically efficient war. As a nonpolitical figure, he should not be burdened with extraneous political considerations. His sole aim was the complete destruction of the enemy's forces—in short, military victory. The enemy needed to be punished for provoking war. Only his total defeat would achieve this aim. Only in this way could the nation's principles be safeguarded. America's full power, if necessary, had to be applied to destroy the aggressor who threatened these principles. Deliberate self-restraint was, in these circumstances, a betrayal of America's national honor. Evil must be wiped out; to allow its continued existence was intolerable. Such compromise implied weakness or softness. To accept it was "un-American."

The reaction to the Korean War was thus twofold. On the one hand, the public demanded a return to an "American" policy, a "dynamic" or "positive" policy which would brook no compromises with the enemy and would withstand Allied pressure to "appease." Such a "tougher" policy, it was hoped, would restore America's dignity, prestige, and initiative on the world scene. On the other hand, the public wanted relief from the almost constant foreign-policy involvements and costs of the past few years. This meant a lowering of international tension, ending the Korean War, reducing U.S. commitments, and cutting expenditures. The contradictory nature of these aims was symptomatic of the intense desire to return to the traditional way of conducting foreign policy: either to concentrate on domestic affairs and to abstain from all foreign policy, or to assert America's power without fear or compromise. It was this double and paradoxical legacy that the Eisenhower administration inherited from the Truman administration.

chapter 5

the strategy of "frontiersmanship"

EISENHOWER LIBERATION

During the Presidential election campaign of 1952, the Republicans cleverly exploited the public's frustration with containment—a frustration grounded in the popular illusion of national omnipotence. America's great insecurity and its present involvement in the Korean War, they asserted, were the result of the "tragic blunders" that Roosevelt and Truman had committed at the Teheran, Yalta, and Potsdam conferences with the Russians. It was there that the Democratic leaders had deliberately and stealthily paved the way for Communism's postwar expansion by selling out Eastern Europe and betraying Chiang Kai-shek. The two presidents had, according to the Republican Party platform, "flouted our peace-assuring pledges such as the Atlantic Charter, and [they] did so in favor of despots, who, it was well known, consider that murder, terror, slavery, concentration camps, and the ruthless and brutal denial of human rights are legitimate means to their desired ends. Teheran, Yalta, and Potsdam were the scenes of those tragic blunders with others to follow. The leaders of the administration acted without the knowledge or consent of Congress or the American people. They traded our overwhelming victory for a new enemy and for new oppressions and new wars which were quick to come." In other words, America's wounds were self-inflicted.

Similarly, the Republicans charged that Truman's postwar foreign policy was self-defeating. It underwrote the false premise that American power was limited and committed the United States to continued coexistence and constant involvement in foreign policy. As John Foster Dulles, the chief Republican spokesman on foreign policy, put it: "We are not working, sacrificing, and spending in order to be able to live *without* this peril—but to be able to live *with* it, presumably forever." The administration's policies were "treadmill policies, which, at best, might perhaps keep us in the same place until we drop exhausted." The failures of containment were many: It was a negative policy; it surrendered the initiative to the enemy; it merely reacted to counter the Communist danger wherever and whenever the latter chose to attack; it was so costly that it would bankrupt the country; and it aimed only at preserving the *status quo*. In short, Dulles condemned the policy of containment as "negative, futile, and immoral."

The aim of American foreign policy, Dulles stressed, should not be to coexist indefinitely with the Communist menace; it should be to eliminate that menace. The purpose of American policy should be a rollback of Soviet power. The United States had only to proclaim its stand for freedom and announce that it would never be a party to any "deal" that confirmed Soviet despotism over alien peoples. Such a declaration would preserve the courage and hope of the satellite peoples and prevent them from accepting the Soviet regime. In Dulles's words, the United States "should make it publicly known that it wants and expects liberation to occur. The mere statement of that wish and expectation would change, in an electrifying way, the mood of the captive peoples. It would probably put heavy new burdens on the jailers and create new opportunities for liberation."

Never had the illusion of American omnipotence received a greater tribute. America's cause was righteous, and in order to be victorious it need only publicize this cause by launching a moral crusade. Right would then again prevail over might. The Republican program of action apparently envisaged the future secretary of state, John "Joshua" Dulles, marching around the walls of the Kremlin empire, sounding the call of freedom upon his trumpet. The walls would then come tumbling down, the enslaved peoples would be liberated, and Soviet power would be forced to retreat. The world would once more be safe for democracy.

The Republicans thus appeared not only to promise an eventual end to the cold war—they also pledged themselves to do it at less cost. For they claimed that the Democrats' foreign policy of indefinite coexistence, with its vast outlay for armaments and economic aid, would undermine the nation's economy. The Republicans asserted that it was Russia's aim to destroy America by forcing the country to spend itself into bankruptcy—an aim furthered by Democratic policy. America's defense had to be provided with a healthy economic foundation. This would require a sharp cut in the present huge foreign aid and military expenditures. The Republicans, in brief, promised the nation at one and the same time an offensive strategy, a balanced budget, and reduction of taxes. They pledged a rollback of Soviet power on the one hand and, on the other, a cut in the appropriations for America's defense.

Such goals were not only incompatible; they were unattainable. The mere enunciation of the doctrine of liberation would not free any Soviet satellite; good intentions, unsupported by concrete political and military policies, possess a notorious impotence on the international scene. But perhaps this did not really matter, since the policy of liberation seems to have been devised primarily to roll back the Democrats in the United States, not the Red Army in Eastern Europe. And for this domestic purpose, liberation was a highly effective strategy.

The country desperately wanted a more vigorous and forthright anti-Communist policy that promised an end to the cold war. At the same time, it was unprepared to take the risks involved: That is, a policy that actively sought the liberation of the satellite states would have to accept the very definite risk of all-out war with the Soviet Union. In these circumstances, the only kind of dynamism the country could afford was a verbal dynamism. And this was all the people seemed to want. It allowed them to delude themselves that the United States once again pursued a vigorous and forthright policy that would defeat its opponent. Liberation was the Republican Party's therapy for a public that refused to accept the facts of America's limited power in the world and rejected any changes in its traditional approach to foreign policy. That this policy of liberation was probably never meant to be more than a verbal appeal to the American people was clearly demonstrated at the time of the anti-Communist revolt in East Berlin and other East German cities in June 1953, and during the national uprising in Hungary in late 1956. In neither case did the Eisenhower administration act—except to condemn the Soviet Union for its suppression of Germans and Hungarians and to express its sympathy for the victims of Soviet despotism. In Berlin, it substituted food packages to the East Berliners for liberation; and in Hungary, it even reassured the Soviet Union that it had no intention of intervening. The *status quo* was thereby reaffirmed. Liberation had returned to the "womb" of containment.

The administration did, however, carry out its promises of military and economic retrenchment. This involved three measures. The first of these was to end the Korean War, which would allow the administration to cut the size of the army and avoid the cost of maintaining large standing ground forces. The second was to draw a clear line, or "frontier," around the entire Sino-Soviet bloc. The Democrats had already drawn such a frontier from Norway to Turkey; the Republicans expected to strengthen and extend it to the Middle and Far East. The third measure was to preserve this global boundary around the Communist world with the deterrent power of the Strategic Air Command. The Russians and Chinese could cross the line only at the risk of total war with the United States; the fear of total destruction was expected to deter them.

This reliance upon strategic air power was also expected to appeal to the American public. In the first place, "massive retaliation" simply sounded more dynamic than containment; at the same time, it made possible a reduction of overall military expenditures. It was obviously considerably cheaper to concentrate military spending upon a one-weapon system than to build up and maintain large balanced forces to meet any contingency. The second appealing feature of massive retaliation was that it, in fact, rejected the concept of limited war, or "half war," and reasserted the old American doctrine of either abstaining or fighting an all-out war. This return to the more traditional American approach to war was natural in 1952. The Republicans had been elected largely because of the deep popular revulsion against the Korean War; it was clear that the people wanted no more Koreas.

Basically, then, Eisenhower's policy was not to be very different from his predecessor's: containment of Communism by drawing a frontier around the Sino-Soviet periphery and supporting that frontier with nuclear air power. But in one essential aspect the new administration's policy was different—and this difference was crucial. Truman and Acheson had also relied upon air-atomic striking power to deter a total attack upon either the United States or America's "first line of defense" in Europe. But in Asia, once the Communists had faced them with a limited aggression, they had met this challenge with local ground resistance. The Eisenhower administration also expected to deter an all-out war with the threat of massive retaliation. But, unlike the Truman administration, it would not fight local ground wars. It proposed to prevent any future limited attacks by threatening to retaliate against the Soviet Union or Communist China. This basic policy decision reflected Secretary Dulles's own strong conviction that the only effective means of stopping a prospective aggressor was to give him an advance warning that if he committed aggression, he would be subjected to such overwhelming retaliatory blows that his possible gains would be far outweighed by the punishment he would suffer. Dulles believed strongly that Korea would never have been invaded if the Communists had known that their attack would have been met with retaliatory air strikes on Moscow. It was the absence of such a warning that had led the Communists to miscalculate. The Eisenhower administration did not intend to repeat this mistake. It meant to draw the line so clearly that the enemy could be left in no doubt whatsoever of what would happen to him if he crossed it. The expectation was that by going to the "brink of war," the United States would be able to deter future Koreas. This policy, which later became known as "brinkmanship," was to be applied first in an attempt to bring about a cease-fire in Korea.

ENDING THE KOREAN WAR

Truce talks in Korea had begun in the summer of 1951, but the negotiations had dragged on fruitlessly until they reached a deadlock. When the Eisenhower administration took office in January 1953, it decided that if its efforts to gain an armistice failed, it would bomb Chinese bases and supply sources in Manchuria and China, blockade the mainland coast, and possibly use tactical atomic weapons "to provide a tremendous beef-up in the United Nations punch." Dulles conveyed this decision to Prime Minister Nehru of India in late May 1953, on the assumption that Nehru would pass the message on to the Chinese Communists.

In early June, the deadlocked negotiations were resumed, and in late July the armistice was signed. Whether the administration's decisions alone were primarily responsible for the Chinese Communists' willingness to conclude the war is difficult to say. Probably other factors did play a significant role. For instance, Stalin had died in 1953, and his successors were proclaiming their belief in "peaceful coexistence" and trying hard to convince the non-Communist world that they wanted to relax international tension. Agreement on an armistice and an end to the war would provide evidence of their earnestness. But in Dulles's own mind, it was his threat to unleash American air power against China that induced the Chinese Communists to agree to end the fighting; in turn, this reinforced his faith in the utility of the advance warning coupled with the threat of heavy punishment.

South Korea's leader, Syngman Rhee, attempted at the last minute to upset the armistice. Rhee wanted to renew the war in the hope of reunifying his country; he had bitterly opposed an end to the fighting which again left Korea divided. But he failed in his purpose.

Thus, the Korean War concluded just about where it had begun—on the thirty-eighth parallel. It had taken three years of fighting to decide that this line was to become part of the global line dividing the Communist bloc from the non-Communist bloc. In August, the United States signed a mutual security pact with South Korea designed as a deterrent to another attack. This alliance had already been preceded by a declaration, signed by the fifteen nations that had fought in Korea, warning the Chinese Communists that, in the event of renewed aggression, it would probably be impossible to confine hostilities to Korea. And they added this significant warning: The armistice must not "result in jeopardizing the restoration or the safeguarding of peace in any other part of Asia." Events in Indochina were soon to prove the meaninglessness of this statement.

THE FIRST INDOCHINA WAR AND SEATO

After World War II, strong nationalist movements in colonies that had long been ruled by European powers demanded independence for their countries. The British met these demands in India, Burma, and Ceylon. The French did not meet them in Indochina. Returning to Indochina after its years of Japanese occupation, they refused to grant any meaningful concessions to the government which, under Ho Chi Minh, had proclaimed the independence of Vietnam after Japan's collapse. The French, determined to reestablish sovereignty over their colony, recognized Ho's "Democratic Republic of Vietnam" as a free state within the French Union; as a part of the agreement, the French would be allowed to maintain garrisons in Vietnam for five years. But within less than a year, as a result of actions taken by France that the Vietminh considered to be in violation of its agreements, there developed open conflict between the Vietminh and the French, and this soon was transformed into what Bernard Fall called the First Indochina War. When France established an "independent" state of Vietnam in 1949 under Emperor Bao Dai, the Communist-dominated Vietminh became, in effect, "rebels," but with the important difference that they were rebels identified as nationalists fighting for the independence of Vietnam. By contrast, Bao Dai, who spent much of his time on the French Riviera, was seen as a French puppet, and, in fact, he could not have survived one day in office without the presence and support of French arms. The war, therefore, went on unabated. Ho, like Mao Tse-tung in China, conducted a guerrilla operation and met with considerable success, partly because the terrain favored this kind of warfare. The French, who generally held the cities, were at a disadvantage from the beginning, for in the absence of genuine independence, the Vietnamese identified themselves with the Vietminh and saw the French as their colonial rulers. In the long run, France paid a very high price for the war in terms of manpower, material, and morale.

During the first few years of the war, American public opinion was unsympathetic to France's attempt to reestablish its colonial control over Indochina. But two events were to lead to United States involvement in this conflict. The first one was the defeat of Chiang Kai-shek. This was a blow to France, because it meant that the Chinese Communists could now provide assistance to the Vietminh. The second event was the outbreak of the Korean War, which led to an increased awareness of the strategic importance of Indochina as the gateway to the whole of Southeast Asia. In a bipolar world, Indochina could not be allowed to fall.

The administration began therefore to provide France with economic and military aid. By 1954, the United States was paying about 75 percent of the costs of the war. The French position continued to deteriorate, however, especially once the Korean armistice was signed. For despite American warnings, Communist China had now shifted its pressure from Korea to Indochina and was rendering increasing assistance to the Vietminh. On March 13,1954, the entire French position in northern Vietnam suddenly threatened to disintegrate as the Vietminh forces launched an assault upon the French fortress at Dienbienphu. It became painfully clear that the French could not hold the position alone. Only American intervention could save Dienbienphu and the French hold on Vietnam. What was the United States to do?

President Eisenhower had already declared that the fall of Indochina "would be of a most terrible significance to the United States of America," and he had termed Southeast Asia of "transcendent importance" to American security. The secretary of state had issued several statements that rather strongly suggested that America would not stand idly by while Indochina fell. He had warned the Chinese Communists in the same terms he had used after the armistice in Korea: Any aggression—that is, open intervention—would incur "grave consequences which might not be confined to Indochina." This warning also applied to any indirect Chinese intervention—namely, supplying overt assistance in the form of military advisors, equipment, and training for the Vietminh forces. Of prime importance was the strategic significance of Indochina, not whether the Chinese expanded by direct or indirect means.

Dienbienphu was for the administration, therefore, the moment of decision. Eisenhower and Dulles had declared Indochina to be of strategic importance to American security and had cautioned China against direct or indirect intervention by threatening it with massive retaliation. The Chinese had ignored these warnings. The U.S. government now had to "put up or shut up." It shut up; its threats turned out to have been only bluffs.

The reason for this is fairly clear: Because of the nature of American domestic politics, the Eisenhower administration was—despite its recognition of Indochina's vital location—unwilling to involve the United States in another Korea. Moreover, the administration was already cutting the size of the army, and apparently there were not sufficient divisions available for fighting in Indochina. The army chief of staff certainly counseled against intervention on this ground. Only two possible courses of action remained. The first was to stop the Communist advance with air power alone; but this was a wholly unfeasible proposition, since air strikes by themselves could not possibly have halted a ground advance. They had failed to do so during the opening days of the Korean War, and it had been this failure that had necessitated the commitment of the army. And even if such air strikes had been tried in an attempt to stop the Vietminh, they would have been ineffective; for quite apart from Indochina's topography, the Vietminh were fighting a guerrilla war. Thus, the use of ground troops would have been as mandatory in Indochina as in Korea.

The alternative strategy was, of course, to attack China itself. Everything indicates that this is what the administration should have done if it really believed in its own policy of massive retaliation. Its entire strategy was predicated upon two principles of action: first, issuing a clear warning that would allow no doubt of American intentions and no room for Communist miscalculation; and second, if the Communists deliberately ignored the American warnings, punishing the enemy so heavily that he would never again dare challenge the United States. Yet in Indochina the administration did not follow its warning with such punishment.

Why did this happen? The answer is simple: It is one thing to deliver a threat of massive retaliation to an opponent, and quite another for him to believe it. The Russians had not believed it in Korea; nor did the Chinese in Indochina. Both apparently rejected the notion that the United States would risk a total war for anything less than an all-out attack on either the United States or Europe. Thus, the United States was faced for a second time with the terrible dilemma of either doing nothing or risking all-out war (since the Eisenhower administration shared the Truman administration's fear that an attack on China would precipitate Russian intervention).

Truman's experience with Korea had clearly shown that containment could not be successful without the willingness and capability to fight a limited war. Reliance upon strategic air power and an all-or-nothing strategy paralyzed American diplomacy. The United States ability to drop atom bombs on Moscow or Peking was less than useless to defeat limited incursions in areas which the Americans were unwilling to defend at the risk of total war. Ground forces were absolutely necessary if the United States was to escape either defeat or involvement in a total conflict. (Indochina should also have demonstrated—as Americans were to learn a decade later—that a limited war against guerrilla forces also required political, social, and economic measures to alleviate the popular grievances upon which the guerrillas feed.) The Eisenhower administration had ignored these lessons of the Korean War. It had persuaded itself that Korea had happened only because the enemy had not received a previous warning that an attack upon South Korea would bring retaliatory strikes. While such warnings were certainly desirable to prevent enemy miscalculation, Indochina now proved that warnings alone were not enough. It showed that containment was incompatible with heavy budget-cutting.

The result of American inaction was the French government's decision to make the best of the situation by negotiating with the Communists directly for an end to the war. The French people were as weary of the fighting as the American public had been of Korea. Just as the latter had elected Eisenhower to end the war, the French National Assembly had elected Pierre Mendès-France premier to end the Indochina hostilities. The new premier announced that he was willing to conclude the war, and on July 20, 1954, an armistice agreement was reached that divided the country at the seventeenth parallel. The Communists were left in control of northern Indochina; it seemed only a matter of time until they would take over the rest of the country, for the collapse of the Southern rump state seemed imminent.

But the United States prevented this by supporting the new government of Ngo Dinh Diem, a staunch anti-Communist nationalist appointed by Bao Dai after Dienbienphu (Diem later ousted Bao Dai). The Eisenhower administration extended him economic and military aid to help him stabilize the situation in Vietnam. The danger of collapse temporarily receded. The seventeenth parallel, like the thirty-eighth parallel in Korea, became part of the international frontier separating the Communist and non-Communist worlds.

The administration also decided to extend this line to defend the rest of Southeast Asia. Its predecessor had already signed security pacts with the nations lying off the Asian mainland—Japan, the Philippines, Australia, and

New Zealand. The collapse of the French position in Indochina and the rising threat of Communist China made it imperative to bring the line inland. In September 1954, the United States, Britain, France, Australia, New Zealand, the Philippines, Pakistan, and Thailand signed the Southeast Asia Collective Defense Treaty to defend the area of the South Pacific, with the exception of Hong Kong and Formosa. A protocol to the treaty extended SEATO's protection to Vietnam, Laos, and Cambodia. It also provided for joint action to meet aggression; an attack upon any of its members would be considered a danger to the security of all, and each would then act to meet the common danger in accordance with its constitutional processes. In case of subversion, the parties agreed to consult one another immediately and agree on common measures to meet this threat.

SEATO, unlike the NATO alliance, which it resembled, did not possess a unified command or joint forces. The principal force behind the alliance was American sea and air power. The crucial element—land power—would have to be supplied by the member nations if the occasion arose. Moreover—and again unlike NATO—SEATO did not contain within it most of the nations located in the area. India, Burma, Ceylon, and Indonesia would not join. They had just emerged from Western colonialism and were unwilling to be tied again to the West through a military alliance. They preferred to remain neutral in the struggle between the Western powers and the Sino-Soviet bloc. Of the Asian nations that did join the pact, the Philippines did so because of its traditional ties to the United States, and Pakistan because it wished to strengthen itself against India; only Thailand was genuinely concerned with Communist China's expansion, for the French collapse in Indochina had brought Chinese power closer to its borders. But if SEATO was primarily a non-Asian alliance for the defense of an Asian area—a weakness that was to plague the alliance, for the absence of indigenous concern and resistance to Communist expansion could only ensure its eventual failure—its chief purpose was to warn the Communists of the stake America perceived in an area of what it continued to define as a bipolar world. If the United States, therefore, felt its security threatened by direct or indirect Communist aggression, SEATO provided it with the rationale for unilateral intervention to preserve this newly drawn land frontier.

THE FORMOSA STRAITS AND THE OFFSHORE ISLANDS

Another critical situation arose in the Formosa Straits. During the summer of 1954, the Chinese Communists openly proclaimed their intention of taking Formosa and began shelling the Nationalist-held offshore islands (Quemoy is only nine miles outside the harbor of Amoy; Matsu lies almost as close, blocking the harbor of Foochow; and the Tachen islands are 200 miles north of Formosa). In December, the United States and the Nationalists signed a Treaty of Mutual Defense, by which the former guaranteed the

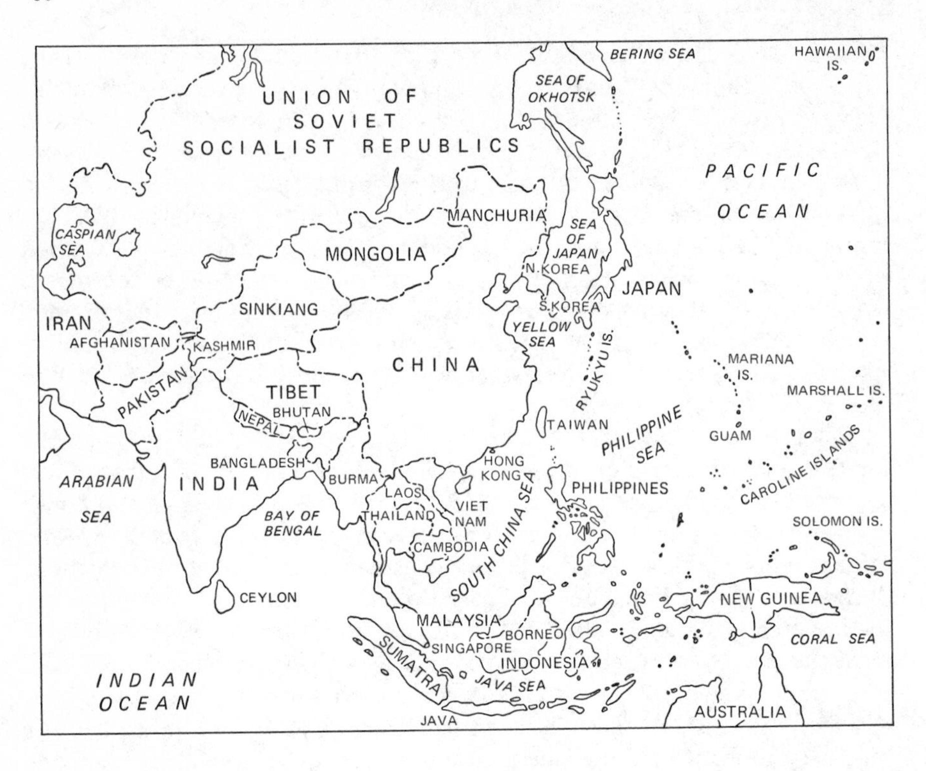

security of Formosa and the nearby Pescadore islands. The Nationalists also pledged themselves not to attack the mainland or reinforce their offshore garrisons without United States consent.

The offshore islands, however, were not included under the terms of the treaty. However, as the situation in the straits grew more tense in January 1955, the president requested and received from Congress the authority to employ American armed forces to protect Formosa and the Pescadores. This authority extended to the protection of "such related positions and territories" as the president judged necessary. In Dulles's mind, Quemoy and Matsu had to be defended to maintain the Nationalist government's morale. Even more important, the islands had to be guarded since the alternative was to cede them; and this would have been interpreted as a sign of weakness by the Chinese Communists, spurring them on to further aggression. Dulles's determination to demonstrate American resolution to the Chinese Communists may have been reinforced by the Indochina debacle. It would seem, therefore, that in case of attack, the administration would have committed American armed forces to the defense of the offshore islands. At least the Communists thought so, and they abstained from any invasion attempts on Quemoy and Matsu. (The Nationalists had, meanwhile, evacuated the Tachens.)

Three years later, in August 1958, the American position became clear when the Communists again began to shell the offshore islands very heavily. The Seventh Fleet—with orders to retaliate if fired upon—escorted Nationalist supply ships to within three miles of the beleaguered islands and helped them to break the blockade; and the Nationalist air force, equipped by the United States with air-to-air missiles, defeated the Communist air force's attempt to establish air supremacy in the sky between the mainland and Quemoy.

Thus, the line remained where it had been before the two Formosa crises —a few miles off Communist China's coast. Some months later, Dulles reaffirmed this line when he firmly rejected Chiang's calls for the reconquest of the mainland. American policy in the straits was committed to the preservation of the *status quo*. Each side should keep what it had and refrain from attacking the other. The Eisenhower administration had finally recognized what neither it nor its predecessor had been willing to admit openly before: that the Nationalist expectation of reconquering the mainland was a myth. At the same time, it tacitly acknowledged the Chinese Communist government as continental China's *de facto* government. It reconciled itself to the Communist conquest of the mainland. Containment had once more replaced liberation. The administration was, moreover, resolved to back up its "disengagement" policy with force. In the straits, it could support its political position with sea and air power; ground forces were not needed.

For the moment, the situation in the Far East had been stabilized—at the thirty-eighth parallel in Korea, in the Formosa Straits, at the seventeenth parallel in Indochina, and at the line drawn by SEATO. Communist attention now turned to the Middle East.

THE MIDDLE EAST AND THE SUEZ WAR

In 1955, the United States completed its line around the Sino-Soviet periphery. Under its sponsorship, Britain, Turkey, Iraq, Iran, and Pakistan established the Middle East Treaty Organization (METO). Thus, the Baghdad Pact (as this treaty was called) extended the NATO line from Turkey to India. But this "northern tier," drawn—except for Iraq—along 3000 miles of Russia's southern frontier, drew a sharp reaction from the Soviet Union. Rebuffed in Iran and Turkey in 1946–1947 by America, Russia had not surrendered its ambitions in this area. The Middle East linked Europe, Africa, and Asia. For Britain, the area—and especially the Suez Canal—had traditionally been the lifeline of its old empire and of its present Commonwealth. Above all, Europe's economy was becoming increasingly dependent upon the Middle East for oil (America was still self-sufficient in oil); without oil, Europe would collapse. The power that could deny it this oil would be able to dictate its future. Soviet influence in the Arab world might thus allow Moscow to neutralize Europe without firing a shot. In short, for Russia the Middle East was the means to outflank and disintegrate NATO. Its opportunity to attempt to do this came as a result of the bitter Arab–Israeli conflict, the only slightly less bitter Anglo-Egyptian quarrel, Egypt's own expansionist ambitions, and the United States attempt to draw the line of containment just south of Russia's border.

Arab antagonism toward Israel is understandable. In 1917, Britain had pledged itself in the Balfour Declaration to the establishment of a "national home" for the Jewish people in Palestine, while also promising the Arabs that the civil and religious rights of non-Jews would not be prejudiced. Zionists took this pledge as promising the conversion of Palestine into a Jewish state; they considered Palestine, a British mandate after the collapse of the Ottoman Empire during World War I, as their ancient and traditional homeland.

Britain's troubles became serious after Hitler's assumption of power in Germany—and impossible after World War II. Hitler had slaughtered 6 million Jews in his concentration camps; few of the survivors wished to remain in Europe, with its unhappy memories. Many emigrated to Palestine. The Jews were now determined to establish a Jewish state, while the Arabs feared that the Jewish immigration would crowd them out of what they also regarded as their rightful homeland. British troops were unable to keep the peace between the Arabs and Jews. Under these circumstances, Britain—already gravely weakened by the war and forced to curtail its commitments throughout the world—decided to end its burdensome mandate over Palestine.

In November 1947, the United Nations decided to partition Palestine into two independent states, one Jewish and the other Arab. The Arabs refused to accept this solution, however; they wanted Palestine to become an Arab state. On May 10, 1948, as Britain ended its mandate, the Jews proclaimed the State of Israel, and the armies of the Arab League (Egypt, Jordan, Syria, Lebanon, and Saudi Arabia) invaded the new state. In the ensuing war, the Israeli army defeated the larger Arab armies. The state of Israel became a fact of political life.

The Arabs, however, refused to recognize it as such. Though they did sign an armistice in February 1949, they refused to conclude a peace treaty. They continued to regard the Jews as infidels who had no right to be in Israel. Moreover, they felt deeply humiliated by their defeat. The Arabs awaited their day of revenge; meanwhile, they continued to proclaim their intention to destroy Israel. They conducted constant guerrilla warfare against Israel—sabotaging, pillaging, and murdering (so did the Israeli army when it intermittently took revenge by launching heavy assaults into Arab territory); they refused to allow Israeli shipping through the Suez Canal and blockaded the Gulf of Aqaba; and they tightened the ring around Israel. In April 1956, Egypt, Syria, Saudi Arabia, and Yemen formed a joint command against Israel under Egyptian leadership, and in October 1956, Egypt, Jordan, and Syria announced another joint command "the principal concern of which is the war of destruction against Israel." Earlier (in late September 1955), Egypt had concluded an arms deal with Czechoslovakia, although the actual agreement was signed with the Soviet Union; under this arrangement, Egypt received a large quantity of arms, including planes and tanks. Egypt now had the tools with which to achieve a decisive military superiority over Israel. This, in turn, raised a very vital question for Israel: Should it strike now or wait until Egypt and its allies were ready for the "second round"? As Egypt solidified the encirclement of Israel, grew increasingly aggressive, and began to absorb the Soviet arms, the Israelis decided to strike before it was too late. All that was needed was the right condition for launching their preventive attack.

This conditon, which was to occur in October 1956, was the product of Anglo-Egyptian antagonism. Britain had controlled Egypt since 1881, when it had established a protectorate over Egypt in order to safeguard its own communications through Suez to India. The 1936 treaty between the two countries had converted this status into an alliance. By its terms, British troops were confined to the Canal Zone, and their presence was declared to be neither an occupation nor an infringement of Egyptian sovereignty. To the Egyptians, however, British soldiers on their soil continued to represent a violation of Egyptian independence, pride, and dignity.

World War II intensified Egyptian nationalism and heightened the demand for a withdrawal of British forces from Egyptian soil. But negotiations on this question broke down, while other postwar events further increased Egypt's anti-British sentiment. The Egyptians resented the Palestine partition plan, for which they blamed Britain as well as the United States. In late 1951, the Egyptian parliament abrogated the 1936 Anglo-Egyptian treaty, and in July 1952, the new military regime that took over the Egyptian government from King Farouk pressed for the removal of British troops with renewed vigor. The Eisenhower administration supported this Egyptian demand. Faced with this opposition, and aware of its own unpopularity in Egypt, Britain signed a new Anglo-Egyptian treaty in 1954, by which it agreed to withdraw all its troops from Suez over a 20-month period. British influence over Egyptian politics had come to an end.

Britain now shifted the focus of its power from Egypt to Iraq, a long-time ally. It therefore joined the Baghdad Pact, of which Iraq was already a member, in order to protect its vital strategic and economic interest in the Middle East. But President Nasser of Egypt did not regard METO merely as a means of containing Russia; he saw it as an instrument to preserve Western domination throughout the area, and, since Iraq had always been Egypt's traditional rival for Arab leadership, he considered it a personal challenge as well. Nasser therefore set out to destroy the Baghdad Pact by forming a counteralliance and undermining pro-Western Arab governments. His means of achieving these objectives was to place himself at the head of the Arab struggle against Israel and Britain. Thereby, he would become the foremost exponent of Arab nationalism and win the allegiance of the Arab masses. Once he had gained this loyalty of the people, no Arab government would dare oppose him, for if it did he would call on the people to overthrow that government. "Revolution in the street" was an accepted Arab method of making and unmaking governments. Moreover, by exerting his influence over the Arab world in this manner, he would gain control over the area's oil resources; this would place him in a position where he could siphon off the oil revenues to help Egypt's economic development. Thus, partly as a reaction to Israel and Britain, but also as a result of his own strong ambitions and the Arab states' domestic condition, Nasser began to use Pan-Arabism as an instrument of expanding his own and Egyptian influence. By turning to nationalism, and thereby asserting the Arabs' pride, sovereignty, and dignity, by humiliating those who had in the past humiliated and subjected them, he consolidated his leadership at home, gained the admiration and enthusiasm of the long-suffering masses in other Arab countries, and compelled their rulers to follow him if they did not wish to be overthrown by popular revolutions led by pro-Nasser forces.

Nasser's influence grew quickly. He formed close links with Saudi Arabia, Yemen, Syria, and Jordan (whose pro-Western government he first successfully overthrew). But the act that really endeared Nasser to the Arab masses was his dramatic arms deal with the Soviet Union. This agreement made Nasser the great new hero, the modern Saladin—the staunch opponent of the West and champion the Arab nationalism. At the same time, the Soviet Union became the Arabs' greatest friend. But this Moscow–Cairo axis frightened not only Israel but also Britain; if Russia and Egypt gained control over the Middle East, Britain would be cut off from its oil supplies, which for it was a question not just of profit, but of survival. The situation thus became inflammable.

Only an incendiary incident was needed to start a conflagration. The United States provided this when, on July 19, 1956, it informed the Egyptian government that it would not help finance Nasser's Aswan Dam, a high dam on the Upper Nile whose purpose was to raise Egypt's low standard of living by irrigating new land and providing electricity for industrial development. The American retraction of its offer to help build this dam was a heavy blow to Egypt's hopes to raise itself by its own "sandalstraps." For the American loan had been a prerequisite for further aid from the World Bank and Britain; these offers, too, were now withdrawn. The Eisenhower administration's action was occasioned by several considerations: Nasser had attempted to blackmail the administration into providing more money by hinting that the Russians had offered to finance the entire project; Egypt had moved too close to Russia and had recognized Communist China; Nasser had also probably mortgaged the funds he was supposed to provide for Egypt's share of the cost of the dam to buy Russian arms—which, in effect, meant that the entire cost of the dam would fall upon the United States and Britain.

Nasser regarded the American decision as a personal and national humiliation. A few days later, on July 26, he announced that he would nationalize the Suez Canal and use the revenues collected from it to finance the dam. Arab nationalists were ecstatic, and Nasser's stature, already strong, reached new heights.

Unlike the crises in Korea and Formosa, however, the consequences of Secretary Dulles's act fell not on the United States but on its allies—above all, on Britain. And its government reacted sharply to Nasser's seizure of the canal. Prime Minister Eden did not trust the Egyptian dictator; although Nasser guaranteed that all ships, except Israel's, could still pass through the canal, Eden feared that the Egyptian would use the canal as an instrument of political blackmail. Moreover, if Nasser could face the West with such a major act of defiance and go unpunished, Western influence would be destroyed throughout the Middle East. Other Arab governments would expropriate Western oil interests, and all opponents of Nasser would be discouraged and come to terms with him. Western prestige—and especially British prestige, since south of America's "northern tier" Britain was the leading Western power in the Middle East—had to be upheld. If it were not, the Cairo–Moscow axis would dominate the entire area and be in a position to strangle Europe. The British were therefore determined to stand up to Nasser, and they insisted upon some form of international control for the canal. But the Egyptians rejected all proposals to wrest their newly won control out of their hands and denounced them as "collective colonialism." All attempts to bridge this gap were therefore doomed to fail.

It was in these circumstances that war broke out. The United States was busily engaged in the last days of its presidential election campaign, and the Soviet Union was concentrating on crushing the Hungarian uprising. On October 29, only four days after Jordan's chief of staff announced that the time had come to launch the Arab assault on Israel, the Israeli army marched into Egypt. The Israelis quickly defeated the Egyptian forces in the Sinai peninsula. The British and the French (who sought Nasser's downfall because of his aid to the Algerian rebels who wanted to free Algeria from French control) intervened 24 hours later. At this point, the United States saved Nasser. Although the administration had pressured Britain to sign the Anglo-Egyptian treaty by which all British troops had been removed from Suez and had withdrawn the Aswan Dam offer, thus precipitating Nasser's seizure of the Canal and the British attack, it now opposed the use of force to settle this issue.

The reason was that despite the administration's disapproval of Nasser's action and the pro-Soviet direction in which he was leading Egypt, it saw his foreign policy in terms of a reaction against Israel and Western colonialism. If Israel had not existed, and if Egypt and the Arab states had not long been subjected and exploited by the Western powers (especially Britain), Arab nationalism would not be anti-Western and pro-Soviet. The administration therefore saw the invasion of Egypt as a golden opportunity to win Egyptian and Arab friendship. When the Jews had originally proclaimed the state of Israel, the United States had, because of domestic political considerations, recognized the new state within eleven minutes. Here was a chance to show the Arabs that the United States was not as pro-Jewish as they thought it to be, and that the country could even be pro-Arab. Since Egypt's actions were also the product of her anti-British resentment, it would be beneficial to oppose the British attempt to reassert control over the Suez Canal. By saving Nasser, the United States could align itself with Arab nationalism; supporting Britain, France, and Israel would have left the Soviet Union as the sole champion of Arab aspirations. American opposition to the invasion would, in short, identify the United States with the anticolonialism of the entire underdeveloped world, and particularly with the anti-Israeli and nationalistic sentiments of the Arab world. Since continued evidence of British power in the Middle East only antagonized the Arabs, the destruction of this power and its replacement by American influence would be in the interest not only of the United States but of all the Western powers. In this way, the West's strategic and economic interests could be more adequately safeguarded.

America's opposition to the Suez invasion was the decisive factor in stopping the fighting. Egypt had already blocked the canal, and the Syrians had cut the pipelines running across their country from Iraq. Britain was therefore dependent upon American oil to replace its losses from the Middle East; and the administration threatened to use this economic sanction if Britain did not cease the attack. Faced with this dire prospect—plus opposition to the invasion within Britain, the Commonwealth (Canada, India, and Pakistan), and the United Nations—the British government accepted a cease-fire and later withdrew its forces; France and Israel had little choice but to follow suit.

It is ironic, however, in view of America's leading role in halting the attack on Egypt, that it should have been the Soviet Union—and not the United States—that was to reap the benefits from America's opposition. After it had become clear that the United States would not support the British and French invasion, Russia threatened "to crush the aggressor"; it sent notes to the British and French governments warning of possible rocket attacks on their countries, and it bluntly told Israel that its very existence was at stake. It even asked the United States to join forces with it to stop the war. And after the cease-fire, Russia and Communist China threatened to send "volunteers." In short, the Soviet Union risked nothing to deliver these threats, but it was the country that received most of the credit from the Arabs for saving Nasser by its threats to exterminate Israel and attack Britain and France. Suez thus resulted in the collapse of British power in the Middle East, the strengthening of Arab nationalism, and the consolidation of Egyptian–Russian links.

Nasser's great political victory—despite a humiliating military defeat at the hands of Israel—increased his self-confidence. Supported by the Soviet

Union—whose aim it was to weaken if not to eliminate all Western power in the Middle East—Nasser continued his expansionist drive. Jordan abrogated the Anglo-Jordan Treaty by which Jordan had received an annual subsidy to maintain its economy; Egypt, Saudi Arabia, and Syria promised to replace the British funds, and Jordan announced that it would seek to establish a federal union with Egypt and Syria. The last two states did, in fact, join together into a union, the United Arab Republic, in early 1958. Attempts to undermine the Iraqi government continued throughout 1956, and in the spring of 1957, the Egyptians organized riots against the government in Lebanon.

The first step taken by the Eisenhower administration after the Suez crisis was the formulation of the Eisenhower Doctrine. This joint resolution of Congress in the spring of 1957 declared that the United States considered the preservation of the independence and integrity of the Middle Eastern nations vital to American security, and that it was prepared to use armed force to assist any nation or nations "*requesting* assistance against *armed* aggression from any country controlled by international Communism [italics added]." It was difficult to understand what this doctrine meant. Russia did not border on any Arab state. Iraq, to the south, was already protected by the Baghdad Pact and, through its association with Britain and Turkey, by NATO; so the doctrine could not be directed against Russia. Moreover, the Soviet Union had already leapfrogged the "northern tier" by establishing close relations with Egypt and Syria. And Suez had demonstrated that the United States did not regard such association as turning a country into a Communist-controlled vassal; if it had, it would surely have supported the invasion of Egypt.

But the administration, viewing Nasser's continued attempts to undermine Western power in the Middle East, his vicious attacks upon all the Western nations, including the United States, and his continued flirtation with Russia, soon reconsidered its views of Nasser. At Suez, it had thought that by demonstrating its friendship, the United States could win his trust. Post-Suez events proved this expectation to have been ill-founded. A reversal of policy was thus in order, and this required a reinterpretation of the Eisenhower Doctrine. First, the term "armed aggression" was no longer to refer only to the direct attack of one nation upon another but also to attempts to overthrow pro-Western governments through internal revolt aided from the outside; and second, "any country controlled by international Communism" was now meant to include nations with close bonds to the Soviet Union.

The doctrine was first applied in Jordan, where King Hussein's dismissal of the pro-Nasser and pro-Communist government led to a general strike, massive street demonstrations, and riots. Jordan's days as an independent state appeared to be numbered. In this crisis, Hussein charged in April 1957 that international Communism was responsible for the efforts to overthrow him. On the same day, the United States announced that it regarded "the independence and integrity of Jordan as vital." And to prove that it meant what it said, the administration dispatched the United States Sixth Fleet to the eastern Mediterranean and extended Jordan $10 million for the support of its army and economy. The Hussein government survived.

In the summer of 1958, an even more serious crisis arose when a group of nationalist officers led by General Kassem overthrew the pro-Western government of Iraq and murdered the king and prime minister. Although the new regime did not withdraw from the Baghdad Pact until some months later, this revolt, in effect, eliminated Iraq, the pivot on which the alliance had been centered. The United Arab Republic immediately hailed the revolution and recognized the new government; and the two countries quickly signed an alliance. There was little the United States could do but recognize the Kassem government. Arab nationalism seemed to be sweeping everything in front of it. Only Lebanon, Jordan, and Saudi Arabia were still outside the Nasser camp, and the first two were teetering on the verge of revolution. The whole Western position in the Middle East seemed to be on the brink of disintegration.

The Eisenhower administration now resorted to force. Lebanon had been plagued for some time with civil war between Muslims and Christians. The Muslims wanted close relations, if not union, with the United Arab Republic, and the Christians favored a pro-Western policy and the continued independence of Lebanon. With the Iraqi revolution, men and arms for the pro-Nasser elements began to be smuggled in over Lebanon's Syrian border. In Jordan, too, the situation took a turn for the worse; the Iraqi example was hardly a happy one for King Hussein, who also had his pro-Nasser masses and army officers. Both countries now invoked the Eisenhower Doctrine and asked for military support. The British sent paratroopers into Jordan, and the United States sent 14,000 men into Lebanon. The large size of the American contingent seems to have been deliberate. Apparently, it was meant to warn the new Iraqi government against nationalizing Western oil resources. Kassem quickly gave the assurance that he had no such intention, and possible American intervention in Iraq was thereby forestalled. Loud Soviet hints of intervention also turned out to be hollow when countered by resolute American action. Both Britain and the United States withdrew their troops in late October.

The Anglo-American action had saved, at least temporarily, Lebanon and Jordan. But it was also intended to have another important effect: to show Nasser and the Arabs that there were limits to Soviet willingness to come to their aid. Nasser's personal ambitions were, by themselves, relatively unimportant; the decisive factor that had reaped success for Egypt's Pan-Arab policy was Soviet power. The Western powers, in thinking of counteraction against Egypt, could never eliminate the possibility of Soviet intervention. This, in turn, further encouraged Nasser's expansionist drive. The Anglo-American action in Lebanon and Jordan disabused the Arabs of this notion. Prior to the intervention, the Russians had again threatened to send "volunteers" to oppose the Western "imperialists" and had carried out conspicuous military maneuvers in Soviet Central Asia and Transcaucasia. The firmness of the American position, and the failure of the Soviet Union in the face of Eisenhower's determination to do more than to denounce the intervention and call for a diplomatic settlement, made it very clear that there were limits to Soviet willingness to bail the Arabs out of trouble. This had a dampening effect on Nasser's anti-Western drive.

There was another unexpected turn of events which influenced this situation. The new regime in Iraq, instead of turning out to be pro-Nasser—as almost everyone, including Nasser, had expected—took an anti-Nasser position. It was not long before it began to challenge the Egyptian ruler's leadership of Arab nationalism. Nasser quickly recognized this threat of Egypt's traditional rival and attempted to overthrow the Kassem government. But the revolt by a group of pro-Nasser officers was quickly squashed. At the same time, the Soviet Union gave economic and military support to the Kassem government. Nasser was becoming increasingly isolated in the Arab world: Jordan, Lebanon, and Saudi Arabia had remained independent; Libya and the Sudan had resisted his attempts to subvert them; Syria was restless in the United Arab Republic; and Iraq had become a rival for Arab leadership. Nor was this situation materially changed by the events of the early 1960s: Kassem was overthrown and Syria revolted to quit the United Arab Republic. Despite the common Pan-Arab aspirations of Egypt, Syria, and Iraq, a real Arab union remained as elusive as ever. Syria and Iraq were unwilling to permit Nasser to dominate them; and Nasser was unwilling to form a union he could not control. The Egyptian leader's new emphasis on domestic reform —or what he called "Arab socialism"—therefore became crucial to his fight for Arab leadership, even though he continued his attempts to overthrow traditional pro-Western regimes and remained generally anti-Western in his policy positions.

Meanwhile, the United States had almost become a full-fledged member of the Baghdad Pact (now renamed the Central Treaty Organization) by joining its economic, military, and countersubversion committees; it was also bound to each of the three Muslim states individually by bilateral defense agreements. But behind these developments remained all the essential problems that had given rise to the turmoil after 1955: the conflicts among the Arab states, the Arab–Israeli quarrel, the overshadowing competition between the United States and the Soviet Union, and, above all, Arab nationalism with its frequent xenophobic overtones. Despite the vast oil wealth, the Arab masses remained very poor and suffered from illiteracy, malnutrition, and disease. Social discontent and political instability were the result. While the area settled down to relative quiescence, the American attempt to fill the vacuum left by the reduction of British power and draw another "frontier" was unsuccessful. Ironically, it was the attempt to do this that drew Russia and Egypt together to destroy the "northern tier," permitting the former to jump over the line that was supposed to contain it.

WESTERN EUROPEAN UNION AND THE COMMON MARKET

In Europe, the defense line had already been drawn by NATO. But the strength of this line on the ground depended upon supplementing NATO forces with West German troops. EDC was the means the Allies had chosen to achieve this goal. But in August 1954, the French National Assembly rejected EDC by a decisive majority. Fear of Germany remained too great, and French nationalists wished to maintain France's identity and honor. This was a real blow to the efforts toward creating a situation of strength in Europe. The whole basis of NATO strategy and European integration was suddenly imperiled.

The response of the Eisenhower administration was a self-righteous one. Instead of taking the lead in finding a way out of this impasse, it simply withdrew from the problem and waited for the European powers to resolve it. Secretary Dulles only repeated his threat that the United States would make an "agonizing reappraisal" of its NATO commitments if the deadlock were not broken. It was Britain's Prime Minister Eden who initiated averting such a reappraisal and seeking a way of rearming West Germany with French approval. He found it in the forgotten Brussels Treaty.

This organization was now to be revised by the inclusion of Germany and Italy. The new alliance, which pledged all its members to come to one another's aid if attacked, would be known as the Western European Union. Yet WEU was not really an alliance, no forces were assigned to it, and it had no responsibility for formulating a strategy to defend its members. These remained within the functions of NATO. WEU's role was to channel West German troops into NATO, while at the same time maintaining a set of controls over West Germany similar to those included in EDC. Furthermore, Britain agreed to keep a minimum number of troops—four divisions and a tactical air force—on the Continent. Britain's pledge was a formalization of its responsibilities under the Dunkirk, Brussels, and NATO treaties. But to the French it seemed an important new commitment; they now felt assured that they would not someday be left to face German troops alone.

These commitments, embodied in the Paris Pact, came into force in May 1955. Thus, ten years after Germany's defeat, the occupation came to an end, and the Federal Republic regained its sovereignty and entered NATO via WEU. West Germany's military power could now be added to Western strength. Two important declarations were appended to these Paris agreements. In the first, the West German government subscribed to the principles of the United Nations, undertook "never to have recourse to force to achieve the reunification of Germany or the modification of the present boundaries of the German Federal Republic," and to resolve all disputes between itself and other states by peaceful means. In the second, however, the United States, Britain, and France declared that they recognized the Federal Republic as the only freely and legitimately constituted government entitled to speak for all of Germany—which indicated a policy of nonrecognition of the East German government. In addition, the Allies would pursue German reunification by peaceful means—which meant that the alliance with West Germany, while revisionist in its political objective, was conceived of as being defensive in nature. Finally, the Western powers stated that they would continue to exercise their responsibilities with regard to the security of West Germany and West Berlin.

With Germany safely enrolled as a member of NATO, the WEU members now took a momentous step toward further economic and political integration. The six states that composed this Little Europe had gained increasing benefits from this movement. On June 1, 1958, they established the European Economic Community, usually referred to as the Common Market, whose objective was to join them together into an economic union. Their plan was to achieve this in a twelve- to fifteen-year period. During this time, all six states would completely eliminate the tariffs and quota systems still hampering trade among them (agriculture was to be the exception—the Market expected to develop a common policy of subsidies and price supports, and eliminate discriminations among farmers within the community); they would also abolish restrictions on the movement of labor, capital, and services among them, although this commitment was qualified. But these moves, the "Six" realized, would not suffice. A government might abolish a tariff, but it could compensate its producers through subsidies or impose internal taxes that would discriminate against foreign products. Production costs also reflected national regulations on wages, hours, working conditions, and social welfare programs; producers in nations with lower standards would have an obvious advantage against foreign competition. Thus, to ensure maximum free competition in the Common Market, subsidies were forbidden (except for use in developing backward areas); discriminatory taxes, price-fixing, and division of markets by cartel arrangements were not permitted; and the need to equalize hours, wages, and working conditions was recognized as urgent.

What were the chances for the development of this market? The economic benefits suggested that they were excellent. As trade barriers were lowered and then disappeared, the increasing competition would result in the growth of efficient companies and the elimination of the less efficient ones unless they modernized or converted to new lines of production. All members would also gain from the capital funds. Italy would receive capital for the development of its southern area; France and its overseas territories would also receive development capital. While Germany would contribute a large share of these funds that would benefit its partners, it would in return receive access to their European and African markets—and Germany was in the strongest competitive position of the Six. A final factor was that the community expected to receive advantages against third parties. It would be in a strong bargaining position to demand reciprocal lowering of tariffs. All these advantages outweighed the burdens each nation would suffer as a result of economic dislocation and hardships, which would, in fact, be minimized by being extended over a twelve- to fifteen-year period (the plan's initial successes were to cut this period down by several years) and by being shared among all members.

Above all, the principal advantage of the Common Market would be political. For a common market needs common policies; only one set of rules—not six—can govern its competitive behavior. One nation cannot be allowed to pay its workers considerably lower wages than its neighbor in order to achieve a competitive advantage. There would therefore have to be some standardization of wages, as well as of such related items as overtime, hours worked per week, and various welfare benefits. In the long run, if the Market developed successfully, it would therefore also undoubtedly lead to the adoption of common fiscal policies to control the ups and downs of the business cycle, a common currency, and a central bank. Thus the economic "spillover" —from a common market in coal and steel into a common market for all sectors of the economy—was expected by the Common Market's founding fathers to stimulate political unification as economic integration compelled the Inner Six members to harmonize their social and economic policies. Economic union was expected to encourage increasing political integration. It was precisely this objective to form a political union that had originally inspired ECSC.

EEC was the culminating act of the movement, initiated by France and strongly supported by Chancellor Adenauer, to tie Germany so closely to a European community that it would never again be able to use its power for purely national ends. The formation of the Inner Six was nothing less than the last link subjecting Germany to European restraints and responsibilities. Its success would make it impossible thereafter for Germany ever again to pursue a unilateral course. The Common Market was also the end product of France's desire to supplement its own strength with that of a united Europe, so that it would gain an equal voice with Britain in the Atlantic Alliance and not always remain subservient to the United States. France did not want to pursue a NATO policy dictated largely by Anglo-American interests; it wanted the alliance to take its interests into account as well.

It was hardly surprising that Russia reacted quickly against the Common Market and attempted to break up this potential united states of Europe. A strong and united Europe, economically prosperous and politically stable, would not only prove to be a powerful barrier to Soviet expansionist ambitions, but it might well threaten the Soviet *status quo* in Eastern Europe. The existence of a free Germany had already had an unsettling effect upon the whole satellite system.

West Berlin, especially, has had a tremendous impact in this respect. The existence of this city, alongside Communist East Berlin, had hampered Soviet control of East Germany. Through West Berlin escaped many young, skilled, and professional men and women of East Germany; it was an escape hatch that was depopulating East Germany of the very people it needed to run its society. In West Berlin, the United States, Britain, and France had, moreover, established agencies to gather intelligence about Eastern Europe. There was a constant flow of information about the West from West Berlin into the Russian-controlled satellites; this defeated one of the major purposes of the iron curtain, which was to stop incoming information that might lead to comparisons of the Communist and free systems. West Berlin, in short, affected the political stability of all of Eastern Europe. If the existence of West Berlin and West Germany made the Communist *status quo* insecure, how much greater the Soviet apprehensions of a united Europe must have been.

The stability of the Soviet position in Eastern and Central Europe, as apparently seen by Moscow, depended upon two factors: one, gaining Western recognition of the East German "Democratic" Republic; and two, destroying the freedom of West Berlin. To achieve these objectives, the Soviet Union announced in November 1958 that at the end of six months it intended to end the four-power occupation and would hand control of East Berlin and the routes leading into West Berlin over to the East Germans. The clear implication was that in the future free access to Berlin would require that the Western powers deal directly and officially with the East German government. The Russians also repeated their former proposal for the unification of Germany: that East and West Germany should join in a confederation. This, too, was a tactical device to gain the Federal Republic's recognition of East Germany. The Russians obviously wanted to entice the West Germans to start negotiating with the East Germans on the issue of unification; at the same time, it was also clear that the Russians were not in the least interested in any form of unification. Their proposal was, in fact, so constituted that it precluded Western acceptance. A confederation half democratic and half dictatorship was a contradiction in terms and was totally unfeasible. How could a government of such a confederation ever agree on economic policies? Most industry in East Germany was owned by the government; West Germany was a booming private-enterprise state. The G.D.R. had recognized the Oder–Neisse line as Germany's eastern frontier; West Germany did not yet acknowledge the permanent loss of the territories Poland received from Germany at the end of World War II. As if to ensure the rejection of their terms, the Russians also demanded that East Germany, with a population of a little more than 17 million, and West Germany, with a population of more than 53 million, should be equally represented in the confederated government. The Soviet Union naturally did not want the East Germans to be outvoted —with the possible result that East Germany would be voted out of existence —but Khrushchev could hardly have expected the Western powers or the Adenauer government to accept such equality. This lack of Russian interest in German unification was made explicit in 1960, when the Russian Ambassador to West Germany stated that the precondition for German reunification was not German neutrality but the nationalization of West German big industry, the "breaking up of the power of monopoly capital," and the "domination of the working class." None of the Western powers, let alone the Federal Republic, was likely to accept these conditions.

If the Soviet proposals, then, were meant to elicit Western recognition of East Germany, this goal still remained subsidiary to the primary aim of strangling West Berlin. What the Russians were actually calling for when they declared the end of the four-power occupation was an Allied withdrawal from West Berlin, turning it into a "free city." This was, in effect, a demand for the incorporation of West Berlin into East Germany. Once Western troops had left the city, the West Berliners would feel isolated and unprotected, abandoned and completely helpless. They would be surrounded by the Russian army and the East German army and police. In these circumstances, the defenseless West Berliners would have to come to terms with the East German regime. On the other hand, if the West would not sign a treaty turning Berlin into a "free city," the Soviet Union would then sign a separate peace treaty with East Germany, thus automatically abrogating the West's right to be in Berlin and making any further Western stay dependent upon the terms that could be negotiated with the now "sovereign" German Democratic Republic. This would mean that the West would remain in Berlin by the consent of East Germany, which could then gradually intensify its pressure and gradually undermine the West's position until it became untenable.

At this point, one way or the other, the Russians would have eliminated a very troublesome thorn in their side. They would then be in a far better position to stabilize the *status quo*. But the destruction of West Berlin would not only have accomplished the Soviet Union's defensive aims; it would simultaneously have attained Russia's long-standing offensive purpose of weakening its opponents, perhaps fatally. If the Russians could drive the Western powers, especially the United States, out of Berlin, they would also be able, first, to cut off the development of the Common Market before it gathered too much momentum, and second, to shatter the NATO alliance. It was, above all, American power that guaranteed the freedom of the 2 million Germans living in West Berlin. If the United States were to abandon these people under pressure, faith in America's protective power and willingness to live up to its commitments would collapse in Europe. The Germans would be the first to read the lesson: that since America could not guarantee their security, they must approach the Russians independently. Whatever the nature of the terms the Russians would offer them, they would certainly include clauses demanding the abandonment of all Germany's political, economic, or military ties to the West. But without Germany, there could be no Common Market, since Germany's partners were dependent upon it for much of the capital required for their economic development. And if Germany pulled out of the Atlantic Alliance, American troops would have to be withdrawn back to the United States, since it would be politically and strategically impossible to station them in France. Yet, these troops were a symbol of the American commitment to defend Europe; they were psychologically and politically indispensable. No written guarantees could be substituted for this living embodiment of America's stake in Europe. Certainly, the withdrawal of U.S. ground forces at that time would have indicated to the Europeans that America was no longer willing to defend them now that the United States was itself becoming increasingly vulnerable to a Soviet nuclear attack.

This was, in the final analysis, the fundamental issue posed by the Berlin crisis. The Soviet proposals had included the ultimatum that if West Berlin's status had not been "renegotiated" *à la Russe* within six months, the Russians would place the East Germans in control of the railroads and highways leading into West Berlin. If the East Germans then interfered with Western traffic, the West would have to employ force to break any blockade; and Khrushchev stated that any such Western attempts would meet Soviet resistance. The defense of West Berlin therefore posed the definite possibility of total war. But would the United States be willing to take this risk, when it no longer possessed an atomic monopoly? Threatening the Russians with SAC might, at a time of increasing nuclear bipolarity, be ineffective. The Russians, too, were acquiring a capability for massive retaliation. Was Berlin worth the devastation of many American cities and 50 million to 100 million dead and wounded? The Russian challenge was a clever one: It faced the United States with a limited challenge and offered it the choice of surrendering West Berlin or fighting a total war for its preservation. It was America's will that was thus really at stake in Berlin, and a failure of this will would disintegrate the entire American position in the European rimland.

Berlin was thus a major test of postwar American policy. Nor was it a repeat of the 1948 situation. At that time, Stalin had acted upon two assumptions: first, that the far larger Red Army contingents would deter an Allied attempt to break through on the ground; and second, that the United States and Britain could not keep West Berlin alive. The first assumption proved to be correct, but the second was mistaken. When Stalin realized this, he had either to call off the blockade or shoot down Allied planes and risk a war. America's atomic monopoly favored the first solution. By late 1958, the Soviet Union did not have to feel as worried about America's nuclear arsenal; it had a stockpile of its own, and it had just tested the world's first Intercontinental Ballistic Missile (ICBM). American brinkmanship, given this circumstance, would thus be riskier. Yet, if the United States would not accept this risk to prevent Russia from slowly strangling West Berlin to death, the question inevitably arose: What objective was worth the cost of total war? If not Berlin, what was? Berlin was thus a crisis of massive retaliation; for the Soviet action questioned the very feasibility of basic American strategy. Could strategic air power, upon which the Eisenhower administration depended almost exclusively to preserve the line around the Sino-Soviet periphery, fulfill this task in an age of nuclear plenty, when World War III was merely a pseudonym for suicide? The answer seemed to be that too great a reliance upon SAC was gravely weakening the American ability to preserve this line. Nuclear bombs were just *too* powerful; they were *too* enormously destructuve to be used in any situation but the ultimate one. U.S. strategic power was—ironically—*so* great that it tended to paralyze the will to use it; it therefore paralyzed diplomacy as well.

The Berlin crisis, a limited Soviet challenge but one which had enormous stakes for the United States, was the most serious challenge Washington had confronted since 1948–1949. The Truman Doctrine, Marshall Plan, Berlin airlift, and NATO had made it very plain to Moscow that Western Europe was an area of vital American interest. Soviet domination over this Western rimland of the Eurasian continent was no more tolerable to the United States than German control. To prevent such hegemony by a great power whose strength, greatly enhanced by its control of Eastern Europe, had consistently been seen as a threat to the United States, and whose antidemocratic political orientation was viewed as a danger to the preservation of an international environment in which democratic values would not only survive but flourish, the United States was prepared to fight. Presumably this knowledge had deterred the Russians in the late 1940s, and it was this fear of war which had led them to redirect their challenges to Third World areas between the so-called free and Communist worlds. But now, ten years after the first Berlin crisis, the Soviets had once more challenged the West in Europe. Indeed, the reopening of the Berlin issue—and especially that for the first time in the postwar era they were publicly demanding that the Western powers abandon territory they controlled and were threatening them with an ultimatum—suggested a new Soviet confidence in the ability of their power to achieve their stated political aim of converting the Western half of Germany's former capital into a "free city." Not only did the West not have a capacity for a limited response to a limited challenge but, worse, the strategic balance appeared to be changing. The Soviets were claiming that they were mass-producing their new ICBM. America's deterrent bomber force, they said, was now vulnerable and its deterrent capacity declining. The Central Intelligence Agency seemed to agree by forecasting a missile gap as the United States entered the 1960s, and many Americans, both in and out of government, became concerned that Khrushchev might be right. Clearly, he was attempting to cash in on what the Soviet leader already asserted was a changing distribution of power which had become favorable to Russia.

chapter 6

berlin, cuba, and the crisis of massive retaliation

MUTUAL DETERRENCE AND SUICIDE

No policy could have been more typically American than massive retaliation. It was a strictly military one, completely divorced from political considerations. The separation of force and diplomacy was, indeed, twofold. First, should it ever become clear that the diplomats had failed to keep the peace, the military would take charge and their aim would be total victory. The enemy was to be punished by completely defeating him. A maximum of violence was required to achieve such a military victory, making nuclear weapons ideal for this task. A combined attack upon the enemy's major population and industrial centers would paralyze the entire country and reduce it to a mass of rubble and radioactive dust. Massive retaliation, in brief, carried the American doctrine of war to its logical culmination. Second, in "peacetime," massive retaliation's function was strictly the deterrence of all-out war. For less than a total challenge, therefore, American diplomacy was unsupported by any usable power. This eliminated any incentive for the Soviet leaders to arrive at any compromise arrangements over the issues that had precipitated the cold war, such as the division of Germany or the incorporation of Eastern Europe into the Soviet empire.

Nor, since the United States had renounced the use of force except in retaliation against a direct attack, could the Soviet Union be deterred from constant probing actions. Indeed, the irony of the situation was that throughout this whole period the Russians were constantly probing, seeking to expand their influence by means short of total war—by guerrilla warfare, *coups d'état,* internal Communist parties, anti-Western nationalist movements, "volunteers," and satellite armies. The only thing they had to avoid was an attack upon the United States itself or upon those areas the United States had designated as of vital interest to its security; short of that ultimate provocation, the Soviet Union, the strategically weaker party during the first decade of the cold war, could raise tensions and challenge the United States.

If this was the pattern during the period of America's atomic monopoly and greater strategic power even after Russia had acquired its own atomic bomb, the possibility of challenges in areas vital to the United States—such as Europe—increased as Russia's nuclear stockpile and capacity to hit the United States increased during the late 1950s. As massive retaliation became a two-way street, the Soviet Union's growing ability to impose catastrophic damage upon America meant that the two nuclear states would increasingly stalemate one another's strategic striking power. The "balance of terror," as Churchill called it, would ensure the peace; indeed, in President Eisenhower's words, "there is no alternative to peace." His participation at the 1955 summit conference in Geneva with Soviet Premier Bulganin (Khrushchev was at that time not yet premier but first secretary of the Communist Party of the U.S.S.R.) was generally recognized as testimony to this fact. War was no longer a rational instrument of national power; by simply meeting, the leaders of the two most powerful countries of the world were said to have "signed" a tacit nonaggression pact.

Actually, American policy handed the Soviet Union the opportunity to break this stalemate. For the age of atomic plenty has increased America's strategic dilemma. The Eisenhower all-or-nothing strategy has meant that each limited Soviet challenge confronted Washington with the question of whether the defense of the objective under attack was worth the destruction of most of America's cities and their inhabitants. Faced with this prospect, if it responded to the less than total Soviet challenges, the American government had a strong incentive to do nothing. This meant that Moscow could gradually turn the nuclear balance of power in its favor by imposing a series of piecemeal defeats upon the West. It could erode the *status quo* by nibbling away at it bit by bit, without ever once facing the United States with the one kind of challenge for which it was prepared. According to Henry Kissinger in 1957:

> It can be argued that the fear of all-out war is bound to be mutual, that the Soviet leaders will, therefore, share our reluctance to engage in any adventures which may involve this risk. But because each side may be equally deterred from engaging in all-out war, it makes all the difference which side can extricate itself from its dilemma *only* by initiating such a struggle. If the Soviet bloc can present its challenges in less than all-out form it may gain a crucial advantage. Every

move on its part will then pose the appalling dilemma of whether we are willing to commit suicide to prevent encroachments, which do not, each in itself, seem to threaten our existence directly but which may be steps on the road to our ultimate destruction.

To be sure, we shall continue to insist that we reject the notion of "peace at any price." The price of peace, however, cannot be determined in the abstract. The growth of the Soviet nuclear stockpile is certain to widen the line between what is considered "vital" and what is "peripheral" if we must weigh each objective against the destruction of New York or Detroit, of Los Angeles or Chicago.

Was Berlin still a "vital" interest? Or was Berlin now a "peripheral" interest? These were the stark questions which confronted the United States in the late 1950s.

MASSIVE RETALIATION AND NATO

The question raised by the Soviet challenge was further underlined by the lack of sizable shield forces on the Continent. The original tasks assigned to these troops were twofold: first, to strengthen deterrence by assuring the Russians that an attack upon Europe would break the tripwire and unleash SAC; and second, in case deterrence failed, to implement the "forward strategy" and hold the Red Army at the Elbe while SAC was laying Russia waste. The success of the deterrence of total war, however, dictated yet a third operational assignment for NATO forces: to conduct limited operations and thereby deter less than total challenge. It was preposterous to assume that the United States would continue to risk suicide no matter what the level of Soviet provocation. Would it really be willing to initiate an all-out nuclear war if the Russians seized a small portion of Turkey? Would it really precipitate a total nuclear exchange if the Red Army or satellite East German troops seized all or part of West Berlin or a small enclave of West Germany? Would suicide in these instances be preferable to accepting limited losses? Only a capacity for limited war would allow the United States and its allies to escape this dilemma.

But it was exactly this capacity to respond to limited challenges that was missing in Europe. In a large measure, this was a result of the Eisenhower administration's determination to "maximize air power and minimize the foot soldier." By January 1960, NATO had only 17 or 18 ready divisions. Apart from the numerical deficiency of NATO ground forces, their equipment with atomic tactical weapons raised the same question as did SAC: Would they be used? Would NATO not grow increasingly reluctant to rely on these forces to respond to Russian moves? When the original decision to equip Allied forces with atomic weapons was taken, it was believed that the Soviet Union would have few, if any, atomic tactical weapons. Thus, the damage caused by the tactical weapons could be absorbed—particularly since East Germany and Poland would have to absorb most of it, and Soviet and satellite troops would have to suffer the atomic blows. The picture changed, however, when the Russians, too, acquired these weapons and thereby ensured that their use would be reciprocal. In these circumstances, the advantages that atomic arms were supposed to confer upon the West began to diminish, if not to disappear.

Nuclear weapons would not protect Europe; they would devastate it. Europe is densely populated; its cities are too close to one another; civil, military, tactical, and strategic targets are all intertwined. A nuclear ground war would be a catastrophe for Europe, probably spelling the end of European civilization. The distinction between limited atomic war and total atomic war was for Europeans meaningless. NATO's capacity to fight a limited tactical atomic war would therefore not allow the West to escape the dilemma of suicide or appeasement. A limited war in Europe was meaningless unless it also limited the devastation. But the concentration on massive retaliation—on NATO's sword—had reduced the apparent necessity of raising sufficient ground forces and strengthening the NATO shield. This, in turn, reinforced the need to stake Western survival on each issue, no matter what the level of provocation, since America was left with no weapon but strategic air power with which to respond to the Soviet challenge in the heart of Europe.

THE BERLIN RETREAT

It was this reliance upon SAC that made it very difficult for the Western powers, especially the United States, to impress the Soviet Union with NATO's unity and resoluteness. On the one hand, the United States was determined to stay in Berlin; on the other hand, having stated that it would defend Berlin by massive retaliation, it simultaneously sought to escape the consequences of its own military strategy. This it could do only by granting concessions. Shortly after the presentation of the Soviet ultimatum, Secretary of State Dulles talked of accepting the East Germans as "Russian agents" at the checkpoints on the routes leading into Berlin. The Secretary also declared that the reunification of Germany could be brought about by means other than free elections. Both statements threatened a complete abandonment of the previous and long-held American positions of nonrecognition of the East German regime and Germany's right of self-determination. The administration, already pressured by the British, also accepted the standing Russian call for a summit conference. But it insisted on the prior fulfillment of two conditions: withdrawal of the Soviet six-month ultimatum and a foreign ministers' conference to lay the basis for a settlement of the Berlin and the general German issues. The purpose of a "meeting at the top" was, in the administration's opinion, essentially to ratify decisions already reached at a lower level; Eisenhower definitely rejected a meeting that would settle nothing and end in a fruitless propaganda debate.

The Russians reluctantly accepted the precondition of a foreign ministers' conference and at the same time denied that the six-month ultimatum was an ultimatum. But they refused to budge from their position at the foreign ministers' marathon held in Geneva in the spring and summer of 1959. It was the West that offered the concessions. In the first place, the United States allowed an East German delegation to sit in on the deliberations and thereby took a step toward *de facto* recognition of the Soviet-installed regime. The Soviet Union had threatened not to negotiate at all if the East Germans were not permitted to attend. Second, the West abandoned its plan for the reunification of Germany at the first sign of Soviet opposition. Third, the foreign ministers then took up the problem of an interim settlement for Berlin. In short, after years of stating that it was the Soviet division of Germany that was the cause of European instability, the United States and Britain accepted the Soviet definition of what constituted the principal source of European tension. Furthermore, they offered two concessions: The West would not arm its forces in Berlin with nuclear weapons and would not install missile bases in the city; and the Allies promised to curb their propaganda and intelligence activities in their sector if the Russians would halt similar (and anti-Western) activities in their zone. These proposals were unacceptable to the Soviet Union.

The Russians simply refused to renew their endorsement of Allied rights in Berlin and reasserted that they would end the occupation regime. The Allies thus failed to obtain the Soviet guarantee they sought, but the fact that they had attempted to arrive at an interim arrangement for Berlin at all, and were willing to grant concessions to obtain it, is eloquent testimony to the dilemma in which American strategy had placed them. For, in effect, the Western powers—in this case, America and Britain—were willing to transform the Western position in Berlin merely in return for the withdrawal of the Soviet threat to the city. In an attempt to extricate themselves from the dilemma of suicide or surrender, the two countries were placing themselves in the humiliating position of calling into question their well-established rights in Berlin. No wonder Khrushchev felt that all he had to do was maintain a high level of tension.

His bellicosity and rigidity were thus paying handsome dividends. The more menacing he sounded and the more inflexibly he stood, the greater the number of voices in the West that called for more Western "flexibility" and "new approaches" to the Soviet Union on the whole problem of Germany. Policies which had almost become "untouchable" over the years were suddenly placed in flux and condemned as dangerous. The West was torn apart by precisely this kind of controversy. The British denounced Chancellor Adenauer's "rigidity"; the Germans, in turn, accused the British of "appeasement." Franco-British relations cooled considerably. And both Adenauer and

De Gaulle demonstrated increasing suspicions of United States intentions and resolution. America's apparent willingness to discuss Berlin with the Russians seemed to the French and German leaders to show little American conviction or courage to uphold a previous position; to them, Eisenhower was showing far too much flexibility.

As if to prove Khrushchev's theory that his threats of war against the West would have rewarding consequences, and to confirm De Gaulle's and Adenauer's apprehensions, President Eisenhower issued an invitation to Mr. Khrushchev to visit the United States in September 1959. This invitation represented a major Soviet tactical victory. Such a summit *à deux* would show Khrushchev's equality with the American president and convincingly demonstrate to the world Russia's status with the United States as one of the two great superpowers. And, as Khrushchev knew, it would deepen the divisions within Western ranks by increasing the Allies' apprehension of a separate United States–Soviet agreement at their expense, and conversely, would persuade President Eisenhower that the crisis was caused by the rigidity of certain Allied leaders who were opposed to the "normalization" of relations. It is noticeable, for instance, that after the conference had ended, the president described the Allied position in Berlin with the same word Khrushchev constantly used—"abnormal." This unwittingly strengthened the Soviet leader's diplomatic hand. If the Allied position in Berlin was indeed "abnormal," the Soviet demands then seemed "reasonable," and the Western powers should alter their position to "normalize" the situation. This heedless use of a single word was characteristic of the manner in which Khrushchev was being allowed to set not only the pace of the negotiations, but also the context within which these took place.

The Eisenhower–Khrushchev meeting did result in the Soviet Union's withdrawal of its threat to take unilateral action in Berlin, in return for American willingness to negotiate on the problems of Berlin and Germany at a four-power summit meeting. For American policy-makers, this meant another postponement of the day on which they would have to decide the painful question of whether Berlin was worth the cost of a total war. But if the administration believed that the crisis had been ended, that from then on it could leisurely negotiate on these issues and, if the Russians did not accept its terms, preserve the *status quo,* it was soon disabused of this notion. Mr. Khrushchev was soon reiterating his threat to sign a separate peace with East Germany.

Shortly before the scheduled Paris summit conference in May 1960, an event took place that was to shatter the summit conference after only one session and further postpone future negotiations on Berlin. On May Day, 1300 miles within Soviet territory, the Russians downed an American U-2 "spy plane" loaded with photographic equipment for the gathering of intelligence data. The Eisenhower administration reacted to this unexpected and unhappy turn of events with considerable diplomatic ineptitude. When

Khrushchev initially announced only the shooting down of the U-2, the U.S. government responded that the plane had been engaged solely in meteorological observation and speculated that the pilot must have flown off his course. When the Soviet premier then revealed the real mission of the flight and produced an alleged confession by the pilot, the administration reversed itself. In a move unprecedented in diplomatic history, it admitted that the U-2 pilot had been taking aerial photographs of the Soviet Union and that it had lied in its previous announcement. Nor did the administration stop there. It claimed that similar flights had been sent into Russian skies for several years and strongly intimated that such flights would continue. The reason advanced was that Soviet secrecy made it necessary to gather information by this means in order to prevent a surprise attack. But it is one thing to be caught red-handed in spying and to admit it; it is quite another thing to assert that you will continue to do so in the future. In effect, the United States claimed the *right* to fly over Soviet territory (one need only imagine the uproar in the United States if the Russians were to announce calmly that they had the right to fly over American soil and take photographs of military installations).

Such a challenge could hardly have been left unmet. For the Soviet premier to have bypassed this claim would have been equivalent to acknowledging to the world, to his people, to his domestic enemies, and to his allies that he had surrendered to the United States the right to violate Soviet territory. Khrushchev could not have survived such an admission. The alternative course he took was to strike a belligerent pose in Paris. He launched a blistering personal attack upon President Eisenhower, demanding from him a personal apology for past U-2 flights, a promise that no such flights would be undertaken in the future and punishment of those responsible for the spying operation. Eisenhower's promise that no more reconnaissance missions would be undertaken during his term of office did not satisfy Khrushchev; he apparently considered this to mean merely a temporary suspension. The other conditions demanded by the Soviet premier were rejected outright by Eisenhower. Khrushchev thereupon suggested that the summit conference be postponed for a period of six to eight months, and he bluntly told Eisenhower that he would not be welcome if he came to the Soviet Union in June to return the premier's previous visit to the United States. In short, Khrushchev said that he wanted nothing more to do with Eisenhower and that he would wait to negotiate the Berlin problem with the next administration. A new crisis had been put off for a little while longer.

It was inevitable, therefore, that the Berlin problem would be raised again by the Russians once the new administration had established itself in power. Khrushchev was still convinced that the global balance was shifting in his favor, and he remained confident that he was strong enough to acquire West Berlin. President Kennedy, fearing that Khrushchev might miscalculate, therefore journeyed to Vienna to emphasize America's determination to defend West Berlin; the United States would stand firm and protect the free half of the city. Khrushchev, however, took these warnings lightly. His response was characteristic: to test the president's resolution by reviving the original threat that the Berlin situation would have to be resolved within six months —that is, before the end of 1961. The fruits of the Vienna summit meeting were thus precisely the opposite of what was intended: the very type of Russian brinkmanship against which Kennedy had sought to caution the Soviet leader.

Kennedy was thus confronted with a crisis. On the one hand, he fully realized the significance of Berlin. While he declared his willingness to negotiate, he also stated that he did not expect the Soviets to confront him with the accomplished fact of a treaty with East Germany. The United States was not willing to discuss merely how the West would withdraw from the beleaguered city, thereby leaving it for the Communists to swallow. The West's right to be in the city stemmed from its victory over Nazi Germany. Western presence and access to the city, and the freedom of West Berlin, therefore were not negotiable. In the president's words: "We cannot negotiate with those who say: 'What's mine is mine, and what's yours is negotiable.' " More specifically, he asked, if the West refused to meet its clear-cut commitments in Berlin, where would it meet them? Yet it was also clear on August 13, 1961, when the Communists built a wall dividing the city, that they had eliminated the escape hatch for East Germans, ended West Berlin's usefulness as a "showplace for Western capitalism," and violated the quadripartite status of Berlin. But the West did not react by resisting the erection of the wall with bulldozers and tanks for fear of military conflict with Communist—especially Soviet—forces. This passivity intensified Khrushchev's conviction that the United States would not fight and that he could, slowly but surely, increase the pressure on NATO and drive the West out of Berlin.

It was this latter conviction, and the consequent American fear that the Russian leader might miscalculate Western resolve and thereby accidentally trigger a war, that accounted largely for the difference between Kennedy's and his predecessor's reactions to the Berlin crisis. Unlike Eisenhower, Kennedy used the tensions over Berlin to further the build-up of American military power; the new president was determined to show Khrushchev that the United States was not bluffing when it declared its intentions to defend West Berlin. Kennedy had actually begun his move to increase the nation's military strength shortly after assuming office. His first consideration had been to reduce SAC's vulnerability during the changeover from bombers to missiles that began in the late 1950s. Bombers located at known sites were highly vulnerable to surprise attack. Thus, even in a situation of mutual deterrence, the possibility that many or most of the enemy's bombers might be surprised and destroyed on the ground remained an incentive to attack. If they could be destroyed, the retaliatory attack by a small remnant force might not be fatal to the attacking nation. In a crisis situation, this possibility could tempt either side to launch a preemptive strike in order to forestall a possible blow by the other side—even if the other side actually had no intention of striking. But solid-fuel missiles, like the air force's Minuteman, could be widely dispersed and protected, or "hardened" underground, instead of being concentrated on a few bases, as bombers were; and the navy's Polaris missiles could be moved underwater so that the enemy would at no time know where to strike them. Missiles were not yet too accurate.

The importance of the dispersion, the "hardening," and especially the mobility of missiles lay in the fact that it deprived a surprise attack of its rationale. When the opponent's retaliatory power consisted entirely or primarily of mobile, solid-fuel, long-range missiles, it was impossible to know all the sites at which to hit him in order to destroy his retaliatory capacity. Obliterating the enemy's cities would benefit the aggressor very little if the enemy still retained this capacity. Surprise, therefore, no longer confered any significant advantage to the side that struck first. Indeed, there was no need any longer to hit preemptively, since enough of the missiles could survive an initial strike and still retaliate fully against the aggressor in a second strike. A first strike in these circumstances—which American policy-makers generally conceded to the Soviets—would be completely irrational.

Yet this change in strategic weapons was a long-range program. Kennedy, as cautious as his predecessor, vacillated between his determination to stay in West Berlin and his equally strong determination to avoid conflict. Thus, like Eisenhower, he was willing to offer concessions and negotiate with the Soviets alone if West Germany and France remained "inflexible." The meager results of these bilateral American–Soviet negotiations were primarily due to Soviet unwillingness to concede the right to any Western presence in Berlin, which, in turn, was in all probability due to Khrushchev's conviction that he need only maintain Soviet pressure finally to evict the Western powers from the Communist-surrounded and divided city. If during this early period of the Kennedy administration, as during the late years of the Eisenhower era, the Russians were unwilling to risk the final test, they had shown they were not hesitant to push the issue to a point of high tension. If the United States upheld the *status quo,* the manner in which it questioned its own position in Berlin and the concessions it offered in the name of flexibility demonstrated a lack of will and sense of purpose, which augured ill for the future if: (1) the Soviet leaders could keep their challenges below the level of provocation which might arouse an American nuclear response (while the exact level of tension could not be known to them, they did keep well below it); and (2) the Soviets confined their challenges to the periphery of Western power, and especially such isolated outposts as West Berlin. As long as they followed these two fundamental precepts, they could seek to exploit the dilemmas of American strategy.

It was the second rule that they failed to follow when Moscow shifted the challenge to 90 miles from the American mainland—to Cuba—where the United States had no choice but to respond in defense of what Washington conceived to be its vital interests.

CASTRO AND THE MISSILE CRISIS

Cuba's revolutionary government had been established on January 1, 1959, after its leaders had overthrown the tyrannical Batista dictatorship. During his struggle against Batista, Castro had identified himself with both democratic government and social and economic justice and had gained widespread popularity among the Cuban people. This public support ensured the victory of his guerrilla army against the larger government forces. The Castro revolution was essentially a social revolution. In the opening months of its rule, the new government moved to remedy the conditions of the people by instituting land reforms and by building low-cost housing, schools, and clinics. But some features of this social revolution were bound to clash with the United States. Castro was highly nationalistic, and therefore anti-American because of past American domination of Cuba. Although the United States had been instrumental in freeing Cuba from Spain, it subsequently passed the Platt Amendment, which granted the Americans the right to intervene at any time in Cuba for the preservation of Cuban independence, for the protection of life, property, and individual liberty, and for the discharge of Cuba's treaty obligations. By 1934, when the amendment was repealed, the United States had intervened militarily three times; it also had established a naval base at Guantánamo Bay. American capital was even more effective in controlling Cuba. By 1956, the United States controlled 80 percent of Cuba's utilities, 90 percent of its mines and cattle ranches, nearly all its oil, and 40 percent of its sugar. It was thus not surprising that the Cuban revolution should in large part direct its long-pent-up nationalism and social resentment against "Yanqui imperialism." America's support of the Batista dictatorship until the moment of its collapse only intensified this anti-American sentiment. "Cuba, si! Yanqui, no!" became the Castro regime's rallying cry, the ceremonial burning of the American flag its ritual, and the confiscation of American property its reward.

This anti-American nationalistic feeling—deliberately fostered by Castro to increase the popularity of his regime—led to an increasing identification of Castro's government with Communism. Before long, the regime became a dictatorship with centralized control over all phases of Cuba's life. All parties were abolished except for one—the Communist Party, upon whose organizational strength Castro had become increasingly dependent. It was simply a matter of debate as to whether the Communists dominated the government. The real point was that the Communists actively supported Castro's revolution, convinced that it was only a transitory stage to Communism, and that the Castro government linked itself to the Communist bloc—and then consolidated these political, military, and economic links. The Soviet Union supplied Cuba with vast amounts of arms and accompanying military advisors. Cuban airmen were sent to Czechoslovakia to learn how to fly Soviet fighters, and a large number of Cuban technicians were trained in

Communist countries. Cuba's armed services soon ranked second only to America's as the largest in the hemisphere. Diplomatic relations were established with all Communist countries except East Germany; and economic agreements were signed with many of the same countries, including East Germany. Cuba's economy became integrated into that of the Communist bloc; 75 percent of the island's trade was with countries behind the iron curtain. In January 1961, the United States cut off diplomatic relations with Cuba. If Castro had only now attempted to seize the Guantánamo base, there would have been an excuse for open American intervention.

Castro was much too shrewd to do so. Consequently, the United States supported an attempt, in April 1961, by a small force of Cuban exiles—many of them former Castro associates who had become disillusioned by the Premier's tyranny and his Communist sympathies—to land in Cuba and attempt to overthrow Castro. Plans for this operation had been begun during the Eisenhower administration, and Kennedy decided to support them when he came into office. The U.S. intelligence community believed that, once the exiles had gained a beachhead in the Bay of Pigs, some units of Castro's army and Cuba's population would welcome the invaders as liberators. But when the American-organized and -financed operation was launched, it turned out to be a dramatic and appalling failure. America had bungled because it launched a major foreign policy move involving American prestige—whether it intervened directly or not—on the glib assumption that a feeble beachhead operation would result in a mass uprising of Cubans against their government. But such an operation was bound to fail without adequate planning and preparation inside Cuba itself, without the binding together of the different anti-Castro factions, and amid conditions in which popular anti-Castro sentiment had not yet ripened. The rumors and press reports, which conveyed the impression of a major invasion, only made the failure appear to be even greater.

If nothing succeeds like success, it can also be said that nothing fails like failure. American prestige, already lowered by Russia's man-in-space achievement, sank to a new low. In Cyrus Sulzberger's succinct sentence, "We looked like fools to our friends, rascals to our enemies, and incompetents to the rest." The administration had fallen victim to its own half-heartedness. The results of an unsuccessful invasion could have been predicted: an increase in Castro's domestic support, a revival of Latin American fears of "Yankee imperialism," a blunting of Kennedy's initially successful attempts to identify the United States with anticolonialism, and a loss of confidence in America's leadership by its allies.

Finally, Cuba survived as a Communist base from which the Soviet Union could threaten the United States itself and subvert the security of the other nations of the Western Hemisphere. It was in the fall of 1962 that U.S. intelligence suddenly discovered, to its great surprise and consternation, that the Soviets were building launching sites for approximately 70 medium- and intermediate-range ballistic missiles. The very fact that Khrushchev had dared to move his missiles so near the United States, and apparently expected no counteraction beyond ineffective diplomatic protests, was a dangerous sign. The great danger of all-out war is war by miscalculation; to prevent such a miscalculation is therefore an absolute necessity. But American actions had seemingly convinced the Soviet Premier, the apostle of "peaceful coexistence," that the United States would not fight to protect its vital interests. He probably recalled more recent events: the desire of Kennedy to eliminate Castro, but his unwillingness at the moment of truth to send in American forces and, in Berlin, Kennedy's paralysis when the Soviets built the wall. In each instance, Khrushchev had seen the fear of conflict deter the United States. Thus, he apparently came to believe that he could install his missiles in Cuba with impunity; the United States would rather accept this result than risk the use of force.

For Khrushchev, the stakes were high. American failure to respond to his move would have proved to its NATO allies what they feared already—namely, that the United States, having itself become highly vulnerable to attack, could no longer be relied upon for the protection of their vital interests in Europe. Inaction in the face of Soviet missiles installed only 90 miles away from the American coast would have emphasized this consequence of the nuclear stalemate in a most dramatic fashion. And the promised renewal of Soviet pressure on Berlin after the midterm U.S. congressional elections, together with the likelihood of an even more cautious American reaction than before, would only have reinforced this impression. This time, the Soviets would probably have issued an ultimatum to get out or else—and the "else" was the fact that the Soviets could for the first time cover a large part of the North American continent with their missiles, which would come flying in over areas where there was no adequate protection against them. The early warning systems against bombers and missiles were in the north, since a Soviet attack had always been expected to come in over the Arctic. American vulnerability to attack had therefore risen. Furthermore, the U.S. position in the Western Hemisphere would have been undermined as well. The sudden and unchallenged appearance of another great power in the area where the United States had long been paramount would have eroded America's authority and status and encouraged the spread of Castroism throughout Latin America. All anti-Castro forces, including the indispensable and all too few genuinely democratic reformers, would have been demoralized and perhaps paralyzed by Washington's inaction.

The political and psychological implications of Khrushchev's limited challenge were thus enormous, for the global distribution of power could well be gravely affected. But Khrushchev had for once overplayed his hand. He had raised the pressure on the United States too quickly and too near the United States itself for Washington to be able to avoid the test. Particularly if previous American actions and inactions had convinced the Soviet leader that he could "get away with it," it was imperative to set him straight about this issue. Such confidence on Khrushchev's part could only be the result of a conviction that the United States no longer possessed the will to defend its interests. Such a notion was dangerous, for, if it remained uncorrected, it could lead to an even greater challenge, for example, in the center of Europe; and if the United States did respond, a violent clash, possibly a nuclear war, would be the result. Characteristically, the Soviets had not committed themselves irrevocably in Cuba. They were willing to gamble for a big payoff, but they were also willing to suffer a serious loss of face in order to avoid a catastrophic clash. American firmness and determination left Moscow little choice. For once, therefore, it was the Soviets who had to decide whether to fire the first shot—to break the American blockade of their missile-carrying ships—and thus risk a possible escalation of the conflict. The Kremlin backed down. The level of tension having been raised, it also was rapidly lowered once American determination and the willingness to use American power became clear. In Secretary of State Rusk's picturesque phrase, "We were eyeball to eyeball, and the other fellow just blinked." Interestingly enough, particularly in view of Kennedy's critics who felt a Soviet humiliation in Cuba would compel the Soviet leader to recoup his lost prestige by forcing the West out of Berlin (with the clear implication that the United States should let him do so or desist in Cuba), Khrushchev called off *both* challenges. America's superior power, as demonstrated in the Caribbean, could also be marshaled in Berlin, and it therefore seemed advisable to terminate the tension over the Western half of the former German capital city as well.

AMERICAN STRATEGY AND FRONTIER DEFENSES

The recurrent crisis over West Berlin from 1958 to 1962, plus the Cuban missile crisis, held several lessons if the United States wished to preserve the frontier line around what was then still considered a cohesive Communist world. First, despite U.S. retaliatory power, the Soviet leadership, when it thought circumstances propitious, did not hesitate to raise international tensions with limited political challenges in order to compel the United States to make unilateral concessions. While Moscow was fully aware of the dangers of nuclear war and the consequent need for the avoidance of acts that would expose the Soviet Union to nuclear conflagration, it had not allowed this recognition to deter it from seeking to exploit the West's fear of nuclear war to transform the *status quo* in its favor. The Soviet leadership has felt confident that it could raise tensions *without* provoking the United States; as long as this tension was not raised too high, it could control the risk of war. To ensure that tensions would not escalate beyond control, the Soviets either left themselves a diplomatic escape hatch or were willing to make timely withdrawals in case they underestimated the American reaction. A Soviet-initiated rise in tension did not, therefore, when met by a determined countermove, spiral this tension further upward; Soviet concern to preserve a ceiling on this tension, lest it precipitate an American nuclear response, tended to lower tension and possibly end the specific crisis. The Cuban missile crisis in 1962 was testimony to the Soviets' confidence that, short of a major provocation, which they were not willing to offer, they could challenge the United States without fearing a nuclear response; their rapid retreat was even stronger testimony to their intense concern to avoid a further upward spiral of tension that might possibly reach the ceiling level.

Second, mutual deterrence was clearly not automatic, needing little attention to maintain it. For technology particularly can upset the stability of the deterrent balance. Simply possessing the bomb was insufficient. The key to a *stable* deterrent balance is an invulnerable retaliatory force; if one's force is vulnerable to attack, it may tempt its possessor to strike preemptively lest his forces be caught on the ground, or lead the adversary to strike first since he fears such a preemptive strike if he does not himself preempt. In the late 1950s and early 1960s, the Soviets were claiming that they were mass-producing missiles that made American bombers vulnerable. If this were true, it meant that the capacity of the United States to deter Russia was declining. This was bound to affect policy-makers in Moscow and Washington, emboldening the former and making the latter more cautious. Russia's willingness to challenge the United States in Europe again after a period of ten years and the manner in which America reacted were symptomatic of this perceived change in the balance by the superpowers. Only in Cuba in 1962, after it had become clear that Khrushchev had been bluffing—that he was not mass-producing ICBMs, that the United States was now ahead because in reaction to Khrushchev's claim Kennedy had started a massive missile build-up on land and sea—did Washington once more regain its confidence and, given the immensity of the stakes, react vigorously. Preserving stable deterrence is thus a continuing, never-ending task.

Third, even before the stabilization of the "balance of terror," the United States refused to invoke its great strategic forces to respond to limited challenges; hence the need for limited-war forces. An all-or-nothing option was no option at all. Theoretically, a series of piecemeal defeats could turn the balance of power against America. At some point, the United States would be compelled to take a stand to prevent further deterioration of its position. But the Soviets were not likely to believe in the firmness of this commitment, massive retaliation and the threat of suicide being less and less credible. If, however, America were willing to accept that risk, the Soviet challenge would precipitate a war by miscalculation. Thus by its reliance on massive retaliation the United States could in fact bring about the very war massive retaliation was ostensibly supposed to deter.

Fourth, massive retaliation foreshadowed the gradual weakening of the bonds of America's foremost alliance, NATO. Its European allies had joined

NATO to gain the protection of U.S. power, particularly SAC. But in an era in which the United States no longer held a nuclear monopoly, what ally could truly be expected to put its very survival behind the defense of its allies' interests? Baldly stated, what would be the U.S. response to limited Soviet demands in Europe? If America did react all out, Europe would be "saved from Communism" by being reduced to rubble. On the other hand—and this seemed more likely—if America was unwilling to risk its existence for specific issues the Europeans deemed vital, then the alliance was meaningless and the Europeans would have to acquire their own national deterrents. Yet such a diffusion of nuclear arms within the alliance would in turn threaten to disintegrate NATO even further.

Finally, as Berlin and Cuba again demonstrated, the chief function of a military power was to delineate and protect "frontiers." These frontiers had been clearly drawn: along the Elbe and through the middle of Berlin; at the thirty-eighth parallel in Korea and the seventeenth parallel in Vietnam; along the coast of China at Quemoy and Matsu; and, more tenuously, at the "northern tier" from Turkey to Pakistan. Any attempt to cross these frontiers, openly by direct attack or covertly by guerrilla warfare, would risk hostilities. Admittedly, the lines drawn outside of Europe were extremely tenuous. METO and SEATO were alliances in areas where nationalist forces opposed the Western-formed and -led alliances. These therefore had little popular support, even in those states which were members. The result was that the Russians could leapfrog the line, as in METO, or that the governments seeking to maintain this line were, despite American help, unable to mobilize the requisite indigenous morale and support, as was to become evident in Vietnam during the 1960s. Indeed, it might well be that the United States would have been better off had it not created what turned out to be poor replicas of NATO. That organization had been formed in an area in which nationalism supported containment against a clearly perceived potential external aggression; the METO and SEATO alliances were organized in non-Western areas where containment was widely perceived as an attempt to preserve Western influence and reactionary regimes. Nevertheless, because the lines drawn created a great danger of conflict, particularly of an American–Soviet clash, this process of delineation had in the 1950s turned the attention of the superpowers increasingly toward the Third World as an area where they believed that the bipolar balance could be transformed in either America's or Russia's favor.

chapter 7

the third world during the cold war years

THE REVOLUTION OF RISING EXPECTATIONS

'Four areas in the world," Guy J. Pauker wrote at the height of the cold war, "are at present or potentially major power centers: the United States, the Soviet Union, Western Europe, and Communist China. In all four, productivity is on the increase, and the political system performs relatively well its integrating and decision-making functions. Despite major differences among them . . . these four areas are likely to be in a position to play major roles in political, economic, and cultural international affairs in the coming decade. In contrast, the Middle East, Southeast Asia, tropical Africa, and Latin America are apt to remain power vacuums during this period, owing to their lack of unity, political instability, economic stagnation, and cultural heterogeneity. It seems highly improbable that ten years from now any of the areas mentioned above will cease to be, respectively, a power center or a power vacuum."

During the 1950s and 1960s such possible vacuums in the Third World, composed largely of ex-colonial, economically underdeveloped countries, were viewed in Washington as dangerous. For in a bipolar world, the two superpowers felt compelled to compete for the support, if not the allegiance, of the new emerging states who were not politically and militarily aligned with either one. Moscow perceived the anticolonial revolt against the West as part of the disintegration of the international capitalist order and an opportunity for attracting the underdeveloped countries into partnership with Russia in the building of a new Soviet-led Communist international order. The challenge of Russian Communism and Chinese Communism in the Third World was, therefore, seen in Washington as stemming not so much from some conspiracy or military takeover as from the totalitarian model for modernization which Communism offered the underdeveloped countries. The majority of the world's population lived in those countries. If those people in their search for the freedom President Franklin Roosevelt had once called "freedom from want" turned to dictatorial means, it would profoundly affect whether the democratic or the totalitarian way of life would flourish throughout the world. Their choice was therefore seen as critical to American security and, more broadly, an international environment in which open societies and democratic values would be safe. Thus it was vital to help the new countries develop; it was a matter of basic self-interest rather than humanitarian concern for the poor. Said a leading scholar: "Whether most of these countries take a democratic or Communist or other totalitarian path in their development is likely to determine the course of civilization on our planet."

It was a paradox that the distintegration of Western colonialism after World War II afforded the most eloquent testimony to its success. For the Western powers, including America in the Philippines, had justified their imperial domination in terms of bringing the backward peoples of the earth the benefits of Western democracy, medical science, and technology. It was the "white man's burden," or duty, to educate the natives so that one day they could govern themselves. The colonial powers had clearly taught their lesson well. They had ruled their colonies autocratically, while simultaneously propagating the virtues of democracy. It was in the name of these ideals that the Western powers had come as colonizers; it was in their name, too, that the nationalist movements challenged their rulers and asked them to practice what they preached. The leaders of these nationalist movements had invariably been educated in Europe or America, or in a Western school in their own country. They fought the European powers in terms of the principles of democracy and national freedom that they had learned in the West. They saw that these principles were incompatible with imperialism.

Once these countries became independent, however, they were left with a legacy of poverty, illiteracy, and disease. Rarely in these nations did the annual per capita income attain the $100 level. Because this condition of economic underdevelopment, compared to that of the economically developed nations (indeed, we generally refer to this division as one between the poor and rich nations) was so startling, economic development—often equated with industrialization—was the generally recommended remedy. Industrialization modernized—that is, transformed a backward, traditional, agrarian society into a twentieth-century industrial urban community. More specifically, industrialization would help consolidate the rather tenuous bonds holding the infant nation together as a political entity. For industrialization requires a high degree of specialization. The resulting division of labor between the various sectors of the economy located throughout all regions of the country and the need for all these branches of industry to cooperate would forge new cohesive links and place the still fragile political union upon the base of an interdependent economic union. Industrialization was also expected to create greater welfare for all of the nation's new citizens. This, too, would be a fact of great political significance. The people in the underdeveloped countries were familiar only with their immediate surrounding area, and they were loyal to this region; national loyalty was unknown. Consequently, the newly formed nation must prove to them that it could offer them something they could not otherwise attain. This "something" is an improvement in their standard of living. By achieving this, the nation would demonstrate its utility and, in turn would be expected to receive from its people the popular support and allegiance it needed to survive and grow.

Yet the question confronting the new countries in the 1950s—as today—is whether they can develop themselves economically. The answer will to a large extent depend upon whether their economic progress will be faster than their population growth, or whether their "population explosion" will eat up any increase in national income. The world population by mid-1970 was 3.6 billion. In 1830, it had been one billion; by 1930, it had doubled. Thus, while the first doubling took 100 years, it took only 40 years more to add another 1.5 billion. Experts predict 6.5 billion by the year 2000. In 1900, there was one European for every two Asians; in 2000, the ratio will probably be one to four. In the Western Hemisphere, there will, perhaps, be two Latin Americans for each North American. Despite later reports in 1978 that population growth was slowing down somewhat, these countries may still come face to face with the Malthusian problem: constant hunger and grinding poverty which result when the population grows faster than do the means of subsistence. More than 150 years ago, the Reverend Thomas Malthus, who was also an economist, predicted this fate for the Western world—unless the population growth were limited by either "positive checks" such as wars or epidemics, which result in a high death rate, or by "preventive checks," which result in a low birth rate. Yet, despite the huge population increase since 1800, the West made great economic progress: Agricultural production provided a plentiful supply of food, and industrial production raised the standard of living to heights never before attained. The West's recent history would thus appear to refute Malthus's gloomy prediction.

Unfortunately, the conditions that faced the underdeveloped nations were quite dissimilar from those experienced by the West. One of the chief differences is that the Western countries had far smaller populations when they began industrializing, and their population increase did not outdistance the economic improvement. But India set out on its modernization with a population of more than 400 million, which is expected to reach 1 billion people by the year 2000. China was expected to reach this staggering total much earlier (in 1979, the C.I.A. predicted that China's population would approach 1.5 billion by the end of the century). If the United States after the War of Independence had had a population density equivalent to that of Egypt, it would have today a population exceeding 2 billion people instead of over 200 million. Under these circumstances, it would hardly have become a "developed" nation.

The European nations were also aided by the New World and by their colonial empires, which provided them with outlets to relieve their population pressures. About 60 million Europeans emigrated during the nineteenth and early twentieth centuries. The United States and Canada, rich in resources and fertile land, easily absorbed millions of immigrants and still increased their living standards; Australia, New Zealand, and South Africa experienced similar population and economic expansions, although on a smaller scale. From 1650 to 1950, the European population (excluding Russia) increased by approximately 300 million. By the 1950s there were about 400 million people of European descent living outside Europe. The colonies thus served Europe as a frontier similar to that of the American West, which absorbed population that might otherwise have overcrowded the Eastern seaboard and thus added materially to the nation's wealth. But the underdeveloped countries can generally find no such relatively empty and rich spaces to absorb their surplus populations (although Mexico exports some of its unemployed to the U.S. and economically backward countries like Greece, Yugoslavia, Turkey, and Spain export workers to the Common Market countries).

In the West, moreover, the Industrial Revolution made possible the use of machinery in agriculture. This permitted a great increase in the food supply; efficient agriculture also meant that food could be produced by a smaller farm population. Excess labor from the land was thereby forced to go to the city, where it was used in the factories; this, in turn, accelerated the industrialization process. Quite apart from modern technology, however, Europe was blessed with sufficient sunshine and rain. Temperate lands are more favorable to food production than the tropical and monsoon areas that make up many of the underdeveloped countries. Europe could thus grow sufficient food for its multiplying population; what it could not produce, it imported from the colonies and the New World in exchange for industrial products. This enabled some European countries to support larger populations than their domestic food resources would otherwise have permitted. By contrast, in the nonindustrialized nations, the majority of the population is still engaged in a primitive agriculture. Many of the new countries' governments equate development with industrialization and therefore have neglected agriculture, which to its leaders often remains the symbol of their former colonial status as agrarian, raw material producing nations—which they are trying to get away from in their quest to be modern. In some countries more intensive farming of land already under cultivation—that is, using better seed, more chemical fertilizers, and insecticides—may yield enough food to keep pace with the population growth. But many countries cannot feed themselves sufficiently for yet another reason. "If our population continues to increase as rapidly as it is doing," a former president of Pakistan said, "we will soon have nothing to eat and will all become cannibals."

If this statement appears exaggerated, it nevertheless dramatizes the underdeveloped countries' problem of overpopulation. There are simply too many poor people. This might have been all right if the sleeping masses had not awakened—if they had continued to accept their miserable lot as natural and not suddenly become conscious that it was not a fate ordained by God but a man-made one, if they had not made this discovery and therefore demanded to eat more and live better. It is this "revolution of rising expectations" which creates the problem, for it will be impossible to fulfill these expectations unless there is a reduction in birth rates. The population pressure keeps the masses living close to subsistence; and such widespread poverty makes it very difficult to accumulate enough capital to stoke industrial growth.

In the West, the birth rate declined after 1850; with industrialization and the growth of cities came the spread of literacy and knowledge of artificial birth-control techniques. Malthus was thus right even for the West, because preventive checks were adopted. But the Third World has not yet reached a similar level of economic development, and knowledge of birth-control methods has spread only very slowly.

It remained questionable, therefore, whether the birth rate would significantly decline in the near future. This means that the pace of economic development had to surpass the fast-rising populations. But these countries simply did not have enough capital. Internal savings in sufficient amounts could not be squeezed out of peoples living at subsistence level—at least, not without totalitarian controls. An alternative means of obtaining capital was to earn it by trade. The underdeveloped areas are exporters of primary products or raw materials, such as coffee, tea, rubber, and tin. But it was precisely this fact that in the past had limited the earning capacity of many of them; for these exports rose or declined with every fluctuation in Western prosperity. A major Western recession lowered the demand and price levels of natural resources; the resulting losses of income tended to exceed the Western aid extended during the same period. Furthermore, markets may become glutted with certain items because of overproduction or substitution. A nation may have sought to raise its income by increasing production, but the fact that its competitors had done the same only resulted in further lowering world prices; or the Western industrial nations, whose ever-increasing demand for raw materials was supposed to furnish the capital for economic development, may no longer have needed them because of the development of synthetics. The lack of stabilized international commodity prices, similar to the parity prices paid to American farmers, plus the inventiveness of modern technology (which may in the 1980s start extracting resources from the ocean's seabeds) thus hampered the prospects of financing industrialization via trade.

Foreign investment was the third source of capital for economic development. Private capital has, however, been in short supply for the kind of long-range development that the underdeveloped nations need. Most private American investments outside the United States have been made by a small group of oil companies to build refineries and to discover and pump out oil fields in Latin America and the Middle East. The reasons for this lack of private Western—and especially American—capital for foreign investment were not hard to find. The American economy experienced a boom for most of the cold war period. Investment capital stayed mainly at home. This was true for Europe as well. European capital concentrated on rebuilding, modernization, and expansion of its own capital plant. American capital that did go abroad often went to the Common Market. Private capital is drawn to investments that will return sizable and relatively speedy profits.

But perhaps the basic reason that private funds were so small for the new nations was that public funds were so small. Businessmen could not be expected to invest in hospitals, ports, schools, and roads. The returns from such projects were insufficient; and even if there were any profits, it would take too long to reap them. Optimists who felt that this first stage of economic development could be undertaken by private funds forgot that in the West the speedy economic growth of the nineteenth century, financed largely by private enterprise, rested upon an economic base developed by the mercantilist state; in brief, it was political authority, the state, that initiated the process that transformed the underdeveloped Western economies into the highly modern, industrialized economies we know today.

Modernization, then, was the new nations' principal task. But this became increasingly seen as *not* essentially an economic undertaking. More and more, modernization, of which economic development is a major ingredient, was viewed as a political, social, and intellectual task. Moreover, it was a revolutionary process frequently marked by political instability and violence rather than evolutionary peaceful change. One reason for this, in addition to their low level of economic existence, was that most of the nations that so recently gained their independence lacked administrative and political cohesiveness. Generally, the peoples had no single common culture or language; tribes were opposed to one another; different areas were in conflict with one another. There was no natural loyalty to the state, no tradition of cooperation except, of course, on the one overriding issue of eliminating the colonial ruler. But once that struggle for independence ended, power tended to fragment. Thus, colonial India disintegrated violently into Hindu India and Muslim Pakistan following independence, and the latter dissolved further into Pakistan and Bangladesh—with the help of India, which may itself fragment further; the Congo (now renamed Zaïre) fell apart when the Belgians withdrew; Cyprus divided into Turkish and Greek factions; and Biafra split from Nigeria, only to lose the subsequent civil war. Even where actual disintegration has not occurred, religious, linguistic, and racial differences and antagonisms tend to tear apart the fabric of these states with their lack of any history of nationhood. In Burundi in 1972, for example, Tutsi tribesmen reportedly slaughtered 120,000 Hutus. Nation-building thus becomes their first task.

The absence of a strong sense of national consciousness was soon reflected in the manner in which many of the leaders of the new countries built themselves up as symbols of nationhood. It was not too difficult for them to do this, since their prestige was usually high as a result of the roles they had played in leading the nationalist movements for independence. But the task was an essential one. With Louis XIV, they said, *"L'état, c'est moi."* For they *were* the state; without their presence as its symbol, the nation would not hold together as a unit. One-party rule or military governments exist almost everywhere in the Third World. In Africa, for example, the world's last continent to be freed from colonialism, three-fourths of its 345 million people by the late 1960s already lived under single-party and military rule ten years after these nations had become independent.

Such policies might seem undemocratic, but they were widely perceived to be necessary. Loyalties in the new nations were less to the state than to ancestors, family, village, or tribe. Wherever the opposition represented these centrifugal forces, an American-style democracy would lead not just to a change of government but to the disintegration of the state. The alternatives facing the leaders of these countries have often been not democracy or dictatorship but statehood or disintegration.

Another reason that modernization was increasingly seen in an essentially political and revolutionary context is that the nationalist revolutions direct their opposition not only against the dominating foreign ruler but also against the domestic ruling elite. Many underdeveloped countries were split into two main groups when they gained independence. The first is the ruling minority, usually composed of the landlords, tribal chiefs, priests, and great merchants, sometimes fronted by an old-regime king. The second group, which constitutes about 80 percent in most underdeveloped nations, encompasses the peasants, villagers, small artisans, and shopkeepers—those whose efforts have been concentrated largely on the sheer struggle for day-to-day survival. It is this group, which has for centuries borne its hardships silently, that has awakened and is now demanding a better life. It is the urban intelligentsia, educated in Western ideas and committed to modernization, that voices these resentments against the old way of life and proclaims the new aspirations most articulately and loudly. Change, and more change is the demand of the day.

Without such social change—that is, the overthrow of the old ruling elite which is often identified with foreign influence and control, if not imperialism —modernization will be inhibited. This is not a matter of "reform" but of revolution because the crucial issue relates to power: Who controls the nation

—the old ruling elite, committed to the preservation of the traditional, religiously oriented, preindustrial society, or those who seek to secularize, modernize, and industrialize the nation? Only one thing was certain: Few who rule yield their dominant political, social, and economic position without a struggle.

Instability is promoted even where economic development occurs, where national bonds do not disintegrate, and where a secular modernizing elite is in control. The cause of this is that the slowly rising standard of living does not normally create an increasingly satisfied—and therefore happy and peaceful—population. Capital for investment can only be saved from money not paid to the workers; low wages militate against mass consumption and allow the reinvestment of the capital saved into further economic expansion. While there may be some improvement in living conditions, it will probably not suffice to satisfy the "revolution of rising expectations." Dissatisfaction will result from the fact that the population, knowing that it no longer has to live in the poverty and filth of the past, that man can create a better life for himself here on earth through his own efforts, will be frustrated by the continuous gap between achievement and expectation, which becomes particularly aggravating when the modernizers live well, even ostentatiously, while the rest of the population still lives in poverty. When this comes on top of the resentment produced by the uprooting of a large number of people as they shift from the countryside to the city, whose factories need manpower, the bewilderment resulting from the anonymity of the city, and anger caused by a miserable existence in the slums, social discontent and an increasingly sullen, hostile, and more radical mood are bound to rise.

The resulting growth of social instability and turmoil is further enhanced by the intellectual and cultural changes that accompany the transformation of a traditional, static, rural society into a modern, dynamic, urban-industrial state. Many of the old customary and religious values that helped man to accept his place in society and conduct himself throughout life simply collapse and the individual becomes disoriented, torn from his age-old moorings for which he has not yet found a substitute. Robbed of the status and function of his ancestors, he is left as an isolated and insecure atom in a rapidly changing environment which he neither made nor comprehends. Secular values, emphasizing material values and progress, replace religious values denying the importance of earthly existence and material possessions. A society in which individual effort is rewarded and a man can rise socially into a higher class replaces a society with a rigid social structure in which birth determined his place and religion his code of conduct. Nationalism replaces local loyalty, and modern means of transportation and communication bring the individual to an awareness of the larger society in which he must now live and work. Impersonal ties to people far away in "his" country replace former face-to-face relations with neighbors, and he must learn new skills and ways of thought. In short, he must forget many of his old ways and cut long-time ties and adjust, readjust, and adjust once more. In the best of circumstances, this is a difficult and agonizing process even if it does not arouse effective opposition from the traditional elite (as, for example, in Iran in late 1978 and early 1979, when the religious leaders led a powerful opposition movement to the Shah and his modernization so that they could restore the Islamic Republic).

DOMESTIC INSTABILITY AND INTERNATIONAL TENSIONS

It is hardly surprising in these circumstances that the domestic transformation of the underdeveloped nations had international repercussions that tended to destabilize an international system largely defined by the frontiers drawn between the two superpowers and by the nuclear stalemate. For when the internal difficulties of the countries of the Third World spilled over into the external arena of international politics, they attracted the Soviet Union and the United States, thus leading to possible confrontations with their attendant danger of military conflict. The reason these difficulties attracted the two superpowers is that they could bring to power a group one country likes and the other dislikes or result in regional expansion and influence that may be perceived as benefiting one and hurting the other. If one of the two nations is unwilling to tolerate what it may, in terms of the global balance of power, consider a local or regional setback, it will intervene; or, if it fears that if it does not intervene its opponent might, the result may be a preventive intervention. In both cases, it risks counterintervention.

If a new nation disintegrates into two or more parts, those who seek to reunify their land or establish their new splinter states may appeal for help to sympathetic states who, for reasons of their own, may wish to see a nation preserve its unity or fragment to support a favorable faction in power. Such appeals were—and continue to be—addressed especially to Russia or America. One of the more dramatic examples of the manner in which the survival of the new states as national entities involved the superpowers was given when, in 1960, the Belgian Congo became independent and Patrice Lumumba, leader of the nationalist party, became the country's new premier and Joseph Kasavubu its first president. Almost immediately, the Congo began to disintegrate into disorder. First, the rich mining province of Katanga, upon whose copper and cobalt exports the Congo was largely dependent as a major source of revenue, split off into a separate state. In this venture, Katanga's president, Moise Tshombe, had the support of the powerful Belgian mining interests, anxious to protect their investments. Then the army began to revolt because it resented the continued presence of its Belgian officers and wanted them replaced with native leadership. In a wild spree, the soldiers began to attack white women (including nuns) and children. The Belgian settlers' reaction was to flee. Among their numbers were the experts the Belgians had expected to leave behind in order to help the Congolese in their early period of self-government. All public services now collapsed because the Congo lacked an educated native elite. The Belgians had never trained one.

In the midst of this situation, the Belgians flew in paratroopers to protect their nationals. Lumumba, however, saw this move as a Belgian attempt to restore colonial rule, and he appealed to the United Nations to send forces to help him against the Belgians. It was at this point that the cold war was injected into the Congo. For the United Nations troops, whose composition did not include any forces from the Great Powers, did not compel the Belgians to evacuate their paratroopers or agree to Lumumba's demand that they help him reestablish control over Katanga Province. Secretary-General Dag Hammarskjöld ordered that the international organization's forces were not to be involved in the internal squabbles of the Congo or employed by the different contending political factions for the purpose of gaining power over their rivals. This, however, had the effect of underwriting the divisions of the Congo, and the country could not survive without Katanga. Since no leader likes to preside over the disintegration of his nation—particularly when that disintegration is being encouraged by the former colonial power seeking to preserve a base of control—Lumumba turned against the United Nations, bitterly attacked the secretary general, and accused Belgium and the Western powers, especially the United States, of conspiring against him; in these attacks, Lumumba resorted increasingly to antiwhite racial appeals and finally asked the Soviet Union for help to prevent the disintegration of the Congo. He received Russian diplomatic backing, military supplies, and offers of troops or "volunteers"; several neutrals, especially the United Arab Republic, Guinea, and Ghana, also extended their sympathy and support.

The United States now supported President Kasavubu (who dismissed Lumumba) and his army commander, Colonel Mobutu, who established a caretaker government composed of the Congo's only 15 university graduates. Mobutu also infuriated the Soviet Union by driving out all Communist-bloc personnel, who had been aiding Lumumba. The Russians insisted that Lumumba was still the Congo's legitimate ruler and demanded his restoration; so did the neutrals, who supported this demand by threatening to remove their contingents from the U.N. army. This would have left the Congo in utter chaos. The United States, however, refused to budge and continued to give its support to Colonel Mobutu, in whom it saw the best means of eliminating Soviet influence in the Congo and possible Communist penetration into the heart of Africa.

Soviet–American differences now became extremely bitter. The Russians, thwarted in the Congo for the time being, made two demands: the resignation of Dag Hammarskjöld and a veto over the secretary-general's activities. These demands were rejected. But by early 1962, after all efforts to unify the Congo had failed, the international organization reversed its original stand. It finally adopted the policy of forcefully squashing the opposition. Although it was still to be many months before the country was "unified" through the deposition of Tshombe and his Belgian advisers and foreign mercenaries, this task was eventually accomplished, although not without bloodshed. Ironically, this restoration of national order, accomplished with U.N. support, proved to be a posthumous victory for Lumumba, who had in the meantime been assassinated. (The CIA reportedly had assassination plans for Lumumba too but was beaten to it.) If the central government had not received American and U.N. support and had been unable to reunite the Congo, it, like Lumumba, would have been compelled to turn toward the Soviet Union. National disunity was clearly dangerous with its superpower interference, attempts to impose "their" factions upon the country, plus the possibility of a military clash. But bipolarity extended superpower competition to all continents.

Even if a new nation with tenuous bonds does not disintegrate, the political leaders may well invoke the only emotion the people ever shared in order to hold the nation together. This emotion is, of course, the nationalism born of the hatred of the former colonial power and directed against both that country and, more broadly, "Western imperialism." The granting of independence has not meant that colonialism was no longer an issue; rather, to preserve national unity the fight against colonialism and imperialism had to continue. The same technique may be invoked by a country with the even more common condition of a stagnant economy in which the "revolution of rising expectations" is turning into a "revolution of rising frustration." The political leadership will then be tempted to preserve its power by externalizing domestic dissatisfaction; foreign scapegoats will be needed to relieve internal stresses and strains. It is simply easier and therefore more attractive for leaders to play a prominent and highly visible role on the international stage before their countrymen than to undertake the hard and difficult work of modernizing their nations. The people can take pride in their leader's—and hence, their nation's—new status and identity in an international society which, under colonialism, had been denied importance and dignity as a nation and a people. Nkrumah of Ghana, Sukarno of Indonesia, Ben Bella of Algeria (until their deposal by military regimes), and Nasser of Egypt were among the most prominent and skillful practitioners of the art of channelling domestic grievances into international strutting and adventures during the 1950s and 1960s.

The most dramatic example of the dangers this can hold for the peace of the world was given by Nasser, who, as in 1956, provoked a war with Israel in 1967 when he confronted increasing economic hardship at home and a militant anti-Israeli Arab nationalism in Syria, a notoriously politically unstable and stagnating country. Nasser, increasingly compelled after 1958 to turn his attention and energies inward to "Arab socialism" in his fight for Arab leadership, had after more than a decade of rule still not managed to launch

Egypt on a path of self-sustaining economic growth. Egypt was desperately short of funds to finance its development, buy food, support its sizable army, and provide enough jobs for its unemployed and underemployed population. The national debt in 1966 was estimated at $2 billion; more than $100 million was overdue to Western states; foreign credit was very tight, and the balance of trade was declining. The second Five-Year Plan, already extended to seven years, was shelved. An estimated 30–50 percent of the productive capacity of the government-owned industry was idle because of a lack of money to buy parts. The growth rate, which in the early 1960s was 6–7 percent, had fallen to an annual 2–4 percent, hardly sufficient to keep up with the population growth. The birth-control program had failed to have any significant impact; the birth rate added 800,000 people annually to a population of over 30 million. The pace of inflation was approximately 15 percent a year. Nasser's program of nationalization and expropriation had brought domestic investment to a near halt and discouraged foreign investment. And his virulent anti-American attitude resulted in a cut-off of the American surplus food shipments. So he had to buy his food elsewhere and use up funds that might have been invested in the economic development of Egypt. The heavy expenditures on military equipment, probably amounting to one-third of Egypt's annual budget, also diverted funds from development.

Arab socialism, having lost its glamour and thereby weakened Nasser's claim to Arab leadership, left him only the arena of foreign policy in which to recoup his prestige and hold on the Arab masses. But here, too, his stature had declined. He had reached the height of his self-proclaimed leadership of Arab nationalism at the time of the seizure of the Suez Canal a decade earlier. Nationalism had also affected Nasser's neighbors. Iraq refused to subordinate itself to his direction, and Syria quit its short-lived union with Egypt in 1961. Nasser then resumed his verbal attacks on the traditional monarchies of Jordan and Saudi Arabia; Egyptian forces also helped the revolutionary forces who had overthrown the Yemenite monarchy supported by Saudi Arabia. He was clearly seeking to extend his influence southward into the sheikdoms and sultanates of South Arabia, a British protectorate scheduled to become independent in early 1968. This would give him control over the Red Sea entrance to the Suez Canal. But the Egyptian army was unsuccessful in destroying the royalist supporters. By 1967, the pressure of intra-Arab rivalries was thus added to the pressure of economic failure for Nasser to reassert his leadership of Arab nationalism.

First, he had to act if he was to be successful in establishing his influence in the former British protectorate of Aden upon its independence. Second, the Jordanians, in response to Nasser's hostility, taunted Nasser with hiding behind the U.N. forces stationed between the Israeli and Egyptian forces at the close of the Suez War. Third, the Syrians, trying to displace Nasser as the leader of Pan-Arabism, openly and repeatedly called for Israel's destruction and stepped up their terrorist raids into Israel. After a retaliatory Israeli raid, the Syrians even claimed in May 1967 that the Israelis were assembling their forces for an invasion of Syria. This rumor, reportedly also brought to Nasser's attention by the Soviet Union, which was seeking to exploit the Arab–Israeli–Western quarrel for its own purposes, was found to be untrue by U.N. observers. But Nasser, the great hero of the Arab peoples, either felt compelled to act or saw in the invasion rumor his opportunity to restore his leadership of Arab nationalism. Since Arab nationalism competed in terms of who was the most anti-Israeli—Israel being alleged the extension of Western "imperialism" into the Arab world—there was bound to be trouble. This was particularly true because, after eleven years of receiving Soviet training and arms, Nasser seemed very confident that his forces could beat Israel, which this time would be fighting by itself, without the aid of France and Britain.

The Egyptian leader therefore made several moves. He moved reinforcements into the Sinai Desert. Next, he demanded and obtained the withdrawal of the U.N. peace-keeping forces; Egyptian and Israeli forces thus confronted each other for the first time since 1956. In addition, he proclaimed the blockade of the Gulf of Aqaba, through which Israel received its oil and other goods. Israel had long declared this to be a vital lifeline, since Nasser barred its shipping from the Suez Canal, and he knew Israel had stated that it would consider a blockade intolerable and an act of war. In short, Nasser was deliberately provoking a military conflict. Finally, he signed a pact of alliance with Jordan. This meant that Arab armies were surrounding Israel: Syria in the north, Jordan with its highly regarded army directed to cut Israel in two at its narrow waist, and Egypt in the south. All these moves were accompanied by increasingly shrill calls for a holy "war of liberation" and the extermination of all of Israel's inhabitants—in brief, genocide.

In these circumstances, war was inevitable, unless Israel was willing to accept a major political defeat, an unlikely prospect. Whether peace could be preserved, primarily by Nasser's "unblockading" the Gulf of Aqaba, depended now on the United States and the Soviet Union. Washington was, however, caught in a dilemma. On the one hand, it had recognized Israel's right to send its ships through the gulf after compelling it to withdraw in the wake of its 1956 victory. But it also recognized that if Nasser did not relent, a forceful test might be necessary; seeking support from other maritime powers, it found the major nations were reluctant to use force. On the other hand, it was deeply involved in Vietnam and therefore reluctant to become engaged in a second conflict with Egypt. Furthermore, a key question for American policy-makers was whether such a test would precipitate a clash with the Soviet Union, which had with great fanfare sent warships into the eastern Mediterranean, fully supported the Arabs in their aims, continuously denounced Israel as an aggressive tool of American imperialism, and perhaps even spurred Nasser on with the false story of an imminent Israeli invasion of Syria.

For Moscow, the Arab–Israeli conflict had, as earlier, not merely regional but global implications. If Western influence could be expelled from the

Middle East and if Russia could establish itself as the dominant power over this oil-rich region, Europe might possibly be weakened and perhaps even neutralized. Soviet political support and the naval show of force undoubtedly contributed to Nasser's intransigence. Certainly it helped restore his reputation in the Arab world, and, had the blockade been successful, the Soviet Union would have earned the Arabs' everlasting gratitude, since it would have been chiefly responsible for Egypt's political victory, having demonstrated its ability to inhibit the American navy and having eroded American commitments to Israel. Thus Moscow was unwilling to restrain Damascus or Cairo.

Since Washington was unable to arrange a diplomatic solution, the Israelis, tired of waiting for one, attacked. Routing the air forces of their Arab opponents in a brilliantly coordinated set of air strikes in the first hours of hostilities, they defeated the Egyptian army in short shrift and reached the Suez Canal in three days—two days ahead of their 1956 record! They then routed the Jordanian army and captured half of Jerusalem and the western bank of the River Jordan. Finally, they turned on the Syrian army and eliminated the bases from which Syria launched the terrorist raids and shelled Israeli settlements. Nasser's dreams of an Arab empire were shattered, despite his efforts to salvage his reputation by blaming his defeat on alleged American and British air intervention on behalf of Israel. The Soviet Union reaped an ambiguous legacy. On the one hand, the Arabs were bitter because they felt that Moscow had deserted its friends when the situation became critical. On the other hand, the humiliating and complete defeat of the Arab armies left Egypt and Syria more dependent on the Soviet Union for political support, economic help, and further military aid and training, since they had by their own propaganda alienated themselves from the West. Arab nationalism and intra-Arab quarrels had once again intensified the Arab–Israeli conflict and precipitated war; and the bipolar competition for influence in the Middle East had once more turned the area's problems into the "Balkans of the twentieth century," an inflammable area of political instability, regional rivalry and Great Power conflict likely to explode at any moment and spread the resulting war far beyond the immediate area. Domestic Arab problems only aggravated the tendency of leaders to engage in adventurism, export internal dissatisfaction and grievances, strike tough and inflexible poses, and expose the world to the dangers of a superpower clash.

Even more broadly, Washington defined the greatest danger to American security as stemming from the new states' functional—not ideological—attraction to Communism. Confronting an amalgam of political, social, and cultural changes, (not just an economic transition), experiencing revolutionary transformations (not just evolutionary progress), the non-Western nations have no guarantee that they will successfully climb what Robert Heilbroner has termed the Great Ascent; even the attempt may well call for some sort of left-wing authoritarian rule. In this context, the Soviet Union represented itself as a model of development. The Soviets could point to the

Soviet experience and say: "In 1917, Russia was also underdeveloped but now, within the space of one generation, it has become militarily one of the two superpowers, the second largest industrial country in the world. You, too, can be industrialized quickly and live a better life." To people who already suffered from chronic hunger and poverty, it presumably would not matter greatly that the Soviet Union achieved industrialization by means of totalitarian governments that brutally squeezed the necessary sacrifices out of the people; the loss of liberty would not mean much to people who had never known it anyway, who have lived for centuries under authoritarian governments, whether domestic or foreign. Soviet totalitarianism would provide the organization and efficiency to extract the sacrifices from the masses, the discipline to hold the nation together, to speed up the pace of the cultural revolution while controlling the social tensions produced by the early stages of development, and, where necessary, to ruthlessly depose the traditional ruling class blocking the path to modernization. In short, just as capitalism was the chief means of modernization in the nineteenth century, Washington feared that Soviet Communism would be able to present itself as a successful model for modernization for the new nations seeking to enter the twentieth century. (After the Sino-Soviet schism, China too promoted itself as a model for modernization, one superior to European Russia.)

Thus, Communism was seen not just as a military threat. In the newly politically aware and poorer areas of the Third World, Communism was viewed as attractive because it appeared to promise a fairly rapid and disciplined way of bringing about political, social, economic, and cultural changes. The competition with the Soviet Union was in terms of improving the conditions which allegedly breed Communism. Poverty, ignorance, hunger, and social injustice lead to the growth of Communism; curing these conditions and giving people hope for a better life was the response, then, to defeating Communism. This would be achieved once the new nations' development had gained a self-sustaining momentum. Communism, therefore, had only a short time during the initial phase of modernization to enhance its appeal; during this period, Communists would act as "the scavengers of the modernization process." But with Western help, it was optimistically believed, more modern, urbanized, and industrial societies which would look Westward could be created.

GLOBAL INEQUALITY, FOREIGN AID, AND SOCIAL POLITICS

It was in terms of this competition of models that the United States and other Western states first offered economic aid and technical assistance. For, in the final analysis, the fundamental problem was perceived to be the growing division of the world between the rich and poor nations. Western aid was intended to close this gap, modernize the new nations without compelling them to resort to totalitarian methods, satisfy the revolution of rising expectations and thereby create politically and socially stable societies—and possibly lay the basis for democracy—which, in turn, was expected to create a more peaceful world by giving these developing societies a vested interest in the international order and Western values. Thus, in the rationales for sympathy and material and political support for the countries of the Third World, it was clear that besides simple humanitarian sentiments for peoples living in such abject poverty, squalor, disease, and ignorance, security considerations were uppermost. A world divided into rich and poor nations was said to be an explosive one, for it set the majority of the poor against the privileged minority. Such a gap was no more acceptable internationally than it had been within each of the Western nations 100 years ago.

The two situations were believed to be so similar that the "lessons" of the previous experience were applied to the international division of wealth. As the Industrial Revolution gathered momentum in each of the European countries and America, it created a privileged minority which owned most of the wealth. The distribution of income was, to say the least, unequal. Laborers, including many children and women, worked 14 to 16 hours per day, six or seven days a week, earned little beyond what was considered a living or subsistence wage (and sometimes less), and lived in overcrowded slums. The rich got richer and the poor got poorer. This trend was so obvious that Disraeli talked of England not as one nation but as two.

But the prevailing *laissez-faire* philosophy argued that nothing could be done to alleviate this situation. Government intervention, whether to end the grosser forms of exploitation such as child labor or to redistribute the income to help the poor lead a decent and dignified life, was rejected as contrary to the "iron laws of economics." Any outside interference with the workings of the market would stifle the private incentive and initiative that stoked the competitive capitalistic system. These "laws," which condemned a large section of the population to a hopeless and miserable existence, received even further support from Darwin's theory of evolution, with its emphasis on the "struggle for survival" and the "survival of the fittest." This philosophy, called social Darwinism, argued very simply that the rich were wealthy because their success in the competitive struggle had demonstrated that they were the most fit; conversely, the poor were destitute because they were unfit. It never occurred to social Darwinists to ask themselves whether everybody had had an equal start or opportunity in this struggle.

These philosophical justifications for leaving the poor very poor were ultimately rejected in all Western societies. The long working hours, the unsanitary and unsafe working conditions, the teeming slums were a blot on the West's conscience. They were also politically shortsighted and economically foolish. Politically, the division of people into "haves" and "have-nots" could only end in revolution, with the bourgeoisie being overthrown by the working class or proletariat; or, if it surrendered its democratic beliefs and values, the bourgeoisie could perhaps retain its power by establishing an authoritarian government and crushing any proletarian protests and uprisings. Neither of these alternatives was a very happy one for the ruling middle classes. Nor did this policy of squeezing the workers for maximum profit make sense economically, since the less money people have, the fewer things they can buy. Thus, social justice made sense—morally, politically, and economically.

In every Western society, government in the late nineteenth century began to intervene increasingly in the economy. Growing public awareness of social problems and ills eventually led to the regulation of business; the passage of minimum-wage and maximum-hours legislation and the abolition of child labor and "sweatshop" working conditions; the organization of trade unions, thus enabling workers to bargain collectively with their employers for better wages and terms of employment; measures to counteract the swings of the business cycle; the implementation of the progressive income tax; and the initiation, during depressions, of unemployment insurance, public-works programs, and other "pump-priming" projects to increase the purchasing power of the people, thereby stimulating renewed demand and production. These measures, especially in the United States, widened and raised the base of wealth, giving rise to the twentieth-century mass market. They also led to a discovery so simple and yet so hard to understand that Europe, particularly continental Europe, learned it only after 1945: namely, that a worker is also a consumer. If he is paid a good wage, he will also buy the goods he produces. This is profitable all around: The worker is economically satisfied and therefore gains a vested interest, politically, in the social and economic order; capitalists earn handsome profits by selling volume at reasonable prices, and they retain their social status and political influence.

It was this same problem of an inequitable distribution of income that was seen as once again plaguing the world. Only this time the problem did not exist within nations, but *between* nations. The rich countries were becoming wealthier, the poor ones more poverty-stricken. The iron laws of economics seem to hold the same fate in store for them that they once did for the Western working classes. Had the Marxist prophecy that the exploited proletariat would overthrow the bourgeoisie been defeated domestically only to reappear internationally and defeat the West on the global plane? Would the poverty-stricken nations of the world, the international proletariat, rise up in revolution against the privileged and wealthy Western countries, the international bourgeoisie? Modernization was expected to give the new states a stake in the international system and help create a world in which Western values would be more secure.

Although the nature of the problem seemed clear to many policy-makers, the rationale for economic aid to assist the new nations develop never attracted the degree of public support that the more easily understandable military preparations against the Soviets did. What was probably required, as Barbara Ward (among many) had suggested, was a progressive international income tax by which all the advanced Western nations would contribute 1–2 percent of their annual national income for this development process. The World Bank's Pearson Commission in 1969 endorsed the 1 percent figure. But no Western country was giving sums amounting to that percentage by that time. Despite the rapid economic growth of the industrial states during the 1960s, their foreign aid spending had declined. This was particularly true for American aid. At the time of the Marshall Plan to Europe, the figure had been 2.75 percent of the gross national product (GNP); for the underdeveloped countries, this figure was always less than 1 percent. In short, at a time when the American GNP had risen by hundreds of millions of dollars, the national effort was puny compared to its increasing capacity to pay and to the growing gap between the rich and poor nations.

Indeed, the term "economic aid" was itself something of a misnomer. After 1950 and the eruption of the Korean War, most economic aid was, in fact, military aid. Moreover, since Western Europe's recovery, most of this aid was channeled to allied countries: Turkey, Pakistan, South Vietnam, South Korea, Jordan, and Nationalist China. Even of the sum designated for economic assistance, a good part was "defense support"; this provided money to sustain the economies of allies like South Korea or South Vietnam, which, in the absence of this support, could not maintain their standing armies. And the final sum actually allocated to economic development, was also concentrated in relatively few countries. Most underdeveloped nations got next to nothing.

Apart from the lack of public support for foreign aid, the existing aid programs suffered from three other liabilities. One was that American dollars were all too often offered with the explicit or implicit assumption that the recipients should associate themselves with U.S. cold-war policies; that even if they do not formally ally themselves with the United States, they should often thank it for its generosity, praise it for the morality of its anti-Communist stand, and certainly refrain from criticizing it. The United States has been reluctant to give dollars to nations that would not join its side. After all, could any nation really be neutral in a struggle between right and wrong? Was not democracy good and Communism evil? If countries wanted U.S. money, surely the least they could do was "to stand up and be counted." The basic aspiration was to concentrate their attention and energy on internal matters, to raise their standard of living and strengthen their independence, and to minimize their involvement in the cold war. Most therefore preferred to remain nonaligned in the struggle between the West and the Communists, avoiding all "entangling alliances." Attempts to use economic aid as a means of forcing them into an American alliance system only failed.

In preferring a generally nonaligned position, the underdeveloped nations were following America's own earlier experience. After it had gained its independence, it, too, abstained from all entangling alliances and preoccupied itself with internal developments; as an underdeveloped country itself, it was very much aware that its newly realized independence meant very little until it had gained economic and political strength. Moreover, having just thrown off the shackles of colonialism, the Americans had no desire to be once more tied to the European powers. For they knew that if they joined any alliance system, the European powers would again have a large voice in their affairs, simply because they were the far weaker party. The United States would become involved in their quarrels and wars; and this would mean that it would have to maintain a sizable military establishment, which, in turn, would divert much-needed capital from its economic growth. It was for these reasons that Washington, in his Farewell Address, advised the country to isolate itself from Europe's conflicts until it was strong enough to "choose peace or war, as our interest, guided by justice, shall counsel." It was for the same reasons that John Quincy Adams, when he was secretary of state to President Monroe, advised against accepting the British bid for joint action against the Holy Alliance if it attempted to reimpose Spain's control over its former Latin American colonies. The United States, Adams said, refused to become a cockboat in the wake of the British man-of-war. Adams knew that he could safely reject the British bid, since Britain's own interests would make it necessary for it to oppose the Holy Alliance—economically, because it had trade interests in South America, and politically, because a Holy Alliance powerful enough to extend its power across the Atlantic was a coalition strong enough to dominate the European Continent and threaten Britain's security. Adams therefore unilaterally declared the Monroe Doctrine with every confidence that the British navy would enforce it.

The American position was also severely handicapped by the continued discrimination which prevented blacks from realizing their full measure of civil rights and equal opportunities in American society. To a world in which the vast majority of the population is nonwhite, the persisting segregationist practices and exploitation of blacks in the South and the North were flagrant violations of the democratic principles of freedom and human dignity so often proclaimed by the United States. The peoples of the underdeveloped areas not only claimed equal status as nations but also sought equality as human beings; when they heard about segregation in America, they could only be reminded of the old days when the white man had treated them as inferiors simply because of the color of their skins. This situation began to change during the Kennedy and Johnson Administrations, as blacks listened to Martin Luther King articulate their aspirations for a life of more dignity and full participation in American life, as the ghettos exploded, and as the government itself began to act by removing certain discriminatory practices against blacks, as well as providing greater opportunities in such areas as jobs and housing. However, racial problems continued to haunt the United States on the foreign front. In Rhodesia and South Africa, minority white-controlled governments determined to stay in power used abhorrent methods such as apartheid and the strictest police surveillance. The United States, despite its often expressed disapproval of these policies, did not follow through in its actions. Rhodesian chrome was imported for years despite a U.N. embargo, and in South Africa American companies, although often providing their black workers with better working conditions and pay than local companies, continued to invest. America, the world's first state to insist that all men were created equal, seemed all too often to say to the world that there was a qualifying phrase "except black men."

A third attitude which especially hampered United States relations with the developing states was the American lack of understanding of class struggle and social politics. America, "born free" as a bourgeois democratic society, had managed to avoid the kind of domestic conflicts over basic values that the countries of Europe experienced and that now plague many of the underdeveloped nations.* Not having experienced a genuine social revolution at her own birth—only a War of Independence and a set of institutions which were "given" to her by the Founding Fathers and which have been remarkably adaptable to the changing needs of the American people as the U.S. grew from a small rural to a continental urban-industrial society—America was not particularly sympathetic to revolutions and tended to identify revolutionaries with radicalism. Deviations from what were generally considered to be middle-class American values were likely to be condemned as "un-American" and sinful, to be rooted out so that the "American way of life" would remain pure and unadulterated. The principal challenges to these values have indeed not come from within the system, but from outside the U.S. borders, and the United States has reacted to foreign threats—German, Japanese, Communist—in two ways: internally, by hunting for "subversives" that inevitably has infringed upon civil liberties and endangered the security of traditional freedoms; and externally, before the atomic bomb, by the total destruction of the hostile regime so that American principles could continue to live untainted.

Thus, domestically, the Communist threat in the early 1950s led to McCarthyism, a search for heresy in which the goal of eliminating alleged un-American attitudes and behavior justified any means, including disregard for "due process of law," which is the basic guarantee of all civil liberties. At times, this hunt went to frightening lengths, as when the U.S. Information Agency actually burned "suspect" books—and, even worse, when the careers and lives of people were jeopardized and sometimes ruined. In foreign policy, the reaction to the Communist threat to the American way of life was to support almost any "anti-Communist" regime. Therefore, the United States associated itself with traditional regimes whose days were numbered because they had alienated mass support: Chiang Kai-Shek in China and Bao Dai in Indochina were two such examples. This attitude was typical of American absolutism and inability to understand the deeper social struggles of Asia and the Middle East. In the attempt to contain Communism—that is, to preserve the global *status quo*—the United States became committed to the domestic,

*See Chapter 1, p. 6.

social, and political *status quo* in these countries. Thus America, in seeking stability, was paradoxically trying to preserve freedom by supporting ramshackle autocracies that were unrepresentative of their peoples' aspirations. But this internal contradiction within the U.S. alliance system had eventually to resolve itself. American support for traditional regimes only bottled up the social and political resentment and ferment even more, thereby adding to the explosive forces that someday would burst forth and further upset the global balance of power.

THE EXAMPLE OF LATIN AMERICA

Latin America was a good example of the manner in which U.S. foreign policy, even when realizing the need for development aid, became a prisoner of its own domestic experience. Much was said in this country in the 1960s about Cuba as a base for subversion of other Latin nations. If such subversion were successful, this would constitute a great threat to the United States. But the possibilities for success were enhanced by a number of factors: resentment against a history of past American interventions in the Caribbean and Central America; vast-scale private American capital investments and economic control of many Latin American economies; frequent American support for the privileged few who, usually closely linked to American capital, sought to preserve their position by ignoring social grievances and establishing right-wing military dictatorships; and finally, the misery, poverty, and mass illiteracy of the vast majority of the people, who, although they lived in the countryside, were landless.

Latin America, in short, shared two aspirations that were sweeping through all the underdeveloped areas: the urge for a better life for the mass of people who, dispossessed and exploited, were filled with deep and bitter social resentment; and the desire of countries to determine their own national destiny and become free of colonial rule—in this instance, America's. The United States has exercised its colonial domination by indirect means, usually an alliance with the wealthy and privileged native governing class. Americans may believe that they were free of Europe's taint of colonialism, but it has not disguised this fact for Latin America. The Monroe Doctrine turned the southern part of the hemisphere into a U.S. sphere of influence; America did not have to resort to direct rule. Invested American capital spoke louder than guns; and political orders were unnecessary when a nation was a "banana republic" or an economic satellite. The economies of many Latin American nations remained backward, undiversified, and agrarian; they therefore continued to depend for a livelihood on the export of one or two raw materials to the United States, their largest market. In good years, they earned money; in bad years, the normal measure of unemployment, poverty, and hunger increased. Their very lives depended on the fluctuations of the business cycle, as well as, of course, their obedience to American political wishes.

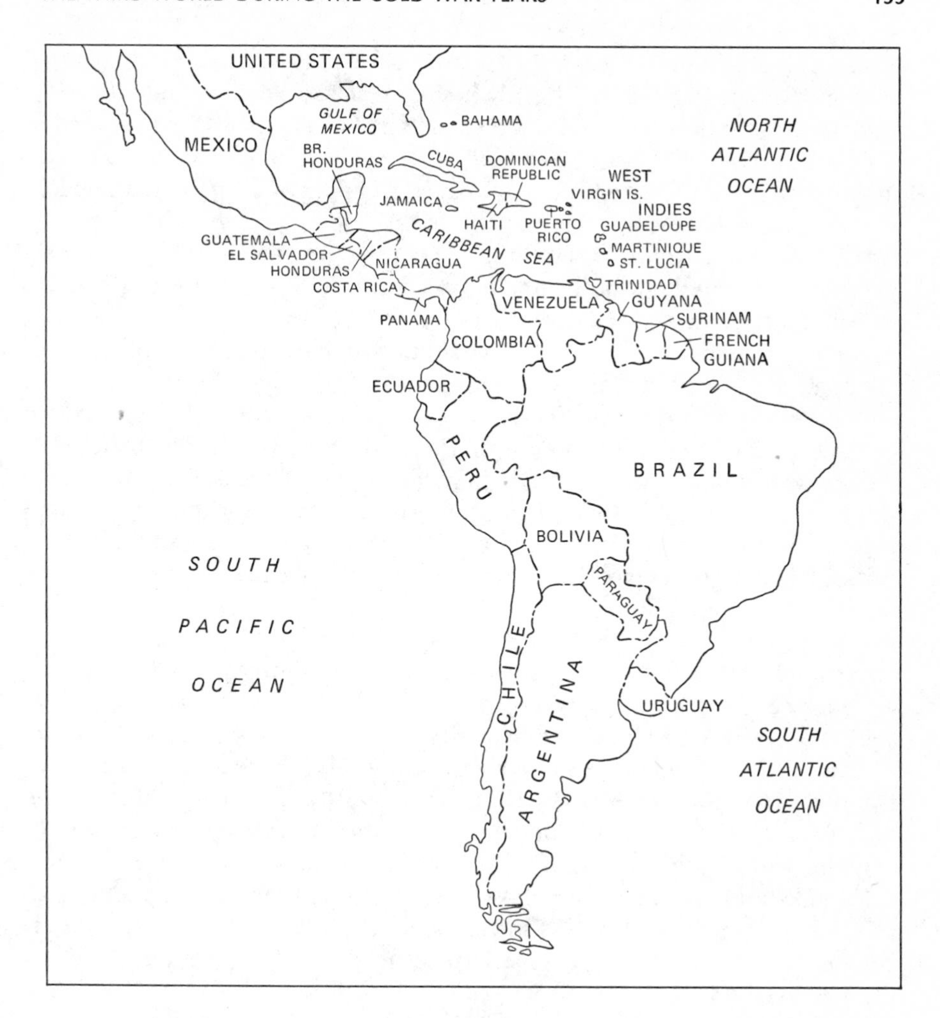

In these conditions, the success of Castroism was thought to depend on two factors. First, it would depend upon the Latin American governments themselves: whether they would undertake large-scale social and economic reforms or cling to their privileges; whether these privileged few were wise enough to understand the need for internal changes or whether they would prefer to commit suicide after fearfully clinging to their fading power for a few more years. Public pressure for change was rising. The only question was whether this change would be revolutionary or evolutionary. If the ruling classes remained as hostile to reform and as irresponsible toward public welfare as in the past, Castro might be able to export his revolution. For wherever there is social injustice, destruction of the *ancien régime* will appear as the sole way of gaining a job, a piece of land, or enough food. Revolution and a "radical solution" will seem the only hope for a better life.

Second, the success of Castroism would depend on the effectiveness of an

American policy directed toward alleviating the conditions that fostered popular resentment in Latin America. Whether America would be able to guide this revolution, however, was another matter. For it was a task that would require American support of non-Communist left-wing movements and acquiescence in the expropriation of American property, neither of which would be easy because of the frequent identification of democratic "socialism" with revolutionary Communism. Moreover, the United States was expected to invest billions of dollars in the Latin American economies in order to help them achieve a self-sustaining rate of economic growth, to develop conditions in which private capital would be attracted to projects other than raw materials extraction, and to aid in the transformation of backward societies into modern, urbanized, industrial nations. Latin America's projected 50 percent increase of population during the next 25 years—approximately 90 million people—only underlined the urgency of this developmental task. In the absence of an adequate effort, the already far too low standard of living would probably deteriorate even more. This would probably assure the success of future radical revolutions and the complete alienation of Latin America from the United States.

It was to meet the challenge of the Latin American "revolution of rising expectations" that President Kennedy, soon after assuming office, called for an Alliance for Progress between the United States and the nations of the south. He pledged $20 billion of primarily public capital over the next decade to Latin America and, even more significantly, placed great emphasis upon the need for social politics. In the absence of the necessary reforms, he realized, the possibilities of economic and political development were slight. The alliance, in short, was a post-Castro attempt to abort any future Castros.

Would the ruling oligarchies, however, surrender their power, status, and prestige, or commit themselves to fundamental reforms? In the words of a veteran observer of the Latin American scene at that time, Herbert L. Mathews:

> In the whole of Latin America, the rich are getting richer and the poor poorer. This is the worst, the most difficult and the most dangerous feature of the area. The Alliance for Progress was created primarily to tackle this essentially social problem but social imbalances (as the United States is discovering in the case of segregation) are devilishly hard to correct.
>
> The most serious feature of this problem centers around agriculture and land reform. The frantic urge to industrialize that seized Latin America after the Second World War was, in part, satisfied at the expense of the agrarian sector. Yet virtually all the countries are from half to three-quarters agricultural. Latin exports are overwhelmingly agricultural and mineral.
>
> The abnormal and dangerous urbanization, caused by the flight of impoverished peasants from the rural areas to the urban centers, has led to some of the largest cities in the world and some of the worst slums. Countries with plenty of land were, and are, importing food at high cost.

> Most landowners are resisting the reforms that their governments and the Alliance for Progress desire. . . . Much will depend on whether the ruling classes see the need to make drastic structural reforms. Much, also, will depend on the state of the world and the world markets for raw materials, not to mention the ability of the United States to invest and to aid. . . .
>
> There are revolutions and revolutions. The fascist-military type in Latin America comes from the right; the socialistic-communistic from the left; and in between is the sort of peaceful, voluntary, gradual but genuine type of revolution which the Alliance for Progress is trying to promote.
>
> Latin America is such a dynamic area of the world that it is bound to have revolutions. The only unknown factor is: what kind?*

The paralysis imposed on the alliance by Castro was abundantly illustrated at the time of the Dominican intervention. The background for this event was the overthrow in 1961 of the cruel 31-year-old Dominican dictatorship of Rafael Trujillo. Following a brief intervening period of political turmoil, Juan Bosch, a man of genuinely democratic convictions, had been elected to the office of president. Seven months later, Bosch was overthrown by a military *coup d' état* whose leaders announced that they would reestablish a "rightist state." In April 1965, the pro-Bosch forces revolted against this right-wing military government. But the leadership of this revolution swung increasingly, according to Washington, in a Communist direction. Communists were thought to be active in the antijunta movement, and Washington feared they would gain control of the pro-Bosch forces and that the result would be a second Cuba in the hemisphere. The rebels claimed that while some Communists might support their movement, their revolution was led by non-Communists who only sought a return to constitutional government. President Johnson, however, ordered American intervention before the evidence was clear that the revolution was in fact Communist-controlled—even though this action would once more raise the old specter of American intervention, so common in the days before Franklin Roosevelt's "Good Neighbor" policy. But in 1965 the problem was that the U.S. fear of a Communist capture of the Bosch movement would lead Washington to intervene on behalf of a right-wing military junta. In short, the United States would be siding with the very forces who supported the *status quo* and opposed the Alliance for Progress. At the same time, by opposing non-Communist reformers, Washington might drive many other Latin Americans who had hopes for democratic reform into an anti-American direction. If the United States were willing to risk intervening and alienating the very people whose support was needed for the Alliance for Progress, it might at least have waited to see if the "Castro-Communists," as Washington called them, would capture the pro-Bosch movement. If it were in America's interest to avoid the establishment of a second Cuba, a firmer case for intervention would then have been

***The New York Times*, March 15, 1965.

laid; it might even have diminished the criticism and consequences of such an action.

What the Dominican intervention did in fact demonstrate was that the Alliance for Progress continued to be haunted by the Cuban leader. Castro was responsible both for the alliance and for its failures. Without him, there would have been no large-scale efforts to seek the democratic development of Latin America. But the American fear that any Latin revolution might end up being Communist-controlled and that this required preventive action would also not have sprung up without Castro. The overt United States intervention—the first in 50 years in Latin America—therefore resulted in undermining the Alliance for Progress which had tried to persuade the region's ruling elites that they ought to reform the *status quo* if they wished to avoid revolutionary violence. Latin America's ruling classes could now relax for there was an alternative: American intervention would save them from the consequences of their own folly in holding onto an unjust *status quo.* United States policy, south of America's border as in other areas of the world, thus continued into the middle 1960s to be motivated by a bipolar image of the world. Nowhere was this to be more evident than in South Vietnam and the American interpretation of the nature of that war and the reasons for the American intervention. Also, no experience could more searingly and searchingly have compelled the country to reassess its foreign policy and note that bipolarity was itself in the process of change.

WAS UNITED STATES' THIRD WORLD POLICY IMPERIALISTIC?

Especially since the American involvement in the Vietnam war, some radical writers, often referred to as the New Left, have said that American actions as in Cuba and the Dominican Republic were hardly accidental; nor was the failure to provide meaningful economic aid for the modernization of the new nations a mere oversight. Indeed, this line of argument maintains, while these nations may have been new in the sense of formal political independence, they were in reality economically controlled by the dominant economy in the "global capitalist system," the United States economy; the so-called new and independent nations thus in fact remained colonies. "Neocolonialism" was the term popularly used to refer to their alleged status. Whereas in European eighteenth- and nineteenth-century colonialism the European state had usually invaded a piece of territory and established direct rule of the newly acquired colony, American imperialism in the contemporary age of nationalism controlled its colonial appendages through less visible but equally binding economic chains: corporate investments, economic aid, and the needs of the Third World countries for advanced technology and for markets in which to sell their raw materials. And, of course, the United States supported reactionary political and social elites who survived only with American backing which, when necessary, was supplemented with American training and arming of local police and military forces, CIA bribes, subsidies for private armies, and all sorts of "dirty tricks," including assassinations and *coups d'état.*

Why all this bother about the poor countries of the world? Because they are, according to this radical critique, enormously profitable. They are sources of cheap raw materials to stoke Western industry; they constitute potentially sizable markets for Western goods; and they provide places for the investment of private capital at large returns. Capitalist economies like that of the United States, the leading Western capitalist state, constantly need profits; without them, unemployment would increase, standards of living decline, and the struggle between capitalists and those who worked for them resume. This struggle is muted in the capitalist country where some of the enormous profits reaped by the capitalists, basically from exploiting the underdeveloped countries, trickle down to the workers in the form of higher wages and living standards, thereby drawing their revolutionary fangs and winning their support for capitalism. Without this trickle, the class struggle would resume. Therefore, even with the best of intentions, America, as a capitalist society and guardian of Western capitalism, could not surrender its "neocolonial control" over the less developed states. It was structurally necessary; if capitalism was to be preserved and domestic social revolution avoided, the Third World countries had to be maintained as profitable dependencies and raw material suppliers. Hence the American pursuit of counterrevolutionary and interventionist policies.

In fact, this economically imperialist interpretation of postwar American foreign policy is testimony to the significance of faith and attitudes over facts. Little evidence supports such a purely economic interpretation. The vast bulk of American private investments has been made in the American economy; and of the approximately 5–6 percent of American investment that was made abroad, most, even at the height of the Vietnam war in 1968, went to Western Europe, Canada, and Japan. In short, investment in non-Western economies was hardly significant for the welfare of the American economy. In trade, the pattern was identical. The United States trades primarily with the other industrial countries. They have something to sell to each other. Again, the Third World states are not essential to the well-being of the American economy. It is primarily in the area of natural resources that the dependency argument carries a degree of plausibility, for clearly America, like other Western industries, needs raw materials. But even here, with the possible exception of oil, the case is far from persuasive. Substitutes, alternative raw materials, the domestic availability of vast array of raw materials, the finding of new resources on the world's seabeds, in fact make the country less dependent upon the Third World than the imperialist interpretation would suggest. (Admittedly, the cost of materials from domestic sources will be higher than from the less-developed countries, although not necessarily higher than the prices these countries hope to get or, in the case of oil, are already receiving.

Even in oil, as the price continues to rise, alternative sources of energy or oil from deeper wells become economically more feasible.) The United States, in fact, possesses many of the raw materials it needs, including energy resources, especially coal.

What is equally clear is that the imperialist interpretation which suggests that capitalist countries either exercise control of Third World economies in order to make a profit, or have no control which leads to a collapse of capitalist economies, could not be more wrong. The Western states that, since 1945, have achieved the highest rates of economic growth are countries like Japan, West Germany, and those of Scandinavia, states that obviously had no colonies and that exercised no "control" over non-Western countries. They bought what they needed. Imperialist control was completely unnecessary for these states with "capitalist" economies; indeed, such control was inversely related to their prosperity. It was former colonial states like Great Britain and the last colonial state of all, Portugal, whose economies fared the worst of all Western economies. Thus, domination of the underdeveloped countries for the purpose of having access to their raw materials is not required. Indeed, and no doubt disillusioning to radical critics who would like the Third World countries to withhold their resources to bring down American capitalism, these nations, radical or not, sell their resources to all Western countries—if the price is right.

But to return to the main point: The picture of the United States controlling Arab oil countries or even Latin American states is ludicrous. As became clear in 1973 with the Oil Producing Exporting Countries' (OPEC) fourfold increase of oil prices, and should have been clear even before that historic date, the Third World, country after country, has been expropriating American investments and property. Nationalization has been the trend in this age of nationalism, and there is little that can be done about it except to acquiesce and officially protest—with anger sometimes, but not too much—and seek some compensation for the expropriated industry. But the United States does not send marines in or overthrow governments to save a corporation's sugar fields or banana crops, not even to lower oil prices. Economic and other pressures, as well as covert operations and overt interventions, have been resorted to only where Washington perceived the stakes to be far broader than simple expropriation—that is, where the stakes were not simply those of corporate property, indeed where the stakes were perceived to be far broader than merely economic ones. In Guatemala in 1954, in Cuba in 1961, in the Dominican Republic in 1965 (and later, as we shall see, in Chile in the early 1970s), the American government intervened—even if, as in Cuba, unsuccessfully—because it viewed the governments in these countries and their international orientation in the context of cold war bipolarity. All these countries seemed to be slipping into or aligning themselves with the Soviet camp. This appearance, which led to the U.S. interventions, may have been in error, but, it needs to be noted, it is not one that stems from an *a priori* antileft or anti-Socialist animus; the United States has allied itself and cooperated with Democratic Socialist or Labor party governments in many countries, especially in Europe, as well as with nondemocratic Communist regimes in countries such as Yugoslavia and China.

American policy in the Middle East is probably the strongest refutation of the imperialist interpretation. If the corporate capitalists did indeed control Washington, it is impossible to understand why the United States has since 1948 so strongly supported Israel, alienated most Arab states, jeopardized access to the oil needed so badly by Europe and increasingly by America, and risked the nationalization of Western oil companies (almost everywhere now controlled, even if not yet totally owned, by OPEC). In fact, what this policy shows is that economic considerations, if present and important, are not at all necessarily predominant in the making of the nation's foreign policy. If only the United States did control Saudi Arabia, Iran, Kuwait, and Venezuela! (In fact, if the imperialist theory *were* correct, the Western industrial states would be in the process of becoming the colonial appendages of OPEC.) American motivations in foreign policy must be sought elsewhere than in the economic realm, primarily in security considerations and fear of Russian power and the identification after 1946–1947 of the expansion of Russian power and influence with the expansion of Communism. In a bipolar era of two relatively cohesive alliances, NATO and the Sino-Soviet alliance, this identification was easy to understand, even if it was not always correct.

chapter 8

vietnam and the collapse of containment

AMERICA AS "GLOBAL POLICEMAN"

The world that emerged from World War II and dominated most of the twenty years from 1945 to 1965 was bipolar. The United States and the Soviet Union, plus their allies, confronted one another directly and globally. In a series of crises, they drew the "frontiers" between their worlds and extended their competition to the Third World. This bipolar world was very dangerous, because the distribution of power in the state system between two poles is extremely sensitive. Both are constantly alert to the slightest shifts in power lest they upset the equilibrium and give one adversary a superiority of power. Each side perceives a gain of power and security for one as a loss of power and security for the other. Each views the opponent's moves, even if alleged to be defensive, as deliberate and offensive; and moves in areas of secondary importance are ranked as significant and countered because they are seen as symbolically vital.

The first characteristic of the resulting American containment policy was its involvement on all continents of the world, thereby becoming what some of its critics called a "world policeman." Thus initially in the Eastern Mediterranean and Western Europe, then in Asia and Middle East and, to varying degrees, in Africa and Latin America, Washington sought to contain what it saw as Soviet and/or Chinese attempts to exploit power vacuums, intraregional conflicts, and differences between Western countries and the Third

World. As a result, the United States, the formerly isolationist nation which felt that no quarrels anywhere affected its security, developed into the world power that became involved in all regions (except sub-Sahara Africa), drawing "frontiers" around the areas it deemed vital.

The second characteristic of the American role was the continuous vigilance and effort needed to protect these "frontiers." Strategic deterrence was the principal means of preventing a major incursion of Western Europe and subsequent strike against the continental United States. Limited challenges were met by a variety of means: nuclear blackmail by a mixture of military and diplomatic tactics and actual frontier crossings by "frontier wars."

A third feature was that these challenges normally have taken place at the farthest point from the U.S. This is, of course, where frontiers meet and where the opponent finds it easiest to cause trouble and the defender is likely to show the least resolution. The frontier is far away and may not seem clearly related to America's security interests of the center; it is also nearer to the opponent, and its defense therefore may involve great risks and costs. Indeed, such peripheral involvement may seem like an overextension of the center's power, which, it will be claimed, is not only dangerous but also expensive and unnecessary. Yet these frontiers have been guarded by America's armed forces. When the occasions have arisen in the ex-colonial areas of the world, the two superpowers have agreed to allow U.N. forces, staffed primarily by nonaligned members, to keep the peace in order to avoid a clash between themselves.

A fourth and key characteristic of the American role is the U.S. belief that in a bipolar system deterrence, total and limited, requires the opponent to believe that this country will honor its commitments. It follows that if commitments to maintain a particular frontier are no longer credible—no matter how distant or unimportant this frontier may seem to some—the adversary may come to believe that other frontiers too may be crossed with impunity. It may be true that one frontier is more vital than another, but how is the opponent to know which one? The failure to honor a commitment in one area may thus be seen by the adversary as an indication that another commitment elsewhere may also not be honored and tempt him to test the defender's will. A commitment, whether eagerly sought or reluctantly accepted, therefore becomes a matter from which it is presumably virtually impossible to withdraw without dangerous consequences.

This is also because, fifth, America's allies and friends know that their defense depends upon the United States and they are therefore constantly alert to signs of a weakening will. Precisely because they are keenly aware of their geographic location and know that the defense of their security may at times seem either hazardous or unimportant to their imperial protector, they will live in a continuous state of apprehension lest they be left undefended; if they are, they may well consider approaching the opponent and bargaining for the best terms possible. As President Kennedy said with regard to Soviet policy on Berlin: It was designed to neutralize West Germany as a first step toward the neutralization of Western Europe. If the United States did not meet its commitments in the divided city, it would mean the destruction of NATO and a resulting dangerous situation for the whole world. All of Europe was at stake in West Berlin.

VIETNAM AS A "FRONTIER WAR"

The United States became involved in the Vietnam war in Southeast Asia because, first of all, it was a frontier war. In the words of Eugene Rostow, formerly of the State Department,

> In Indochina the North Vietnamese government has broken the first and most basic rule of Peaceful Coexistence: That the frontiers of the two systems not be altered unilaterally, or by military action. To cite a clear parallel, it has been deemed self-evident in Washington and in Moscow that it would be unthinkably dangerous for either East Germany or West Germany to attack the other, either openly or through infiltration. Yet what North Vietnam, with Chinese backing, is attempting in Indochina—to conquer a country the United States has agreed to protect—is the precise analogue of such a hypothetical German conflict, or of the Korean war of 1950–53, or of the Soviet Union's early postwar probes against Greece, Turkey and Iran.

Second, it was a war fought at a great distance from the center, in a place where the frontier was very accessible to the enemy. South Vietnam was a badly divided society: refugees (approximately 1 million, about half of them Catholic) against indigenous South Vietnamese; Buddhists against Catholics; lowlanders against *montagnards;* and peasants against urban inhabitants. Loyalties were, as in most new nations, primarily local. Hostility to a central government was deeply ingrained since, as in most underdeveloped countries, the government historically has been that of the colonial power, as represented by the tax collector and recruiting sergeant. Transportation and communication were primitive and industrial development nonexistent. In addition, this was a new state that had emerged from the 1954 Geneva conference concluding the First Indochina War between France and the Vietminh forces, with no established political institutions and a precarious economy. Not surprisingly, the Vietminh expected South Vietnam to collapse: The Geneva agreement called for a general election to be held in 1956, and it was assumed by Hanoi that a majority of the 12 million South Vietnamese would vote for the man who had led the nationalist struggle against the French, Ho Chi Minh (who obviously could have delivered most of the North's 15 million votes). Thus the country would be reunited under Communist control.

It was for this reason that neither the United States nor the new Diem government in the South favored the election; the former wanted the seventeenth parallel to be accepted as the new frontier, and Diem, a fervent Catholic and anti-Communist, was not about to eliminate himself. Their opposition was decisive, irrespective of the issue as to whether the unsigned Geneva declaration about the election was politically binding. Thus Hanoi's chances for a peaceful takeover of the South ended, and so did its stance of reasonableness and restraint. At the time of the Geneva settlement, approximately 5000–6000 local hard-core guerrillas, presumably the Vietminh's political and military elite, went underground and became anonymous peasants. About 90,000 others went north (to be infiltrated into the South again later) while about one million northerners, mainly Catholics, went south. Within a few months, the guerrillas who had stayed in the South began to murder village chiefs and other government officials. The Second Indochina War had started; the immediate guerrilla objective was to isolate the central government from the majority of its population and substitute Vietcong control over the peasantry by killing the government's local representatives.

This war, in short, started in quite a different manner from the Korean War. Korea had begun with a clear-cut, aggressive attack which aroused the American public and united the principal Western allies against the common threat. It had also been a conventional war in which regular Communist forces had been checked by regular South Korean, American, and U.N. troops. By contrast, Dienbienphu had been a decisive moment in contemporary history, for, apart from defeating France and throwing off French colonial shackles, the battle demonstrated that *guerrilla warfare* could defeat the larger, stronger, conventionally equipped army of even a major power. It also showed that nuclear weapons would be useless in countering the tactics of such a war. An internal uprising by guerrillas, directed and organized by the North, was therefore a shrewder manner of "crossing" the seventeenth parallel. It would lend the resulting struggle the aura of a civil war, which, if taken at face value by the United States and the West, would paralyze any united response and cause domestic doubt about the morality and wisdom of fighting in such a conflict. Diem's increasingly autocratic rule and his failure to enlist the support of his population, especially the peasantry, through political, social and economic reforms helped prepare the ground for a successful guerrilla campaign and lent support to the view of the conflict as a civil war.

Yet the war was seen in Washington as a test of its will, which was believed to be necessary to maintain all frontiers. The Asian balance depended upon the United States until the non-Communist states of the area became economically developed and possessed sufficient capabilities of their own. Commitments—and the administrations of Presidents Eisenhower, Kennedy, and Johnson all considered the United States to be committed to the defense of South Vietnam—were interdependent. The United States could not choose to defend West Berlin and Quemoy but not Matsu and South Korea (an American protégé which did not even have a formal treaty of defense with the United States). Washington believed that it could no more forego the defense of the frontier in South Vietnam than in Greece and Turkey, in Western Europe and Berlin, or in Korea and Cuba. If one country fell it would, in its turn, knock down the next one and so on down the line; the political and psychological impact of an American pullout would be felt throughout the area, if not in other regions as well.

THE MISCONDUCT OF COUNTERGUERRILLA CONFLICT

During the Kennedy and Johnson administrations, therefore, justifications for an increasing military commitment to South Vietnam were made in terms of America's global responsibilities for maintaining the general peace and stability of the international system. Despite this, the wisdom of the policy was debatable. During his years as president, Kennedy sent 16,500 military advisors; Johnson, beginning in the spring of 1965, augmented this number to more than 500,000. Particularly significant during the years of piecemeal commitments was that at no point did policy-makers in Washington ever sit down, take time, and ask themselves some fundamental questions about Vietnam: Was it vital to American security interests and, if so, how vital? Could the situation in South Vietnam be saved militarily, given the nature of the Saigon government and its seeming lack of popular support? If American forces should be sent, in what numbers? And how could they be effectively used in an unorthodox type of war? What cost, if any, was South Vietnam "worth"? As incremental commitments were made whenever conditions in South Vietnam appeared ominous, these questions continued to be avoided. During the Kennedy period, military advisors managed to prevent total collapse, but by 1965 his successor—who had spent his time since Kennedy's assassination passing a major domestic reform program and getting reelected—could no longer operate on this basis and avoid the central question of what the United States ought to do. South Vietnam was about to be cut in two, and the Vietcong would then be in a position to mop up first one part, then the other. In the face of this reality, Johnson sent in 200,000 troops that year, extending U.S. involvement and turning an incremental policy into a long-term commitment. After years and years of neglect and procrastination and with the situation growing worse daily, Washington had neither the time nor the inclination to make a carefully calculated basic decision; when the crucial decision was made, it was made by a new president—whose primary interest, experience, and skill were domestic—on the advice of the Kennedy staff and cabinet he had inherited. Long-range policy had thus become the prisoner of a number of prior short-range decisions that had been made to tackle immediately critical problems.

The key to the successful deployment of American arms—the political structure of South Vietnam—was virtually ignored. For years, the United States had supported Ngo Dinh Diem, whose increasingly authoritarian rule and aloofness from his people had alienated most of them. By the time the military overthrew Diem, with Kennedy's knowledge and tacit blessing, the Vietcong already controlled much of south Vietnam; the social, political, and economic reforms needed to win the war had for too long been disregarded. The very fact the United States acquiesced in the coup against Diem should have alerted future administrations; that Kennedy had himself said Diem had "gotten out of touch with the people" testified to the political bankruptcy in Saigon, as well as to the questionable wisdom of having begun the military commitments in the first place. Diem's successor governments proved no more able to rally popular support for a vigorous prosecution of the war against the Vietcong. Saigon's succession of corrupt, reactionary, and repressive regimes apparently never reawakened thoughts in the minds of U.S. policy-makers of Chiang Kai-shek and his Nationalist government in postwar China.

The Truman administration at the time had decided China could not be saved, except perhaps—and it was only *perhaps*—at an enormous military and economic cost. Thus, it felt the American public would not be willing to pay; in addition, this would have diverted the nation's resources and efforts from its area of primary interest in Europe where these could be productively used to enhance American security. In Secretary Acheson's words at the time: "Nothing that this country did or could have done within the *reasonable* limits of its capabilities" could have changed the result in the conflict between Mao and Chiang [italics added]. In short, containment could not be affected through a sieve. By attempting it in South Vietnam, Truman's successor Democratic administrations were in fact risking major domestic discontent. They were also risking a public questioning of the fundamental assumptions of American postwar foreign policy which had led to the war.

Certainly, the possibility of achieving a quick victory over the Vietcong was remote, for a guerrilla war is anything but the traditional type of Western warfare. Its aim is to capture the power of the government from within, and to do so by eroding the morale of the army and by undermining popular confidence in the government. To achieve this objective, it is necessary neither to inflict complete defeat on the government's forces nor to compel them to surrender unconditionally. Indeed, until the final stage of the war, guerrillas do not even meet these forces openly, and then they do so only to apply the *coup de grâce.* Guerrilla forces fight a guerrilla war because they are compelled to; in the initial phases, they are the weaker side militarily. Guerrilla war is therefore a protracted conflict in which the guerrillas resort to hit-and-run tactics—here, there, everywhere—and engage only those smaller and weaker government forces they can defeat. In order to cope with such tactics, year in and year out, the government troops must be dispersed to guard every town, every hamlet, and every bridge against possible attack. Unable to come to real grips with the enemy and impose a heavy defeat upon him as in a conventional and set battle, suffering defeat after defeat, however small, the army is subject to great loss of morale and its mood becomes defensive.

Although such tactics gradually weaken the military strength of the army, the guerrillas' main effort remains directed at the civilian population. As they are the weaker side, the guerrillas' principal aim becomes one of wresting the allegiance of the population from the government. Without popular support, the government will simply collapse. The guerrillas proceed to do this in two ways. First, by their increasing control of the countryside, where the vast majority of the population live, and by their defeats of government forces, they demonstrate to the peasants that the government cannot protect them. The execution of the village headmen, who are generally government representatives, and of any persons who may have helped the government forces proves this most vividly. Second, and even more important, the guerrillas exploit any exisitng popular grievances. Communist guerrillas do not pose as Communists, and they do not receive popular support because they are Communists. The populace will support them because it believes the guerrillas will oust the government with which it is dissatisfied and that a new government will meet its aspirations. Mao Tse-tung said that guerrillas need the people as fish need water; without popular support, the guerrillas would not receive recruits, food, shelter, and, above all, information on the government forces' disposition. Thus, in contrast to conventional warfare, in which each army seeks the destruction of the other's military forces, in guerrilla warfare the guerrillas seek to win the support of the people. A government that has the allegiance of its population does not provide fertile soil for guerrillas; the outbreak of guerrilla warfare is therefore one indication that a government is unpopular. The guerrillas gain the support of the peasantry because they successfully represent themselves as the liberators from colonialism or foreign rule, native despotic governments, economic deprivation, or social injustice.

Counterguerrilla war is therefore not a purely military war, but a political war as well. While the defeat of guerrillas in the field must be vigorously pursued, the principal task is to tackle the political, social, and economic conditions that bred the support for the guerrillas. Fundamentally, counterguerrilla warfare is therefore an extremely difficult and sophisticated form of war to wage—far more so than the traditional clash of armies—because the war cannot be won without thoroughgoing reforms. Yet these have to be carried out in the midst of battle. Such a war is also likely to take years; five to ten years is not at all out of the ordinary. And finally, it takes approximately 15 counterguerrilla fighters to one guerrilla—in short, a sizable army, and one trained not in conventional fighting but in counterguerrilla tactics. What all this meant was that the United States would find such a war extremely difficult to fight. America likes its wars "strictly military." A war that is concerned primarily with social and political reforms—and thus opens itself up to all the usual domestic criticisms of "socialistic," "pro-Communist," and "do-gooder" reforms—runs completely counter to the American approach. Its length would also cause great frustration, because the United States likes to get its "boys home by Christmas"; not a lengthy, drawn-out affair, but a quick and happy ending à la Hollywood is the American way of fighting. If this new kind of warfare did not yield swift and successful results, the American temptation would be either to pull out or to seek a short-cut to victory by purely military action.

American policy-makers, however, misplaced their confidence in the nation's military prowess and its ability to change the guerrillas' "rules of the game." In 1965, the illusion of American omnipotence had not yet died. Had not the United States successfully confronted the Soviet Union in Cuba and compelled it to back down? Could there really be much doubt that its well-trained generals in command of armies equipped with the newest and latest weapons from America's industry and under the leadership of that most efficient Pentagon manager, Secretary of Defense McNamara, could beat a few thousand "peasants in black pajamas"? Could America not, with its sizable forces and its superior mobility and firepower, find the enemy's troops and destroy them, compelling that enemy to desist from taking over South Vietnam? Characteristically, then, the principal emphasis was strictly military.

In a war that required forces to secure villages and to stay there in order to root out the Vietcong cells and possibly give Saigon the opportunity to prove to the villagers that "their" government did care for them, the military carried out massive search-and-destroy operations. The guerrillas, even when defeated (as they usually were when they were found), returned after the helicopters had left and continued to control the countryside. Since such large-scale operations could hardly be launched without preparation at the base camp and were usually preceded by airstrikes and artillery bombardments of the area in which the troops would land, the Vietcong generally disappeared and the whole operation ended in frustration.

The American military clearly did not understand the political nature of counterguerrilla war. They had been trained for conventional battle and their strategy was to bring maximum fire power to bear, even when, for example, by destroying a village from which a few shots had apparently been fired, they alienated the villagers without whose support the war could not be won. The government, too, tended to become increasingly enamored of the military approach—probably because the political nature of the war remained so elusive and difficult to grasp. The military "kill" thus became the prime aim, because that seemed tangible and attainable. The war was also extended by air to the North. The purpose in the beginning was clearly not primarily military. Guerrillas can live off the land and capture many of their weapons from their enemies; and, in any case, the sustained American attacks on

Chinese supply lines in North Korea during the Korean War had shown that air power alone was unable to stop the flow of supplies to the fighting zone. The aim of the attacks was political—to persuade North Vietnam to call a halt to the war. The gradual extension of these attacks was intended to stress the fact that the United States meant to protect South Vietnam and would not withdraw; that the price Hanoi might have to pay for victory would be disproportionally costly, and therefore that it had better desist. But the bombing did not weaken Hanoi's will to prosecute the war, cut the supplies sufficiently to hamper the fighting in the South, or greatly reduce troop infiltration. This, is turn, led to increased military and political calls for *more* air strikes and against new targets. These calls did not acknowledge that air power could not by itself win the war; rather, they insisted that it could win the war only if it were used with maximum efficiency. Air power, in short, came to be seen by some as an immaculate way of fighting the enemy, of efficiently inflicting great destruction on him, throttling his supply lines, breaking his morale, and finally compelling him to seek an end to the conflict.

This objective, however, remained unattainable. Even the more stable Thieu–Ky military regime, which sought to legitimate itself in the election of 1967, failed to implement a program of social and economic reform; it was particularly remiss in not carrying out a necessary redistribution of land from the usually absentee landlord to the peasant. Without such reforms, the ground could not be cut out from under the Vietcong. Militarily, every increase of American forces was met by increased infiltration of both guerrillas and conventional troops from the North to the South. Nevertheless, optimistic battle reports and forecasts of victory were frequent. It was the 1968 Tet (or Vietnamese New Year) offensive that was to be the Johnson administration's Dienbienphu. Tet showed once and for all—and Americans could see it nightly on their television sets—that, despite the repeated optimistic predictions of the past, the enemy had again been badly underestimated. He had launched a major countrywide offensive and penetrated Saigon, Hué, and every other provincial capital; a Vietcong squad had even penetrated the American Embassy compound, thereby scoring a significant symbolic victory. Above all, the Vietcong had clearly demonstrated that neither an American army of a half-million men nor Saigon and its vastly larger army could give the people living in the urban areas security—and the Communists already controlled much of the countryside.

American power and its effectiveness in unorthodox warfare were revealed as greatly exaggerated. Tactically, American forces had seized and retained the offensive, claiming the destruction of large numbers of enemy soldiers, but strategically the Vietcong had maintained the upper hand. The Americans were still very much on the defensive and, by using about 80 percent of their forces to find and destroy North Vietnamese troops in the relatively unpopulated central highlands and frontier regions, they were unable to secure *and* protect the 90 percent of the population living in the Mekong Delta and coastal plains. The pursuit of victory through physical attrition clearly could not be transformed into military and, especially, political advantages. Indeed, in question was not just America's protective capacity but also its wisdom. Having left the cities unprotected, except for elements of the South Vietnamese army (Tet revealed Saigon's impotence dramatically), allied forces then had to fight their way back into the hearts of the various cities and towns the Vietcong had infiltrated. If, after almost three years of American help, South Vietnam was still that insecure and the enemy that strong, the wisdom of continuing the war, let alone sending further American reinforcements, was bound to be intensely debated.

This was particularly so because many Americans increasingly perceived the war to be morally ambiguous, if not downright immoral. There had never been a clear-cut crossing of the seventeenth parallel dividing North and South Vietnam; this made the accusation against Hanoi as an aggressor less believable. The undemocratic nature of Saigon's government and its apparent lack of popularity gave credence to the view of the war as a rebellion or civil war against Saigon's repression. (Interestingly, in 1950, the South Korean government had a similar autocratic reputation, but the attack across the thirty-eighth parallel focused attention on North Korean ambitions and justified the American intervention. No one in the United States raised questions about defending a "corrupt dictatorship.") The massive and often indiscriminate use of American fire power leading to widespread destruction of civilian life and property, the creation of thousands of refugees, and, allegedly, the hostility of the very people upon whose support military success depended had already pricked the conscience of many Americans concerned with their nation's historic image as a compassionate and humane country. The tanks rumbling into cities after Tet, the dive-bombing of apartment houses, the civilian suffering and personal tragedies left many a television viewer asking himself whether there was any point in destroying a country in order to defend it.

Within the United States, Tet coalesced the opposition that had been growing throughout 1967 as the war had continued, seemingly without end, and President Johnson's initial support eroded on both right and left—the former demanding an end to the war through escalation and the latter through deescalation, if not outright withdrawal. (Sometimes, in fact, the same people held both views.) The articulate opposition to the conflict by a number of liberal and moderate Republican and Democratic senators, especially the chairman of the Senate Foreign Relations Committee, J. William Fulbright, made the opposition of other politicians, some university professors, many students, and a number of editorial writers and television commentators respectable instead of "un-American." Indeed, after Tet, Fulbright and his committee became an alternative source of interpretation and policy recommendations to the president.

At the same time, two senators from the president's own party, Eugene McCarthy and Robert Kennedy, were contesting Johnson's renomination as the Democratic standard-bearer. Running as "peace candidates," they provided a rallying point for the ever larger numbers of Americans disenchanted with the war. Then, in March 1968, at the end of the speech that laid the basis for the Paris peace talks, the president announced that he would not run for a second term. In the words of the political commentator Tom Wicker of the *New York Times,* Lyndon Johnson's tragedy was that he "came into office seeking a great society in America and found instead an ugly little war that consumed him." The changing American mood was evident in the 1968 election campagin. Vice-President Humphrey, nominated in Chicago after bloody clashes between police and antiwar students (many of them McCarthy supporters) and bitter disagreement among the delegates over the Vietnam platform, was mercilessly heckled during most of the campaign. As a member of the administration, he found it difficult to disavow the war; when he did take his own "risk for peace," it was very late in the campaign. In these circumstances of Democratic disunity, former Vice-President Nixon, a long-time hawk, found it inexpedient to charge the Democrats with a "no-win" policy; instead, he softened his views on the war. Indeed, in his speeches the menace abroad suddenly ran a poor second to the "moral decay" at home. Generally, candidates from both parties fell over themselves in their eagerness to abandon both anti-Communist slogans and the war, offering instead hopes for an "honorable" peace in Vietnam and for "law and order" at home. Halting Communist aggression was abandoned as an issue; stopping further costly foreign adventures—"No more Vietnams"—became the issue.

"CONTAINMENT" REEXAMINED

Vietnam raised two major questions for the future of American foreign policy. One was whether the United States could in the future pursue a strategy of limited war. The direct result of Vietnam, this question remains even if the necessity of an alternative to suicide-or-surrender in the face of a limited external challenge is acknowledged in the abstract. The other, and more fundamental, question was whether the United States would continue to implement the containment policy. Vietnam was widely perceived as the product of U.S. global policemanship; the assumptions underlying that role were therefore subjected to rigorous examination, with the result that a more limited role was prescribed.

Vietnam, even more than Korea, seriously strained the domestic consensus required for the conduct of "frontier wars." One lesson it has taught is that, apparently, in a democratic country committed to the territorial *status quo,* public support for military action requires the presence of widely understood imperatives. The most important of these is the existence of a "clear and present" danger to American security. But a limited war fought across an ocean seems far away, the danger to the country is less apparent, and public concern and fear are much smaller. Only a total threat, like World War II, or limited challenge close to American shores, like that in Cuba, pose so overwhelming a menace that public opinion unifies in support of whatever political and military actions are required, that criticism is largely muted and that, above all, domestic considerations remain subordinated to foreign policy commitments.

The second imperative is identifying the opponent. As a nation of predominantly European immigrants, the United States is "nearer" to Europe than to other continents. Germany, especially Nazi Germany, could therefore arouse American opinion. Distant non-European antagonists whom Americans hardly know, and with whom they cannot easily identify in terms of a common culture and past history, fail to elicit the same intense hatred or fear. In Korea, by marching across the thirty-eighth parallel, the North Koreans left no doubt that they were the aggressors. In Vietnam, by calling for an uprising in the South and infiltrating troops and supplies across the seventeenth parallel, North Vietnam avoided such a clear-cut identity; by exploiting the seeds of revolt in South Vietnam, Hanoi was able to give the struggle in the South the appearance of a civil war.

The third imperative is that limited wars avoid massive involvement and costs, particularly the danger of a nuclear war. But, in reality, limited wars may become less limited. Korea escalated as the United States advanced into the North and precipitated Chinese intervention. Subsequently, strong pressure was exercised upon President Truman to attack China, regardless of the risk this entailed of a very much enlarged war. Johnson escalated the air attacks on the North, which it was hoped would quickly bring Hanoi to its knees. Open interventions by the North Vietnamese regular army and by the Chinese were constant possibilities. And the costs of these limited wars in lives and money, domestic inflation and higher taxes, and, in Vietnam, great social tension and morale, after several years appear increasingly excessive compared to the limited goals pursued.

Finally, limited wars must be won quickly while domestic opinion, which "rallies around the flag" initially, is still largely disposed to support the president. Yet a counterguerrilla war is, by its very nature, drawn out. For many years, therefore, Hanoi showed itself uninterested in a negotiated settlement. Basicially betting that the fragmented, war-weary South Vietnamese society would collapse, it also hoped that domestic pressures in the United States as a result of the rising costs of the war would compel the abandonment of Saigon. The split of the Democratic Party and Johnson's withdrawal from the presidency were incentives for Hanoi to wait things out and erode American support for the war. But the fact that Korea had destroyed Truman and Vietnam had consumed Johnson raised the question not only of whether the American public would ever tolerate another "frontier war," but also of whether it would continue to support the containment policy that had twice in 20 years resulted in limited wars and that had continuously since 1945 threatened to involve the nation in various conflicts and quarrels around the globe.

Ironically, it was the former supporters of containment who turned into its critics. American power, they asserted, was very great, but the United States was not omnipotent and therefore could not pursue global commitments: It simply did not have the wealth to take care of all possible foreign policy obligations and at the same time handle its pressing domestic needs. Policy-makers therefore had to carefully rank the external priorities—usually Europe and Latin America are considered of primary importance—and concentrate on these. By being selective in commitments, the nation could bring the ends of policy and the means of its implementation into balance. Vietnam was thus seen as a tragic product of an indiscriminate anti-Communism which led the nation to overextend itself. It also was seen as a chastening experience which would result in the reduction of American commitments, a concentration on urgent domestic problems, and a generally more sober and restrained international behavior.

After Vietnam, these broad prescriptions were probably useful reminders to policy-makers, but had they in fact been ignored in the earlier conduct of foreign affairs? In looking backward over two decades of containment, the first thing that can be said is that American policy-makers, during World War II and in the immediate postwar years, had been aware of the nation's limited power, of its need to be selective in making commitments according to some criteria of priorities and to apply power discriminately. Indeed, during the war they had planned no overseas obligations whatsoever. The whole point of Franklin Roosevelt's policy toward Russia was to overcome Stalin's suspicions of the West and win his friendship for, and commitment to, postwar cooperation. The expectation was that the United States, the Soviet Union, Great Britain, and China would, in a new era of goodwill, jointly keep the peace. America's partners would preserve it in Eurasia; the United States would limit its responsibilities to its own hemisphere. It was the disintegration of these hopes, as Soviet hostility became apparent and England and continental Europe collapsed, that left America as the only countervailing power to Russia. Even then, American responses were limited to those countries and areas where the Soviets challenged the territorial *status quo* left by World War II.

Aware of the need to be selective, the Truman administration decided that priority should be given to Europe, the cradle of the American heritage, the area where an imbalance of power had twice in this century sucked the United States into total wars. This focus on Europe was the chief reason the United States did not intervene in any major way in the Chinese civil war. While the United States furnished the nationalists with some economic and military assistance, limits to its intervention were dictated by the resolve not to become militarily engaged. Similarly, in husbanding the nation's resources and trying to keep a balance between America's commitments and "limited power," troops were withdrawn from South Korea. Continental Asia was strictly of secondary interest and the American defense perimeter in the Pacific was publicly defined in terms of the island chain, including Japan, off the Asian coast. The Soviets and North Koreans apparently drew the logical conclusion that the United States had written off the Republic of Korea. Consequently, in June 1950, the North Korean army marched southward across the thirty-eighth parallel, and America was suddenly and unexpectedly engaged in its first "frontier war."

Why did the United States fight in South Korea if it was not a vital interest? Was it only because Korea was a protégé? The answer was that while the southern half of the peninsula was not in itself significant—and certainly the Americans were not legally obligated—the political and psychological consequences of inaction would affect the global balance. In Asia, reestablishment of a balance after Chiang Kai-shek's defeat depended upon creating an American–Japanese alliance; a demonstration of fear or indifference to the fate of a friend would hardly win Japan to an alliance. A nation that permitted Communist power to establish itself 100 miles across the water from Japan was hardly to be relied on. Similarly, the United States had just committed itself through NATO to the protection of Europe; if Korea were allowed to fall, the newly acquired European allies, who still recalled America's post-World War I withdrawal and isolationism and who still were apprehensive about a recurrence, might disregard NATO and try to bargain for the Kremlin's best terms. In short, it was believed that the impact of not defending South Korea in a bipolar world would result in the neutralization of Japan and Europe. Suddenly, American security was recognized as very much involved in this area of secondary interest. Thus a noncommitment, deliberately excluded from the defense perimeter because it did not seem vital, overnight became a primary commitment; yet a prior commitment pledging American help in case of attack, supported symbolically by a few thousand troops, might have deterred the Communist invasion and spared the Americans a costly war. (One need but compare the situation in Europe, including the divided city of Berlin, where such a defense commitment has kept the peace for more than 20 years, even though a spark between the confronting American and Soviet forces might well have erupted into a major fire extremely difficult to extinguish.)

The lesson appeared to be, regardless of its preference not to be committed in some areas or countries, the United States as a superpower on occasion still became involved. Despite a nation's best intentions, commitments were not always determined by a priori selection but by contingencies and events over which even a Great Power had little or no control. Thus, twice in this century already the United States had become involved in the two world wars although no commitment of defense to France and Britain had existed. It had little choice on both occasions if it wished to preserve the balance and guard its security.

A second point about containment, suggested by Korea, is that the extensive American involvement was not due to any "arrogance of power" or desire to dominate the world, or quest for capitalist profits, let alone an unawareness of the need for the nation to order its foreign policy priorities; rather, it was due to the postwar bipolar distribution of power. In a reevaluation of containment, it is worth stressing once more that a bipolar distribution of power is the most sensitive of all balances. In a bipolar balance, each power sees its adversary as its foe; for the opposing power is the only one who can hurt it and threaten its security. The balance is continuously seen as being at stake, since each fears that once the adversary has shifted the balance in his favor and gained a superiority of power, the balance may be irreversible. For reasons of security, therefore, when one side sees the other push, it feels compelled to push back. A bipolar balance is, consequently, one of continuous confrontation and frequent crises and occasional limited wars. Even moves in areas of secondary interest will be opposed since each power fears a domino effect; that if one of its allies, protegés, or satellites is allowed to fall, others will follow and that an accumulation of small losses of power—each one of which would be tolerable—would add up to a major loss of power —which would be intolerable and must therefore be prevented.

The Korean War, the rise of Communist China, and the subsequent Chinese intervention in Korea as American armies advanced toward China's frontier, plus the Sino-Soviet alliance, reinforced this bipolar pattern: Russia and China extending across most of the Eurasian continent, versus the United States and NATO on the Western rim of Eurasia, and Japan on the Eastern rim. Not surprisingly, then, after America first bluffed intervention and then accepted the division of Vietnam in 1954, the seventeenth parallel became part of the frontier drawn between the Communist bloc and "free world." Increasingly thereafter, the defense of South Vietnam became seen as a test of the credibility of American commitments, a domino whose fall would result in the loss of further dominoes. Containment was, therefore, applied in South Vietnam and not reassessed in the late 1950s and early 1960s when the Communist world showed increasing signs of divisions as nationalism eroded the cohesion of a group of countries who claimed that their unity resulted from sharing a common ideology.

Three, it was this bipolar distribution of power which led to the militarization of containment. Although during the first few years the policy of containment was in existence its implementation was mainly economic, the attack upon South Korea and the resulting fear that the Soviets might try something similar in Europe led to vast American and Western rearmament. After Korea, the concept of deterrence as a drawing of frontier lines and a threat of major retaliation if these were crossed was extended from Europe to the Middle and Far East. Because the rise of nationalism in these areas was frequently accompanied by anti-Western overtones, the alliances formed to support such lines proved relatively useless as containers, caused a great deal of turmoil among the nations of these regions, frequently drew the United States into their quarrels, and led the nation to support some rather despotic regimes in the name of defending freedom. This emphasis on drawing lines of containment by establishing military alliances—multilateral ones like NATO, SEATO, and CENTO, as well as bilateral ones like the American alliances with Japan or Taiwan—largely followed from the bipolar division of power. Given the great sensitivity of the superpowers to any changes in the balance, especially of the United States which saw herself as essentially on the defense against Soviet (and for a while, Chinese) expansionism, the essence of the cold war in which neither felt it could advance without risking nuclear war or retreat without risking political collapse was the drawing of "frontiers," to mark off their respective spheres of influence and then defend the resulting territorial *status quo.*

Not totally surprisingly, this defense led both superpowers to search for allies, primarily as a means of delineating the areas of vital interest to them and communicating this to their adversary in order to deter an attack; to maintain the cohesiveness of their respective alliances and prevent defections, even if this required military or covert intervention; and perhaps most symbolically, to engage in an intense arms race spurred by the fear that with rapid changes in the technology of modern weapons the opponent might achieve a technological breakthrough which he would then exploit to gain a perhaps irreversible superiority of power. A bipolar balance in which two powers constantly confront one another, and often push each other in attempts to shift the balance and push back to maintain the balance, is indeed more dependent than any other distribution of power on military power to preserve an equilibrium.

Fourth, what was the role that anti-Communism played in American foreign policy? There exists today a widely accepted belief that had America not been so passionately anti-Communist after 1945, it would not have undertaken so many commitments. Was American globalism not really the offspring of the nation's penchant for crusading against opponents who had provoked it? The presumption of anti-Communism as a principal motive of postwar American foreign policy assumed that the cold war was somehow not the typical power struggle inherent in an anarchic state system that left each state to be its own protector and therefore compelled it to concern itself with its power status relative to other potentially hostile states. The record of U.S. foreign policy since 1945 was, in fact, less that of a crusader than that of a practitioner of the ancient art of power politics. The purpose of containment, the American synonym for a balance-of-power policy, was precisely that—to contain Russia and, after 1949, Communist China—by establishing a central strategic American–Soviet balance supplemented by regional balances where required. The aim of American policy was not the launching of holy anti-Communist crusades to overthrow the government in Moscow or Peking. Passionate anti-Soviet and anti-Chinese speeches and talk of "liberation" were not translated into policies.

In other words, American policy had been "limitationist," and the power behind it had on the whole been used with restraint, as shown for example in Berlin, Korea, Hungary, Cuba, and Czechoslovakia. It was the anti-Communist rhetoric that had tended to create the widespread public impression of a policy lacking moderation and proportion, and pursuing instead an ambitious and often wasteful adventuristic world role. Nonetheless, despite extravagant declarations of intentions, the objective of containment was what George Kennan had called the mellowing of Soviet power; presumably this logic also applied to China. If they could be prevented from expanding, both Communist countries would, in time, become derevolutionized, no longer acting as messianic powers with a secular mission to convert men to the true faith.

As a nation which had put isolationism behind it, and as a state which, once it had become actively engaged in international politics, quickly learned to play power politics as had others before it, the United States was never so blinded by an allegedly indiscriminate anti-Communism that it could not adopt the age-old technique of divide and rule. Thus, within a year of the Truman Doctrine, the United States, offering help to Communist Yugoslavia after Tito's break with Stalin, demonstrated that American policy was anti-Soviet not anti-Communist. Even in China after the war, the United States first sought to arrange a coalition government composed of the Nationalists and Communists to stop the civil war and unify China; and once the Communists had won the civil war, Washington, already seeing the possibility of conflict between Russia and China, expected to exploit this schism when it occurred. Even after the Korean War had embittered Sino-American relations, the United States negotiated with Peking whenever Washington felt its interests were involved (as in ending the Korean War and the first Indochina War), even though it maintained its policy of nonrecognition of the new regime on mainland China.

Anti-Communism has thus been less a motive explaining American foreign policy than a tool used by American leaders for mobilizing public support. As suggested earlier, the United States is essentially an inwardly oriented society. Nor is this accidental, for, quite apart from the historic tasks of westward expansion and modernization, a political system in which the people vote and the governors must therefore be responsive to mass preferences is a system that concentrates upon domestic affairs and welfare issues rather than on a burdensome, costly, and distracting foreign policy. To arouse the public to support external ventures, the struggle for power and security inherent in the state system must be disguised to appear as a struggle for the realization of the highest values. From the beginning of its existence, the United States has felt itself to be a post-European society—a New World standing as a shining example of democracy, freedom, and social justice for the Old World. Anti-Communism fitted beautifully into this traditional dichotomy. America could thus practice *Realpolitik* as long as it could be disguised as *Idealpolitik,* which fitted its national style of conducting foreign policy; power politics needed ideological justification in a nation that had always felt that the use of power internationally was evil. Domestically, power was legitimated by the democratic purposes for which it was used; so, externally, its employment had to be justified in terms of making the world safe for democracy.

Fifth, while anti-Communism served well as an instrument of internal mobilization, its "feedback" upon the foreign policy it was intended to serve was, because of the competitive nature of American party politics, frequently harmful, if not disastrous. Once an administration had aroused the public by promising to stop Communism, it laid itself open to attacks by the opposition party in case of setbacks, even if the latter occurred for reasons beyond America's ability to control. The out-party could then seek to exploit foreign policy issues by accusing the in-party of "appeasement" and being "soft on Communism." This in turn made it difficult to recognize a Communist regime, build bridges to Eastern Europe, and especially to discriminate between the defense of areas of vital and secondary interest. Democratic administrations were particularly affected because they recalled that it was their party which had been in power when Nationalist China had collapsed, it was they who had been accused of "treason" and "selling out" China, and it was they who had lost the 1952 presidential election. The desire to avoid accusations of being soft on Communism had affected Truman's decision to advance northward across the thirty-eighth parallel before the 1950 midterm elections; it had made it impossible for Truman to negotiate any settlement of the war that would leave Korea divided; made it impossible for Kennedy, who had campaigned on a tough anti-Castro platform, to reject the Eisenhower-initiated invasion plan about which the new president had serious qualms; led the Kennedy and Johnson administrations to make their piecemeal commitments in Vietnam, lest the Democrats be charged with the "loss of Indochina" as well as China; influenced Johnson to bomb the North and finally escalate the war by sending in the army; and persuaded him to land troops in the Dominican Republic to prevent "another Cuba" from being established.

These examples illustrate the high price the U.S. consistently paid for the need to moralize power politics: overreaction, diplomatic rigidity, and overt or covert interventions which it might otherwise never have launched. National style, in brief, was a principal reason for the nonrecognition of Communist China, the failure to understand the nature of "Asian Communism," including the nature of the war in Vietnam; it was also responsible for the subsequent intervention. It was because the domestic costs of losing a China or Indochina or any other place were so high that those in power felt compelled to intervene with the CIA, marines, or army in order to avoid such losses. The desire not to face accusations of appeasement, of betraying the nation's honor, of weakening its security, was keenly felt; the costs of intervention, by contrast, appeared far smaller—especially just before elections (and, of course, there was always an election coming up)—than the domestic costs of nonintervention. These costs should not be underestimated. The president would lose prestige; in turn, this would affect his ability to gain support for the rest of his foreign, as well as domestic, policies. In short, he would be vulnerable to congressional attacks and his entire program for the nation, abroad and at home, would be jeopardized. Thus far more than the president's personal reputation, his ability to be reelected, and his party's electoral future were at stake, although these were hardly minor stakes. The basic rule of domestic politics during the cold war years, therefore, was to avoid what appeared as major losses to Communism overseas.

Only conservative—Republican—administrations seemed less vulnerable to such attacks. Eisenhower was the first president during the cold war to meet the Soviet leaders; he signed the same peace in Korea that Truman could not; nor did he feel compelled to intervene in Indochina in 1954 and, although he supported the new Diem regime in Saigon, he carefully limited United States support; and it was Nixon who could do what a rational foreign policy would have done years earlier—seek a rapprochement with China and try to exploit the Sino-Soviet schism. Neither president could credibly be accused of being "soft on Communism."

Sixth, if our national style on important occasions greatly hampered the conduct of American foreign policy, it needs to be stressed once again that the purpose of United States policy—to preserve the balance of power—was not an end in itself. It was the means to the end of preserving the security of a democratic America; in turn, successive administrations felt that this required the maintenance of an international environment congenial to the survival of democratic societies. The fundamental orientation of American foreign policy was, therefore, to support the democracies, old and new, in Western Europe and Japan through alliances—and one state, Israel, which had no formal alliance with the United States (although, for all practical purposes, it might as well have). Admittedly, the United States also acquired a set of dictatorial allies and friends, usually of right-wing coloration, which appeared to weaken Washington's democratic rationale and lay its foreign policy open to the charge of hypocrisy. One reason for this has been, as we just saw in the case of South Korea, that the security of Japan required the defense of the authoritarian regime in the southern half of the peninsula. Similarly in Europe, the desire for air and naval bases to strengthen NATO, composed of the principal remaining democracies in the world, led to the inclusion of Portugal as an ally and Spain as an associated power. It might be preferable to have democratic allies, but in a world most of whose states are not democratic it is not always possible. Security and democracy are therefore bound to appear on occasion as conflicting values; which is to be given priority is the difficult and often agonizing choice. If in the name of security a democracy somewhat indiscriminately picks up a large number of dictatorial allies to enhance its power, acquire strategic position, or play off one country against another, it may indeed sully its purposes; on the other hand, if in the name of democracy it refuses to align itself with any undemocratic regimes in order to keep its hands clean, it may remain pure but weaken itself against its principal adversary. Thus, in the real world, a democracy must at times sup with a dictatorship, be it of the Right or Left, although when it does so it should remember to eat with a long spoon.

The question is not whether a democracy should ever ally itself with an undemocratic government or come to its rescue if it sees that its *own* security is involved—as, for instance, Great Britain did when it went to the rescue of an undemocratic Poland attacked by Nazi Germany in 1939 or the United States when it sought to bolster undemocratic Turkey and Greece against perceived Communist expansionist pressures from Russia in 1947—but how often, for what purposes, how long, for what ends, and at what level of commitment such an association should be forged. On these issues, honest men can and do differ vigorously. In the absence of war, it cannot be proven that America's relations with Portugal and Spain, for example, contributed to the prevention of hostilities and therefore the protection of Western Europe; perhaps war would not have occurred without them and we need not have stained our cause. Perhaps the United States could have achieved its diplomatic objective of restraining Russia even without aligning itself with Tito's Yugoslav dictatorship after 1948 (or, after 1972, with Mao's totalitarian regime in China to exploit the Sino-Soviet schism).

Interestingly enough, however, although not a single Communist state has ever evolved into a Western-style democracy or been overthrown by force from within in favor of a parliamentary form of government, some of America's authoritarian allies, as those on the Hispanic peninsula and Greece, were overthrown, collapsed, or began to evolve in a more democratic direction—which, in itself, suggests an essential difference between Communist totalitarian and right-wing authoritarian regimes in terms of the degree and permanence of governmental control and subjugation of population, despite similarities such as arbitrary government or the loss of civil and political rights in both types of regimes.

In any event, the principal thrust of American policy since World War II, as before the war, has remained the preservation of a balance of power that would safeguard democratic values in the United States and other basically Western countries. Indeed, this has been a consistent policy since World War I, whether the threat came from the expansionism of the Right (Germany twice) or the expansionism of the Left (the Soviet Union once). American policy-makers in the twentieth century have opposed both types of regimes, for they threatened not just our security but, more broadly, the international environment in which democratic values could prosper. And this remains the crux of American opposition to Soviet Russia: that Russia's great power is a threat to Western values and Western-style open societies. Indeed, Communism, as reflected in the organization of all Communist societies, remains the antithesis of societies that believe in individual freedoms, whether of speech or religion, free-party competition and genuine political choice, and a distinction between state and society. The basic purpose of American foreign policy, after all, is the protection of a democratic social order in a hostile world and it is America's counterbalancing power which has protected its own democracy; without that power, Soviet power and the Soviet Union's social values and order would have prevailed. As Henry Kissinger, while secretary of state, succinctly expressed it, "If we do not lead, no other nation that stands for what we believe in can take our place."

A NEW MOOD

Whatever the validity of the criticisms of America's cold war policies and the value of advice about ordering of priorities, what was clear was that they reflected a mood of weariness, disillusionment, and retraction from global commitments and involvements. One feature of this mood was the attempt to curb presidential power in foreign policy, especially the power as commander-in-chief to commit American forces to battle. Under the Constitution, the president is chiefly responsible for the conduct of foreign policy; it is not surprising that those opposed to these policies focus their attention on him. Just as conservatives during the 1950s wished to limit presidential authority because the president was, in their minds, not anti-Communist enough and might, therefore, upon the advice of the "pro-Communists" in the State Department, sell the country down the river (as the State Department had already "sold" Eastern Europe and Nationalist China), so liberals started in the late 1960s to seek to restrain his authority because in their opinion, he, the military-industrial complex, and the C.I.A. supporting him were too anti-Communist, intent on involving the country in too many places, in too many costly adventures abroad. Conservative or liberal, the remedy for the "imperial presidency's" alleged abuse of its authority and its virtually solo determination of foreign policy was identical: to reassert the control of Congress in the formulation of external policy and to restore the constitutional balance that had purportedly been upset. Thus, the president would presumably be restrained so that he would no longer be, for conservatives, able to "appease" America's enemies or, for liberals, able to act in an interventionist and warlike manner. The abuse of power by Richard Nixon, a conservative president, reinforced the liberal sentiment to curb his powers and compel him to conduct a more restrained and moderate policy.

A second symptom of the new mood was that greater attention should be paid to the nation's domestic problems. These became very clear as the affluent society began to reveal its seamier and more violent sides in the 1960s, such as urban slums, air and water pollution, and the dissatisfaction of the poor, who were composed primarily of the discriminated-against sections of society—blacks, Puerto Ricans, Indians, Chicanos, and Orientals. It was on such problems that critics of the war wanted to spend money to improve the quality of American life for all citizens and prevent the fabric of their society from being torn apart. Instead of crusading for democracy abroad, they argued, the United States should start crusading to make *America* safe for democracy. Liberal critics of the war in Vietnam quoted Edmund Burke to the effect that "example is the school of mankind, and they will learn at no other." The example should be one of a free society enjoying its freedom fully; yet these blessings could not be fully realized in a nation whose excessive preoccupation with foreign affairs drained its powers and resources, both human and material. A "strong" foreign policy was unlikely to bring with it any lasting greatness, prestige, and security; rather, the constant expenditure of energy in foreign adventures would ruin the domestic base. The cold war preoccupation was corrupting the very nature of American society. Institutional imbalance was eroding constitutional processes, particularly when powerful and energetic presidents in the name of national security not only committed the nation to war but also appeared to sanction plots to assassinate foreign leaders such as Castro (with Mafia help), lied to the American people and Congress about what they were doing or why they were doing it, acted secretly (even bombing Cambodia secretly for years), and in various ways violated the constitutional rights of some American citizens. And the large-scale devotion of the country's financial and intellectual resources to its external commitments meant a corresponding neglect of domestic issues. Foreign policy, in short, was tainting the American promise and vision; the priority of foreign policy, therefore, had to be ended. This had always been the heart of the old isolationism: America could only take care of her own needs and remain pure in a morally wicked world if she stayed out of or minimized her political involvement in it. The domestic consequence of playing an extensive role internationally was to endanger the very democracy such a role was intended to protect.

Perhaps the most revealing symptom of America's reaction to Vietnam was the reassertion of the deep-seated attitude toward the exercise of power internationally as immoral and corrupting. Once power politics could no longer be moralized in the context of the democracry–dictatorship dichotomy, the sense of guilt awakened by its employment returned. Vietnam seemed to prove again that in the exercise of power the nation had forsaken its moral traditions and violated its own democratic and liberal professions. Not surprisingly, sensitive men deeply committed to humane values—and daily watching the exercise of power in the form of violence in history's first televised war—repented their former support of containment-through-power as if in giving that support they had been unknowing sinners. Thus Senator Fulbright, who had been a leading advocate of postwar foreign policy while it could be disguised as a moral conflict, now attacked America's global role as evidence of an "arrogance of power." He did not merely assert that the United States had overextended itself and that its commmitments needed to be cut down to its capacities. Nor did he say that Vietnam had been an unwise commitment although the basic policy of containment had been a correct one. He stated something far more fundamental: that all Great Powers seem to have a need to demonstrate that they are bigger, better, and stronger than other nations, and that it was this "arrogance of power," from which the United States now suffered, which was the real cause of international conflict and war. In brief, it was the exercise of power per se that, regardless of a nation's intentions, made it arrogant. Power itself is a corrupting factor; even if justified in moral terms, its use is immoral except in clear unambiguous cases of self-defense. No title for a book could have been more characteristically American. Power is evil and its exercise is tantamount to the abuse of power; abstention from power politics, providing an example to the world of a truly just and democratic society, is a more moral policy. America should be loved for its principles and for practicing what it professes, rather than feared for its might. Democracy and "power politics" were simply incompatible.

If Vietnam and the consequent mood had not led to a reappraisal of America's foreign policy role and objectives, the result of the bipolar distribution of power and the intensive concern with security, the changes in the international system would have required such a reassessment. Vietnam perhaps speeded up this process of reappraisal, but it was in fact already going on at the time of the military intervention. Two changes were particularly significant and were to have a profound impact upon American–Soviet relations: the erosion of NATO's once cohesive bonds and the disintegration of the alliance between Russia and China, as the former "Sino-Soviet bloc" or "Communist world," including Eastern Europe, became increasingly polycentric.

chapter 9

the passing of bipolarity

THE EROSION OF NATO

Having committed their wealth and manpower to the defense of Europe, Americans deemed the states of Europe, particularly the Continental states, ungrateful since during the 1960s they increasingly questioned America's authority to speak for the alliance. But the NATO partners had good reason for doing so. First, the European nations had recovered their economic health and sense of confidence; and their continuing economic integration still held out the possibility that someday Europe would emerge as another superpower. To be sure, this union might not turn out to be the federation envisaged by the functional advocates; for the establishment of a European supranational authority could not, as expected, be an automatic result of the spillover process. The spillover could work "automatically" only if all the member states agreed to form a federal union. During the 1960s, however, General de Gaulle opposed a union in which the Six would lose their individual identities. He therefore sought a "Europe of Fatherlands" in which power would remain in Paris, Bonn, Rome, the Hague, Brussels, and Luxembourg; the Six were, however, to coordinate their political policies through regular meetings of the chief executives, foreign ministers, defense ministers, and other ministers. But if Europe's future as a confederation or federation remained undetermined—and a confederation could, as in the case of the American Confederation, be only a stepping stone toward federation—its future as a closer union seemed less in doubt, despite differences among the Six. For Europe was no longer the weak, divided, and demoralized continent of 1945.

When NATO was formed, Europe had been almost powerless. The imbalance of power within the alliance resulting from Europe's virtually exclusive reliance upon the United States for its defense had placed Washington in a primary and Europe in a subordinate status. Washington's voice had been the voice of the alliance. It was Washington that had determined overall Western foreign and defense policies. While Washington had taken into account its allies' objections and had on occasion adjusted its policies to their wishes, its voice had nevertheless remained the determining one. If France objected to West German rearmament, Paris could delay but not prevent it. If France and Britain acted to defend what they deemed their vital interests, as at Suez, and the United States disagreed and opposed them, they had to withdraw in humiliation. The final decisions were made in Washington in terms of what the United States defined as the West's vital interests. But once Europe had recovered, and even surpassed, its prewar economic vitality, it demanded recognition as America's partner plus a greater share in the determination of NATO's political policies and strategic decisions.

This desire for equality with Washington—and with London, as head of the British Commonwealth—had, of course, been one of the original motives behind the French proposals for European integration. Not surprisingly, therefore, once a more equitable distribution of power had been restored within NATO, the French insisted that the political relationship between the United States and its allies had to be changed, too; and they claimed to speak for Continental Europe. The subsequent Franco-American differences may well be ascribed to de Gaulle; but Gaullism, in the sense of what could then be called a nascent European identity, was paradoxically both the product of America's postwar policy of rebuilding Europe and proof of its success. Just as once the youthful American republic strengthened its unity by rejecting Europe, so the embryonic Europe of the Six consolidated its bonds by opposition to its "outside" ally, America; this opposition was consistent with the changing distribution of power within the Atlantic community. It would have been unnatural for the Six not to rebel against their subordinate, or "satellite," status in an alliance controlled by Washington with its junior partner in London.

Besides equality, however, the Europeans also sought a greater voice in alliance policy formulation because of fear. As the United States became more vulnerable, they had to ask themselves whether they could continue to rely—ten or twenty years ahead—upon American protection against the Soviet Union. Without sufficiently large and credible national nuclear forces of their own, they would continue to be completely dependent upon American power for the most important aspect of their existence, their national security. But, as Soviet power grew, what would happen if the Soviets ever made demands considered vital by the Europeans but not by Washington, either because this was its true assessment of the demands or because it did not consider the demands worth the possible price of all-out war? Could the small British or French strategic force be relied upon to deter the Soviet behemoth?

Finally, the loosening Western alliance reflected to some degree the different geographic position of the partners and to the diverse historical roles played by the United States and Europe in the postwar period. Both factors contributed to, and underlined, all of the other differences within the Atlantic Community. From 1945 onward, each of the major European countries, including Great Britain, had relinquished or been divested of its colonies until, by 1960—with but a few relatively minor exceptions—their extra-European role had come to an end. By contrast, during this same period the United States had become a global power. Hence, at a time when its allies were essentially looking inward, seeking a new role, modernizing themselves, and groping toward a larger political organization and identity, the United States found itself having to become concerned with those areas of the world previously under the controlling hand of Europe. Undoubtedly, the European powers resented their reduced role. Tensions were inevitable.

Perhaps more important, the nations of Europe were deeply concerned over any major diversion of American resources and attention away from Europe and to such underdeveloped areas as Korea and Vietnam. They were equally concerned over the possibility that the United States, in its new global role, might involve them in an all-out war resulting from a head-on confrontation (as had seemed possible in Cuba) or from the escalation of an ongoing limited conflict (such as the Vietnam war). Conversely, U.S. resentment over their lack of sympathy and support for its extra-European ventures merely deepened the already existing American disappointment over the failure of the Europeans to take on a far greater share of their own defense.

The resulting European "revolt" against American hegemony largely revolved around the issue of nuclear weapons, since these have played a triple role within NATO: as the symbol of Great-Power status, as a means of influencing Washington's policy (by contributing to American strategy, which has relied so heavily on nuclear weaponry), and as a means of defense. But it was in the nuclear field that the United States was not willing to surrender its primacy and the accompanying political dominance that the virtually exclusive possession of nuclear weapons gave it. Partly, Washington had become too used to wielding the determining voice in the alliance, and consequently, when its protective capacity was questioned, it tended to react with hurt pride, as if the issue at stake were a matter of American honor. Partly, too, Washington feared the diffusion of nuclear weapons, which would seem to increase the opportunities for accidents and miscalculations that might trigger nuclear war. In brief, such a diffusion would tear the alliance apart. For almost two decades the United States had possessed the power to determine an issue on which Europeans might have to die; but now that France, for example, could decide for which issues Americans might die, the United States balked. What this meant was that the issue of more than "one finger on the trigger" tended to rupture the American–European partnership. The bonds of internal cohesion of the "entangling alliance," and therefore the external security the alliance provided for its members, were thus coming apart under the pressure of this ominous question: How does an alliance preserve its unity in the nuclear age when each major crisis poses the risk that actions by one member may precipitate a nuclear holocaust for an issue that the other members may not consider worth so high a price? Washington, particularly during the Kennedy years, had therefore been insistent on maintaining its nuclear monopoly and the political supremacy of the alliance.

One of the principal ways it sought to do so was by supporting Britain's bid to join the new Europe. British membership, it was hoped, would mean that one of the leaders of the resurgent Europe would be a close friend who would act as the spokesman for the American point of view. This would result in a more harmonious American–European relationship. Britain had already achieved its national deterrent and, unlike France, whose atomic development was vigorously opposed by the United States, had received extensive U.S. help. Britain's reasons for developing a deterrent were exactly the same as those stated by France in its quest for nuclear arms—namely, to gain prestige, security, and particularly a voice in Washington. Indeed, it was the "special relationshp" between nuclear Washington and nuclear London that had been the incentive for France to follow Britain's lead.

But continental Europe no longer recognized Britain's leadership. Even throughout the 1950s—before de Gaulle—it had been somewhat suspicious of the intentions of America's junior partner. Since the end of World War II, Britain had stayed out of all European integration schemes for two main reasons: first, because it considered its close ties with the Commonwealth and, more generally, its global interests to be incompatible with integration into Europe; and second, to preserve its special position as America's closest ally. The only European organizations Britain had joined were those that committed America to Europe. On the other hand, Britain was so dependent for its livelihood on trade that it could not afford to be shut out of the Common Market. To reap its advantages, Britain had therefore proposed that the Common Market be included in a large free-trade area including Sweden, Norway, Denmark, Switzerland, Austria, and Portugal. Members would abolish the tariff barriers among themselves, but they would establish no common tariffs against third parties. The British purpose was clear: to eliminate tariffs on industrial goods but not on agricultural commodities, which it received from the Commonwealth countries under preferential tariff arrangements. Thus, London wished to exploit the economic benefits of the Common Market for which it was in a strong competitive position. At the same time, it also wanted to maintain the advantages it derived from its

Commonwealth association. Needless to say, the Common Market countries did not take too kindly to this attitude, especially the fact that London seemed little concerned with the Inner Six's primary purpose of forming a closer political union.

Britain's position therefore continued to deteriorate. The Commonwealth, traditionally an outlet for British goods and in this respect Britain's own common market, was buying fewer and fewer British industrial and consumer goods, either manufacturing these themselves or receiving them more cheaply from the United States or Common Market countries. But by the early 1960s, after the searing experience of Suez in which London had been forced to desist from its course of action by pressures from America, presumably its close colleague, Britain had begun to realize the advantages of a European political union. Increasingly, in the scale of world powers, London's voice would be heard less and less in comparison with those of Washington, Moscow, Brussels (the new Europe's capital), and Peking; nations would pay principal attention to these centers of power, not to a comparatively feeble London. Britain therefore sought entry into Europe. But de Gaulle and Adenauer were suspicious of Britain's bid. What they feared was that if Britain maintained its special relationship with the United States, continental Europe would remain in its subordinate status in what they felt was an Anglo-American dominated alliance.

The crucial task for Britain was therefore to prove its loyalty to the Europe it had shunned at the time of ECSC, EDC, and EEC. Instead of shattering EEC, as it had tried to do, it had to demonstrate that this time it was wholeheartedly committed to the political aspirations of European union. This is exactly what it failed to do in a year and a half of negotiations. Entry into Europe meant accepting the Six's common external tariff, which would, in effect, have ended the preferential tariff relationship Britain enjoyed with the Commonwealth countries—and this tariff was the economic link that had become the Commonwealth's principal bond. Yet, month in and month out, Britain sought special arrangements, arousing, as before, the suspicion that all it wanted from the Six was the Common Market's economic benefits. Confronted by a choice between the Commonwealth and Europe, Britain hesitated, implying all too strongly a choice for the Commonwealth.

London's stand on the nuclear issue reinforced this anti-European impression. Since it was economically weak, Britain's only real bargaining point with the Six was, in fact, its nuclear force. If Europe was in the long run to have an economic and political identity, it also needed a nuclear one. As a potential great power, this was fitting; for bargaining, this was essential; for defense, in case of American nonprotection, this was vital. For France, still developing her nuclear deterrent, Britain's help in this area, plus the contribution of its bombers, would have been very important. By breaking its special nuclear relationship with Washington and offering its nuclear knowledge and deterrent to the new Europe, Britain would have demonstrated that it was sincere in its application and that it wished to help build this greater Europe politically, economically, and militarily. But, in late 1962 at Nassau, Britain made its choice between Brussels and Washington in 48 hours and chose the latter. To maintain its "independent" national nuclear force, Britain became absolutely dependent upon the United States, which promised to supply Britain with the Polaris missile, for which Britain would build its own submarines and warheads. London's decision ended the negotiations and Britain's bid for entry into the Common Market. Just as it had chosen the Commonwealth as between the Commonwealth and Europe, it had now made its choice between the United States and Europe. The logical conclusion of Britain's continuing "special relationship" was de Gaulle's veto of Britain's entry in January 1963.

Thus, by the middle 1960s, the members of NATO had arrived at a turning point of their relationship. On the one hand, it was quite clear that the United States retained its predominant position in the alliance. It possessed overwhelming nuclear superiority and this was reinforced, starting in the 1960s, by American business which, with its immense amounts of capital and technical and marketing skills, wished to profit from the Common Market by establishing industries behind its tariff barrier. America, because of its world power and the huge sums of money spent on research and development, had a lead in computers, electronics, space, and rocketry. Although the subsequent American-owned industries in Europe were not to account for more than 5 percent of the total business activity in any one country, they were concentrated in a few highly technological sectors that not only shaped the contemporary economy—such as chemicals and oil—but also tended to reshape the environment of the future: U.S. companies at that time manufactured 75 percent of all computers in Europe, 33 percent of all cars, 35 percent of Britain's tires, 40 percent of France's farm machinery, 70 percent of its sewing machines, 75 percent of its electrical and statistical machines, and 90 percent of its synthetic rubber. There were, of course, many reasons for Europe's technological lag—for example, national markets and industries had been too small in the past, not enough money had been spent on research and development, even by private enterprise, managerial training and skills had been inadequate, as were the general and higher educational system. Moreover, beyond this technological gap was a psychological, political, economic, and social gap.

On the other hand, the Europeans were in revolt against America's political primacy. Even Britain, which reapplied for Common Market membership in 1967, only to be turned down again by de Gaulle, had become more "European." And although a majority of British public opinion remained opposed to going into Europe, Britain's government, led by Conservative Prime Minister Heath, who had conducted the Common Market negotiations from 1961 to 1963, finally took the island nation into the Europe whose divisions it had historically exploited in order to assure her own security. Together with Ireland and Denmark (Norway voted to stay out), Britain's 1973 entry substituted the Europe of Nine for the Europe of Six. Whether this enlarged Europe would once more give impetus to the movement for a monetary and eventually a political union remained to be seen; so did the answer to the question of whether this would lead to greater friendship and closer relations with the United States once more or to more intense political competition and major economic and financial rivalry. A confederation could not balance American power in NATO or economic strength in Europe. Only a Europe with economic vitality and a government politically able to establish a European foreign policy and the military strength to support it could in the long run define and support its interests and once more play a major role in the world.

As the 1960s ended, Europe had, however, shown no sign that it even wished to play such a role again. Its growing economic and financial strength, like Japan's, had not yet been translated into political and military terms that looked much beyond Europe. Political unification, even cooperation on forming a joint European foreign policy, still seemed far off. French–British nuclear cooperation for the establishment of a possible European deterrent had not started; and the role of West Germany in such a venture—a Germany that if left out would feel discriminated against and resentful, but if involved might scare many of its partners away and arouse intense Soviet opposition —had scarcely been given any thought. The European countries remained preoccupied with their individual affairs.

THE SINO-SOVIET CONFLICT

The disputes between Russia and China, paralleling those among the Atlantic alliance, stemmed from the tendency of China, first, to assert its equality with the Soviet Union, and second, to take independent actions in foreign policy. Peking's first major opportunity for the former came during the East European crisis in late 1956. The Hungarian revolt had overthrown the Communist regime, and only intervention by the Red Army had kept Hungary within the Communist bloc; and Poland had also struck for a measure of independence from Russia under the leadership of a man whom Khrushchev had personally attempted to keep out of power. For a while, it looked as though Russian power in Eastern Europe might collapse. At this point, the Chinese came to Russia's rescue. They did so by issuing a statement approving of Russia's suppression of the Hungarian "counterrevolution" and by sending Chou En-lai to Europe to reconcile Moscow and Warsaw. In Stalin's time, such Chinese intervention in Europe would have been inconceivable; now the Chinese were actually helping Russia stabilize its position in its own satellite sphere. They achieved this by stressing the unity of the Communist bloc under the leadership of the Soviet Union and at the same time supporting the aspirations of the East European states for greater control over their domestic affairs. This position was not as incompatible as it might seem. The Chinese argued that the Communist states must stand together against the capitalists, and since Russia was the strongest Communist nation, it was the obvious leader. But Russia's primacy did not mean that the other Communist states (including China) could not take "different roads to socialism."

The idea that this assertion of China's independence might lead to a break with Russia gained support as China began to take a different stand on international issues with increasing frequency. For instance, in late 1959 and 1960, the Chinese took actions in opposition to Soviet wishes. First, they crushed a revolt against their rule in Tibet; perhaps remembering Hungary, the Russians did not criticize this Chinese act. But they openly criticized China's dispute with India. The quarrel with India, which involved minor military skirmishes, was over the precise location of the Sino-Indian frontier in the Himalayan mountains. This was a clear test of strength, and the Chinese were apparently determined to press their point of view in an attempt to inflict serious damage on the prestige of their main Asian rival for power. China's actions were a shock to Asia. Up to then, the Asians had interpreted the Chinese Communist revolution largely in terms of their own experience. Chiang Kai-shek had been tied to the landlord class; his overthrow was therefore a blow for social progress. The Nationalist leader had also been allied to the West; his defeat was therefore an advance toward national independence. Now the Chinese were showing themselves to be aggressive. This hurt the Communist cause in Asia, and no one realized it more keenly than Premier Khrushchev. He made no attempt to hide his annoyance. Few things could have mattered less to him than a few square miles this way or that on the Indian–Chinese frontier. Compared with the need to make a favorable impression on the underdeveloped countries, this matter was picayune; for the issue at stake was a triumph of Communism throughout the formerly colonial world and a shift away from the West in the global balance of power.

The Chinese did not really disagree. They merely believed that the Communist victory must be won in a different way. It was on this central issue of the proper strategy with which to win the global victory that Russia and China differed with increasing vehemence; and their "debate" focused on the two interrelated issues of war and peace, and policy toward the leaders—the so-called national bourgeoisie—of the underdeveloped countries. The Soviet position was that in a nuclear war the Soviet Union would not only destroy its enemies, but be destroyed itself; therefore, unnecessary risks were to be avoided—or so the Soviets argued after Cuba—and the two nuclear superpowers even had to cooperate on some arms-control agreement to avoid nuclear accidents and miscalculations. Consequently, the main line of the Soviet attack upon the West's position had shifted to Asia, the Middle East,

Africa, and Latin America; great energy had been devoted to the encouragement of the revolutions raging throughout the underdeveloped areas.

The aim has been obvious: the establishment of friendly political relations with the nationalist regimes, whose emotional dispositions are generally anti-Western. The Soviet Union has tended to encourage their nonalignment (often a pro-Soviet nonalignment in fact, as Nasser's Egypt) in the cold war. This was clearly a tactical device. If Russia opposed their wish to remain disassociated from the cold war—even if some of them wished to exploit the bipolar superpower antagonism to advance their interests—the new nations might become alienated. An attitude of "if you're not with us, then you must be against us," an attitude Stalin and Secretary Dulles had both frequently expressed, might drive these states back into the capitalist camp. If their neutrality were supported, however, their separation from the West would be reinforced and world capitalism would be further weakened.

The Chinese Communists had a somewhat different point of view. They seemed far more willing to risk war. It was often said that this attitude was probably shaped by China's gigantic population. It could afford to lose 400 to 500 million people, in which case it would still have a population of 200 million or more. No other country in the world could survive such mammoth losses. "On the debris of a dead imperialism," Peking had itself pronounced, "the victorious people would create very swiftly a civilization thousands of times higher than the capitalist system and a truly beautiful future for themselves." Nor did China yet possess a large industrial establishment, as did Russia, whose destruction its leaders would be unwilling to risk in a total war.

Simultaneously, the Chinese had grown increasingly skeptical of aiding the new nationalist governments not under Communist control. Though often anti-Western, these governments were also bourgeois—and thus by nature anti-Communist. Economic aid and technical assistance therefore only built up nations whose true colors would sooner or later come to the fore. Consequently, the Chinese preferred to encourage local Communist parties to seize power. In any case, they held that the Soviet Union should channel its aid exclusively or primarily to Communist countries, especially to China.

These Sino-Soviet disagreements over tactics, however, exaggerated the differences between the two Communist powers. Even if nuclear weapons had not existed, the Soviets would not necessarily have been eager to attack the West. Neither Lenin nor Stalin thought of the world revolution in exclusively, or even primarily, military terms. Khrushchev's policy of "peaceful coexistence" was hardly novel. The Communists have been coexisting peacefully with the non-Communist world since 1917. Communists think of victory over capitalism in long-run historical terms; and history, according to them, is determined by economic forces. Hence the struggle will be conducted in primarily social and economic terms, not military ones. This does not mean that the role of military power is unimportant. But its principal use besides defense is political—to harass, pressure, gain limited objectives, not to precipitate an all-out war that would risk the security of the bastion of the world revolution. This was as true in the prenuclear period as it is in the nuclear one. And it was equally true for the Chinese as well.

Peking might well talk of several hundred million Chinese surviving a nuclear attack, but it was also very well aware that such a war would endanger Communist control of the country. The Chinese might talk of constructing a superior postnuclear civilization, but they had also been anxious to avoid any major clash with the United States. In Korea, they warned the United States several times not to advance to their frontier and they finally intervened only for defensive reasons. In the Formosa Straits, they had not even invaded the offshore islands when the United States openly supported the Nationalist troops on these islands. The whole Chinese approach was, in fact, that of protracted guerrilla warfare rather than direct military attack. In the final analysis, for all the Chinese leaders' militant talk, they had acted with great caution. And for all his talk of peaceful coexistence, it was Khrushchev who had threatened to attack London and Paris during Suez, who had precipitated the Berlin crisis, who had broken the test-ban moratorium, and who had sought to install missiles in Cuba.

The real difference between the Russians and the Chinese had not been that one favored peace and the other desired war. Rather, the key issue that divided them had been how much pressure should be exerted against the United States, how far Washington could be pushed before it would react. This was the vital question. For the answer determined both the opportunities that could be exploited and the consequences that might have to be suffered. If not much pressure were applied because of the high risks, then the gains would be small, if any; this is why the Chinese charge the Russians with betraying the cause through a cowardice that led them to "kowtow" to the United States. If a great deal of pressure were exerted, the "profit" might also be far higher, but so were the risks; this was why the Russians accused the Chinese of a recklessness that could end in suicide by provoking the United States. Wisdom in these circumstances counseled caution.

The issue of strategy toward the West and the underdeveloped nations was, furthermore, closely related to the issue of leadership of the Communist bloc. The Soviets had long dominated the Comminist world. As the capital of the first Communist-controlled nation, Moscow had since the early 1920s controlled the international Communist movement; and it had been Moscow that had formulated the movement's policies. After World War II, it established control over the states of Eastern Europe, which were unable at that time to pursue an independent policy. Only Yugoslavia had not been controlled by Moscow, and when it did oppose Stalin's efforts to control it, Tito was read out of Stalin's empire. Communist China's birth—another state controlled by the indigenous Party—had thus presented a real problem for the Soviets. Potentially far more powerful than Yugoslavia, China was determined to be Russia's equal, not its subordinate, in the Communist bloc.

Peking had therefore sought to share Moscow's authority to formulate bloc policies. But Khrushchev would have none of this. Moscow, like Washington, had too long defined the policies for its followers and thus become a poor alliance-manager. Instead of sharing authority with Peking, Khrushchev acted as Stalin had—and ironically, he did so first on the issue of de-Stalinization! He had decided to de-Stalinize at home and within the bloc; China was expected to adopt the same policy. It was not that the Chinese had been particularly fond of Stalin, for they had not. Nor was it that the Chinese did not recognize the need for de-Stalinization, particularly some relaxation of the Soviet grip on the satellites and permission for each to travel its own "road to socialism"; they did recognize this need. What offended the Chinese, and therefore initiated the Sino-Soviet dispute, was that Khrushchev pronounced policy for the entire Communist bloc without even bothering to consult them.

This debate over authority, then, was a key issue of the Sino-Soviet conflict. If to this extent it was comparable to the Franco-American conflict, it has also proved to be totally different in one respect: Unlike the French and Americans, the Chinese and Russians conducted their struggle in ideological terms. And because of this, the struggle held more ominous implications for the Communist bloc. Paradoxically, the very ideology that bound them together also tended to divide them. On the one hand, Moscow and Peking interpreted the world through the same ideological framework; Communism provided both of them with a *Weltanschauung*. Both held the same view of man, society, and history. They both saw world conflict in terms of class struggle and the final triumph of Communism, and they both defined capitalism as their common enemy.

On the other hand, precisely because of the intimate relationship between ideology and action—ideology providing the framework through which events in the world are analyzed and defining the general purposes of the movement—ideology became a divisive factor. Moscow had long been the Communist Rome, and the ruler in Moscow therefore became the Communist Pope when he assumed power. If an ideology claimed to represent the truth, there could only be one correct interpretation of that truth. Thus there could be only one center for the interpretation and application of the doctrine. No ideological–theological movement can tolerate two Romes and two Popes. A schism—and a fight for the leadership of the movement—had therefore to develop, since one of the Romes and one of the Popes must per se be heretical. Hence Moscow denounced Mao for having deserted Marxism–Leninism and, by fragmenting what had been a united Communist front against the United States, for having aided the devil's cause, imperialism. Denouncing the actions of the Soviet Communist Party as "Khrushchevism without Khrushchev," the Chinese charged that it had been seized from within by "revisionists" who were in fact capitalists, cooperating with Washington in order to contain China! Peking called for the overthrow of the Soviet leaders.

Since Mao attributed the caution of the Soviets toward the United States as well as their hostility toward China to the *embourgeoisement* of the Soviet leadership, he launched his Cultural Revolution after 1965 in order to purify his nation and keep it loyal to the true Marxist–Leninist faith. All persons, no matter what their positions and functions, were to be rooted out if they were suspected of "taking the road back to capitalism." Purges—especially by mobs of youths called Red Guards—were conducted in the army, government, industry, agriculture, even the Party itself. The president of China and the general secretary of the Party were among those deposed as the conflict between Mao and his followers on the one hand and his opponents on the other raged on for several months. Central authority seemed to have broken down. In these circumstances, the army increasingly came to the fore, restoring national unity and central control.

The Sino-Soviet schism was, by the late 1960s, dramatically clear. The epithets hurled between Peking and Moscow reached a ferocity unknown since the early days of the American–Soviet cold war. Thus, the Russians called Mao China's Hitler and compared the Chinese with the Mongol hordes who overran Russia a millenium ago; and the Chinese talked about the "Soviet revisionist clique" as a "dictatorship of the German fascist type," and quoted Marx as saying already in the middle of the last century that Russia's aim had been, and always would be, world hegemony. For Mao and his followers, the struggle against Russia became increasingly primary. The infidel had to be eliminated first before resuming the conflict against the evils of imperialism; internal betrayal within the Communist movement had to be rooted out lest those who had strayed from the true faith corrupt and weaken the movement beyond repair for the ultimate struggle. Thus, avoiding conflict with the United States became important. During Vietnam, for example, China continuously counseled Hanoi that revolutions had to be self-sufficient and repeatedly stated that only an American attack on China itself would precipitate Peking's intervention. In brief, North Vietnam should not and could not count on active Chinese help to help defeat American forces in South Vietnam. Mao's policy was therefore militantly anti-American rhetorically, but restrained in its behavior.

Even after Mao's death a complete Sino-Soviet reconciliation was impossible for, quite apart form any ideological issue, these two powers remained divided by the same issues that divided NATO: differences of power, of geographic position; different evaluations of international problems; and the obvious conflict between a power with global interests and an ally whose capabilities were essentially regional. Russia and China also had a long history of conflict which antedated their becoming Communist states and still affected the intensity of their antagonism. Peking was bitter about Russian retention of lands seized by the tsars when China had been a weak state exploited by all the major Western powers, especially by Russia. But Moscow considered these lands Russian, regardless of how they were acquired. The two large Communist states also had a number of clashes along their 4500-

mile border, the longest in the world. Both had heavily reinforced their troop strengths; the Soviet army, larger than the one in Eastern Europe, reportedly possessed large quantities of tactical nuclear weapons.

The Soviets even had to bargain with the East European "people's democracies" because, as a result of the Sino-Soviet conflict, these increasingly nationalistic states gained a degree of independence from Moscow in return for their support of Moscow against Peking. Indeed, it is doubtful that most can any longer be called satellites. Their conflict with the Soviet Union, moreover, has taken on a dynamic of its own. Romania is the most defiant of the people's democracies; in 1968, Czechoslovakia was also moving rapidly toward greater independence when Soviet fears that Prague's reforms would jeopardize the survival of Communism in a country bordering on West Germany (Romania, which does not share a frontier with the Federal Republic, is also, internally, a quite orthodox Communist regime) led to the Red Army's intervention. Yet, even while this intervention reminded the East European nations of the limits of Soviet tolerance, none of them is as completely subservient as it was during Stalin's reign. Indeed, they increasingly looked westward for economic–technological assistance. Concomitantly, they needed a relaxation of international tensions; a return of the cold war would reduce their links to the West and bring back greater Russian control and intervention in their affairs. On the whole, therefore, they approved of the changing nature of American–Soviet relations "from confrontation to negotiations," which had been going on throughout the last half of the 1960s and which was to become dramatically visible with the advent of the Nixon administration.

A BACKWARD GLANCE

Twenty years after World War I, a new world war had already started. Twenty-four years after that war, in 1969, the two superpowers, while they remained in conflict, were keenly aware of their stake in preserving the peace. Even before the Nixon administration, the "hot line" between the White House and the Kremlin for use in case of crises and emergencies, the limited test ban, the agreement to outlaw nuclear weapons in space, the antinuclear proliferation treaty, and the outlawing of biological weapons had been among the fruits of this awareness. But there was additional evidence, especially the changeover from "soft" to "hard" strategic weapons which had enhanced American and Russian national security during the 1960s by stabilizing the bipolar strategic equation. The Soviet–American Strategic Arms Limitation Talks (SALT) of the 1970s were to be particularly significant and symbolic of the new "adversary partnership" emerging between the two nations.

These "arms-control" measures—safer weapons systems and strategies—were supplemented by other actions. The United States restrained Chiang

Kai-shek from attacking mainland China; it did not intervene on behalf of the Hungarian rebels in Russia's East European security belt; it compelled its two closest allies, Britain and France, to desist from their attack upon Egypt because it was in America's interest to keep Nasser from being overthrown, an act that might have compelled the Soviets to intervene and would have tainted the Western anticolonial stance; it negotiated with Moscow bilaterally on Berlin when its allies opposed such negotiations for fear of an agreement at their expense. In its turn, the Soviet Union tacitly cooperated with the United States in the United Nations in the establishment of a peacekeeping force to be stationed between Egyptian and Israeli forces in 1956, and did not intervene when Israel defeated the Arabs in 1967; similarly, despite harsh verbal attacks on the United States and on the U.N. secretary-general, the Soviet Union acquiesced in the dispatch of U.N. forces to the Congo a few years later; it did not support Chinese Communist attempts to capture Formosa; it signed the limited test-ban treaty despite Chinese Communist opposition (just as the United States signed despite French objections); it supported India when China attacked it and constantly denounced Chinese militancy; and during Vietnam, it negotiated with the U.S. on such key items as the nonproliferation treaty and SALT.

In retrospect, then, could it not be said that this period, despite all the crises, was remarkably stable and "peaceful" in the sense that conflicts in the international system were resolved and adjusted without triggering a world war? And was it, in fact, not the simple and direct confrontation of the two great nuclear powers that accounted for these conditions? When one nation pushed, the other had to push back; and this occurred no matter how distant the arena from Moscow or Washington. The two superpowers, precisely because their attention was riveted on each other, were constantly on guard against any disturbances of the balance between them. The recurrent confrontations in the postwar period, as Kenneth Waltz has pointed out, were in this context an essentially healthy sign, since they meant that attempts at expansion were being met with counteraction. "Rather a large crisis now than a small war later is the axiom that should precede the statement, after made, that to fight small wars in the present may be the means of avoiding large wars later." Furthermore, the general caution and responsibility in handling crises was reinforced by each power's knowledge that if it miscalculated, it might be risking suicide; whereas in an earlier age, a nation in its power calculations could easily overestimate its own strength and underestimate that of its opponent, nuclear arms have compelled policy-makers not to commit such errors, and this has had a restraining effect. A *Pax Atomici* it was, but it was precisely this *pax* that constituted the principal restraint upon the superpowers and transformed their relationship to one of a more "limited adversary" nature, which stressed not only their continued competition for influence in the world but their cooperation if that world were to survive and each of the powers' interests were to be relatively satisfied.

chapter 10

from cold war to détente

FROM *IDEALPOLITIK* TO *REALPOLITIK*

Vietnam had left the nation disillusioned with anti-Communism as a rationale for American global involvement. The war having been justified in its name, the reaction was that the price was too high. Before Vietnam, the nation could be mobilized to stop Communist aggression; after Vietnam, the concern became avoiding engagement in further adventures overseas. Even more basically, anti-Communism had been weakened by the increasing pluralism of the formerly cohesive Sino-Soviet bloc. In the bipolar world, it had been relatively easy to moralize about power politics precisely because the bipolarity had been one of power *and* values. Globalism, which had made sense as long as any Communist expansion meant an addition to Soviet strength, could thus be explained in terms very understandable to Americans, that is, democracy versus dictatorship. But it was one thing to "fight Communism" as long as there was only one Communism to fight; once Communism became a many-splintered thing, which Communism were they to "fight"? Were all Communist states, because they were Communist, their enemies? Or did they now have to distinguish among them, determining which was hostile, which friendly, which neutral—in short, which posed a threat to American interests? More specifically, in these new circumstances, what changes in the distribution of power could America safely allow, and where, if anywhere, and against whom did it still have to draw "frontiers"? Quite apart from the fact that the answers to these questions were more difficult to arrive at than during the simple days of bipolarity because each situation would now confront policy-makers with alternative policies, thereby arousing great debates and possibly intense controversy, anti-Communism would no longer be very useful as a means of eliciting popular support, since the United States might well be supporting one Communist state against another.

One crucial question this posed for the future conduct of American foreign policy, therefore, was whether, in the absence of anti-Communism, the United States would "dirty" its hands by playing straight and unadorned power politics. While *Realpolitik* was synonymous with *Idealpolitik,* it had been easy to be a leader and organize various coalitions whose basic task was to push back when pushed. The state system's requirement to keep the balance could, in other words, be performed by the United States government as long as it could disguise from its own people what it was doing and pretend it was engaged in a noble task. *But could a nation that historically has condemned power politics adapt its outlook and style to a world in which justifying foreign policy in terms of ideological crusades was outmoded; could it "play the game by no other name" in an increasingly multipolar world?* More specifically, how could the United States, disabused of anti-Communism and disenchanted with a world in which the forces of good could no longer crusade against the forces of evil, mobilize congressional and popular support for the continued conduct of its foreign policy? Or would America, no longer believing it had an ideological mission to perform, sway from occasional fits of moral passion and crusadism to moralistic isolationism—or, if that were no longer possible in the late twentieth century, a major withdrawal from the world? Would the country, having enjoyed its drug of anti-Communism and the resulting "high" of global responsibility and exercise of world power, now swing to the "low" state of reaction and withdrawal?

The incoming Nixon administration in January 1969 thus confronted a novel postwar situation: how to conduct foreign policy without a consensus. The administration thought it could substitute a policy based on the traditional logic of the state system. This dramatic shift away from a style which stemmed from the nation's domestic values and experiences to a balance of power rationale was somewhat surprising because the president, as congressman, senator, and vice-president, had been an exponent of virulent anti-Communism, the "illusion of American omnipotence" and an inflexible moralism which tended to reject having anything to do with Communists lest one be tainted with an "un-American" virus. But as president, he and his national security assistant Henry Kissinger, a German-born Jewish immigrant and Harvard professor, who later also became secretary of state, both rejected the traditional American justification for participating in foreign affairs. International politics was not a fight between the good side and the bad side. All states had the right to exist and possessed legitimate interests, a right as true for Communist as for non-Communist states. A nation, therefore, did not launch crusades against an adversary on the assumption that differences of interests represented a conflict of virtue and evil. The better part of wisdom was to learn to live with other states, defend one's interest if encroached upon, but also attempt to resolve differences and build on shared interests. Nor would such differences be easily or quickly resolvable, for when states held conflicting views of their interests these views were usually deeply held and not easily relinquished. Summit meetings were important as part of a negotiating process, but one summit did not all problems solve, and to raise false hopes that it would was to produce the cynicism and disillusionment that would endanger diplomacy itself. Good personal relations among leaders might smoothe this process, but they were not a substitute for hard bargaining; accords basically reflect the ratio of power between the nations the leaders represent.

And what about dealing with a Communist dictatorship whose values and practices were abhorrent to us? The most the United States could expect was to influence its international behavior in a responsible direction; American power was too limited to transform another nation's domestic structure, and to make agreements dependent upon such a transformation would be counterproductive and raise tensions. American demands would be resisted, and this, in turn, would jeopardize accords on international issues which might otherwise have been resolvable. The United States was not omnipotent and had to abandon its habit of crusading to democratize adversaries. Negotiating with a Communist regime like Russia's was not a matter of morality which required an internal purification preceding discussions; it was a matter of dealing with a powerful state with which the United States had to discuss issues if peace was to be preserved. And in the nuclear age, maintaining the peace was itself a moral goal. In turn, peace could be kept only by a balance of power and that balance also, of course, protected democratic nations. Within the parameters of that balance, however, it was necessary to try and accommodate the legitimate needs of the principal disturber of that peace. Power neutralizes countervailing power, and satisfying the interests of other Great Powers would be more likely to produce acceptance of the present international system than continued frustration and hostility to an international system in which they had little vested interest. No state could be completely satisfied, but it could be relatively satisfied.

The focus of the Nixon– (and later, Ford–) Kissinger view, then, concentrated on the powerful actors. Although the rhetoric and style of American foreign policy were to be different and were to reflect more candidly and publicly the operational norms of the international system rather than domestic values and experience, there was to be an essential continuity in policy. The Russian–American balance remained the preoccupation; it was still Russia, as a Great Power, whose influence needed to be contained and behavior moderated. This unity of rhetoric and action—the explanation of United States policy in terms of power, balances, spheres of influence, prestige, national interests, and the limits of American power, as well as the specific rejection of ideological justifications and crusades—represented the socialization of American foreign policy by the state system. The United States now finally explained its actions on the international scene in the same terms as all great powers before it—that is, in terms of the logic of the balance of power.

Indeed, this task was considered more necessary than ever before for three reasons. One was the American mood of weariness with the nation's global role in world politics since 1945. Despite the victory of World War II, there had been no respite, only more conflict. And all the subsequent years of involvement and commitments had not apparently brought peace and security any nearer; they had led to Vietnam instead. The cost of being a world power was too great. Public opinion polls at the time showed that a majority of Americans would agree only to the defense of Canada! In these circumstances, a relaxation of tension or *détente* became necessary until the nation would "recover its nerve" and be ready once again to play the extensive role the Administration judged as still necessary. In the meantime, Moscow could hopefully be restrained.

A longer-term reason for *détente* was that by the time President Nixon assumed office, the Soviet Union had attained strategic parity. The balance of power between the two superpowers had been between the U.S. Strategic Air Command, later supplemented by the navy's nuclear submarines, and the Red Army. The American bombers and missiles deterred Russia by threatening to destroy her cities; the urban population was hostage for the Kremlin's restraint. By contrast, Russia did not gain an intercontinental capability and capacity to destroy the United States until the massive build-up which began after 1964. From the 1950s to the middle 1960s, America's strategic power was balanced not so much by Moscow's bomber and missile force, which was small by comparison to that of the United States, but by the Red Army. It was Western European and American forces stationed in that area which were hostage for Washington's restraint. The powerful Russian army, it was believed, would overrun Western Europe; NATO forces could be quickly defeated.

In brief, the American–Soviet balance had been an asymmetric one; the United States held strategic superiority and an intercontinental reach, the Soviet Union conventional superiority and a regional reach. However, by 1970 the balance had become symmetrical; Russia's strategic power had caught up with that of the United States and she could now hold America's population—no longer Western Europe's—directly hostage.

But this balance was a dangerous one because of technological innovation in missiles. In the early 1960s, it had been believed that the hardening and dispersal of missiles, as well as making them mobile, would mean: one, that deterrent forces could be made invulnerable; and two, that once one side had sufficient missiles to destroy the other's society, there was no need for acquiring more missiles. In short, since massive retaliation was unavoidable, there would be no nuclear war; and the arms race would end. But the MIRVing, or multiplication of warheads whose accuracy was continuously being improved, meant an increasing capacity to hit the other side's land-based missiles; the earlier expectation that these forces, the backbone of deterrence, were invulnerable, became increasingly less true. Thus the balance was again threatening to become unstable, as it had been when both sides had relied for deterrence on vulnerable bombers. American–Soviet *détente* and what Nixon called "negotiations instead of confrontations"—especially arms control negotiations to stabilize the deterrent balance and lower international tensions in general—were therefore very important. America and Russia had become interdependent in the nuclear area. Politically competitors, they were compelled to cooperate by their mutual desire to avoid suicide—a possibility that had been increased by the Soviet acquisition of nuclear parity.

Lastly, there was the Soviet Union's emergence as a global power. Although her leaders' ambitions might be worldwide—Soviet Russia considered herself the nucleus of a new and more humane postcapitalist world, as well as a Great Power—the reach of Russian power had been limited essentially to Eurasia. Attempts to extend her power beyond Eurasia had been largely unsuccessful; in the Congo and Cuba in 1962, where Russia, confronted by America's strategic superiority and local conventional (naval) superiority, had to retreat, were painful reminders that Russia was not, like the United States, a power with a worldwide capacity. The Soviet Union of the 1970s had apparently concluded from Cuba that strategic power paid off politically because it could be used not only to deter but to intimidate and compel the adversary to retreat. In addition, within the context of this growing strategic power, the Soviet Union had also engaged in a parallel massive conventional build-up, particularly of a modern surface navy and airlift capability. This meant that as her ability to neutralize America's nuclear power grew, her capacity to project her power beyond Eurasia grew also. Would Russia, in these new circumstances, continue to seek to expand her influence only on land and in territorially contiguous areas? Or would she, as a result of her new might, feel a confidence that had been absent before and act more boldly and take greater risks, reopening old issues and challenging the United States in new areas further away from Russia? Would the United States, by contrast, now that she had lost her strategic superiority, be more cautious and hesitant to react? Just as Moscow now could stare America down, so Washington, in any situation involving American interests, now had to calculate whether Russia would also intervene and, if she did, what the risks and costs would be.

Kissinger compared Russia's emergence as a world power to Germany's development at the turn of the century. In both cases, the challengers were land powers. The symbols of their aspiration and determination to find their "place in the sun" were the navies they built; nothing could have been more symbolic to Great Britain and the United States, the two greatest naval powers in their respective times. Germany's emergence and the desire to be a world power resulted in World War I. How could Russia's newly-gained power be managed peacefully while simultaneously safeguarding American security interests? Should these be jeopardized, the United States might feel compelled to react strongly and risk war. Thus the question of Russia's massive military build-up raised questions not just about the military balance and its stability but, more fundamentally, about her ultimate intentions and whether the emergence of a peaceful "structure of peace," to use Mr. Nixon's phrase, was possible.

Détente *was thus a consciously chosen strategy for managing the superpowers' adversary relationship which would seek to secure American interests at a lower level of tensions and at a lesser cost than the extensive involvement, high-cost policy of cold war confrontation and frequent crises.* The American–Soviet balance would still be bipolar, but one which was somewhat more complex and fluid than in the earlier cold war era. And it was here that the stylistic difference was to become more apparent. Nixon's predecessors, as we have noted, also pursued a balance of power policy but felt compelled to justify their policy in terms of the past crusading style; thus they—and especially Democratic presidents—were frequently trapped by their own anti-Communist rhetoric and had to be more inflexible and interventionist than they would have been had they not had to pose as the guardians of the true faith against the barbarians from without. For twenty years the United States had therefore been unable to abandon the fiction that Taiwan was China and establish a formal diplomatic relationship with the real China on the mainland. The Nixon–Kissinger balance was to include Communist China. As Moscow's bitter rival, Peking could be used to provide the Soviets with an incentive to act with restraint and a greater willingness to compromise if it wished to avoid closer Sino-American relations and cooperation against the Soviet Union. The Nixon tripolarity was thus a tactic in order to make the superpower bipolarity work more smoothly and securely.

This balance was, furthermore, to be supplemented by a network of agreements and a set of rules of mutual restraint beneficial to both powers. Cold war bipolarity had been based on the fundamental assumption that what benefited one side would hurt the other and had, therefore, to be prevented by counteraction; this kind of bipolar competition, while still relevant on some issues, was, however, to be supplemented by agreements and rules profiting both, thereby presumably enhancing each country's stake in cooperation with the other. The Kissinger word was "interdependence." If a series of agreements and understandings cutting across the broad range of issues affecting American–Soviet relations could be arrived at, the Soviet Union, the more expansionist-minded state, would gain a vested interest in continuing stable and good relations with the United States. While Russia was to be faced with a continued balance and a strong American military that would provide an inducement for restraint in foreign policy, this "stick" was to be supplemented with enough "carrots" to make that restraint more appealing. There was another word: "linkage." This referred to the fact that the various issues would be linked together diplomatically. Progress on one front would be tied to progress on another; the Kremlin could not expect to make gains on one issue that interested it but refuse to meet American interests on other issues. If it did so, there would presumably be a penalty exacted in the form of nonprogress on issues of interest to Russia or the withholding of benefits Moscow was seeking. This linkage was often explicitly declared to exist during the Nixon–Ford period (although not necessarily followed in practice); it was officially denied by the Carter administration (although, it was on occasions pointed out, certain Soviet actions could not but affect American public opinion or congressional support for administration policies). Cooperation and mutual concessions were obviously preferable. The adversary part of the relationship, was to be balanced by the partnership element in a new adversary-partnership. The overall purposes were to lower tensions between the superpowers, to confront fewer crises, and to encourage diplomatic negotiations; it did not mean an end of American–Russian conflict and competition. A *détente* was not an *entente cordiale.*

DISENGAGEMENT FROM VIETNAM

Nixon's perception of power relations among the Great Powers heavily influenced his thinking about acceptable terms for the U.S. withdrawal from the war in Vietnam. An option he had upon becoming president, one that would have brought him much public acclaim, was to pull out all American forces immediately on the grounds that the United States had more than magnanimously fulfilled any obligations it had had to Saigon; that after many American deaths and immense amounts of American money, Saigon should stand on its own feet. But in President Nixon's view the central issue was, as he repeatedly pointed out, not getting out of Vietnam—that was a foregone conclusion—but *how* the country would get out. If the United States withdrew quickly, the events it had fought to prevent might well occur; if South Vietnam collapsed and Hanoi unified Vietnam under its control (and presumably eventually Laos and Cambodia as well), the credibility of the American commitments and power would be weakened, perhaps gravely so.

Thus the new administration was from the beginning determined not to accept any settlement that was tantamount to a defeat, namely, a coalition government in Saigon controlled by the Communists. For it was Nixon's view that establishing a *détente* with Russia and a rapprochement with China would not be feasible if America's prestige—reputation for power—was badly impaired. It was the president's aim to modify U.S. relations with the two large Communist states, especially Russia, the more powerful of the two. Why should the Soviet Union, rapidly building up its strategic power, settle for parity and mutually acceptable peaceful coexistence if she sensed that America was weak and could be pushed around? Why should China tone down its revolutionary rhetoric and conduct a more traditional state-to-state diplomacy, and indeed reorient its policy closer to the United States, if it could not count on American strength and determination to resist what it saw as Soviet attempts at hegemony in Asia? In short, the country had to "hang tough" in Vietnam in order to normalize relations with Russia and China.

Was this policy not contradictory, deciding on the one hand to improve relations with the giant Communist states while on the other hand fighting hard against a Communist pigmy which, unlike Russia and China potentially, could never constitute a threat to the U.S.? Nixon's answer, like Kennedy's in 1962, was no. For Kennedy too had won the presidency determined to achieve what is now called *détente* with Russia. But it gradually had become clear to Kennedy that Khrushchev misread Kennedy's restraint in foreign policy as weakness and lack of resolve to defend American interests. The Missiles of October crisis had been only the latest and most agonizing of Khrushchev's challenges to Kennedy; to fail to meet this test and not disabuse the Soviet leader of his misperceptions of the president would therefore be extremely dangerous. Only if Khrushchev gained a healthy respect for Kennedy's will would there be an opportunity to negotiate fairly, compromise on outstanding issues, and relax international tensions.

President Nixon and Henry Kissinger, therefore, devised a twofold strategy. First, American ground troops were to be gradually withdrawn to cut the costs of the war and make further hostilities tolerable for the "silent majority," which Mr. Nixon felt was loyal, even though fatigued, and would support him in a search for an "honorable" ending of the war. Thus, in terms of domestic strategy, he would contain his critics. In terms of his Vietnam strategy, the continued involvement of United States forces, especially in the air while the army's participation in the ground fighting progressively diminished, would hopefully provide an incentive for Hanoi to negotiate an end to the war. This incentive would presumably be all the stronger if the president's strategy worked at home, for he would then remove Vietnam as a principal issue in the next election and presumably be reelected. Thus Hanoi, confronted with the prospect of a lengthy war that might last longer than four more years, would have every reason to settle the war diplomatically.

The second part of the president's policy was the "Vietnamization" of the war. South Vietnam's forces were to be trained better and supplied with modern arms so that they could bit-by-bit take over the ground fighting. Assuming that the South Vietnamese army could hold its own by 1972, although supported by American air and naval power as well as economic and arms aid, Hanoi's ability to win on the battlefield would dim as the cost of tenaciously pursuing the war increased. The offer of a negotiated settlement would therefore double its attractiveness.

But could Nixon win the time internally and persuade Hanoi externally? Criticisms and pressures remained strong in the United States. During Johnson's tenure, the critics had focused their demands on cessation of the air war against the North to clear the way for what were anticipated to be fruitful negotiations to conclude hostilities; during Nixon's days, the critics concentrated their arguments on the abandonment of the Thieu regime in Saigon, since Hanoi had made it clear that it was not willing to cease fighting unless Thieu was replaced. No coalition government with him was acceptable; indeed, no coalition government, even without Thieu, in which the Communists did not control the key positions appeared acceptable. Hanoi remained as adamant as ever in the belief that it was the rightful successor to French power in Vietnam, indeed Indochina. Thus in Congress, on campuses, and elsewhere, the calls for faster troop withdrawals and forsaking Saigon multiplied. But the president, by appealing to his silent majority, seemed to be quite successful in using Vietnamization to pull the sting out of the peace movement.

The danger inherent in the president's strategy was, however, that as American troops were withdrawn but before the South Vietnamese were ready to meet the enemy in battle, the North Vietnamese would attack. So, for example, in March 1970, Cambodia's Prince Sihanouk, who had tolerated the Communist troops and supply lines in his country, was overthrown by a military regime that wanted Communist troops out of it. The president, aware of North Vietnamese activity in Cambodia and now dealing with a regime that was friendly toward an American presence, decided to expand the war. On April 30, 1970, American and South Vietnamese troops were given a six- to eight-week period and ordered to clean out the North Vietnamese sanctuaries in Cambodia–South Vietnam border areas.

The critics were quick to pounce. The president had not consulted—or even informed—Congress before announcing his move into Cambodia. If the move was indeed short-term, the North Vietnamese could be expected to move right back into the sanctuaries after the troops had pulled out. Dissension spread: within the president's cabinet (the secretaries of state and defense reportedly had been among those opposed); within the State Department; in the Senate; and on campuses, where demonstrations and riots erupted. In one such demonstration, four students were shot to death by the Ohio National Guard. The Cambodian invasion and the shootings at Kent State led to strikes on many campuses, with the complete shutdown of a number of colleges and universities. Protesters once again turned out for a peaceful mass demonstration in Washington. The reaction to Cambodia made it clear that it would be foolhardy for the president to repeat such an action.

Saigon's army was unfortunately the key to the success of the president's strategy. In the spring of 1972 came its first real test when North Vietnam launched an unexpected attack across the DMZ (the demilitarized strip between North and South Vietnam). It was a broadscale conventional assault by almost all of North Vietnam's divisions supported by heavy weapons, including artillery and tanks. American commanders, experts in orthodox warfare, would have welcomed precisely such an enemy onslaught in the days of half a million American troops; but, with some exceptions, the South Vietnamese army performed poorly and, among other results, lost the northern provinces. Only American air support staved off even worse losses.

President Nixon was thus in a quandary on the eve of his visit to Moscow. The Soviets had supplied Hanoi with its modern arms and, whether or not it had been informed of the date of the North Vietnamese offensive, it should —according to Nixon—have restrained its Asian ally if it wished the summit conference to proceed. As a Great Power itself, it must have known that a major South Vietnamese defeat would be humiliating to its adversary on the eve of vital negotiations from which Moscow had as much to gain as Washington. The president was unwilling to negotiate under this shadow of defeat.

"Vietnamization" being in danger, he "re-Americanized" the war by once more initiating extensive bombing of the North and blockading North Vietnam's ports with mines. The point was to stop the supplies from coming in; since the war was now a conventional one, dependent on oil and heavy weapons and large amounts of ammunition, air power might be more effective than during guerrilla operations in halting them. Simultaneously, Nixon also offered Hanoi just about all it could reasonably expect to be given: "the complete withdrawal of all American forces from Vietnam within four months"—that is, the end of blockade, bombing and all other American military activities in all of Indochina—if all prisoners of war were returned and an internationally supervised cease-fire were arranged. The Communists could, in other words, keep their forces in the South, a significant concession previously offered only in secret talks. Equally important, the president did not insist on the survival of the Thieu government. Not only did he not mention Thieu, but he specifically said that the United States withdrawal "would allow negotiations and a political settlement between the Vietnamese themselves." This new set of proposals was, at the very least, a concrete and serious basis for negotiations. But Hanoi rejected the offer. It appeared to want the president to do the one thing he refused to do—guarantee Communist control in Saigon. His proposal, in fact, had seemed to suggest that the North Vietnamese do this job for themselves, if they could do it.

The North Vietnamese thus confronted a dilemma. Despite the heavy bombing and blockade, the Soviet Union had gone ahead with its summit meeting with Nixon. Clearly, Russian interests were far more important to Moscow than North Vietnam's interests. Communist China too was no longer the fervent advocate of continued revolutionary warfare and opponent of a negotiated cessation to the war that it had been earlier. Moscow and Peking both gave priority to their relationships with Washington. Thus Hanoi was pressured to try Mr. Nixon's offer. Yet the North Vietnamese leaders had hung onto their goal of unifying Vietnam for so long, paid such a very high price for it, and been so often cheated out of the fulfillment of their dream by their adversaries that they were naturally suspicious of Mr. Nixon's offer and resentful of Russian and Chinese pressures. But suddenly in the middle of October, less than a month before the American presidential election, Hanoi signaled its apparent willingness to accept something less than a total victory and by late October negotiated a tentative Indochina settlement. The terms included an internationally supervised cease-fire that would halt all American bombing and mining and bring about withdrawal of all United States forces within two months (two months less than the president's earlier proposal); separate future cease-fires were expected in Laos and Cambodia. Prisoners of war would be exchanged. A series of mixed political commissions, composed of elements from the Vietcong, the Saigon government, and neutralists, would then be established to work out a new South Vietnamese political order leading to a new constitution and the election of a new government.

The Nixon administration felt it had achieved an "honorable peace." The North Vietnamese, after having for years declared that the Thieu government would have to be dismantled as a precondition for a cease-fire, now accepted him as the leader of the government faction; and Thieu remained in control of a sizable army and large police forces with which he administered most of the country and all the urban centers, leaving only minor areas and a small percentage of the population under the control of the Vietcong and the approximately 145,000 North Vietnamese troops. Thus the Thieu faction seemed to have a good chance to compete politically and militarily with the Communists after the fighting ended.

But Thieu stalled against the tentative October 1972 settlement to pressure the United States to demand the withdrawal of the Northern army and recognize Saigon's authority over all of South Vietnam, including areas that Communist forces held. But President Nixon felt that Hanoi's willingness to allow Thieu to administer the territory he now controlled was a crucial concession and that Hanoi, having fought for so long to unite Vietnam and sacrificed so much, could not be expected to end the fighting without an opportunity to gain some political influence, even if it were less than the original goal; and militarily, he felt that even further prolonged fighting could not compel these forces to withdraw from South Vietnam. Thieu could procrastinate, but he held no veto.

One of the fascinating questions about the negotiations between Hanoi and Washington is why the former was willing to change its mind about Thieu after years of insistence that it would not do any business with him. One suspects that the North Vietnamese did not retreat from their earlier demand and agree to a settlement of the war to reelect President Nixon; more likely, they too were familiar with American public opinion polls predicting a landslide victory for the president over his Democratic rival, Senator McGovern, and they feared that with four more years guaranteed Nixon would raise his demands. Therefore, it would be more profitable to reach a settlement, or at least the outlines of a settlement, before the election. Hanoi thus leaked the terms negotiated during October, thereby seeking to place the responsibility for the continuation of the war on Washington and Saigon; more significantly, it also elicited a public acceptance by the Nixon administration of the basic outlines of a settlement. By the end of the second round of negotiations before Christmas the administration's chief negotiator, Henry Kissinger, stated that 99 percent of the settlement had been agreed upon, but on that 1 percent the negotiations broke down. Anxious to end the war, or at least American disengagement from the war, Nixon resorted to very heavy B-52 bombing of Hanoi—partly to demonstrate to the South Vietnamese government that despite its concerns about the Northern troops that would remain in the South the United States continued to support it and would maintain a hard line with Hanoi, partly to show the North Vietnamese the kind of heavy punishment they could expect if they did not sign a cease-fire and end the war. In late January 1973, this American disengagement became possible as the war was formally concluded, although this was only a prelude to a continuing political military struggle among the Vietnamese themselves for control of South Vietnam. But for the administration the disengagement allowed it to concentrate more of its attention on its two large Communist adversaries.

DÉTENTES WITH CHINA AND RUSSIA

When the Nixon administration had come into office in January 1969, Communist China was still outside of the bilateral relationship. The Chinese Communists were still adamantly opposed to resuming relations with the United States while the latter defended the Nationalist regime, rival to legitimate power over China, on Formosa, Chinese territory. But the new president recognized the changing circumstances and considered it vital to bring mainland China into the diplomatic constellation. Calling the regime by its chosen name, the People's Republic of China, ending regular patrolling of the Formosa Straits by the Seventh Fleet, lifting trade and visitation restrictions against China, Nixon opened the way for a visit to China. This visit served in part to symbolize to the American public and Congress, long hostile to dealing with Peking, the dramatic shift of American policy and in part to begin clearing away mutual misperceptions and defining the real nature of some of the more outstanding issues and problems impeding improved Sino-American relations.

Thus, to talk of *détente* and to refer to it as if it encompassed only American–Soviet relations is a mistake. There were two *détentes*, one with China and one with Russia. Indeed, it may be argued that the *détente* with China was the greater one because of the high degree of hostility that had existed between the two countries since 1950; at least with Russia, the earlier period of high tension, confrontation, and recurring crises, particularly since the Cuban missile crisis, had been supplemented and mitigated by an increasing degree of cooperation in the area of arms control. In any event, it is probably correct to argue that *détente* with China was a prerequisite to *détente* with Russia. At the very least, it would increase the Soviet Union's incentive for *détente* with America, for it would serve to bring pressure to bear upon Moscow to be more conciliatory on such prominent and substantial issues as arms control for offensive and defensive strategic missiles, *détente* in Central Europe, especially Berlin, and other key issues such as the continuing Arab–Israel hostilities to which the Kremlin had contributed by sending Soviet fighters and pilots, Soviet ground-to-air missiles with crews, and vast military supplies for the Egyptian military and military training mission.

For the United States, then, the Sino-Soviet split permitted Washington to pressure Russia if the latter proved to be diplomatically inflexible and demanding; the clearly implied message to the Soviet leadership was that Soviet obstinacy would compel Washington to align itself more closely with Peking. To the Soviets, already fearful of China, such an alignment and the encouragement it would provide China to be more hostile, as well as renewed tension on Russia's other front in Europe, had to be a nightmare. Similarly, Peking had for years complained loudly about alleged American–Soviet collusion to isolate and contain China. But as the Soviet Union began to move huge numbers of troops eastward to defend its frontier with China, and on occasion let a rumor slip about the possibility of an attack on China, Peking —apparently convinced that Nixon was pulling out of Vietnam—was interested in detaching Washington from any possible cooperation with Moscow against China. Even more important, better relations with United States would presumably restrain Russia from attacking China, especially with nuclear weapons, for the Kremlin could not be sure that Washington in such a contingency would not support Peking. In the Shanghai communiqué released at the end of Mr. Nixon's historic visit, the United States and China declared their opposition to the hegemony of any power in Asia; it was clear that the power they meant was Russia. Thus Sino-American relations began despite Formosa, to which the United States reaffirmed its defense commitment. But it also declared that it would gradually remove all its forces and installations from the island and not interfere in a "peaceful settlement" between the Communists and Nationalists of their differences, including the future of Formosa, which the administration acknowledged to be a "part of China."

The stakes of both the Communist powers in their relationship with the United States were perhaps most evident when, after his visit to Peking and just before his visit to Moscow in the spring of 1971, President Nixon ordered the mining of North Vietnam's harbors, particularly Haiphong, to stop Russian supplies of oil and tanks for the massive, successful conventional-style North Vietnamese army invasion of South Vietnam. Both Peking and Moscow formally denounced the mining; but China continued to oppose shipments of Soviet arms across its territory, and Russia neither tried to break the "blockade" nor called off the president's visit. To prevent a closer Sino-American relations was the negative incentive for Moscow to go ahead with the summit conference: to move toward *détente* with the United States was the positive incentive.

One of the most important benefits for Russia as well as the United States was to be the Strategic Arms Limitation Talks, which in the West were widely seen as the centerpiece of the *détente*. Clearly, only a relaxation of tensions could provide the diplomatic atmosphere that would enable the two nuclear giants to arrive at an arms agreement that would leave them feeling secure, sanctify the strategic "parity" between them, and avoid another intensive and costly offensive and defensive "arms race"; by the same token, a failure to arrive at an agreement, or continue the SALT dialogue, was bound to have a deteriorating effect on their overall political relationship. SALT, in brief, became a symbol of *détente*. Without it, there would have been no SALT; but without SALT *détente* could not survive.

It was the bomb that had been largely responsible for this shift away from cold war. Bipolarity had been the most dangerous of all international systems, leading to continuous confrontations and crises; the possibility of a preemptive strike was ever present in a system in which to come in second was not to come in at all. But it was the enormity of the catastrophe that would occur if nuclear warfare broke out that had placed the emphasis on deterrence, limited war, and crisis management. Increasingly, the two superpowers felt the need for a mutual antisuicide pact, which took the form of a series of arms control agreements. But their relationship was subject to two opposing sets of pressures. On the one hand, the two superpowers remained in conflict and needed to assure themselves of protection; because both were highly industrialized and capable of applying great financial resources, scientific effort, and technical skills to their security needs, their great fear of a technological breakthrough that would upset the deterrent balance was well based. On the other hand, their equally compelling fear that a continuing arms race fueled by an ever-changing technology would upset the balance and increase the possibility of nuclear war led them to attempt to negotiate a freeze of defensive and offensive weapons in SALT. Such a freeze would allow each to acquire the arms necessary for its security while at the same time preserving a stable balance that would prevent either from acquiring a first-strike capacity.

By the late 1960s and early 1970s, military technology was rapidly changing. One matter of concern was that the antiballistic missile (ABM) system the Soviets had built around Moscow—as well as the more sophisticated ABM they were presumably working on—might be so effective it could shoot down enough incoming ICBMs to ensure that the damage inflicted on their territory would be held to an "acceptable level." Were this so, the Soviets could undermine the U.S. deterrent capacity. It was this fear that stimulated U.S. development of the Multiple Independent Reentry Vehicle (the "space bus"). MIRV would carry multiple warheads that could separate in flight, change trajectory, and fly independently to assigned and dispersed targets. By sheer numbers, the next generation of strategic missiles—Minuteman III and Poseidon, with three and ten warheads on each, respectively—would thus be able to penetrate any ABM defense. For their part, the Soviets had developed their own version of MIRV—the SS-9. Unlike its American counterpart, whose warheads were relatively small and could destroy vulnerable urban targets only (thereby, however, strengthening SAC's retaliatory capacity), the Soviet SS-9 reportedly could carry one 25-megaton or three 5-megaton warheads. It was on the basis of this information that the Nixon administration concluded that the SS-9 was a first-strike weapon aimed at America's land-based missiles, endangering the Minuteman's survival. President Nixon therefore recommended development of a "thin" American ABM system that would protect enough missiles to ensure that U.S. retaliatory capacity could never be eliminated.

Technology, then, was about to upset the stability of the deterrent balance and threatened a new and very expensive defensive and offensive missile race that would, paradoxically, probably leave both superpowers less secure. The danger was twofold: one, that the United States would also develop a second generation of MIRVs that, fitted with larger and more accurate warheads, would constitute a first-strike weapon; two, that once both powers possessed first-strike MIRVs, their mutual fear of a preventive war and, especially, of a preemptive strike during a crisis would make both jittery, possibly precipitating a nuclear war. Thus, the United States and the Soviet Union had arrived at a critical moment.

In May 1972, President Nixon and Soviet Communist Party leader Brezhnev signed two arms control accords that had taken two and a half years to negotiate. The first pact, a treaty, limited each nation's ABMs to 200 launchers (later to be reduced to 100 each; although the United States was to abandon the whole system, since such small ABM forces could not prevent a catastrophic strike by either side on the other); the second, a five-year interim agreement, essentially froze the then current number of offensive missiles each side possessed. This meant 1619 ICBMs plus 740 on nuclear submarines for the Soviet Union, 1054 ICBMs for the United States plus 656 on nuclear submarines. Bombers, in which the United States had in 1972 a numerical superiority over Russia of 460 to 140, were not included in the accords. Given the American lead in MIRVing, the offensive accord meant that the larger number of Russian missile launchers was matched off against the technological superiority of American missiles. Each side had the right to make qualitative changes—to improve its weapons—within the overall quantitative agreement, thus preserving a "parity" (or, perhaps better, a "sufficiency") of strategic arms acceptable to each adversary. While no on-site inspection to check against violations was decided upon, both sides pledged themselves not to interfere with each other's reconnaissance or spy satellites, which would be the principal means to check compliance with both accords. In addition, further negotiations were to be held in order to negotiate a final overall offensive missile treaty; clearly, the nuclear warhead ratios, estimated to be 5700 for the United States to 2500 for the Soviet Union by the beginning of 1973, would change as the Soviets replaced their current missiles, including the SS-9, with even larger missiles capable of carrying more warheads.

SALT II was thus crucial in the effort to give each side a sufficiency which it felt would be safe and which decreased each one's fear that the opponent had gained a significant enough advantage that he might risk a challenge and seek to intimidate his adversary into making vital concessions. It was President Ford, after Nixon's resignation, who arrived at the guidelines for SALT II with Soviet leader Brezhnev at a Vladivostok meeting. Each power would have an equal number of strategic weapons for each side: 2400 missiles and bombers and, 1320 of these delivery systems could be MIRVed. SALT I plus Vladivostok were thus widely perceived as important steps toward trying to stabilize the arms competition by the United States and the Soviet Union, who needed to work together to avert the ultimate catastrophe that might be precipitated by their continuing rivalry and distrust. The length of these negotiations and the fact that SALT II remained uncompleted after the 1972 interim agreement had expired, that nevertheless the agreement was being kept, and that the negotiations continued, reflected these contradictory pressures of conflict and cooperation. Militarily, the two superpowers had become interdependent and that is why, fundamentally, after often difficult and frustrating negotiations in which it changed its mind on several occasions, the Carter Administration in 1979—almost seven years after SALT I—signed SALT II (although ratification of the SALT II treaty depended upon the confirmation of the Senate and this was by no means assured, especially after the issue of an armed Soviet brigade in Cuba and its removal was raised in the Senate as a possible precondition.)

This treaty did reduce strategic force levels, including land- and sea-based missiles (ICBMs and SLBMs, respectively). While not significant in numbers, this reduction of the Vladivostok ceilings from 2400 to 2250 strategic launchers by 1981 not only resulted in a reduction of 150 older ICBMs for Russia and none for the United States but set a precedent for SALT III, one of whose principal American aims has been declared to be a major cutback in strategic launchers. SALT II also allows the United States to deploy the new mobile land-based MX missile to help offset the increasing vulnerability of the land-based Minuteman force by the growing Soviet counterforce capability. (The projected 200 MX missiles will be moved around on train tracks among 4–5 bunkers). In addition, the air force can deploy its extremely accurate, long-range air-launched cruise missiles (ALCMs), about 20–28 on each plane.

Approximately 120 such planes, each counted as a MIRV (for a total of 2400 to 3360 warheads), are allowed—they can be B-52 bombers with an average of 20 ALCMs and/or Boeing 747s or DC-10s adapted for carrying an average of 28 ALCMs—because the limit on land- and sea-based MIRVs is 1200 while the overall MIRV ceiling remains at the Vladivostok 1320 figure. The United States will also be permitted to deploy its huge new and superior nuclear submarine, the Trident with 24 tubes each (as opposed to the Polaris and Poseidon with 16 tubes). While these enormously expensive submarines are being slowly built, the over 4000-mile range Trident I missile can be deployed in the Poseidon submarines; testing will continue on the over 6000-mile Trident II.

The key question, however, remains: Does SALT II help stabilize mutual deterrence and will it constrain future arms competition? The answers are bound to be ambiguous. SALT cannot be expected to undo what technology and prior political decisions have done. For example, having developed MIRV first in order to overcome possible extensive Soviet ABM deployment, the United States still went ahead with the MIRV after Moscow had agreed to the virtual elimination of the ABM. That decision came back to haunt the United States. The Soviet Union's 1400 land-based missiles would not be capable of threatening the vulnerability of our 1000 Minuteman force if each missile possessed only one warhead. The increasing American vulnerability stems from the combination of heavy Russian missile launchers with the large number of warheads they can carry. SALT can at best ameliorate this consequence and has attempted to do so by limiting the number of Soviet land-based MIRVs to 820 and the number of warheads per missile. Still, 300 huge MIRVed SS-18s and about 500 MIRVed SS-19s remain a danger to the Minuteman's survivability and the assuredness of American deterrent capability. Nor is it certain that the "arms race" will be slowed down much, if at all, for the precedent is that as this race has become less quantitative with the establishment of ceilings on strategic arms it has become more qualitative. It is in the area of the increasing sophistication of weapons—for instance, multiplying warheads and enhancing their accuracy—that the arms competition has been channelled. The United States long ago decided to forego the very heavy missile with large warheads for smaller warheads plus accuracy. American warheads, as a result, are becoming very accurate, and United States ICBMs will possess an increasing counterforce capability—which will grow when the MX missile, with 10 warheads on each, is deployed. The cruise missile too has such potential, especially if over the years it will combine its extreme accuracy with supersonic speed and multiple warheads.

Thus, while the United States and the Soviet Union have achieved parity in their deterrent forces, the threat of strategic instability is real and potentially very dangerous as each side acquires an increasing first-strike capacity and the other's deterrent capability becomes more vulnerable. Yet the theoretical instability is probably far greater than the real one. Planning an attack upon the United States deterrent would be extremely difficult because it would simultaneously have to hit the ICBMs, SLBMs, and bombers that compose the American triad. Even if all ICBMs were destroyed, they represent only about 25 percent of American strategic power. The two other elements possess an enormous retaliatory capability of their own, one that is moreover growing; and should even 100 to 200 MIRVed ICBMs survive, that retaliatory capacity is greatly enhanced. Will any leader in the Kremlin really take the chance of launching a first strike, gambling that Soviet forces can destroy a sufficient number of America's deterrent forces so that they will no longer be able to inflict overwhelming losses on Russia's population and damage to Russia's society? Will he, in Defense Secretary Brown's phrase, gamble on this "cosmic roll of the dice"?

Thus, SALT II probably did as well as could be expected under these circumstances by stabilizing the size of both superpowers' strategic forces; setting a precedent for future negotiations with small but perhaps symbolic reductions; limiting to some degree the destabilizing consequence of MIRVs by setting a sublimit of 820 on the major element of Soviet strategic forces threatening the American deterrent; and by gaining 120 "free" cruise missile-equipped aircraft under the 1320 overall missile-bomber MIRV limit (since Russia has no such long-range air-launched cruise missiles yet and remains limited to the 1200 MIRVed ICBMs and SLBMs). SALT II and the continuing SALT dialogue, the administration claimed, also remain testimony to the Soviet and American recognition of the dangers of an unrestrained arms race, that an agreement which both sides consider relatively fair and equitable can help reduce superpower tensions to some degree and provide an opportunity for further negotiations to enhance strategic stability; it also demonstrated that in the American government (and in the Soviet government?) national security planning takes into account arms control considerations. How much effect the growth of Soviet strategic power and the increasing vulnerability of the U.S. Minuteman will have on the perceptions of the Soviet–American balance in Moscow and Washington, on the confidence of the former to challenge the U.S. and the latter's willingness or hesitancy to respond to any challenge, remains to be seen and is, in any event, beyond the purview of SALT.

In 1972 and 1973 the two powers had underwritten their agreements and negotiations on arms control by setting down certain principles or standards of conduct to guide their relationship. The "structure of peace," in the American view, put a special obligation on the two nuclear giants. One principle summed it up:

> The U.S.A. and the U.S.S.R. attach major importance to preventing the development of situations capable of causing a dangerous exacerbation of their relations. Therefore, they will do their utmost to avoid military confrontations and to prevent the outbreak of nuclear war. They will always exercise restraint in their

> mutual relations, and will be prepared to negotiate and settle differences by peaceful means. Discussions and negotiations on outstanding issues will be conducted in a spirit of reciprocity, mutual accommodation and mutual benefit.
>
> Both sides recognize that efforts to obtain unilateral advantage at the expense of others, directly or indirectly, are inconsistent with these objectives.

The basis of peaceful coexistence, then, were: the necessity to avoid confrontations; the imperative of mutual restraint; and the rejection of efforts to gain unilateral advantages.

American policy-makers were willing to fortify the incentives for Soviet political and military restraint with economic help; the Soviet economy as it entered the decade of the 1970s seemed in serious trouble. The industrial growth rate had fallen off from 7 to 4.5 percent in a 10-year period. The economic decline was particularly notable in those branches of industry associated with the Second Industrial Revolution: computers, electronics, and petrochemicals. In short, in those branches most important for the growth of industry in the last part of the twentieth century the Soviet Union was falling behind the West. The implication of this could hardly be ignored in terms of Russia's appeal as a socialist state in the world in general, its power competition with the United States, and, not least, unrest within Russia at the continuing shortages of consumer goods. Even in agriculture the growth in production had fallen sharply below expectations and official plans. Workers on the land, like workers in the factory, fell quite a bit behind their American counterparts in per capita production. The problem of a superpower experiencing continued difficulties feeding itself bountifully—indeed, in some years just avoiding widespread hunger—was not just the result of weather conditions but the ideologically determined organization of an agrarian economy administered by a rigid bureaucracy.

The Soviet concern about falling behind in the scientific–technological revolution led the Kremlin to look westward for a "technological fix" to help stimulate their economy. In the absence of basic structural reforms of the highly centralized and bureaucratic system, Western technology, industrial machinery, and credit to buy them with were the only recourse; and Russia particularly desired American assistance. In return, since it had little to sell the United States, it offered to let the industrial nations develop and exploit the huge Soviet deposits of raw materials, especially in Siberia; the American capital to help finance this extraction would presumably be repaid in oil, natural gas, and other mineral resources in the future. Politically, the administration thought that this was not a bad deal. Quite apart from profits for the American businesses involved, the Soviet need for American help would provide a powerful material reinforcement for a foreign policy of restraint and accommodation made necessary by the desire to prevent closer Sino-American "collusion," achieve strategic arms agreements to stabilize mutual deterrence, and recognize Soviet parity and equal status with the United States. As Henry Kissinger put it negatively: "Economic relations cannot be separated from the political context. Clearly, we cannot be asked to reward hostile conduct with economic benefits even if in the process we deny ourselves commercially profitable opportunities."

DÉTENTE: CHANGE OR TACTIC?

The general mood of *détente* was soon to be questioned widely in the United States and other Western countries. A number of events were to occur which raised the central question whether the more moderate Soviet behavior in foreign policy was genuine or whether *détente* was more a tactical adaptation to a new international environment, but still part of an expansionist policy. Was *détente* for the Soviets merely a continuation of the cold war by other means? Did it reflect a Russian willingness to live and let live with the West on the basis of strategic parity, acceptance of the *status quo* (including the same nonintervention with regard to Western Europe that the West had practiced toward Eastern Europe, the Soviet sphere of influence) and mutual restraint? Or, having learned from experience that a hard line and fist tended to arouse and unite the West, was *détente* with its summits and smiles itself a way of relaxing the West's guard, shifting the balance, and gaining—slowly but surely—a superiority of power by lowering Western defense budgets, inducing withdrawals of American troops from Europe to weaken NATO, gaining legitimation of the *status quo* in Europe while confronting China, and acquiring Western technology and economic assistance? The great Russian writer Alexandr Solzhenitsyn, exiled from the Soviet Union for his dissidence, and the "father" of the Russian atomic bomb, Andrei Sakharov, another critic of the Soviet system, somberly warned the West that *détente* was a tactic: Soviet objectives remained expansionist, and when the Kremlin had gained new economic and military strength with Western help, it would once more confront the West, only from a position of superiority. Many Western critics of *détente* felt it was really a "selective *détente*" in which the Soviet Union reaped general benefits from the lowering of tensions while unilaterally and with impunity exploiting situations and opportunities that advanced its interests against the West and especially the United States.

The situation that first and most dramatically raised the above central question about *détente* was the Middle Eastern war of 1973. Only a few months after the second summit, which had reaffirmed the general rules of conduct between the two superpowers, Egypt and Syria attacked Israel on Yom Kippur, the highest of all Jewish religious holidays, the Day of Atonement. What shocked Washington and other Western capitals was the Soviet role immediately before and during the hostilities, even though the war may have seemed justifiable to the Arabs. Egypt was now ruled by Anwar Sadat, an Egyptian nationalist who had succeeded Nasser, an Arab nationalist or Pan-Arabist, upon his death. The country had become increasingly frustrated by Israel's continued occupation of Egyptian territory up to the east bank of the Suez Canal. This territory, captured by Israel in the Six-Day War in 1967, precipitated by Nasser, looked as if it might remain in Israeli hands for a long time since Israel had no incentives to surrender it. After the war in which it had established its independence, Israel had had to fight for survival again in 1956 and 1967. The Arab states continued to be hostile to its existence, and Nasser, the only Arab leader of stature who could have mobilized popular support throughout the Arab world for a compromise settlement recognizing Israel's right to exist, refused to play the role of peacemaker. Even after having lost the war of 1967, he refused to sit down with Israel and negotiate a settlement; Israel's victory did not therefore bring peace, only another cease-fire.

But Israel thought it was a peace of sorts. It was militarily superior and therefore not likely to be attacked. The American–Soviet *détente* also benefited Israel since the United States did not exercise any pressure on it to give up the captured Egyptian and Syrian territories. The Soviet Union, needing American technology, investments, and trade for its own ailing economy and wanting a SALT agreement, was also in no position to exert pressure upon Israel or to give active political and military support to the Arab states. Moscow, by limiting its support for North Vietnam despite the American blockade and bombing in the spring of 1972, had achieved better relations with Washington and was not about to permit Cairo to jeopardize these relations any more than it had allowed Hanoi to do so when the latter had launched its spring offensive. Indeed, having supplied North Vietnam with the arms that had helped it launch the offensive which had almost jeopardized better Soviet–American relations, Moscow made sure that the offensive arms Cairo wanted for an attack on Israel were not delivered; only Egypt's defenses were bolstered. The territorial *status quo* thus became frozen.

But Sadat was unwilling to live with this *status quo.* He was subject to domestic pressures, especially from the army and university students, to seek revenge against Israel; external pressures from the more militant Arab states, like Libya, and nonstate actors, such as the various Palestinian guerrilla movements, were also severe. Thus Sadat, an unglamorous figure succeeding the beloved and charismatic Nasser, was in danger of being overthrown; pro-Soviet Egyptian leaders were particularly anxious to replace him as Sadat first reduced and then eliminated their influence and undertook measures to attract foreign, including American, private capital to rescue Egypt's stagnant economy from Nasser's "Arab socialism." Above all, Sadat realized that if Israel was to be compelled to abandon the Arab territory captured in 1967 he had to look elsewhere than Moscow. Only the United States, Israel's friend, could help him achieve this goal; and this emphasis on the return of the 1967 territory suggested a reciprocal willingness to recognize Israel's existence. But

Israel, skeptical after its previous bitter experiences, subject to constant guerrilla attacks, continuously denounced by Arab militants, did nothing; to Israel, Sadat was merely talking, wanting the return of territory that, once returned, would only strengthen him for yet another war. The United States, too, did nothing after Sadat in 1972 threw some Soviet military advisors out, thereby trying to entice Washington to take the initiative in seeking a peace agreement.

Sadat, frustrated, his power endangered, therefore launched the Yom Kippur War, which took Israel by surprise and achieved initial success in crossing the Suez Canal and driving into the Sinai Desert. The Arab armies could not have achieved the successes without considerable Soviet arms shipments and bridging equipment. While it seems relatively clear that the Soviet Union did not wish to risk *détente* by helping to precipitate another Arab–Israeli war as it had done in 1967, it is also obvious that once informed of the Egyptian–Syrian determination to go to war it was unwilling to risk losing influence in the Arab world by opposing this move and withholding arms and advisors to train the Arab forces. Instead Moscow stepped up its delivery of arms; not only that, it supplied the most modern arms, including ground-to-air missiles and antitank missiles of great accuracy, which would inflict serious losses upon the Israeli air force and armor and greatly improve the chances of an Arab victory. When, indeed, the Egyptian and Syrian armies proved successful in the opening round of fighting, the Soviet Union began a huge airlift of war material and opposed any cease-fire calls that were not linked to a pullback by Israel to the 1967 frontiers; Moscow was proposing a settlement that the Arabs could achieve only by a major military victory, which they had not yet won. Moscow also called upon other Arab governments to join the war against Israel and approved the OPEC oil embargo against the United States. And when the United States finally began its massive airlift of military supplies (because the Soviet Union refused to match the American restraint) in the face of enormous Israeli fighter plane and tank losses, its denunciations of the United States were stepped up. There could be little question that despite the new code of conduct the Soviet Union was seeking energetically to exploit *détente* unilaterally in a favorable situation created by its client states.

Once Israel recovered from its shock and had driven the Syrians back from the Golan Heights, however, its forces concentrated on Egypt, crossed the Suez Canal to the West bank, and moved to cut off supplies to the Egyptian forces on the East bank and encircle them. At this point, the United States and Russia agreed upon a cease-fire resolution in the U.N. Security Council, the United States because it felt that no peace could be arranged if Egypt were again humiliated in war—indeed, the psychological boost derived from its initial successes had to be preserved if it were expected to make any concessions in a peace settlement—and Russia to avoid an Egyptian defeat that might compel Moscow to enter the war to rescue its client state. But the shooting continued and the Israelis drove to encircle and destroy the Egyptian army on the Eastern side of the Suez Canal. Sadat now requested the United States and the Soviet Union to use their own forces to impose their cease-fire resolution. When the United States declined to intervene with its forces and Russia threatened to do so unilaterally, the two superpowers confronted one another as American military forces were placed on a worldwide alert. Thus Moscow had supplied the arms before the outbreak of the war; had not pressured the Egyptians and Syrians to abandon their plan for war; had not informed Washington that hostilities would occur; had opposed a cease-fire which did not reward the Arabs' initiation of the war; had called upon other Arab states to join the war; had begun a huge airlift of arms to exploit the initial Arab military successes; had endorsed the oil embargo against the United States (and after the war criticized moves for its removal); and had almost confronted the United States over the cease-fire when the Arabs were losing. None of these actions were compatible with the spirit of *détente.*

Nor was Moscow more helpful in the American attempt after the war to move forward a peace that would avoid future wars with their ever greater chance of a Soviet–American military clash. The Middle East with its unstable governments, militancy, and high emotions, and its ability to suck the superpowers into its regional quarrels, increasingly resembled the Balkans at the turn of the century. The Nixon (and later Ford) administration resolved to avoid the past pattern in which the Israelis won the military victory but were unable to translate that victory into a political settlement, leaving the Arabs humiliated and resentful, more determined not to accept the right of Israel to exist and to prepare only for another round. The 1973 war had, in the American evaluation, shown a number of things: the fact that Israel could be caught by surprise; the ability of Arab armies to learn how to use modern weapons effectively; the intolerable cost in manpower losses to Israel of a war lasting longer than a few days; the grave difficulties for the Israeli economy when much of its manpower is mobilized; and the political isolation of Israel in a world in which even the Europeans (except the Dutch) were fearful of the Arab oil weapons and cowered before the people whom shortly before they had governed. All these factors spelled further trouble for Israel, whose only friend in the world was now the United States; but in the face of oil embargoes and ever higher energy costs, could Israel continue to count on American support—not for the existence of an Israel within its 1967 borders but for an Israel still holding the captured territories?

For the administration with its Jewish national security assistant who had also become secretary of state (which he had been in fact, if not in name, prior to his appointment), the urgency of attempting to reach a Middle East settlement was obvious. And the moment also seemed more favorable than at any earlier time. Sadat had declared his willingness to accept the existence of Israel and make peace with it on the basis of the 1967 frontiers. Sadat had also been able to organize Arab support for the Egyptian war effort from regimes spanning the spectrum from the ultraconservative to the revolutionary left. Of the former, Saudi Arabia, even wealthier now that oil prices had quadrupled, was the most influential. Anti-Israeli but also anti-Communist and pro-American, the Saudis bankrolled more moderate regimes like Egypt and made even militant regimes like Syria's more dependent upon Saudi money, especially for weapons. Egyptian leadership in the Arab world plus Saudi money made a potent combination, one that the Nixon administration wished to exploit. Finally, the Arab armies for the first time had shown bravery and skill and recovered some Arab self-esteem; diplomatic concessions in these circumstances might be easier. Defeat had only led to inflexibility.

Kissinger's strategy was a step-by-step approach. There were too many issues to be settled. To attempt to solve these issues at one time with all the parties present would be impossible. In a public conference to meet at Geneva, cochaired by the United States and the Soviet Union, the most extreme Arabs would set the pace; to take a moderate position would in this atmosphere seem to betray the Arab cause. The presence of the Soviet Union was likely to lend support to the militants, because it profited from continued turmoil in the area; without turmoil the Arabs would perhaps not need Russia much. And such a conference would openly bring out Israeli–American differences. A step-by-step approach would start with the "easier" issues and proceed gradually to the hardest ones. The initial task was the disengagement of the Israeli forces and the Egyptians and Syrians after the war; next would be a further Israeli withdrawal in the Sinai and then on the Golan Heights; the last two issues would be the hardest and most emotional—the establishment of a Palestinian state, a cause espoused by the terrorist Palestine Liberation Organization (PLO), with whom the Israelis would not even talk directly, and the control of the old city of Jerusalem. By successfully resolving the initial issues, a momentum would be established to help resolve the more difficult ones; and success would divide the moderates from the more militant regimes, strengthening the former and weakening the latter.

Kissinger was successful in achieving two unprecedented interim agreements, the first the disengagement of the hostile forces on the Egyptian Sinai and Syrian Golan fronts, and later a further Sinai withdrawal by the Israelis from two strategic passes and an oil well. Throughout, the Russians denounced Kissinger. Becoming cooler toward the Egyptians, to whom it was beginning to seem that the Americans could pressure the Israelis to withdraw and succeed where the Russians had failed, the Soviets increasingly threw their support behind the more militant Syrians and the PLO. As the Israeli government, constantly subject to pressures from its own right, which opposed virtually any concessions to the Arabs, became increasingly inflexible, and Egypt more isolated in the Arab world for having signed the second interim agreement, this strategy seemed to permit the Soviets to recoup their prestige and influence. Egypt by its agreement had, as the Syrians saw it, left them to face Israel all by themselves; it had agreed to let Israeli-bound cargo on non-Israeli ships pass through the reopened Suez Canal, had permitted American technicians to monitor early-warning systems between Israeli and Egyptian forces, and had given general pledges to use diplomacy, not force, in the settlement of Egyptian and, more broadly, Arab–Israeli differences. (This also presumed that further steps toward a settlement would gradually occur since a freezing of the *status quo* short of Israel's 1967 borders was bound to lead to further violence eventually.) To many Arabs, these acts were tantamount to a betrayal of the Arab cause.

Syria and the PLO were the beneficiaries of this attitude; Damascus was increasingly looked to by other Arabs as the spokesman of Arab causes, as Cairo had been during Nasser's days. While Sadat in 1976 broke his 15-year treaty of friendship with Russia and became dependent on America, Syria's Assad repaired his relations with Jordan and established his influence in Lebanon as that country disintegrated in civil war between Christians and Moslems. The former, long the wealthier and politically the more influential, sought to retain their position by suppressing the Palestinians whose presence had become sizable since Jordan's King Hussein had driven them out of his country a few years earlier; sympathetic to their fellow Arabs and their aspirations for a greater say in Lebanese affairs and a better life, the Palestinians, heavily armed, constituted a threat to the integrity of Lebanon. They tended to upset the agreement of the Christians and Lebanese Moslems for a domestic redistribution of power because the more militant left-wing Moslems felt that they could militarily defeat the Christians with the help of the PLO and win all the political power in the fiercely fought civil war which had erupted in that country. Syria, however, was opposed to a solution which would probably lead to Christian secession from Lebanon and establishment of two states, one Christian and one Moslem. It therefore sought Lebanon's survival and political integrity, first through political mediation and, when that proved unsuccessful, through military intervention. Syria did so for several reasons: to boost its prestige; to prevent creation of a Moslem neighbor with a more radical and militant leadership than Syria's own; and to avoid being dragged into a war with Israel by such a leadership at a time of the latter's choosing.

Ironically, therefore, Assad, who had sought to replace Nasser's successor as spokesman for the Arab causes and who had consequently aligned himself with the PLO, now found himself intervening in Lebanon in support of the Christians and against the left-wing Lebanese Moslem–PLO alliance. Moreover, since Moscow continued to support the latter, Syria's relations with Russia became strained as well, (although later, when Syria switched sides again, its relationship with Russia became more amicable once more). In addition, the PLO, fighting for its survival, improved its relationship with Sadat whom it had so recently vituperously denounced as a traitor to the Arab cause. Sadat, in turn, sponsored the PLO to full membership of the Arab

League, even though the PLO, unlike its other members, was not a state. Thus, Middle Eastern politics with its intra-Arab conflicts and jockeying for leadership, persistent Arab–Israeli differences and American–Russian competition for influence, remained a grave danger to regional peace and global stability.

A second test of *détente* came in Portugal. A year after a military revolt had ended a half-century of a rightist dictatorship in 1974, radical officers led by a pro-Communist premier seized power and made the Communist Party the dominant force in what had been a coalition government with the democratic Socialist Party and the left-of-center Popular Democrats. A general election of a constituent assembly to draft a constitution did occur, but the non-Communist parties were compelled to agree that regardless of the election outcome power would remain with the military. The election demonstrated a lack of support for the Communist Party; it could muster only 12.5 percent of the vote, whereas the Socialists received 38 percent and the Popular Democrats 26 percent for a total of 64 percent. Nevertheless, the Communists in cooperation with the radical officers seized many of the levers of power in the army, government, municipal governments, trade unions, press, and broadcasting. The Soviet Union reportedly funded and directed the Portuguese Communist Party in its bid for power.

The struggle continued, however, as Catholics, townspeople, and peasants attacked Communist offices and halted Communist activities in the northern part of the country; the Communists also lost some important trade union elections. The country in the meantime suffered from increasing unemployment and inflation and an influx of refugees from Angola (a Portuguese colony about to become independent). The Common Market refused a loan to help out except to a democratic Portugal. Gradually over a period of months, the election results began to be reflected politically as the Socialists led the popular struggle to isolate the Communists. Settlement of the unrest could come only if the cabinet reflected popular sentiment. The pro-Communist premier was dismissed, the moderate officers deposed most of their radical colleagues, and the Communists were limited to one cabinet post. But the Communists and their military supporters were not yet ready to give up and used huge antigovernment demonstrations to try to paralyze and subvert the government; radical military units refused to obey the government, openly supporting the opposition. Loyal commando troops finally went into action and resolved the issue of whether Portugal's new government would be democratically chosen or a radical dictatorship of the left. It had been touch and go.

What is remarkable about the Soviet role in this affair is its open support of a small minority's efforts to seize power in a country that was a NATO member. The whole point of the earlier cold war had been to draw lines or "frontiers" between the Western and Communist spheres of influence, which were to be off-limits to the other side. As perceived in the West, the basis of *détente's* peaceful coexistence was the mutual acceptance of this arrangement. This had already been American policy during the cold war. The United States had not interfered in Eastern Europe in 1953, 1956, or 1968. And the Soviet Union had certainly left no doubt that it expected the West to continue keeping its hands off this area. Yet Moscow, espousing *détente* and seeking to benefit from it, again saw an opportunity to extract a unilateral advantage in a key strategic area close to the mouth of the Mediterranean. For Moscow, *détente* again seemed to be a selective affair as it intervened in the domestic affairs of an American ally in a manner that it would not have stood for had the United States similarly interfered in Poland, Hungary, or Czechoslovakia.

The third example of selective *détente* came in Angola, as that African country became independent from Portugal. As the Portuguese withdrew, rival factions divided primarily by tribal and regional loyalties competed for power, and civil war erupted. Again, the Soviets intervened, this time with a sizable air- and sea-lift of jet fighters, mortars, rockets, armored cars, ground-to-air missiles, along with military advisors and a Cuban military force of over 12,000 men, in support of a movement for the "national liberation" of Angola sympathetic to Moscow. Russia, which by late 1975 already held military facilities on Somalia on the northeastern coast of Africa, a strategic area for operations covering the entrances to the Persian Gulf (that is, Western oil supplies) and the Indian Ocean, as well as Guinea on the west coast, was thus seeking influence in a country with a 1000-mile-long coastline; this would enhance the ability of the Russian navy and air force to operate effectively in the South Atlantic area should the Russians seek and be granted air and naval facilities. Angola, as well as neighboring states like Zaïre and Zambia, were also believed to be rich in oil and mineral resources. Additionally, Angola was where black Africa divided from "white supremacy" Africa, Rhodesia and South Africa, whose racial troubles were explosive and exploitable, particularly now that Portuguese colonialism no longer protected these racist states from black liberation movements. Another plus was that Russia, as the self-proclaimed supporter of "national liberation" movements and competitor with China for the title of the world's most revolutionary country, was presented by the Angolan situation with an opportunity to establish its credibility throughout the underdeveloped world. Undoubtedly, Russia was also seeking to increase the identification of the United States with South Africa, which sent some troops into Angola, and thus discredit its superpower rival in much of Africa while keeping its own credentials flying high. Indeed, it appeared as if Russia were in a sure-win diplomatic situation in Southern Africa. Concern that Russia and Cuba would also actively support African guerrilla forces in Rhodesia, led the Ford administration to a more active diplomacy to explore whether it was possible to peacefully achieve black majority rule and white minority protection in Rhodesia, as well as independence for South African-controlled South-West Africa, or Namibia, before intense racial violence and possible superpower intervention would erupt.

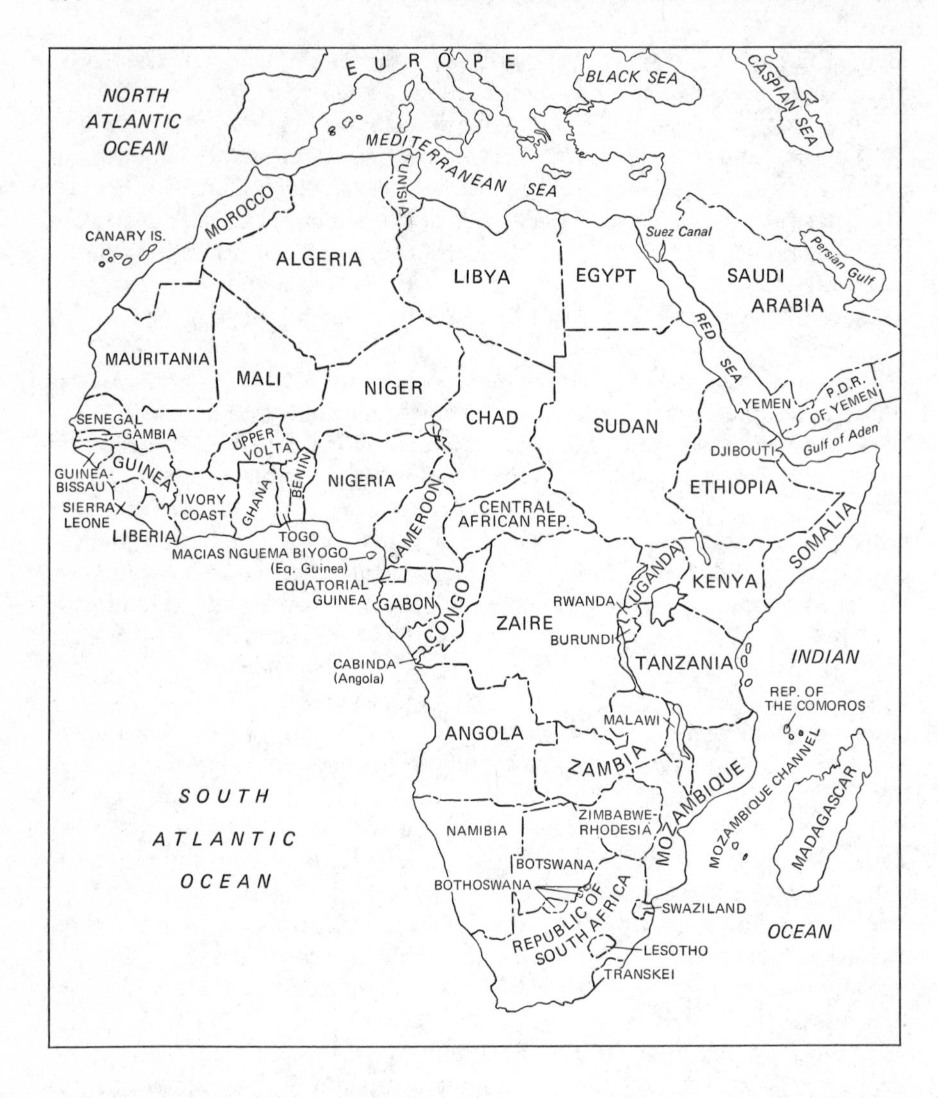

In any event, Soviet intervention in an African civil war for the first time since the Congo 15 years earlier hardly constituted "national liberation," since that had occurred when Portuguese colonialism had ended. To the Ford administration, the Soviet attempt to impose one of the three contending factions for power in Angola on that country smacked of "Soviet colonialism." The result was to reintroduce a measure of Great Power rivalry and possible confrontation into southern Africa. While rejecting any military reaction, Washington denounced the Kremlin's and Havana's acts but limited itself to covert arms aid, purportedly to strengthen the two rival factions, make it impossible for the Soviet-backed movement to win, and compel a negotiated settlement in which power would be shared. But this effort not only did not match that of Russia but further was cut off by the Senate, fearful of another Vietnam in an area that did not constitute a vital American interest. Rejecting the contention that Angola might become another Vietnam, Ford and Kissinger did agree that Angola as such was not a significant American interest. They emphasized, however, that Soviet behavior could not for this reason be ignored. Angola might be far away but, in their view, it was a test case of the superpower relationship. Soviet actions were simply incompatible with *détente;* it was another case of selective *détente,* of the Kremlin's seeking unilateral advantage from the general relaxation of tensions. The secretary of state asserted that America could not be indifferent to Russia's attempt so far from home and so distant from traditional Russian interests to impose a government favorable to Soviet interests. The Soviet response was to defend its behavior by asserting that support of national liberation movements, including armed intervention, was not incompatible with *détente. Détente* did not mean the end of the anti-imperialist struggle. "What's mine is mine, what's yours is negotiable," President Kennedy had once said in summing up the essence of Soviet foreign policy. Had things really changed, *détente* notwithstanding?

This question continued to haunt the Carter administration. The president stated early on that he thought past administrations had been haunted by an "inordinate fear" of Communism. But it was not long before his advisors were divided on whether they should not be concerned over Moscow's continuing activities in Africa. More specifically, her opportunities came as Somalia, the Soviet Union's closest African ally, a country in which it reportedly had a large naval base at Berbera and which it had well supplied with arms, supported a Western Somali Liberation Front in the Ogaden region of Ethiopia (Somali troops were fighters alongside the Front). Somalia had long claimed that this area populated by people of Somali origin was part of Somalia. Ethiopia, already facing disintegration as it confronted other rebellions and secessionist attempts, especially the attempt by Eritrea to establish itself as an independent state, rejected the claim. As other African and Third World nations, she recognized the borders existing at the time of independence—that is, borders drawn by the colonial powers—as her legal national boundaries. Because Ethiopia is about ten times as large as Somalia with its population of just over 3 million, the Soviet Union supported Ethiopia with an estimated $1 billion of military supplies, 1000 advisors, and 20,000 Cuban advisors and troops to squash the Ogaden rebellion. She was willing to risk alienating Somalia and lose her naval base on the Gulf of Aden, built at great expense, as well as some air facilities facing the Indian Ocean, because the stakes were great in Ethiopia, greater than in Angola.

There was an irony in a Soviet-supported Marxist regime attacking another Soviet-supported Marxist regime, which the Ethiopian government had become after the overthrow of Emperor Haile Selassie; as relations with Washington worsened, Moscow saw its opportunity to enhance its influence in the strategic Horn of Africa, the eastern tip of the African continent. Across the Gulf of Aden lay Saudi Arabia. Washington's fear was that the Soviet Union might gain control of the southern entrance to the Red Sea which led to the Suez Canal as well as Israel; and that she would in addition pose a threat to the important oil routes from the Persian Gulf to the West.

The Carter administration's reaction was ambiguous. The president's national security assistant, Zbigniew Brzezinski, like his predecessor Henry Kissinger, tended to see the Soviet–Cuban intervention to help crush the Ogaden rebellion and long-time Eritrean secessionist effort in the context of American–Soviet competition. So did the Defense Department, which wanted to send military aid to Somalia to displace Soviet influence. They argued that American inaction, as in the failure to respond in Angola, would be viewed by Moscow and Havana as a sign of weakness and loss of nerve, thereby encouraging further Soviet–Cuban efforts and discouraging resistance by pro-Western states who felt left in a lurch. Among the states urging American help for Somalia, a Moslem country, were Saudi Arabia, the Sudan, and Egypt, all worried by the expansion of Soviet influence and the need to protect the oil routes through the Suez Canal or around the Cape of Good Hope. Secretary of State Vance, and U.N. Ambassador Andrew Young, the State Department's African desk, however, tended to see the problem as essentially an indigenous one in which American intervention could only be counterproductive and lead to deeper involvement which would be costly and tarnish America's reputation. In a continent where national boundaries, drawn by the colonial rulers, lacked geographic and ethnic logic and where virtually every state had its tribes with separatist hopes, the United States—which, in the early 1960s had supported the U.N. effort to prevent Katanga (now Shaba Province) from splitting away from the Congo (now Zaïre)—could hardly intervene to help Somalia without alienating most African states. Short of Cuban and Ethiopian troops crossing over into Somalia after recapturing the Ogaden, there was little this country could do. The situation, as it existed, simply favored Moscow. Moreover, the Ethiopian government had specifically asked for its help, as numerous governments in the past had asked for America's help. In the long run, it was contended, Russian efforts to establish a foothold in this situation would fail due to the strength of African nationalism, even in Marxist-oriented countries.

The Administration swayed between these two positions. The president on occasions would denounce Moscow and its Cuban proxies and refer to linkages (for example, the chances for Senate ratification of SALT II if these African adventures continued). After alleged Cuban involvement with old Katanganese rebels who had once more invaded Shaba from Angola in 1978, Carter ordered the air force to help airlift Belgian and French troops to the area. (The year before, the United States had not assisted French and Moroccan troops when they intervened to counter the earlier invasion of Shaba by the self-styled Congolese National Liberation Front). But the basic administration position remained that African problems were indigeneous and that the American response should be to resolve these problems on their merits and particularly by encouraging other African states to help in their solution. In short, Soviet–Cuban efforts could best be discouraged by removing the opportunities for intervention.

It was for this reason that the Carter administration became deeply involved in southern Africa, where it was feared that if the guerrilla wars in South-West Africa (Namibia) and Rhodesia (Zimbabwe) could not be ended by political settlements, the Soviets and Cubans might not only provide arms and training for the guerrillas but send Soviet advisors and Cuban troops to help. The West would then be helpless since it could not afford to align itself with white racist regimes. The United States therefore sought to promote Namibia's independence from South Africa, which had governed the former German colony which had become a League of Nations mandate after World War I, and bring about a cease-fire and majority rule under U.N.-supervised elections. Rhodesia was, however, the more critical situation. Its leader was Ian Smith, who had broken away from the British Commonwealth to maintain the rule of 300,000 whites over almost 7 million blacks. After years of resisting any change, Smith was compelled by the increasing cost and drain on manpower imposed on Rhodesia by the black nationalist guerrilla war, as well as economic sanctions, to shift his position. Proclaiming his willingness to accept "majority rule," Smith said free elections would be held before the end of 1978 (later postponed to 1979); even before that date, as a token of his intent, he formed a transitional government which included several moderate black leaders, including Bishop Muzorewa, who were believed to have popular appeal. Had this government moved quickly to abolish racial discrimination, it might have been able to end the war. For Smith hoped that the "internal settlement" would accomplish this goal by attracting black support at home and isolating the guerrillas in their bases in neighboring Mozambique. Presumably, such a settlement would also draw foreign—especially American and British—approval and lead to a lifting of the economic sanctions.

But the government moved too slowly and did little in ending discrimination. The result was to step up the war as the externally-based Patriotic Front rejected the internal settlement as a fraud, asserting that it was a clever device to preserve white privilege and power. Virtually all black African states backed the Patriotic Front led by Joshua Nkomo and the more militant Marxist-oriented Robert Mugabe. In these circumstances, the Carter administration argued against its domestic critics (especially in the Senate), Anglo-American support for the internal settlement and lifting of economic sanctions would be disastrous and end the attempts to arrange for talks between all Rhodesian leaders, including the guerrillas. It also would mean that a new Zimbabwe state would be beholden to Russia and Cuba (since Rhodesia, without the South African army's help, could not long have avoided defeat). The hopelessness of the situation was signified by an emigration rate of over 1000 whites per month, deserted farms in the border areas, and the fact that no road could be travelled, day or night, without a weapon. But American policy was placed in a quandary after the election which was won by Bishop Muzorewa. On the one hand, its representativeness was placed in doubt by the Patriotic Front's abstention and the large number of guaranteed seats for the tiny white minority in the Parliament and Cabinet. The new name of the country, Zimbabwe-Rhodesia, and Ian Smith's retention in the Cabinet appeared symbolic of the whites' continuing disproportionate voice in policy, if not indeed veto power. To many observers, including the Carter administration, the main difference seemed to be that a black prime minister now served as a front for this white domination since the new government included not only white ministers but would be run by an essentially white dominated civil service, army, police, and judiciary. Thus the war was likely to continue, but increasingly it threatened to become a war not of blacks versus whites but a civil war among blacks themselves. On the other hand, the United States Senate by a sizable vote called on the president to lift the economic sanctions and in effect support the new moderate government instead of the more radical guerrillas. The new conservative British government appeared to be moving in the same direction.

In brief, American policy remained driven, after all, by fear of expanding Soviet influence. It may be, as the post-Vietnam critics of American foreign policy assert, that the globalist outlook which interprets and understands all problems as moves in a superpower competition may lead the United States to overlook the significance and reality of local events and produce mistaken policy which hurt American interests (as the critics claimed happened in Vietnam) because the United States automatically backs the anti-Communist side, however unworthy or ineffective it may be. The result is that the United States ends up on the losing side and at great cost, materially and politically. It may be that a wise American foreign policy would not indulge in such spontaneous reactions and involvements and seek to resolve local problems through indigenous forces; that it would first look at the origins of conflict —ethnic, racial, regional, or nationalist—and seek to solve these problems on their merits. Nevertheless, America's new leaders found it hard to ignore the East–West dimensions of the struggles going on in Africa and, while foregoing simple opposition to the Russian–Cuban combination, sought energetically, even if at times hesitantly and with divided counsel, to resolve the problems creating the opportunities for external intervention.

But was this enough? Had not the Carter administration, in criticizing Kissinger for reacting to African problems in terms of East–West competition, perhaps neglected this aspect of local problems too much and perhaps done too little to prevent the establishment of Soviet influence on the Horn of Africa, just across from the Arabian peninsula with its oil wealth on which the West depended so utterly? This question lingered over the administration's African policy in 1978 as a coup in Afghanistan brought to power a

Marxist regime friendly to Moscow, while Afghanistan's neighbor to the east, Iran, which bordered on radical pro-Soviet Iraq to its west, the Arabian peninsula to its south, and Russia to its north, unexpectedly broke out in a popular revolt in late 1978. As traditional Moslem priests led their flock in protest against the Shah's rapid modernization and the accompanying Westernization (which was destroying the traditional religiously-oriented society, as well as eroding their own status and influence), they combined with more secular left-wing forces protesting the Shah's despotic rule and pro-Western policy. Indeed, the Shah was widely perceived by Iranians as a tool of the United States, doing America's bidding. And so he fell and his "foreign" regime was replaced by a more orthodox, xenophobic, and theocratic Islamic republic. This new regime, among its first acts, cut off the oil on which Israel had so long depended and ended diplomatic relations with Egypt after the Israeli–Egyptian peace treaty was signed. The American idea of devolving some of the responsibilities for guarding the Persian Gulf upon a militarily strong and stable monarchical regime thus ended as the Shah took his "vacation" abroad. The collapse of the Shah may well turn out to be a major disaster for the United States and the West. For not only did the reduction of Iranian oil tighten world oil supplies and lead to ever greater and quicker than expected rises in oil prices, thus making it even more difficult to control the world-wide inflation, but it left the impression throughout the world of a collapsing American position and loss of influence in an area absolutely vital for the political and economic survival and prosperity of the non-Communist industrial world. Perhaps symbolic was Pakistan's withdrawal, following Iran's, from the admittedly largely inactive and always rather useless Central Treaty Organization, leaving as members only Britain, Turkey (increasingly feeling alienated from NATO because of the earlier American embargo on military supplies) and the United States, which had been an associate member.

Less symbolic and far more significant was the increased sense of insecurity felt by Saudi Arabia and the other oil sheikdoms as the entire Persian Gulf appeared endangered. Moscow had admittedly not created the troubles in Iran, although she had unhesitatingly exploited the domestic turmoil with anti-American broadcasts, threats of intervention, and may have been involved in supporting the demands of pro-Soviet radical groups seeking greater influence in Iran. But the spread of Soviet influence from Ethiopia across the entrance to the Red Sea—which leads to the Suez Canal—to Southern Yemen (or People's Democratic Republic of Yemen) on the southeastern Arabian peninsula, plus the disintegrating Western position in the Persian Gulf area to the northwest of the Arabian peninsula, demonstrated rather dramatically and depressingly that indigenous problems were difficult to separate from the American–Soviet competition for influence, and that the competition in this key area was every bit as "deadly"—if not, perhaps, more so—than the dangerous nuclear rivalry. After Vietnam, the idea of falling dominoes had been discounted, largely as the figment of previous policy-makers' anti-Communist paranoia; but the events in "the arc of instability" from Afghanistan to the Horn of Africa were a sharp and painful reminder that even if one domino did not automatically and inevitably lead to the loss of a whole row of dominoes, events were related and influenced one another. This was true if only because they were related in the perceptions of a watching world which saw them as gains for one superpower (Russia) and losses for the other (the United States). America's power and resolve in helping its friends and stemming the spread of Soviet and other unfriendly influences came to be widely questioned.

It was primarily for this reason that as Southern Yemen, reportedly strengthened by Soviet and Cuban military advisors, proceeded in early 1979 to attack Yemen (sometimes also called North Yemen) after months of apparent gun-smuggling of Soviet-made weapons to unruly Northern tribesmen, that the United States ordered a carrier task force into the Arabian Sea to both warn the Soviets of the risks involved in supporting the incursion and to impress Yemen's neighbor, Saudi Arabia, of America's concern and determination to defend her. The show of force, plus the military supplies sent to Yemen, were intended to stop the spreading of doubts throughout the Gulf area of the credibility and firmness of American commitments. Thus, after avoiding involvement in the war between Somalia and Ethiopia and cancelling a show of force on behalf of the ill-fated Shah, Washington felt compelled to respond to prevent the further erosion of confidence in the United States by the remaining moderate regimes. But reassurance of Saudi Arabia proved difficult. Worried by the unopposed Soviet efforts to dominate the Horn, and the lack of American support for the Shah as his domestic influence eroded, and upset by Camp David and the Israeli–Egyptian peace treaty in which the Saudis believed that Egypt had given up most of her demands and received little in return—and that this was due to too little United States pressure on Israel—the pro-American and staunchly anti-Communist Saudis suddenly seemed bent on keeping their distance from the United States, the wisdom and forcefulness of whose policies they questioned. In addition to perhaps impressing Washington with a new awareness of the interaction between the superpower rivalry and regional conflicts, the cumulative events in this area were also bound to enhance American cynicism about *détente* and perhaps bring a reassessment as well of the popular post-Vietnam phrase, so often uttered by members of the Carter administration, of "the limits of American power."

ALLIED RELATIONSHIPS

While Americans debated what *détente* meant and what its consequences were for the United States, in an atmosphere more skeptical and cynical than in the early and more euphoric days of 1972, America's relations with many of its allies deteriorated. In the days when all members of the alliance had perceived the Soviet threat as high and threatened them all, the individual members had subordinated their national interests to the collective interests of the alliance; the United States had even promoted Europe's integration for political reasons, although an economically thriving European economy would entail some economic losses for American business and agriculture. In the era of *détente*, however, the various nations were no longer as willing to give priority to alliance interests; Washington, for example, now negotiated directly with the Kremlin on key issues, as relations with Moscow became more important than with NATO members. In these circumstances, economic issues proved to be divisive. Whereas in the immediate postwar era economic policies such as the Marshall Plan had been consistent with and supported American political–military policy, economic relations were now at odds with the other strands of policy. The enlarged Common Market emerging in the 1970s was an increasingly strong economic competitor. European policies hurt in several ways: the barriers against American farm exports and the extension of preferential tariffs by the Common Market to associated members (mainly developing European states like Greece, until it became a full member in 1979, and former colonies). The United States balance of trade suffered. This in turn led to pressures to reduce the dollar drain by withdrawing a sizable portion of the 310,000 American forces in Europe, of which the critical contingent was the 190,000-man army on the central front in Germany.

This pressure, consistent with the post-Vietnam American mood of retrenchment, also raised a more basic question about whether Western Europe, 250 million people strong with its very large industry and military tradition, had the will to defend itself. Twenty-five years after World War II it was still dependent upon America with a somewhat smaller population against a country of approximately the same population—in turn in conflict with a neighbor of 800 million people. Too long defended by the United States, had Europe become too used to being defended? It had the resources; did it lack the resolve? Even after the devaluation of the dollar, as the trade balances improved, this question remained unanswered.

The administration tried to bring some coherence back to NATO in 1973; the year of the American disengagement in Vietnam, as well as the year of the Common Market's enlargement, was also to be "the Year of Europe." Kissinger called for a "new Atlantic Charter" which would subordinate the diplomatic, military, and economic stresses dividing the alliance to its larger collective purpose of defending Western democratic values. Without an overriding sense of direction, Kissinger asserted, the economic rivalry would be carried on without restraint and would tear all the other strands of the alliance. The response to Kissinger's call for a reaffirmation of unity, however, showed how disunited NATO had become. In what was ironically the first success of the Common Market countries in arriving at a common foreign policy position, the Europeans reacted by stressing their "distinctive entity," urged cooperation on an equal basis, and refused even to adopt such American-suggested words as "interdependence" and "partnership" in a proposed joint declaration on American–Common Market relations.

The alliance was to receive one more major blow in 1973. The Yom Kippur War and its aftermath brought the alliance almost to the breaking point. The Europeans, almost totally dependent upon Arab oil for their well-being, were reluctant to antagonize the Arabs and bring an oil embargo upon themselves. Thus, although the Syrians and Egyptians initiated the hostilities, there was little backing for the United States in its support of Israel. Only then still right-wing Portugal permitted America to land its aircraft on its soil (the Azores islands) for refueling during the American airlift. Other NATO members, including Greece and Turkey, would not even grant fly-over rights and made initial supply operations to Israel from American military stocks in Europe, for example on Israeli ships, difficult. Washington, deeply angered, castigated its allies, and the Europeans responded by complaining about the lack of consultation, especially about the worldwide American alert for a possible confrontation with Russia without even warning them. The subsequent quadrupling of oil prices, which confronted all Western industrial societies with economic crisis, strained the alliance even further initially. The year NATO was supposed to talk about improving the allied marriage ended on the brink of divorce.

Europe did confront a new internal problem in the middle 1970s: the possibility that a Western Communist party might receive sufficient votes in an election that it would have to be included in a coalition government. This likelihood seemed greatest in Italy and France. Opinion was deeply divided on the consequences. On the one hand, the Italian and French Communist party leaders declared that they would carry out their countries' obligations to the Common Market and NATO and be faithful to the democratic traditions of social and political pluralism, ideological diversity, and individual freedoms of their societies. They declared their independence from Moscow; they were seeking their own countries' "road to socialism," consistent with their nations' histories.

On the other hand, there were those who were more doubtful. Declaring national autonomy before achieving power was one thing, but once the Communist parties shared power would they really place their own countries' national interests first rather than act as Soviet agents, as so often in the past? How could parties that had always been organized on a Leninist authoritarian basis be committed to the preservation of democracy? Furthermore, if Communist parties did participate in governments of large Western states, would they not stress domestic tasks and deemphasize security commitments and even push for the abolition of NATO and the Warsaw Pact, plus the withdrawal of American forces from the continent? Indeed, if Communists came to power in countries like France and Italy, would not the United States itself pull back its forces since it could no longer justify their presence, or the alliance, to preserve democracy from Communism, which would then be less an external threat than an internal one?

While in Italy and France such coalition governments have not yet come to power as the parties lost some influence in the late 1970s, the external threats did grow and bring back a degree of unity to NATO as each member pledged to increase annual defense spending to strengthen the alliance militarily. For during the 1970s, the Soviets not only augmented their manpower in Eastern Europe but modernized their ground forces with new tanks, and armored personnel carriers and artillery, and updated their air force with new fighters. It was widely feared that the Soviet forces were acquiring the capability to attack from a "cold start" and then drive to the English Channel at a rapid pace. NATO had long depended on receiving plenty of warning time of a Soviet/Warsaw Pact attack in order to mobilize its own forces and hold the attack; if Soviet forces could now lauch an attack without warning signals to alert NATO, the chances of their successfully and rapidly overwhelming the Western armies would be greatly improved. The resulting sense of Western vulnerability did help to alert NATO's political and military leaders to the growing Soviet threat. The question remained whether Western publics shared this concern.

While trans-Atlantic relations were sometimes in doubt, the European Economic Community seemed to be changing its character. With the admission of Greece in 1979 and the prospective admission of Spain and Portugal, the Common Market grew to 10 and would eventually have a membership of 12 countries. But the newer members were all underdeveloped in contrast to the more highly industrialized states who constituted the Market's nucleus. This was likely not only to place a strain on the Community's resources and institutions as, among other things, questions of distribution of these resources had to be settled, but also on the original key issue of achieving political unity. The Common Market was always to be more than a profitable economic organization; its central aim had been the formation of a united Europe. The more members, however, the harder this goal would be to achieve; it would have been difficult enough with the original "Inner Six." Thus, the reason for admitting yet three more states, all of whom could at best be called only semi-industrialized, suggests a new rationale for the Community: the defense of democracy. After the fascist regimes in Portugal or Spain and right-wing colonels in Greece, the Common Market countries see it as their task to help lay the foundation for democratic societies on the "fringes" of the Western European countries whose future was, after all, closely tied to all three of these nations. While the United States through NATO remained the principal provider of Europe security, therefore, the Europeans were apparently going to give more of their attention to the enlargement and stabilization of democracy, to whose defense the Europeans and Americans had long ago committed themselves.

While the future of the European Community and its defense remained somewhat cloudy, some of its past history seemed at least to have been settled. Beginning with West Germany's socialist Chancellor Brandt's efforts, something like a European peace treaty for Germany had been achieved. Brandt negotiated two treaties, one with Poland, the other with Russia, recognizing explicitly Poland's Oder–Neisse border (which included German territory seized by Poland at the end of war to compensate Poland for the Polish territory Russia took), as well as acknowledging Germany's continued division and the existence of East Germany. He also established diplomatic relations with Czechoslovakia, nullifying the 1938 Munich Treaty under which Hitler had annexed the Sudetenland. The American–British–French–Soviet-negotiated Berlin Settlement of 1971, ensuring unimpeded access to West Berlin, was the last link in this overall settlement. The settlement accepted Moscow's demand for the recognition of the territorial *status quo*, in return for which Moscow was willing to make some concessions on Western access to West Berlin. This substitute peace was capped off symbolically with the 1975 Helsinki Conference attended by thirty-five states. The boundaries and the armistice lines which had hardened into boundaries between East and West, and had been accepted as *de facto* by the cold war adversaries, were now blessed with a *de jure* seal, even though Helsinki was not accompanied by any mutual force reductions on either side of the former Iron Curtain or any other Soviet concessions. (It was therefore heavily criticized by many in the United States for its one-sidedness.)

Greek–Turkish–American relations, however, disrupted NATO's southern flank because of a highly emotional and politically explosive situation on the island of Cyprus, an independent state, whose population was both Greek and Turkish. When the colonels then ruling Greece attempted to make the slogan "unity with Greece" into a reality by using the Cypriot National Guard, composed of Greeks and controlled by Athens, to overthrow Archbishop Makarios, who had preserved a fragile peace on the island for a number of years, Turkey became concerned for the Turkish minority on the island and invaded the island for the latter's protection from the Greeks. In the ensuing fighting, Turkey was victorious and the colonels, facing the possibility of a Greek–Turkish War, fell to be replaced by a democratic civilian government. But both Greece and Turkey were also upset with the United States. The Greeks were angry because Washington had not restrained Ankara from invading the island or, after the Turks had protected the Turkish minority, from expanding their territorial control still further and displacing large numbers of Greeks. The Turks were mad because Washington had not used its influence with the military junta in Athens to head off the coup attempt or condemn it after it occurred and, because in retaliation against the extensive Turkish military push into the Greek areas of the island, Congress —strongly pushed by the Greek-American lobby—cut off all military assistance to Ankara (which was not restored until 1978). Turkey was now demanding about half the island for the less than 20 percent Turkish minority; and it refused to budge diplomatically. The southeastern flank of NATO was weakened as Greeks and Turks became embittered toward each other and the United States.

While this tension among three supposed allies was going on, SEATO collapsed completely. Actually, in 1975 it formally dissolved itself after earlier in the year when South Vietnam had unexpectedly disintegrated and the North Vietnamese had finally won power in the South. The collapse of Indochina began with another of the many military clashes between North and South Vietnamese troops, which had occurred since January 1973. All expectations were that Hanoi would, as in 1968 and 1972, make its big push for victory in 1976 during the American presidential campaign. But a rather routine fight turned into a rout as President Thieu of South Vietnam, allegedly short of military equipment and quickly depleting his stockpiles as a result of congressional cutbacks of funds for South Vietnam, sought to withdraw troops from the northern part of South Vietnam and concentrate them in the more populated areas. This withdrawal, improperly prepared and hurriedly attempted by an undisciplined and not highly motivated army, spread panic among the civilians, who clogged the highways in their attempts to flee from the advancing Communist army. Hanoi, undoubtedly as surprised as Washington at the sudden collapse of Saigon's army, quickly sent its troops southward to help keep up with the retreating South Vietnamese. Saigon's fall in these circumstances was merely a matter of time. Thieu had made his decision to pull back in mid-March; Saigon fell April 30. The many leaders of the Saigon governments, who had inherited France's colonial legacy, had been too concerned with their own power, and had relied too much on American assistance and forces instead of developing a social strategy to mobilize the morale and support of its population, now reaped their reward.

The war was finally over. The collapse of an ostensible ally in whom the United States had invested so much in energy and resources could not but fail to affect the politics of the area. Despite a show of force to recoup its perceived loss of prestige when the Cambodians seized the American merchantman, *Mayaguez*, leading to the recovery of the ship and its crew, there was no way to halt the erosion of American influence in Southeast Asia. Shortly after its victory, Hanoi announced plans for the early unification of Vietnam; Cambodian Communist troops also won in that country, and the Laotian Communists gained power politically shortly thereafter in their country. (In late 1978, the Cambodian government, a cruel, inhuman regime which reportedly had killed millions of its own people and provoked Hanoi, was overthrown by the Vietnamese as Hanoi extended its control over Indochina.) Thailand and the Philippines established diplomatic relations with China. Formerly anti-Communist Malaysia had preceded them. Everywhere in East Asia the result of what was seen as an American defeat in Vietnam was anxiety and nervousness. South Korea was highly agitated as North

Korea clearly wished to exploit the American humiliation by invading the South, but China and Russia reportedly discouraged such a plan. Japan too was apprehensive. The United States tried to reassure all these countries of its steadfastness, especially Japan (a reassurance which was later weakened by President Carter's announcement that American ground forces would be withdrawn from the Korean peninsula. Tokyo considered South Korea's security integrally related to its own.)

It was in these circumstances that SEATO did the only thing it could do—bury itself. No one wept at the funeral. It had been an alliance that, unlike NATO, lacked the principal indigenous nations as its members; and it was organized against a threat that the countries of the area did not recognize. Its principal members were Western and white, two of whom had been colonial powers in the area, and the two Asian countries that joined did so for other than anti-Communist motives, the Philippines because of its traditional friendship with the United States and Pakistan to obtain American arms against India. At best, SEATO provided the United States with the justification for unilateral intervention, but the treaty forming the alliance had hardly proved itself to be what Secretary Dulles had once called it, the Monroe Doctrine for Asia. It had been another exercise in overstatement, so characteristic of the rhetoric of crusadism; unfortunately, it had also led the country into a disastrous war.

DÉTENTE: AN EVALUATION

How can *détente* be evaluated? Did the United States benefit by it, or was it advantageous primarily for the Soviet Union? Was *détente* primarily a tactic or was it a symptom of a more moderate Soviet Union in international politics? The critics of *détente* have argued that it was essentially a continuation of the cold war by other means, that the Soviet Union remained an expansionist power but that it had realized that the payoff from smiling was greater than from shaking the fist. *Détente* was thus a tactical change seeking to put the West off its guard and exploiting the resulting relaxation of tensions in order to attain a position of superior power—hegemony, as the Chinese called it. Once achieved, this would lead again to more direct, crude pressures and a renewal of the cold war, only this time the Soviet Union would be the stronger power.

How accurate is this assessment? In part, any evaluation reflects expectations. In the context of America's national style, it is not too surprising that views of *détente* swung from euphoria in 1972 to disillusionment by late 1973–1974. The national mood tended to think in terms of opposites: isolationism or intervention; peace or war; diplomacy or force; harmony or strife; optimism that the United States can reform the world or cynicism about an evil world which resisted reform and in the process corrupted the country—

a course which suggested withdrawal from the world as a solution. Thus, *détente* was widely believed to be the opposite of cold war. The Nixon administration's initial public overselling of *détente,* and slogans like "Negotiation, not confrontation" reinforced the expectation that the cold war was over and that the two superpowers had put their conflicts and crises and the danger of war behind them. Overselling and raising public expectations too high is bound to lead to disillusionment and cynicism when the record does not live up to the original expectations. Each administration tends to package its foreign policy in slogans which emphasize how its policy differs from that of its predecessors; and, anticipating the next election, it wants to make that policy look appealing and successful. The Nixon administration was no exception to this rule. Thus, despite the high degree of continuity of actual policy from Truman to Eisenhower to Kennedy to Nixon, the United States has rhetorically indulged in containment, liberation, frontiersmanship, and *détente.*

Détente as a state of existence which combined both conflict and cooperation was harder, however, to explain and understand than the cold war had been. Both sets of political relationships were a mixture of confrontation and negotiation. The difference between *détente* and cold war is the mixture of the two. In the former there is more negotiation; in the latter, confrontation. As Coral Bell has remarked, the symbol of *détente* has become the summit conference. After 1945, there was no summit meeting until 1955 and it was not until 1961 that the second one was held. The 1955 summit achieved nothing substantively, only the "Spirit of Geneva," which was supposed to usher in a new Great Power friendship, but in fact proved to be the prelude to the Soviet–Egyptian arms deal which helped precipitate the 1956 Suez War. The later Vienna meeting was held because Kennedy wanted to warn Khrushchev that he should not confuse the president's restraint for weakness and cowardice; the Soviet leader, therefore, decided to test Kennedy in Berlin and Cuba. By contrast, *détente* was characterized by frequent summits and diplomatic negotiations at the foreign ministers' and lower levels. But this did not mean that *détente* was the same thing as *entente,* or friendship and harmony, with which it so often appeared to be confused. *Détente,* it was often pointed out, meant a relaxation of international tensions; it did not mean an absence of tension.

Basically, for the United States *détente* was containment for an age of superpower parity and Sino-Soviet schism. The cold war stick was to be supplemented by the carrots of *détente* and issues were to be linked, explicitly or otherwise. Soviet Russia was to be constrained from foreign adventures with force, or the threat of force, plus the withholding of agreements she desired; but hopefully, Moscow, enticed especially by Western economic goods, technology, and credits, would restrain herself to avoid the loss of such benefits, as well as other agreements such as SALT. In other words, Moscow would be given the incentives to practice self-containment! But in reality, the

American–Soviet relationship remains one of cooperation and competition, of agreements and adversary clashes, of common interests and continuing conflicts of interests and values.

A more accurate description is adversary–partnership, in which the mix of these two elements will vary with time and circumstances. In 1972, the Soviets wanted Western, especially American, trade, technology, and credits, a slow-down of the American–Chinese rapprochement, a strategic arms agreement, plus millions of tons of American wheat to help feed their population. But in 1973, the harvest was good, SALT I had been signed but there had been little progress toward SALT II, the Senate had not yet decided what terms of trade and credit to offer Russia and, perhaps most importantly, President Nixon's authority was rapidly eroding as the Watergate scandals unraveled. Whereas in 1972 Moscow withheld the offensive arms Sadat wanted and, as a result, suffered the humiliation of having its advisors thrown out of Egypt, 1973 turned out to be a year the Soviet Union did not need the U.S. for food and was still waiting for the economic pay-off of *détente.* Russia may also have been unsure whether it should still sign any arms agreements with Nixon and felt that he might be unable to react to any challenges; therefore, Egypt received not only the arms with which to launch its war against Israel but the Kremlin's hearty political endorsement.

An additional problem involved in an evaluation of *détente* and the exaggerated expectations it raised may well be the capacity of the American political system to carry out a policy of confrontation and cooperation which relies upon a changing and shrewd balance of sanctions and incentives (sticks and carrots), and—whether explicitly intended or simply the unintended consequence of policy—seeks to link some issues in order to discourage the adversary's belief that he can receive the benefits of cooperation in many areas while at the same time also profiting from the unilateral exploitation of opportunities. *Détente* is not a set of self-denying ordinances. If the Soviet Union is faced with unexpected but favorable situations to exploit, should it shun this opportunity? Self-denial as a policy is asking a lot of any Great Power. The United States itself did not forego opportunities of exploiting the Sino-Soviet schism and, after 1973, of Sadat's westward turn to enhance American influence and reduce Soviet influence in the Middle East.

The question was, therefore, whether in circumstances where an administration believed American interests to be at stake, it will take or is able to take what it deems to be the necessary counteraction. What are the sanctions which are available and applicable? If arms control agreements are in the interest of the United States, should it sacrifice these? If its allies trade with the Soviet Union, how can the United States pressure Moscow by withholding American technology? Or, if the Senate attaches a provision about Jewish emigration to a commercial agreement which is unacceptable to the Soviets; or cuts off funds for arms being sent to the anti-Communist factions in Angola; or the president refuses to use wheat as leverage because he is unwilling to alienate the vote of farmers who prefer cool cash to cold war—

that is, if the carrot or stick is unavailable, whatever the reason, what incentive is there for Moscow to restrain itself when it sees advantages to exploit in the competitive superpower relationship? By contrast, in the Middle East in 1973, the United States was willing to act and compel the Soviets to desist and behave responsibly.

What, then, in this context is the balance sheet for *détente?* One short-term result was to allow the United States to disengage from Vietnam. The American intervention occurred at a time policy-makers still saw the world in terms of the American–Soviet struggle, just as their predecessors in the 1950s. The American forces were withdrawn in a period of *détente.* During the bipolar cold war era, a gain for Communism (Russia and China were viewed as a monolith) was seen as a loss for the United States and the Free World; such a gain had to be prevented. In the postbipolar *détente* period, the vested interests the United States and the Soviet Union had in their relationship meant that Vietnam could be divorced from the central American–Soviet balance. Even the final collapse of South Vietnam in 1975 was accepted without any of the kind of rationales about the expanding power of Moscow and/or Peking which had accompanied the intervention.

Among the longer-term benefits of *détente* is the reduction of the ideological zeal which had marked the cold war and raised so many issues to conflicts of good and evil. Differences were now viewed as differences of interests which were resolvable through negotiations, not a clash of moral absolutes to be inflexibly defended lest one compromise with—and be tainted by—evil. Indeed, one early criticism in the United States of *détente* was that Nixon and Kissinger were too chummy and comfortable with Brezhnev; another was that they were compromising too much and getting too little in return! Both of these criticisms were a far cry from the days when even the slightest signs of an administration's desire to negotiate with the Russians and Chinese were subject to accusations of treachery, sell-outs and "coddling Communism." Soviet and Chinese proposals were then generally rejected out of hand as mere propaganda or tricks to deceive; they were rarely examined for merit or seen as a reflection of legitimate interests. Thus, little negotiation occurred.

Another benefit of *détente* has been the attempts to stabilize deterrence—or at least reduce the degree of instability, the result of prior political decisions and technological innovations—halt the quantitative build-up, and introduce some controls on the qualitative improvements of offensive strategic forces and virtually eliminate the defensive forces. Dangers clearly remain. The strategic force levels remain very high; the far greater "payload" that the bigger Russian missiles can carry means that they may end up with a considerably larger number of warheads which, if accurate, may give the Soviets a first-strike capability and weaken U.S. deterrence. Future negotiations about reductions in numbers of weapons are scheduled for SALT III.

The SALT negotiations remain widely perceived as a barometer of *détente.* Inability to agree reflects not just the difficulties of negotiating an accord but that *détente* itself may be in trouble. Agreements are an indicator, on the other hand, that *détente* is, on the whole, healthy. Quite apart from their substantive content, SALT agreements have gained symbolic value, a token of the parties' commitment to peace and search for coexistence at a lower level of hostility and risk (and, perhaps, financial cost). Yet even the agreements reached have been controversial in the United States because limits on some weapons may be bypassed by replacements or because of qualitative improvements of existing weapons systems which have not been forbidden. Thus, the SALT I offensive interim agreement was attacked because the Soviets were allowed a larger number of missiles, and SALT II was criticized as destabilizing despite the numerical equality of both delivery systems and MIRVs. SALT, in short, remains a symptom of both superpower cooperation and common interest in avoiding suicide, as well as superpower competition and distrust and desire to gain unilateral advantage. In this continuing adversary-partnership, strategic arms control agreements may thus at one and the same time promote *détente* or help undermine it. SALT can cut either way.

A further achievement which *détente* produced was what might be called a German peace settlement. The four-power Berlin settlement, West Germany's treaties with Poland and Russia, the treaty between the two Germanies plus their admission to the United Nations, all capped by the 1975 Helsinki Conference, legitimated the *status quo* that had existed since 1945. Two world wars in this century had broken out in Europe. It was the German issue that had precipitated these conflicts, and it was the same issue that had contributed to the eruption and intensification of the cold war. While the Russians and East Germans could some day reopen the issue of Western access to West Berlin, if Moscow should feel that a favorable shift of power to it had occurred, or America's will and determination to play a great power role had become questionable, the German question seemed largely resolved.

A last benefit of *détente* has been the normalization of relations with the People's Republic of China. President Nixon's trip to Peking in 1972 symbolized a dramatic change in Sino-American relations and, once and for all, ended the irrationality of a situation in which the United States for almost a quarter-century seemed to ignore the existence of the world's most populated country, a nation with great potential power, a significant stake in Asia's future, and an ideological rival of the Soviet Union. And just as Washington, during the 1950s, had feared the Sino-Soviet coalition, and Peking, during the 1960s, had frequently pointed to an alleged Russian–American collusion in an attempt to isolate China, so Moscow now became apprehensive of closer Sino-American relations since, among other things, it gave the United States a persuasive lever—if skillfully used—in its negotiations with the Kremlin. The American shift of policy from Taiwan to Peking was long overdue; domestic politics had too long blocked a rational adjustment and exploitation of the Sino-Soviet conflict, a conflict whose tensions may rise or lower from time to time but one which is likely to continue despite changes of leaders in both countries for their quarrels reflect differences of interest more profound than merely differences of personalities, as the death of Mao in 1976 has amply demonstrated.

Indeed, even as the succession struggle in China continued and President Ford was replaced by President Carter in the United States, progress toward full normalization proceeded. On January 1, 1979, the People's Republic of China and the United States exchanged diplomatic recognition and ambassadors with one another. This was followed almost immediately by an official visit to Washington by China's apparent strong man, Deputy-Premier Teng Hsiao-Ping. The timing of this last step toward normalization had come from Peking which, on the one hand, confronted large modern Soviet forces along its long 4500-mile northern frontier with increasingly obsolete weapons and, on the other hand, had chosen to modernize China and look to the West for economic and technological assistance in everything from building hotel chains and steel mills to oil exploration of China's enormous estimated oil reserves. For the United States, the final shift from Taiwan to Peking meant ending diplomatic recognition of Nationalist China and the mutual security pact, as well as the final withdrawal of the remaining American military personnel. In return, Peking—whose official position is that Taiwan is part of China and that the resolution of the Taiwan problem is a domestic matter—appears to have accepted the reiterated American position that this problem be resolved peacefully and—very significantly—that the United States can continue to supply the Nationalists with military weapons to defend themselves against a possible Communist invasion.

The likelihood of this was not great anyway. For one thing, Peking lacked the air and naval capacity to cross 100 miles of water to launch such an invasion. More important, however, Peking, having turned primarily to the United States and Japan to help it modernize, would hardly risk taking an action which would alienate both of these countries—the United States, which it also needed to balance Russian power, and Japan, which if frightened by such a show of force, might well react with a large-scale rearmament program, including nuclear weapons. That an invasion of Taiwan would be politically counterproductive was further underlined by the fact that Tokyo (which had recognized Peking earlier than Washington) maintained very close and profitable commercial relations with Taiwan; and the United States expected to do the same. In the final analysis, of course, there was nothing to prevent the United States, after it had long insisted on a peaceful resolution of Communist–Nationalist differences, from resorting to force and defending Taiwan should Peking some day change its mind and violate the understanding about the peaceful resolution of this problem.

Thus, having declared in early 1950 that it would no longer intervene in China's civil war, only to do so when the Korean War broke out, the United States had almost 30 years later reverted to its earlier position and taken the final step it had not taken in early 1950: official recognition of the new regime ruling China's mainland. Yet, in reality, it remained tied to Taiwan, even if informally. That Peking was willing to tolerate this situation demonstrated its fears of the Soviet Union and determination to modernize China, including China's armed forces. While the United States had no immediate intention to sell arms to Peking in order not to provoke Moscow, it was willing to let its European allies sell China the arms it was interested, in such as jet fighters and antiaircraft and antitank missiles.

Like SALT, the new China connection could cut both ways. Clearly, the hostility between the two largest Communist states was preferable to a united Sino-Soviet bloc. A strong China, dividing Russia's attention and military power between East and West, could not but benefit NATO. Washington therefore had a vested interest in supporting the new post-Mao Chinese leadership which opposed Moscow and looked Westward, including Japan, and in hoping that this leadership would consolidate its position. Fundamentally, the United States was taking advantage of its adversaries' dilemma and resorting to the time-honored tactic of "divide and rule." Indeed, whereas historically the United States has always had to choose between China and Japan—when it was friendly to China before World War II, Japan became the adversary and, when during the cold war Nationalist China collapsed, the U.S. became an ally of Japan and enemy of the new China—the possibility of closer Washington–Peking–Tokyo cooperation appeared increasingly great since the latter two had already normalized their relationship and signed a friendship treaty aimed against Russian "hegemony." The danger was that the United States would align itself too closely with China. This would be regarded as unfriendly and provocative by Moscow; that, of course, would be true for Peking if, in seeking to improve its relationship of *détente* with the U.S.S.R., Washington pulled too close to the Kremlin.

One dramatic example of this dilemma occurred shortly after the United States had officially recognized the People's Republic of China and its Deputy Prime Minister had toured America vehemently denouncing Moscow. Peking, concerned with what it saw as increasing Russian–Vietnamese collaboration to her south—which it interpreted to be part of a growing Soviet influence and attempt to encircle China—struck at Vietnam. Angered by Vietnam's expulsion of almost 200,000 ethnic Chinese, border conflicts between the two countries, and especially by Hanoi's signing of a friendship treaty with the Russians in late 1977, followed by its invasion of China's friend, Cambodia, and overthrow of its cruel and provocative regime, China decided to punish Vietnam and "teach her a lesson" by an invasion limited to the border areas and by inflicting heavy casualties on her. Not to do so would show up China as a weak, fearful nation. The resulting border war demonstrated once again that a common ideology was not enough to prevent conflict and war between those sharing the same faith and that nationalism was as divisive a force within the Communist world as in the rest of the world. The danger for the United States was the possibility of a Soviet military reaction. An attempt "to teach China a lesson" could affect American interests if it were more than a limited incursion into China and could draw the United States more deeply into the Sino-Soviet quarrel. Moscow already considered Washington's normalization of its relationship with Peking as collusion and tacit support of China's military action, even though Carter explicitly opposed this invasion of Vietnam, as it had Hanoi's earlier invasion of Cambodia. Thus, the possible advantages of "playing the China card" against Moscow was matched by the dangers of China's "playing its American card"; and the possibility of Moscow's someday "playing its China card" against America could not be completely excluded.

A negative result of *détente,* on the other hand, was the erosion of NATO. But the bonds of this alliance had been weakening even before *détente* set in. *Détente* only weakened them further and posed the central question of how an alliance, forged in a period of danger when all the partners perceived the security threat as paramount, can survive a relaxation of tension when the danger has seemingly passed and other issues—often divisive ones, especially of an economic nature—appear more important. The way to unite NATO once more would be to regenerate a perceived common threat. In the absence of a return to the cold war, however, the large-scale build-up of Soviet forces in Eastern Europe, suggesting that these forces could launch a surprise attack without prior mobilization and then quickly overwhelm NATO forces, was the best substitute and provided a unifying element for NATO. The Carter administration's focus on NATO and its attempts to mobilize its allies to make a major effort to match Soviet efforts suggests that this is occurring, at least to some degree.

FOREIGN POLICY WITHOUT A CONSENSUS

Perhaps the major problem to emerge from *détente* was that U.S. policy continued to be conducted without domestic consensus. In the absence of external threat and consensus, America has historically been an isolationist country; when it felt provoked, the country had been easily mobilized and united for its foreign policy crusade. As the cold war anti-Communist consensus had disintegrated in Vietnam and the country had tired of its "global policemanship," the Kissinger abandonment of the missionary style and the moralistic justification for foreign policy seemed very much in order. His emphasis on states and their legitimate interests, instead of moral causes and the division of the world into saints and devils, assumed a clear-cut distinction between a nation's foreign and domestic policies. The United States had an obligation to itself to defend its interests and, in doing so against another great power, it could use a range of diplomatic, military, and economic tools; it could seek to restrain an adversary with carrots or sticks or a mixture of both. But it should abandon ideological goals since they spill over into crusades and hinder the diplomatic process by which states seek to work out the terms of coexistence by making the recognition of, or compromise with, allegedly immoral states virtually impossible. To make changes in the adversary's domestic structure and ideals a part of the negotiating process and perhaps a prerequisite for other agreements is bound to be unproductive—indeed, counterproductive, since it may well harden the opponent's positions and raise tensions. A Soviet leader, Kissinger contended, may well make some concessions in private diplomacy (as Brezhnev did when he arranged with Kissinger to allow a large number of Soviet Jews to emigrate) but to try and compel a Kremlin leader to change the ways he governs the Soviet Union, a sovereign nation, will expose him to accusations of "coddling capitalism" and selling out "socialist interests" and may even endanger his tenure.

Yet, in asking for the abandonment of America's traditional national style which had allowed the country to play its foreign policy roles in the past, what was Kissinger substituting? The answer was basically the balance of power, hardly a very exciting idea which would arouse Congress and the mass public. It was therefore hard to sustain support for a policy which involved elements of conflict and cooperation with Russia, and sought to use tactics which offered carrots and sticks in an ever-changing mix as conditions changed. Personal charisma and diplomatic successes gained public attention and support (for SALT, the opening to China, and the attempts to move the Middle East toward peace) and minimized the criticisms. But the increasing public disillusionment with *détente,* the Watergate scandal, Kissinger's own reported involvements with wiretaps, the succession of an unelected president (and vice-president) with the overall effect of weakening the authority of the presidency, eroded support for *détente* and led to increasing attacks on him. "Superkraut," as he had once been known, had been shot down and American foreign policy continued to operate without a consensus.

Carter sought one in America's self-proclaimed historical role as the defender of democracy and individual liberty. "Human rights" became the platform on which he expected to be able to mobilize popular support; the liberal tradition, which Kissinger was accused of having abandoned, had been reunited with American foreign policy. The nation, it was now proclaimed, once more stood for something, having reclaimed its democratic heritage. Jimmy Carter, the born-again Christian, had become the redeemer of the American tradition. But the policy ran into trouble almost immediately abroad. The Soviets, as Kissinger had predicted, did not care for Mr. Carter's emphasis on human rights which they felt was specifically directed against them. Moreover, they interpreted political opposition, freedom of assembly, and free speech as an attack upon the foundation of their system; a system which claims that it is based upon an exclusive knowledge of Truth is bound to regard those who disagree with it as "counterrevolutionary." Thus the president's human rights emphasis and his support for Russian dissidents—symbolized by his letter to Andrei Sakharov, a leading dissident—was viewed in Moscow as a fundamental attempt to undermine the Soviet system. Predictably, it led to a stiffening of Soviet diplomacy on SALT, a postponement of a final agreement from a time when its approval by the Senate might have been relatively easy, an initial sizable reduction of Jewish emigration from the days when Kissinger handled this problem privately, not publicly, with the Kremlin, and a greater crack-down on dissidents.

Similarly, when the president announced the withdrawal of all U.S. ground forces from South Korea, a move presumably heavily influenced by its government's poor human rights record, Japan—the U.S.'s main ally in Asia—felt a greatly enhanced sense of insecurity since the American army was the principal deterrent to another possible North Korean attack. In addition, the withdrawal, if it is carried out, would hardly help improve South Korea's respect for human rights since that government, feeling increasingly abandoned by its protector, would probably be even more concerned with censorship and arresting its critics as its sense of insecurity rose. Thus, on both grounds of American security and the human rights of individuals living under despotic regimes, the wisdom of the Carter administration's strong emphasis on human rights could be questioned.

Another result of the human rights emphasis was to stress America's double standard of judgment, if not its hypocrisy. One of the early goals of the administration was to normalize relations with Cuba and Vietnam (shortly after the collapse of South Vietnam in 1975, the northern hand behind the origins of the Vietnam war was clearly shown when North and South Vietnam became unified under Hanoi's control). How could that be consistent with "human rights"? Or, how could the president square his human rights stand with normalizing American relations with the most important of Communist countries after Russia, China, whose government was one of the most totalitarian governments in the world?

Even with non-Communist regimes, human rights came to stand in the way of other objectives. One of the key Carter goals was to stop the further proliferation of nuclear weapons. Brazil, for example, seeking to cut oil imports and find other sources of energy, was buying a complete nuclear fuel cycle from West Germany. This would give Brazil, which also had great power aspirations, the capability with which it could acquire nuclear weapons since these could be built from enriched uranium, which was also used to fuel the nuclear reactor, or the plutonium which could be reprocessed from the waste materials. American policy vigorously opposed the sale of the entire fuel cycle. But instead of seeking to influence the Brazilian–West German deal, the Carter administration condemned the Brazilian government for its human rights violations and further strained American–Brazilian relations.

Finally, when in order to gain results as in the SALT negotiations the president toned down his human rights declarations, he cast doubts on the credibility of his commitment to human rights and his control of the policy process. The same doubt about Carter's sincerity was also raised by his support for the Shah of Iran until his demise in 1979. The president publicly praised the man who, while ruling with an iron fist, supplied both the West and Israel with oil and who, the U.S. hoped, would also help stabilize the

Persian Gulf area. No official word was heard about the Shah's human rights violations. And despite his earlier criticism, the president later visited South Korea. Clearly, in all these instances the problem for the administration was one of deciding priorities; failure to decide whether to give priority to human rights or security where these values clashed meant that the pursuit of both enhanced neither.

The dilemma of Kissinger and Carter appeared to be how to combine an effective foreign policy with a domestic consensus. Not only does that dilemma remain, but it raises a more fundamental set of questions: Is a consensus still possible? If possible, is it desirable? And if desirable, is it relevant? The answers to all three questions are probably "no". It would appear that there is probably no single ideological theme around which the country would currently rally in a great burst of enthusiasm. Quite the contrary: an attempt to even formulate one would more likely divide the country with controversy rather than unite it in a consensus. It would also seem that even if such a consensus could be formed, it could be undesirable. In the past, when the country had a consensus which mobilized its energies, it engaged in crusades to totally defeat its enemies; and once its mission had been accomplished, it swung back into isolationism. Like a drug addict, the nation swung from its crusading "highs" to an isolationist "low." These kind of oscillations are hardly desirable in a world which demands a steady, continuous policy. And lastly, the world has become too complex to be managed with ideological slogans. In the security area, how can anti-Communism be invoked when the U.S. is seeking to use China against Russia; or democratic slogans be used when some of America's allies and friends are not democratic? And how can the new economic issues of trade and investment be resolved by moral zeal? In a world in which the United States faces not only Russia but also China, a tangle of indigenous problems in the Middle East and Africa (including the effects of racial problems it had neither created nor could do very much about), and resource problems in the Third World, the issues have become too numerous and too complex to be understood and managed in terms of one or two simple unifying themes. Except in a major war or intense cold war, the days of conducting a foreign policy with a consensus may be over.

Thus, in this more diverse world where the simple foe–friend dichotomy was no longer as applicable as in the earlier era of containment; where the many political, economic, especially energy, racial, and other problems were issues where the United States interests were in conflict not only with its principal adversary but with friends and allies too; and where its own policies were often necessarily contradictory (for example, support of Israel and desire for Arab oil), the conduct of American foreign policy was likely to be more difficult, more subject to domestic controversy and criticism, and the leadership potential of American presidents and United States policy options more constrained.

chapter **11**

conflict with the third world

WITH OPEC TO INTERDEPENDENCE?

A major failing of *détente* was that by concentrating American attention on the Soviet Union and Communist China it led to the neglect of the Third World. The focus was on the nation's adversaries. As relations with Moscow and Peking improved and Washington began increasingly to talk to each of them directly about key problems, even America's European allies felt increasingly neglected. In the context of American–Soviet *détente*, as already noted, the NATO alliance became secondary in contrast to the cold war days when the Soviet threat was perceived as high and the alliance was of primary importance. *Détente* with Russia and China and ending the Vietnam war preoccupied the Nixon administration during its first term; the "Year of Europe" in 1973 was soon swamped by the Yom Kippur War and the subsequent oil crisis, and the growing Watergate scandal which forced Nixon to resign in disgrace in 1974. Thus, it is not surprising that the Third World—with the exception of those areas where Soviet–American competition was perceived as occurring—suffered from "benign neglect." The underdeveloped countries had benefited from the cold war; bipolarity had enhanced their leverage. Basically weak, lacking the basic components of power, they exploited the international distribution of power to acquire influence. Confronted by two powers competing for their allegiance and loyalty, the Third World countries could first lean Eastward, thus attracting Western economic/military aid and political support, and then Westward, thereby attracting similar assistance from the East. The increasing replacement of bipolar competition by the newer adversary partnership meant that their bargaining capacity declined. Nonalignment became acceptable to the United States in these circumstances.

Thus, the change in the structure of the international system was the fundamental reason for the decreased American attention and aid to the Third World. Attitudes from past aid reinforced "donor's fatigue." It had become clear after two decades that the optimistic expectations of "instant development" had underestimated the difficulties and complexities of modernization. Aid seemed never ending. Additionally, aid had not even been particularly successful in winning friends and gaining influence. In the absence of traditional means of control, the friendship of aided countries was unreliable and frequently fluctuating. American aid, as a consequence of all these changes, had not only been reduced to its lowest point—less than half of 1 percent of the gross national product, as already mentioned—but the emphasis had shifted from capital development to technical assistance.

The view that the passing of bipolarity had reduced the underdeveloped countries to a status of only marginal significance exploded during 1973: first in the Egyptian–Syrian–Israeli war stemming from the superpower *détente* which had frozen the post-1967 territorial *status quo,* precipitating Sadat's military action to call attention to his situation and the danger of procrastination; and second, OPEC's dramatic fourfold increase in oil prices. The oil companies, which, according to the imperialist interpretation, were supposed to be such powerful multinational corporations that they dominated the economies and countries in which they operated, were shown to be rather powerless and at the mercy of the governments of the territories under whose soil they operated. And the so-called imperialist states, whose governments are presumably controlled and directed by the capitalists, did not mobilize their military forces to squash the governments that were allegedly their puppet regimes. Confronting a vital threat to their security and well-being from countries that had no military power to speak of, the industrial democracies did not even debate the issue of military intervention. Had this event occurred a few decades earlier, they would not have hesitated to resort to force rather than face the possibility of being destroyed economically. In 1973 they talked of accommodation and acquiesced in this change in the rules of the game, at least in oil and temporarily.

For that was what the OPEC price change was: a change in the rules of the game. The underdeveloped countries had, as they saw it, for years been trying to lift themselves up by their own sandalstraps, but the problems they had faced in their attempts to modernize themselves were for many of them formidable. The hopes and expectations of the 1950s and early 1960s had turned into disappointment, even despair, as much of the underdeveloped world continued to mire in backwardness. The expectation of the nations who had once been the West's colonies that they could realize their dream of a better and more rewarding life for their peoples remained unfulfilled. Poverty, illiteracy, ill-health, and overpopulation, among other things, continued to coexist with dreams of national dignity and material welfare which would provide for man's basic needs.

OPEC's action was, therefore, widely viewed in the Third World as symbolic of a general protest by the underdeveloped countries of their lot. OPEC was regarded as a kind of "vanguard of the (world's) proletariat" or poorer nations. This mood of anger, resentment, and revolt was clearly directed against the West. Perhaps ironically, the effects of the quadrupling of oil prices were felt most in those many non-Western nations who possessed neither large oil reserves nor other mineral resources. Indeed, after 1973–1974, one often talked of the resource-richer underdeveloped nations as the Third World and the resource-poorer nations as the Fourth World. The sharp increase in oil prices threatened the latter with a slowdown of any plans they had to industrialize and handicapped efforts to grow more food with technologically intensive, oil-based, agricultural techniques. But whatever their fears may have been for their futures, the underdeveloped countries stood united with OPEC. Materially and rationally, they should have aligned themselves with the First World to compel OPEC to lower its prices to a level more acceptable to them.

Yet, despite this enhanced suffering, the Fourth World countries did not form a coalition with the industrial states to lower oil prices. This is partly explainable by fear of irritating OPEC, partly by hope for promised but still largely undelivered OPEC economic help (most of it has gone to fellow Moslem nations, which have used much of it to buy arms) and partly by the desire to imitate OPEC. But the basic reason is that the Fourth World identifies emotionally with OPEC. The latter's action, even though it hurt them the worst, was widely perceived by these countries as "getting even" for past exploitation; it gave them a good feeling that for once the weak had reversed the tables and made the strong suffer. The German word *Schadenfreude* says it best: pleasure received from seeing someone who deserves it really suffer, "get his." For in this instance, material considerations, which perhaps should have moved them to align with the West against the Third World countries, were subordinated to far stronger emotional and psychological factors which aligned them with the resource-rich Third World countries against the West. The sight of the rich and privileged nations who had so long ruled them as the "lesser breeds" being humiliated and quaking before their old colonial slaves was just too delicious. While OPEC gained quick immense wealth, the rest of the Third World received an enormously satisfying "psychic income."

The Western states might point out that the causes of the continued poverty of so many of the underdeveloped countries were their own: the continued fragility of nationhood, the low priority given to agriculture and therefore their problems of feeding their populations, the all-too-obvious high birth rate which tended to defeat the most valiant efforts of economic growth, the large amounts of money spent on arms (including in the case of poverty-stricken India, a nuclear explosion), and, all too frequently, widespread inefficiency and corruption. But the non-Western states reject the argument that the responsibility for the inability of most of them to modernize is internal. They point to the external system: the nature of the international economy. In this economy they are the sources of raw material for Western industry. When Western nations' demands decline, or several non-Western suppliers compete with one another for Western markets, or Western industries find substitutes or synthetics, the prices of their resources go down, as does their capacity to earn foreign exchange with which to buy Western industrial products which have tended to rise in price. In short, their earnings decline while the cost of Western-made goods they need rises. In addition, when they do develop some industry and export to the West, they often find that Western industry and labor erect protective tariff barriers. In short, even if they work harder, it is of little help. The structure of the international economy is against them and keeps them in a subordinate position, as cheap raw material suppliers for the rich Western states. Thus, they seem condemned to continued poverty.

They are, as they see it, dependencies. They may have gained political independence, but in reality they remain economically chained to foreign—Western industrialized—economies. Their status remains neocolonial because their own economies are geared not to the needs of their own national markets but the needs of the developed countries' markets. As exporters of raw materials, they are completely dependent upon Western demand and access to Western markets; thus, they are the victims of Western economic policies, obviously made in the interests of the Western countries who are favored by the law of supply and demand. The international market is stacked against the weak and poor and favors the strong and rich nations. That is why after decades of working hard and despite foreign aid, the underdeveloped countries remain underdeveloped and continue to suffer from poverty, unemployment, malnutrition, and inequitable distributions of income within their own countries. For Western nations, their status as relatively cheap raw material suppliers is a matter of self-interest; why should the industrialized world favor their development? Their dependency status in an international economic and political order dominated by the West thus limits, as they perceive it, their ability to grow economically; their integration into this global economy has benefited the dominant Western nations with a high standard of living and left them poor.

Whatever the real mix of internal and external reasons for the continued underdeveloped nature of the Third World might be, the "revolution of rising expectations" had increasingly become the "revolution of rising frustration." That was why OPEC's action inspired so much hope. The suppliers, instead of competing against one another and keeping prices low, organized themselves into a producer-cartel to control access to the oil and its price. Perhaps OPEC had provided the example to the other underdeveloped countries of how they could raise their commodity prices and earn the funds they needed and, in effect, bring about a redistribution of wealth between the rich and poor nations. The Third World was demanding a New International Economic Order. Among the things demanded were higher and stable commodity prices to earn more; indexing these prices to Western inflation rates; more foreign aid; and preferential tariffs so that they can sell their products on Western markets. Basically, the underdeveloped countries felt they had the resources Western industry needed; without them, Western industry and society would be in serious trouble. The rich nations appeared vulnerable and the poor nations finally had seemed to gain real leverage. Increasingly, some observers like Zbigniew Brzezinski, later President Carter's national security assistant, noted the new First–Third World confrontation and asserted that it was becoming at least as important—if not more so—than the First–Second (Soviet-led) World conflict. Indeed, the Second World could sit on the sidelines and exploit the former for its benefit.

Some observers took a rather optimistic view of this First–Third World conflict of interest because they perceived it as part of a broader growing global economic interdependence. One of the critical elements of this interdependence was that the nations of the world were increasingly being tied together by many different economic strands. Nowhere was this interdependence said to be clearer than between the Western world and OPEC, especially between the United States and Saudi Arabia and, to a lesser extent, the Shah's Iran (until 1979). The drastic rise in oil prices in 1973–1974 overnight had had several results: stoked Western inflation; brought on unemployment; created a stagflation, a simultaneous inflation and recession which economists and policy-makers appeared unable to resolve; slowed down economic growth; lowered standards of living; brought about the largest redistribution of wealth in history from the West to the OPEC nations; created large Western imbalances of trade; and perhaps placed Western democracy, tolerance, and social stability in some danger as increasingly in a slowly growing economy some groups in society would enhance their standard of living at the cost of other groups, instead of all groups' being able to share in the benefits of a rapidly growing economy.

This interdependence stemmed not only from the West's need for oil but from OPEC's need for the United States, as well as Western Europe and Japan, both of whom were far more dependent on OPEC for their oil than this country. The West possessed the industry and technology to help the OPEC countries modernize; it could also supply a country such as Saudi Arabia, which felt it had a major security problem, with the most modern weapons and the men to train its forces. In addition, American aid and political support for the Saudi government was desirable because the regime was conservative and concerned with political stability. The government was staunchly anti-Communist and always worried about radical Arab regimes which leaned toward Moscow. Thus, the United States and, more broadly the West, and the modernizing nations of OPEC needed one another. They were interdependent.

Moreover, this interdependence involved the rest of the Third World too, for the effects of the OPEC oil policy was not limited to the countries immediately involved. Recession in the West reduced the demand for raw materials, which lowered their prices, which in turn produced less foreign aid and increased the prices of Western machinery and other goods. With smaller earnings of foreign exchange, their ability to import high-priced oil declined too, unless they borrowed heavily to buy the oil they needed. This threatened their capability to preserve the Green Revolution of miracle wheat, which is highly energy-dependent for fertilizer, irrigation, and transportation for the distribution of food. Thus a food crisis threatened the underdeveloped countries whose agricultural output had not kept pace with the birth rate and which, in years of natural disasters, had been helped by surplus grain reserves, largely in the United States.

One of the consequences of this interdependence was that national planning by itself could not lead to full economic recovery. For example, American attempts to cope with the stagflation depended on OPEC's oil price raises and increases of oil production. Not that domestic policy and discipline in the area of energy consumption could not help. The rapid increases in annual oil imports after 1973 meant a huge outflow of dollars. As too many dollars flooded the international market, the value of the dollar began to decline steadily. The Carter administration at first did nothing to halt this downward slide because it believed that the higher prices of imports would discourage Americans from buying them while cheaper U.S. goods would encourage exports. What happened, of course, is that as imports cost more, American manufacturers raised their prices to earn higher profits instead of undercutting the imports. Thus, domestic inflation continued, more dollars left the country to pay not just for oil but such other goods as European and Japanese cars, the dollar was devalued further, and the cycle continued as overseas money markets lost confidence in the U.S. administration's ability to control inflation. Ominously, OPEC began to talk of being paid with another and stabler currency than the dollar, whose decline in value meant a significant decline in their real earnings. Only in late 1978 did Washington seek to support the dollar; nevertheless, in early 1979 OPEC announced a price rise of almost 15 percent for the year. (The total was to be far higher in fact.) This steep increase, OPEC claimed, was made necessary by the loss of revenues due to the declining value of the dollar. Thus America's continued failure to restrain its oil consumption and the initial Carter policy of allowing the dollar to decline came back to haunt the nation, threaten the administration's belated attempts to discipline inflation and further deflate the dollar as a new cycle of stagflation loomed ominously. Thus, in the final analysis, American economic growth, employment, standards of living, and inflation were beyond strictly national control. In an interdependent world, these matters would be profoundly affected by the actions of other nations.

Why is it, then, that some observers, especially some American academics, are basically optimistic about this growing international interdependence? First, because they claim that in an ironic paradox, nuclear weapons have ensured the peace. The superpowers' strategic nuclear arms are weapons of denial and deterrence; and their existence makes the use of conventional arms less likely because of the danger of escalation. Major war among them, even among their allies and friends, is therefore not high. Attention, therefore, has turned from security to economic or welfare issues. The latter has increasingly gained saliency not only because security seems more assured but because the democratic societies of the West have become more and more preoccupied with economic growth rates, consumerism, and ever higher standards of living, while the underdeveloped countries are bent on modernizing and satisfying their own people's expectations for a better life. The key issues are thus economic and social rather than military, and involve values such as social justice and human dignity rather than violence and destruction.

Second, nations cannot fulfill their socioeconomic goals by themselves. Western societies, for example, run largely on imported oil. The non-Western countries, in their turn, seek Western technology and food. The gap between the rich and poor nations strains, if it does not poison, their relationship, and a similar gap between rich and poor in the underdeveloped states is a cause of domestic tension and political instability which has a tendency to spill over into the international arena. Nations have become interdependent, then, in the sense that they need one another probably more than in any previous period of history to solve their own problems. Whether these problems exist in the affluent West or the poorer nations with their overpopulation, widespread malnutrition, frequent threats of starvation, and often limited ability to earn a living, the response in a world of increasingly finite resources is said to require global solutions. Indeed, just as the United States and Soviet Union have been compelled to cooperate because of their nuclear interdependence on security issues, such economic problems as inflation, currency instability, and pollution cross nations' frontiers, hurting almost everyone. The division of the world between a minority of rich nations and a majority of poor nations, who also happen to contain the overwhelming majority of the global population, is fraught with danger. No nation any longer completely governs its own destiny; and no government can, by itself, meet the aspirations and needs of its people for a better life. Thus, worldwide cooperation is not just desirable but a necessity if such goals as peace, political stability, human welfare, and individual dignity are to be achieved on earth.

Nations' destinies and fortunes are consequently increasingly interdependent. Whereas on the traditional security issue, the state system model posited the separation of states and conflict among them, on these bread-and-butter or welfare issues it appears that only cooperation would enhance each nation's prosperity. Whereas in the former model one nation's increase in power and security would be seen by its adversary as a loss of power and security for itself, in the latter each country's welfare was perceived to depend on the existence of prosperity in other countries as well. Economically, they gained or lost together; one did not gain at the other's expense as on security issues. The OPEC states presumably could not drink their oil; they needed Western markets to sell their oil, prosperity in the First World to safeguard their increasing investments in the West and assure the latter's help for their modernization. The 1973 oil embargo and price hike had shown how easily and profoundly the world's economies—Western and non-Western—were disrupted and lifestyles thrown into turmoil. In an interdependent world, nations can obviously greatly hurt one another by reducing or withholding products or services others need.

Second, precisely because in an interdependent system nations are this sensitive and vulnerable to one another, the need to work out problems is likely to produce a greater willingness to resolve disputes peacefully, if not indeed to attain a higher degree of understanding and international harmony. Unlike cold war security issues, which were bilateral, the issue of oil or other resources or population or environment require multilateral negotiations. Many nations are affected—indeed, usually different nations on different issues. And, by "the logic of interdependence," they have to find collective solutions to their common problems.

Third, and very important, force and the threat of force are said to play a minimal role on these welfare issues, again in strong contrast to the primary role they play on security issues. The downgrading of the use of force in the former is largely attributable to the fact that countries with whom the United States would negotiate on these issues are allies and friends. Saudi Arabia and Iran (until 1979) were not, like the Soviet Union, America's enemies. But even if they were not friendly and the threat or use of force were used effectively once or twice, invoking it frequently could only alienate countries who are needed economically. Although many of the nations with whom the United States must deal on these prosperity issues are comparatively weak militarily, they are hardly helpless and without leverage of their own. They possess commodities which, if production were shut off (and this would surely happen if there were attempts to seize the oil fields), would hurt the consuming nations. Militarily weak states like the major oil exporting nations thus have formidable bargaining power which the traditional type of calculating power by means of adding manpower, industrial capacity, military strength, and other factors, would not reveal. Thus, the old hierarchy of states based upon military power was increasingly irrelevant and the new international order would be a genuinely more egalitarian one.

How realistic is this new model of interdependence? Have welfare issues become as important or more important than security issues? Can countries no longer achieve welfare goals on a basically national basis and, if not, will they cooperate for the common good of all mankind, not because they have suddenly become unselfish but precisely because each nation is selfish and wishes to benefit its own people? Will greater economic interdependence, to the degree it will become all nations' lot, create sufficient mutual vulnerability to act as a constraint on international conflict and provide enough incentive for greater harmony among states? More positively, will countries, out of self-interest, cooperate with one another to close the gap between rich and poor nations and work together to resolve the problems of the world's finite resources, population, food supply, environmental conditions, inflation, and economic stability, before they overwhelm all nations and produce more chaos and violence?

The future may answer these questions which are currently being debated. In practice, there can be no dispute that welfare issues have become more prominent in international politics than they were. Until 1973, the predominant issue was security and the concern was with balances of power, spheres of influence, and military power. Economic issues were subordinate, generally considered nonpolitical and technical. It is also clear that interdependence in trade, investment, and monetary affairs does exist among the Western industrial countries (which include Japan) since they trade mainly with one another and invest in each other's economies. Between the First and Second Worlds, the principal characteristic of their economic relations is independence. Even the increase in trade during the *détente* years hardly lives up to the normal meaning of the word *interdependence.* But between the First and Third Worlds the relationship has been fundamentally one of dependence. Whether that dependence can be converted into interdependence remains to be seen.

On the one hand, the West, including the United States, is importing more resources. Even the United States, which is richer in resources than its major industrial allies, is thus becoming increasingly vulnerable to external pressures. In the middle 1970s, America's population (which constitutes only 6 percent of the world's population) consumed 30 to 35 percent of the world's petroleum (up now to 45 percent and going up), 55–60 percent of its natural gas, 15 percent of its coal, 20 percent of its steel, 35 percent of its aluminum, and 30 percent of its copper. On the other hand, the bargaining power of the oil producers appears to be a special case. Oil is vital and irreplaceable; once burned, it cannot be recycled. There were also only a few countries to organize into a cartel. Even in oil, the cartel could not last—in the long run—as other sources of energy such as coal, nuclear, and the sun, supplemented oil. As non-OPEC oil also becomes increasingly available from Alaska, the North Sea, Mexico (whose supply is estimated greater than Saudi Arabian oil deposits), and someday from China's apparently equally enormous estimated offshore reserves, OPEC would be weakened.

Nonoil mineral resources, by contrast, possess less leverage: There are more readily available substitutes; industrial scraps can be recycled; conservation, stockpiling, and new sources of minerals, including under the sea beds, are available options. Furthermore, there are large numbers of raw material producing nations in most areas which would complicate the task of organizing a united front. However, the most difficult barrier to other Third World producer-cartels is the fact that the underdeveloped countries as the raw material suppliers for the industrial world is in part a myth. The Western countries produce most of the world's resources; so the cartel would have to include its adversaries. The ironic fact is that most underdeveloped countries are net importers of raw materials! Of the nonfood, nonfuel commodities, the Western industrial nations supply 60 percent, the Communist states 10 percent and the underdeveloped countries 30 percent. And most of the world's food exports, as repeated Soviet imports of wheat and the threats of starvation in certain areas of the world during the early 1970s have shown, are from the rich countries, especially the United States. Thus the bargaining capacity of most underdeveloped countries will depend on such factors as how much the First World will import, how critical these resources will be for its economic health, what substitutes are available, and whether OPEC will remain united and stand together with the rest of the Third World to use its persuasive voice for all of the ex-colonial world.

Theoretically, interdependence has also raised a number of questions. Have its proponents not overestimated the likely effects of economic issues on politics and underestimated the impact of political forces and events on economics? It is noteworthy that the model of interdependence assumes, one, that socioeconomic issues can be separated from political issues; two, that the treatment of the former takes precedence; and three, that they will help transform traditional international politics or, at least, make "power politics" less relevant. The emphasis is on cooperation among nations and their common interests, and the prime values to be sought are man's welfare and dignity. While nations clearly continue to exist, their military fangs are to be drawn and their aggressiveness subordinated to the task of building a better future for all mankind. "National interests" are to be dissolved by the greater "human interests." Interdependence, in short, is supposed to restrain national egotism and enmesh nations in the web of interdependence which will compel them to cooperate for the "good of mankind." Interdependence is unquestionably in part a description of current reality, but it is *also*—usually implicitly—a plea to move "beyond the nation-state" to a "world without frontiers" by dissolving, so to speak, power politics in welfare politics and "planetary humanism." In short, without denying the reality of existing economic problems or Third World poverty and hunger, is not the emphasis on interdependence to some degree an attempt to escape from the structure of the state system with its inherent conflicts and dangers, and a plea for mankind to cooperate despite national differences to make "spaceship earth" a truly decent and fit place for all men to live and enjoy life in freedom from oppression and want?

Indeed, what could be more characteristic of America's national style than interdependence, with one, its distinction between economics, which is thought of as good because it is identified with social harmony and man's material benefit, and politics, which is equated with conflict, destruction, and death; and two, the normative commitment to a better future for mankind, to be achieved by a rational response to the allegedly inexorable forces of economics and technology? At one time, free trade was thought to be the answer to war and a unifier of nations because commerce would benefit all of them and presumably give them a vested interest in peace; then economic development was advocated as the key. Is interdependence not just another model in search of a more peaceful and harmonious world, since the previous proposals have *not* done away with "power politics"? Moreover, is the timing of the model of interdependence not coincidental with, as well as a reaction to, Vietnam and the profound moral revulsion of some policy-makers and analysts to that war and "realism" as a way of understanding and conducting American foreign policy? There is certainly an irony of sorts to the advocacy of interdependence. Vietnam created a strong reaction to globalism which was dismissed as an overreaction of the cold war. Yet, under the guise of interdependence, globalism has been resurrected as the best way for nations to coexist and resolve not security issues but welfare or prosperity issues—population, resource depletion, energy, food, and the maldistribution of wealth.

But is interdependence really that new and different from the much-denounced power politics? Interdependence may mean mutual vulnerability but since the vulnerability is not usually symmetrical, does not the resultant asymmetric or unequal relationship give one state "power" over the other? Does this kind of leverage differ from the traditional bargaining among states? Indeed, what about the claims of interdependence? Iran used to be cited as an example: The West needed its oil, the Shah needed the West's technology, civilian and military, and political support. But since Iran's revolution and the ascendancy of an Islamic theocracy, can the Ayatollah Khomeini's assertion that Iran needs the United States less that the United States needs Iran really be disputed? Iran no longer seems bent on as rapid modernization as before, but its oil is needed even more urgently. Yet its productivity remains below the level under the Shah. It seems to have few incentives under its present regime to increase production and exports to the West, and there seems to be little the latter can do to provide either incentives or sanctions. Even the more friendly Saudi regime has made it clear that despite its allegedly mutually beneficial relationship with the United States, it will not increase its oil production to keep up with Western demand. Should analysts not perhaps be more skeptical of claims of interdependence and of exaggerating the effects of interdependence in moderating international conflict and enmity (outside of the relations among Western industrial countries)? Indeed, if on oil, for example, Western vulnerability should prove too great, might the result not be a more violent world if the United States were—despite the assertion of the advocates of interdependence to the contrary—tempted to use force to ensure sufficient oil supplies? Can such a result of interdependence be completely dismissed? And will interdependence not tempt political leaders, especially in the Third World, to avoid making difficult and unpopular decisions (for instance, on population control) which are necessary for their countries' development because they can blame the West for their lot and then leave it to the West to solve their problems? Would this facilitate or hamper more cooperative relations? In short, does interdependence not exaggerate the constraints imposed on national strife and hostility?

None of these observations mean that the demand for changes in the relationship between the First and Third Worlds will in any way diminish. The quest for the New International Economic Order, a system characterized by a major redistribution of wealth and power from the former to the latter, will remain. Since the underdeveloped nations have a public platform in the U.N. General Assembly, where they hold a majority, they can continue to articulate this aim and air their grievances against what they see as the current Western-dominated international economic order. Perhaps more important, the Western nations are increasingly sensitive to the new nations' nationalism and demands for change. In Brzezinski's phrase, America was more and more living in a hostile world where the demand for a genuine equality among states (as distinct from a formal equality) was a principal driving force. As the world's leading democracy and industrial power, could she fail to be responsive? As Samuel Huntington, who served for a time on President Carter's National Security Council staff, put it rather graphically:

> In a sense, the United States is a tenant occupying the largest, most elegant, most luxuriously furnished penthouse suite in a global cooperative apartment house. The hundred or so other tenants occupy premises of varying sizes and degrees of attractiveness. As one tenant among many, the United States does not have any direct concern with how other tenants decorate their apartments. . . . The United States does, however, have a basic interest in the structural soundness of the building as a whole. It is precisely that soundness which is in question. The condition of the building is beginning to deteriorate rapidly, and drastic action is needed to correct crumbling foundations, defective wiring, corroded plumbing, leaking roofs, not to mention overcrowding in some apartments and muggings in some stairwells. Unless these basic repairs and maintenance are undertaken, the building is liable to collapse or to go up in smoke. As the wealthiest tenant in the building, the United States has more to lose than anyone else from the deterioration of the living conditions in the building. The United States has a clear interest in insuring that the structure as a whole is sound and that minimum conditions for decent human existence prevail in the building.*

*Samuel P. Huntington, "Foreign Aid: For What and For Whom," *Foreign Policy*, (Spring 1971), pp. 130-31.

Admittedly, the merit of some of the proposals such as higher commodity prices remained debatable. Would such prices on most nonoil products not drive the consumer nations to new sources of unregulated commodities or alternative resources; and would such prices not benefit mainly the few resource-rich Third World nations plus Western raw material producers rather than the majority of the world's poor states? In any event, most Western states are committed to a free trade philosophy, and while there is some sympathy in the West for the underdeveloped countries' past because of their colonial experience and present poverty, the basic sense of community which exists within Western nations—and which has been the prerequisite for some domestic redistribution of wealth and power—does not exist globally between nations. The pressure for change will undoubtedly, however, persist.

FROM ANTI-SOVIETISM TO SYMPATHY FOR NATIONALISM AND BACK AGAIN

During the Nixon years, preoccupation with Russia and China as well as the Vietnam war meant that events in the Third World received attention primarily when they appeared to have implications for America's relations with the two large Communist powers. One example was the disintegration of Pakistan. A nation divided into West and East with 1000 miles of India lying between the two parts, Pakistan had been born in a burst of communal hatreds in which hundreds of thousands of Hindus and Muslims slaughtered each other. It confronted the issue of survival in 1971, 24 years after its birth, during a period in which India (already hated for its seizure of Kashmir) had tried on several occasions to humiliate Pakistan and destroy it as a possible military threat.

What was to be the breaking point began when Pakistan, ruled for many years by a military regime, held a free election. A majority in East Pakistan voted for autonomy, because under the West Pakistan-dominated government the Eastern half had received less than what it considered a fair share of the national wealth (such as it was) and felt itself to be treated as a colonial appendage. West Pakistan attempted to crush the movement for autonomy with great brutality. The army killed and raped at will, burning village after village; almost 10 million refugees streamed across the border into India to escape this ravaging. The result was the growth of a full-fledged armed independence movement for the establishment of a Bengal Nation, or Bangladesh.

The United States during this period did not utter a single official word of public condemnation against its SEATO partner's brutal behavior (Pakistan, which had joined the alliance to obtain arms against India, had in fact moved away from SEATO toward Communist China as American policy had grown closer to India). In part, America's silence and continued shipment of arms to

Pakistan appeared due to Pakistan's help in opening new relations between Washington and Peking; and in part this support apparently was reinforced during the sensitive period preceding President Nixon's 1972 visit to the Chinese People's Republic by China's strong diplomatic backing for Pakistan. Alone, India supplied arms to the East Pakistan liberation forces and provided sanctuaries for them, thus confronting its traditional enemy, who was greatly angered by India's help for what the Pakistani government, and China and America, considered rebels. Indeed, Pakistan's president had declared that if the rebels seized control with India's help, this would be considered an Indian attack on Pakistan and constitute a cause for war. India turned for support to the Soviet Union and received it in the form of a 20-year friendship treaty intended to deter a Pakistani attack. This move away from India's historic policy of nonalignment was also presumably intended to deter open American support for Pakistan and provide India with the confidence to move against Pakistan. While denying that the new treaty represented a departure from nonalignment, India did have a good short-term reason for wanting to go to war quite aside from the longer-range aim of once and for all eliminating Pakistan as a rival on the Indian subcontinent. This more immediate objective was to end the burden of the millions of refugees, a cost sufficiently great to slow down India's rate of economic growth. In a real sense, a war was cheaper than continuing to support the refugees. Thus, under circumstances in which both sides claimed the other shot first, war erupted. Pakistan lost its Eastern half; Bangladesh attained statehood. India's policy of dismemberment succeeded, Russia reaped the rewards of India's victory, and its influence on the subcontinent reached new heights, while the United States—and to some extent China—lost prestige with the world's biggest democracy by siding with its weaker, military-ruled rival, whose soldiers' brutality had undermined the legitimacy of its cause in the eyes of almost all the world's nations.

In Latin America, American–Soviet rivalry—despite *détente*—was even more conspicuous. American policy showed a strong continuity with a policy that had historically regarded the Southern hemisphere to be America's sphere of influence, and while Washington had gradually been accommodating itself to the increasing nationalism of its Latin neighbors, the United States remained very sensitive to what it perceived to be radical left-wing revolutions and regimes that might bring the principal adversary power, the Soviet Union, into America's so-called backyard. Thus, when in 1970 Chile elected Marxist Salvador Allende to the presidency, the Nixon administration, while publicly acting correctly, sought first to prevent Allende from becoming president and, after that failed, to make life difficult for him and encourage the military to a *coup d'état.* Thus, in a subtler way than Kennedy at the Bay of Pigs or Johnson in the Dominican Republic, the new Republican administration used the Central Intelligence Agency for the same anti-Communist reason as preceding administrations. Yet the reasons for the Chilean coup, when it came, stemmed essentially from Allende's own actions and the domestic reactions these precipitated. The CIA may have helped shorten the time until the coup occurred, but the causes of the crisis were internal; by 1973 Allende's end was merely a matter of time. Indeed, Chile provides a most persuasive example of why the United States should *not* intervene in this type of situation.

While not excusing the intervention, it is important to stress this point because Allende has become something of a martyr, frequently portrayed as the revolutionary who was fairly elected to seek reforms and better the lot of the poor and underprivileged, only to be blocked and finally overthrown by a fascist conspiracy on behalf of a reactionary ruling class in league with capitalist America. Had he in fact lived, Allende's reputation would have been stained by the failure of his political leadership; his suicide at the time of the coup elevated his reputation to a level he could never have achieved had he lived and remained as leader of Chile's "road to socialism."

Allende came to power having won 36 percent of the vote, two points ahead of his next competitor in a three-way race. In the runoff vote in the Congress, he received the support of the centrist Christian Democratic Party. At the start of his rule he possessed opposition support for much of his program, including the nationalization of the American-owned copper mines, banks, major industries, and land reform. While it thus seemed possible to work within Chile's constitutional norms with a democratic consensus, Allende believed in class struggle. He deliberately pursued a policy of polarizing Chileans, which did more to consolidate the professional middle and lower-middle classes in opposition to him than to broaden his worker-peasant base of support. As he pursued his program, his vow to constitutional rule fell by the wayside. Representing a sizable minority, but hardly "the people," he could have governed only if he had gained the majority support in the Congress which he did not possess. In a parliamentary system he would have fallen quickly; in Chile's presidential system he survived by increasingly bypassing Congress and the courts. The Christian Democrats then joined the rightist opposition, and class polarity was then matched by executive–legislative polarity. Allende had eliminated the middle ground of Chilean politics and emasculated the spirit of the constitution.

The nucleus of Allende's opposition came less from any privileged ruling class than from the lower-middle class, which was deeply affected by an inflation of over 300 percent by 1973, shortages of all kinds in the shops (leading to marches by housewives with empty saucepans), and worries that their small businesses might be wiped out by inflation or government takeovers. In 1972 and especially in 1973, small truckers, who owned one or two trucks, went on strike and were joined by shopkeepers, doctors, lawyers, engineers, bus and taxi drivers, and airline pilots (between the strikes even the workers in the largest copper mine struck). It was this, the second truckers' strike, which was reportedly prolonged by the passing of CIA money to the truckers.

The military during this period became increasingly politicized. Asked by Allende at several points to participate in his cabinet to reassure those worried about law and order in the midst of strikes, the street marches of Allende's supporters and opposition, and illegal seizures of land by the president's followers, the military initially served Allende as it had his predecessors (it even crushed one attempted revolt by some military units). What precipitated the military's intervention after 40 years of staying out of Chilean politics was the rapid growth of paramilitary forces among Allende's extreme left-wing followers, who had always believed in armed confrontation with "reaction," and the public call for an insurrection in the navy by a close Allende friend and party co-leader; both events apparently occurred with Allende's complicity. The country was on the verge of civil war when the military struck. It did not need American urging.

Not that the United States had not been hostile to Allende from the start. After the expropriation of American property without compensation, Washington cut off American credit and pressured international financial institutions to follow suit. But Allende more than made up his American losses with credits from Communist states, other Latin American countries, and West European countries. Chile also had rich copper mines. Had Allende been a Nasser, he would have survived American pressure and hostility by arousing his people's nationalist ardor. But that was why Allende did not survive; he rejected a role as president of all Chileans. He declared himself to be president of only some Chileans—against other Chileans. Such polarization of society, a galloping inflation plus increasingly unconstitutional rule, were hardly recipes for political success. Had the CIA practiced abstinence, responsibility for the Chilean coup would properly have fallen on Allende; he destroyed himself politically before he did so physically. The CIA meddling drew attention from this and reaped the blame for Allende's difficulties and fall for the United States. Whatever it says for or against American intervention in its sphere of influence—if such a sphere can still be considered important and relevant in areas far beyond the nearer Caribbean area in this intercontinental age—Chile, like the earlier Bay of Pigs, is a persuasive case for nonintervention. Americans, perhaps because of the democratic nature of their society, seem on the whole rather clumsy at this sort of thing and feel morally uneasy about it. Perhaps most reprehensible and in some ways symbolic were the several attempts to assassinate Castro, involving the Kennedy administration, the CIA, and Mafia figures—certainly an immoral alliance to murder in the name of national security. And, unlike in a television play, this unholy alliance failed in all of its attempts. In Chile, a country as far away from the United States as the Middle East, the question is surely whether the United States had the right to try to upset the election of any political figure who was elected according to the constitutional processes either in the name of American national security or for the broader consideration of the preservation of democratic values—values Washington did not insist on in Chile after

Allende or in other parts of this increasingly nondemocratic globe. One major result, in any event, has been that the United States reaped widespread condemnation for its intervention and that Chile became for many liberal people a *cause célèbre,* as the Spanish civil war before World War II had become a symbol of the conflict between fascist and progressive forces in the world.

A contrary attitude was shown during the negotiations over the acceptance of a change in the status of the Panama Canal Zone, negotiations begun in the 1960s, carried on throughout the Nixon–Ford administration, and finally concluded under Carter. For Latin America, the disposition of this issue was critical. This was not a strictly American–Panamanian issue. For all of the Latin American states—left, centrist, and right—supported Panama in its determination to assert its control over a piece of territory that America treated as if it were America's. Would the United States seek to preserve its control of the Zone, which would lead to violence between the American forces in the Zone and the Panamanians, or would it accommodate itself to the nationalism of not only Panama but all the states to its south? Theodore Roosevelt had created Panama in order to build the canal for the growing American navy at the turn of the century; the 1903 treaty between the two countries had granted the United States "in perpetuity the use, occupation, and control" of a ten-mile-wide zone to build, run and protect the canal, although the sovereignty of this territory was to remain vested in Panama. The result was a virtual colonial situation. The American role in that small country became dominant. The Canal Zone cut Panama in two and was run by the U.S. Army. Panamanians in the Zone were subject to American law administered by American courts. All business enterprises were operated by the United States; Panamanians were denied the opportunity to compete. And the American government held large tracts of zonal land and water needed by Panama's rapidly growing population. What all this amounted to is that the United States acted as if it were sovereign in the Zone when in fact it only possessed certain treaty rights over a piece of Panamanian territory. And to make matters worse, Panamanians felt that they had received rather scanty economic benefits from the Canal; fair or not, the contrast between the standards of living in the Zone and outside it was grating and humiliating. Political discontent had become so high by 1964 that nationalist frustrations burst into riots when Panamanian students tried to fly their country's flag next to the American one at the zonal high school. American students resisted, and 21 Panamanian and three American students were killed in the subsequent explosion. The confrontation had been a symbolic one and a sample on a minor scale of what faced the United States should it seek to preserve its control "in perpetuity."

Time by the middle 1970s was running out. The Canal's economic benefits to the United States were declining with shifting world trade patterns and the increasing use of supertankers and container ships too large to pass through the Canal; even its military value was being reduced by a two-ocean navy with huge aircraft carriers, which could not go through the Canal, and nuclear submarines, which would have to surface to pass from one ocean to the other (providing intelligence to the Russians of their whereabouts). The Canal Zone issue, like the flag issue, had become primarily symbolic. American liberals recognized the need for change to meet Panama's aspirations for territorial integrity and real instead of nominal sovereign control; if denied, Panama might become "another Vietnam." But American conservatives, very strong in Congress, bitterly resisted a new treaty, which would restore the Zone to Panama by the end of the century while ensuring America's right to continued use of and protection for the waterway; if granted, the "American Canal in Panama" would become "another Suez," an indication of a retreat of American power, another instance of a once-powerful America groveling before a tiny country. Common sense in the end did prevail, although not without a struggle in Washington.

The Canal could obviously be better protected with the Panamanians' consent than without—or against—it; the latter would produce sabotage and violence, which would compel the United States to send large military forces to the Zone to protect it from "the natives." The pictures of American troops shooting Panamanians would make ugly headlines. So would the public confrontation in the United Nations, an international forum where Panama has said it would take the issue rather than to the Organization of American States, which it considered an appendage of the United States. In the universal organization, the United States would stand virtually alone against a solid bloc of underdeveloped countries. Thus the symbolism of the issue was domestic and international. While for many Americans, and not just some in Congress, the Canal Zone was "American," anything less than eventual Panamanian control over its own territory was equally unthinkable. A new treaty would therefore be a symptom of change in American attitudes toward the nationalist aspirations of its southern neighbors; it would also constitute a recognition of an American reassessment of its formerly dominant position in this hemisphere. Already Peru, Venezuela, Bolivia, and Argentina had asserted themselves strongly against the United States and American influence throughout Latin American was clearly on the wane. The area was less and less of an American "sphere of influence." The real stake in Panama, in brief, was America's new global image and role. In April 1978, by only one extra vote over the two-thirds required for a treaty, the Senate ended 13 years of negotiations and a lengthy national and Senate debate by voting to turn the Canal over to Panama by the year 2000.

This became part of a new pattern in Latin America. Where President Johnson had intervened in the Dominican Republic to stop left-wing forces from taking over the government, Carter pressured the Dominican generals who tried to oppose the election of a left-wing president to desist. And in Nicaragua, he opposed the Somoza dictatorship and it eventually collapsed; his predecessors had frequently supported other despotisms. The new administration attempted to be equally sensitive to the nationalism of countries in other Third World areas and racial pride of black Africans.

But here it ran into what appeared to be the determination of the Soviet Union to exploit developing situations in order to expand its influence. For Moscow, the underdeveloped world was a natural place to enhance its power. "National liberation" meant the erosion and overthrow of pro-Western regimes—that is, regimes it saw as capitalist, reactionary and (white) racist. This was all part of the continuing "ideological struggle" which the Soviet Union had never claimed would stop during the era of *détente.* The class struggle to free the exploited and the poor was ordained historically. Thus, as the Russians saw it, seizing opportunities for undermining the Western position throughout the underdeveloped world was legitimate and would serve the cause of social justice. Not to do so would be a betrayal of their cause and progressive mankind.

The Soviet Union, it needs to be noted again, did not create these opportunities, such as the collapse of Portuguese colonialism in southern Africa or the white minority governments in Rhodesia and South Africa, or the Somali-supported insurgency in the Ogaden. But she did try and enhance her influence in these situations. In short, the political situation appeared to favor Moscow, and her newly acquired military capability allowed her to act in a way that she could not in Zaïre and Cuba in the early 1960s. She now had a sizeable surface navy and airlift capacity, so that in Angola she flew in thousands of tons of arms and over 12,000 Cuban troops; and in Ethiopia the Soviets delivered even more arms, 20,000 Cuban troops, plus Soviet technicians and several generals to determine the strategy to drive the Somalis out of the Ogaden.

In a way, it was an old pattern. During the cold war already, the problems of the Third World had affected the superpowers and led to several conflicts. Soviet political strategy after Stalin's death had been to support the first generation of nationalist but non-Communist leaders of the newly independent countries. They might be bourgeois but their nationalism was directed against the West. Thus a coalition could be forged to weaken the West. But by the early 1970s many of these leaders had either died or they or their successors had turned against the Soviets, who had often made enormous political, economic, and military investments in the Nassers of the Third World. Moscow lost positions of influence in the Sudan and Egypt which turned Westward; earlier, it had watched in dismay as Indonesia's Sukarno had turned from Russia to China before he was overthrown and Indonesia turned Westward as well. Thus, while this policy of support for anti-Western nationalist regimes was not abandoned where it could still be pursued as, for example, in Iraq and Syria, the Soviets increasingly turned to helping Communist or pro-Communist factions gain power and then defending them. Thus Russia helped the North Vietnamese with arms supplies during the last phase of the Vietnam war; aided the MPLA capture power in Angola; assisted Marxist officers to seize power in Ethiopia; reportedly helped bring pro-

Moscow Marxist regimes into power in Afghanistan and South Yemen; and, by extending a treaty of friendship and cooperation to Hanoi—which presumably would protect Vietnam against China—allowed the former to invade Communist Cambodia and replace the pro-Peking regime there with a pro-Soviet one.

These "pro-Soviet communist regimes in Africa and Asia, imposed by force and backed as they are by Soviet power," to use Donald Zagoria's words,* may of course not necessarily enhance Soviet influence. Communist states, like non-Communist states, have increasingly been divided by nationalism, a force stronger even than Communism—witness, in Asia, the conflicts between Russia and China, China and Vietnam, and until it invaded Cambodia, Vietnam and Cambodia. Thus Moscow might at some point find it has lost influence because it offended the nationalist sensibilities of one or more of its new Marxist allies; but it may not occur and Soviet influence may instead be consolidated.

The results, in any event, are already having two disturbing effects. The first is a regional rise of tensions. In Asia, the Vietnamese conquest of Cambodia and imposition of a Hanoi-controlled government led to China's punitive invasion of Vietnam which, had it advanced toward Hanoi or lasted longer, might have led Russia to punish China by a similar limited border crossing. The dangers were—and remain—obvious. So is the increased danger of Vietnam's expansion and dominance throughout Indochina for Thailand and other Southeast Asian countries. In the area from India to the Horn, the dangers are also several. Pakistan may be faced with historic territorial claims by Afghanistan, and the events in Ethiopia, South Yemen (where in the spring of 1979 there were reportedly already a number of Cuban troops transferred from Ethiopia), and Iran (where the left may yet enhance its power should the Islamic Republic prove incapable of stabilizing its authority and satisfying popular aspirations) may lead Saudi Arabia to put further distance between itself and the United States; in the longer-run, Saudi Arabia may be endangered from without or within with all the ominous consequences for the West that this would entail. These are only a few of the possible examples of increased regional conflict which could affect American interests.

The second result is the impact on *détente* itself. On the one hand, the Soviet Union may well continue to fish in the troubled Third World waters where the potential gains are high and the costs are virtually zero. The problems in Africa or Asia may be regional, but Soviet–Cuban military interventions in Angola and Ethiopia and involvements in coups in Afghanistan and South Yemen have transformed them into the wider Soviet–American competition for influence. Yet no penalties were imposed—in Angola or Ethiopia—and as long as Russia believes that the United States is paralyzed by the memories

*"New Soviet Alliances," *Foreign Affairs,* (April 1979), p. 739.

of Vietnam, Moscow has no reason to desist. But to reject nonintervention as a United States response is not to suggest American military intervention; there are other incentives and sanctions which could be used to restrain Russia. The problems of the Third World, which Moscow is seeking to exploit, are essentially political, and primarily political answers are therefore needed. Thus, while the Carter administration has abandoned the virtually automatic response to Soviet involvement in the underdeveloped areas which characterized American foreign policy during the earlier bipolar cold war days and first few years of *détente,* a lack of understanding of the consequences of Soviet (Cuban) interventions for American interests and the perception of American power and will as weak by an observing world can only be harmful. Increasing sensitivity to the nationalism of the Third World and sympathy for the social struggles and causes involved thus remains an insufficient response. The East–West context continues to intrude. Nowhere has this been more vividly demonstrated than in the Middle East.

THE MIDDLE EASTERN LINCHPIN

It was in the Middle East, however, that America's stake was the greatest. The Carter administration, upon coming into power, viewed the situation in this area with alarm as Egypt appeared to be isolated among the "confrontation states" who had been her allies in past wars. Carter, and particularly his National Security Assistant Brzezinski, believed therefore that the step-by-step approach had reached its end. It had, in their view, some fundamental liabilities. One, Israel was required in each step to give up territory for promises that when all steps had been taken she and her neighbors would sign a peace treaty and Israel be accorded legitimacy. But by then, she would no longer have any bargaining cards to trade. Two, the incremental approach avoided the central problem of the Palestinians, whose grievances would have to be met if a genuine peace were ever to be established; the Kissinger way of trying to deal with the "easy" problems first and then hopefully gaining sufficient momentum and trust among the negotiating parties to resolve the "difficult" issues later frittered away precious time and might thereby jeopardize the possibility of peace. The greatest danger was if the key differences between Israel and the Arabs were not resolved, Sadat would either be outflanked by militant anti-Israeli, pro-Soviet, anti-American Arabs; be overthrown within his own country by a militant; or, in order to survive politically, if not physically, play the role of the new Nasser. Time, in brief, was not on the side of the United States.

It therefore proposed that all parties resume negotiations at Geneva which, in Kissinger's mind, would only have met at the end when all steps had been successfully taken and would then have symbolized the end of Arab–Israeli hostility. This raised at least two serious handicaps. The first was the Palestinians. Who would represent them? How would they be represented? Indeed, would they be represented? It was clear that the Arab states would not even go to Geneva unless the Palestinians were there and that meant the PLO. The PLO, however, was not a state, even if it considered itself a state-in-waiting. This was the rub. Israel had no intention of dealing with the PLO; it considered the organization to be a gang of murderers dedicated to the elimination of Israel as a state. Under no circumstances would it permit the establishment of a Palestinian state.

How were these apparently irreconcilable positions to accommodate each other? The solution adopted was that the Arabs would meet as a single delegation; this would eliminate the problem of how to combine states with a nonstate actor, any official representation of the PLO (and thus the tacit recognition of the PLO by Israel when it sat down with the organization at the diplomatic negotiating table), but it did mean that the Palestinians would be represented. Furthermore, to appease the Israelis, who were insistent only on state-to-state negotiations in order to avoid negotiating with the PLO, it was agreed that after the opening plenary session, the conference would break up and the Israelis would meet with each Arab state separately. Palestinians could be attached to the various Arab delegations. The Israelis, while opposing the presence of the PLO leadership, reportedly promised that they would not, however, check the credentials of the Palestinians attending too closely; this meant others, either low-level PLO members or outside sympathizers approved by the PLO, could represent the organization.

The second obstacle to Geneva proved greater. Kissinger had fashioned his strategy in part to exclude the Soviets; only at the final conference would Russia attend as the cochairman. Carter, determined to call Geneva and to do

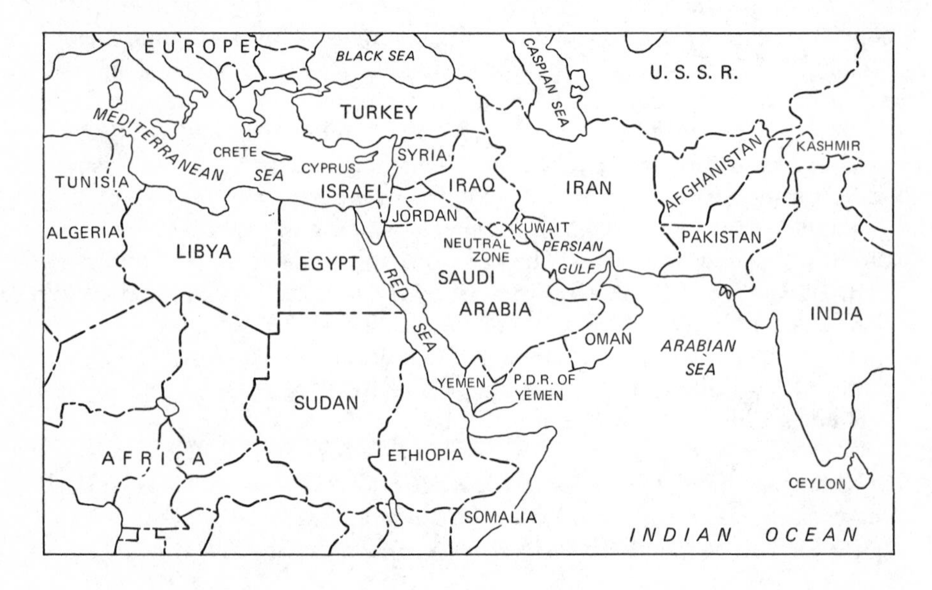

so before the end of 1977, decided to approach the Soviets and enlist their cooperation. Moscow had influence with the more militant Syrians and the PLO and it, therefore, had the capacity to cause a lot of trouble and block negotiations. If, on the other hand, Moscow would help in the peace negotiations by pressuring them to attend and then not just indulge in extreme rhetoric but take practical positions and be flexible and conciliatory, it would presumably retain a degree of influence in the Arab world if and when a peace treaty between Israel and the Arab states were signed, reduce the possibility of a superpower clash in the area they were most likely to clash, and help strengthen *détente* with the United States.

Neither Jerusalem nor Cairo were happy with the Soviet–American accord in late 1977. Even though it excluded any reference to a Palestinian state or a total Israeli withdrawal to the 1967 frontiers, both of which the Russians favored, but did commit both powers to a peace in which all Middle Eastern states were to have secure boundaries, the Israelis objected and the Egyptians were unhappy. It was probably because of this that Sadat, who had broken his ties to Russia, decided to strike out on his own and that the Israelis were receptive to his proposal to bypass Washington and negotiate directly. In a dramatic and internationally televised visit to Jerusalem in November 1977, during which he addressed the Israeli Parliament, Sadat, the leader of the Arab world's strongest nation, in effect extended recognition to the Arabs' archenemy. He expressed his hope that there would be no more war. The impact was euphoric as a comprehensive peace—a peace with all of Israel's Arab enemies—seemed near.

The mood did not last long. Sadat apparently believed peace was easily and quickly achievable since he had taken the significant psychological step to reassure the Israelis that his peace offer was genuine, not a trick. Israel would withdraw to the 1967 frontiers from the Sinai, the West Bank, Syria's Golan Heights, and Jordan's East Jerusalem, recognize the Palestinians' legitimate rights, and, in return for their land, the Arabs would sign a peace treaty and Israel would gain the legitimacy and peace with security she had sought since birth. The Israelis had long publicly asserted that if only the Arabs would negotiate with them directly, implying recognition, they would be willing to return the 1967 territories. Israel had specifically disclaimed annexationist ambitions. The Labor government after the 1967 war had accepted U.N. Resolution 242 committing Israel to the withdrawal from the captured land (or, given some adjustments for security reasons, almost all).

But the new coalition government led by Prime Minister Begin, who had spent his parliamentary life in opposition, had other ideas. He proposed to withdraw from the Sinai desert but he offered the Palestinians on the West Bank and Gaza Strip only autonomy or self-rule, not self-determination. They could elect their own representatives and govern their own affairs but Israeli security interests remained preeminent. The army would therefore remain stationed there and Israel would retain a veto over the question of

Palestinian immigration (the return of the Palestinian refugees displaced by the 1948 war and now living in other lands, such as Lebanon). Begin referred to the West Bank by its ancient Hebrew names, Judea and Samaria; the prime minister claimed that they were not occupied territory to be returned but liberated territory to be kept as a part of the Greater Israel of which Zionists —which Begin was—had long dreamed. The most he would concede was that Israel would recognize that there were other claims to sovereignty over the West Bank and Gaza Strip, that the issue would be deferred for five years and could then be negotiated by the interested parties. But he left the impression that he was irrevocably committed to keeping Judea, Samaria, and Gaza, and that he expected to establish Israeli sovereignty over both areas, each of which contained several hundred thousand Arabs. In the meantime, the Israeli government announced that Jewish settlements in the Sinai and West Bank would remain and began to encourage new settlements.

To Sadat, Begin's plan for the West Bank and Gaza was tantamount to the perpetuation of Israeli military occupation under the guise of autonomy. And without a settlement of the Palestinian issue satisfactory to the Palestinians, and withdrawal of Israel from the conquered Arab territories, he would not sign a separate peace with Israel. To do so would be to brand himself as a traitor and become isolated in the Arab world. Indeed, after his trip to Jerusalem, Syria, Libya, Iraq, Algeria, South Yemen, and the PLO had condemned him and formed a "rejectionist front." Sadat, in turn, had broken diplomatic relations with the five states. But there were limits to his freedom of maneuver. He therefore insisted that the first order of business was to agree to a declaration of principles regarding Israeli withdrawal from all Arab land and self-determination for the Palestinians which would open the way for Jordan and the Palestinians to negotiate the issue of the West Bank's and Gaza's futures themselves. Having gained such commitments from Israel for his "Arab brothers," Sadat felt he could then sign a separate peace with Israel and relieve his country, which had done most of the fighting in four wars, from the burden of heavy defense spending and concentrate on improving the domestic economy and doing something for the people of Egypt.

Since Begin's offer fell considerably short of the concessions Sadat needed, the bilateral negotiations broke down. The fear of what might happen next brought the United States back into the negotiating process. American interests were clear. First, the United States was committed to the security of Israel. But from the American point of view, another war would be even more costly in lives for Israel than the 1973 war and as before, Israeli victory would not bring with it a favorable political settlement; it would only lead to more Arab resentment and humiliation. Of even greater concern was that it might also bring about a Soviet–American clash as had almost happened in 1973 after Moscow declared it would intervene to save the Egyptian Third Army from a complete defeat. Second, the United States, Western Europe, and Japan needed oil to preserve the political, social, and economic viability of their societies. Much of this oil came from Saudi Arabia. If no Arab–Israeli peace accord could be reached, and if a fifth war should erupt, another and longer oil embargo would be very damaging even if an American–Russian military clash were avoided. But war or no war, if Sadat, who had turned away from Moscow toward Washington, failed to achieve a peace which the Arabs would consider fair and just and which could therefore enlist the support of other pro-American, moderate Arab states like Jordan and Saudi Arabia, they would all feel compelled to turn against the United States. In such circumstances, Saudi Arabia, anti-Communist and friendly to the West as she was, would not be able by herself to hold out against the course adopted by the other Arab states to once more seek resolution of the Israeli problem through confrontation. Access to oil and the price of oil would clearly become a weapon in this struggle, particularly because its successful use in 1973 had demonstrated how vulnerable the West was and how much it feared the use of oil as a means of pressuring it. Not only did Washington, therefore, feel that another war was to be avoided but that progress toward a settlement was imperative.

The effect of American intervention in the stalled Israeli–Egyptian negotiations as a mediator, however, was to bring into the open what Kissinger had expected to put off with his step-by-step approach, but had himself not been completely able to avoid during the negotiations of the second interim agreement—namely, American–Israeli differences on how to achieve peace. Carter, like Kissinger, felt that Sadat was offering Israel for the first time in her existence the security and peace she had so long sought, and if this opportunity were not seized the result would be disastrous for Israel and the West, as the Arabs would use their oil weapon and again turn toward Moscow. Israel was already basically isolated diplomatically. Even before the 1973 war, the West Europeans had become increasingly sympathetic to the idea of an end to Arab–Israeli hostilities: recognition by the Arabs of Israel's right to existence for a return of the 1967 territories. The war and the oil threat made them even more sympathetic to the Arab position. The United States had thus become Israel's sole source of diplomatic support internationally, sophisticated military equipment, especially fighters, and economic aid. In 1976, for example, public assistance amounted to $2.34 billion, which meant that the American taxpayer was paying each Jewish man, woman, and child in Israel $700! And the Israeli government now proceeded to alienate Washington as well.

The Carter administration had, upon coming into power, quickly made known what it thought were the ingredients of a solution in the Middle East. One, U.N. Resolution 242 meant the return of most of the Arab territory Israel had captured in 1967. Only minor adjustments for security reasons could be allowed. Two (and in this respect the administration went far beyond any of its predecessors), it boldly asserted that the key to peace was the Palestinian issue. More specifically, it said that the Palestinians had the right to participate in the peace-making process and Mr. Carter himself soon publicly declared that the Palestinians had a right to a "homeland" (a term that was deliberately left vague, but nevertheless the use of the term was symbolically significant). Three, in return for such Israeli concessions, the Arab states had to commit themselves not only to ending their state of hostilities with Israel but also sign a peace treaty followed by such things as diplomatic exchanges, trade, and tourism. The Israelis had been insistent upon this point and the Arabs were balking at such normalization, declaring —as Sadat did—that it would take a whole generation for this to occur after so much bitterness and anger.

The first two positions were clearly at odds with those of Begin, who had proceeded to reinterpret U.N. Resolution 242, accepted by his predecessors, to mean that Israel was not required to withdraw from the West Bank and Gaza. He was also opposed to a Palestinian state which he, and indeed most Israelis, felt would constitute a danger to the existence of Israel. The issue that symbolically played the role of highlighting these differences between Israel and the United States was the settlements policy. Ever since 1967, the United States had consistently opposed Israeli settlements in the occupied lands as illegal. The Carter administration repeated this while it watched almost unbelievingly as the Israeli government actively encouraged new settlements on the land the Arabs were reclaiming. It appeared as if Israel was deliberately setting out to destroy the one chance it had ever had to gain legitimacy and peace; it certainly impressed Washington, as it did Sadat, as an act of bad faith to plant such settlements in the midst of peace negotiations. Secretary of State Vance, a diplomat's diplomat who was careful in his choice of word lest he offend, expressed the administration's anger when he declared that Israeli settlements were not only illegal but an "obstacle to peace."

Repeated American efforts to halt this policy and encourage the Israelis to be more forthcoming and flexible to hold out more hope to the Arabs for the eventual recovery of the West Bank and Gaza were all in vain. It seemed increasingly as if, for a few thousand orthodox and militant Jews, Israel would forfeit this opportunity for peace; indeed, Israeli policy was more and more perceived in much of the world as annexationist and that the government was using Israel's genuine security needs as a disguise for seizing Arab land. For Washington, therefore, the issue was not what Begin accused it of doing—attempting to dictate Israeli policy—but how much longer the American people ought to finance an untenable stalemate which, when it would explode, would hurt not just Israel but the United States and all of its major allies.

By contrast, Sadat appeared reasonable and conciliatory. He had with great courage provided the great psychological breakthrough with his trip to Jerusalem, had shown characteristic sensitivity to Israel's security needs (by being willing to listen to various ideas for demilitarizing or thinning out forces in certain areas, placing U.N. forces between Israeli and Arab armies, and phasing in agreements over 5, 10, and 15 years as Israeli trust in the Arabs' good intentions grew), and been willing to accept Israel's demands for a peace treaty and the subsequent normalization of relations not after 25 years, or even 5 years, but immediately. As an indication of his sympathies for Sadat and Saudi Arabia, without whose support the Egyptian leader could not have survived politically in his solo attempt to achieve an Arab–Israeli peace, Carter tied the sale to Israel of American fighters to fighters for Egypt and Saudi Arabia. Not only had modern and sophisticated American fighter planes not been shipped to these countries before but never had arms for Israel been tied to a shipment for Arab states. Senate approval of this package deal was indicative of shifting American opinion, a disapproval of Israeli policy and support for Sadat's genuine and sincere offer to make peace essentially on bases declared acceptable to previous and less Zionistically zealous Labor governments.

Nevertheless, the stalemate continued. As the three-year second interim Sinai agreement was about to run out in October 1978, Sadat began to sound more pessimistic about a settlement, as well as more ominous. President Carter therefore took a gamble and invited Begin and Sadat to meet with him at Camp David. It was a gamble because had this summit meeting produced no results, the president's prestige, already low, would have been even more seriously impaired, American mediating attempts run their course, and Israeli–American relations set back even further.

But the president, for perhaps the first time in his administration, showed persistence and skill, and emerged after 12 days of patient negotiations with a series of agreements, including a commitment by the two men to sign a peace treaty within three months. Sadat appeared to have made the most concessions for he did not gain, as he had said all along he must, a commitment to an eventual Israeli withdrawal from the West Bank and Gaza Strip, or to full Palestinian self-determination. Begin was still sticking to his formula for autonomy for the Palestinians; while the Israeli army would be reduced from 11,000 to 6000 men, it would still be on the West Bank. Sadat did gain an Israeli commitment, however, to recognize "the legitimate rights of the Palestinians," a pledge that the West Bank and Gaza Palestinians would participate in future negotiations on these areas and ratify or reject a final agreement, and a temporary freeze on Israeli settlements on the West Bank. But Israel kept a veto power over the participation by the PLO leaders in such negotiations or the establishment of a Palestinian state. Thus, on the one hand, it appeared the Israeli position had remained essentially intact. On the other hand, she gained a separate peace treaty with the strongest of her Arab neighbors; the others could not by themselves take on Israel without Egypt. In other words, for a seemingly small investment Israel gained the enormous dividend of a real sense of security, since Jordan or Syria alone or together were too weak to wage war against Israel. That was why, in fact, Syria had opposed Sadat's journey to Jerusalem and the subsequent bilateral negotiations. Once the threat of war with Egypt had ended, there would be no reason why Israel should return the Golan Heights to Syria.

Sadat too, however, may have taken a gamble. Rather than having sold out, he appears to have felt that a momentum would—or at least could—be built up as the West Bank and Gaza Palestinians would gain representation and a degree of power, as well as a voice with which the Palestinians, who could, after all, elect pro-PLO representatives, could state their legitimate aims. This momentum would start with an Israeli withdrawal of the Sinai settlements, an Egyptian–Israeli peace treaty, and a subsequent total Israeli withdrawal from the Sinai. Sadat must also have hoped that Jordan would join the negotiations about the future status of the West Bank and that Saudi Arabia would continue to support him. In brief, as the peace process began in earnest with the initial Israeli pull-back from the Sinai, an irreversible process would begin.

The initial Arab reaction to Camp David was, however, negative. Jordan and even Saudi Arabia now joined the rejectionist frontier of Syria, Iraq, Libya, and Algeria in condemning Sadat. Thus, instead of widening his base of support in the Arab world, Sadat was more isolated than ever. The Egyptian leader therefore insisted upon clearly linking Egyptian ratification of a peace treaty with a timetable for steps toward Palestinian autonomy; but the Israelis resisted, for if the Palestinians were not cooperative (or Israel itself slowed down moves toward Palestinian autonomy as its fears of a Palestinian state grew), Jerusalem feared that there would be no peace treaty.

Subsequent events did not make it any easier to resolve this and other obstacles to peace. The Iranian revolution greatly enhanced Israel's sense of insecurity as Iran both cut off its oil supplies and welcomed with great acclaim the head of the PLO as its first official visitor. Indeed, the possibility of Moslem fundamentalism sweeping through the Arab world—including Egypt—threatened to administer the final blow to the Camp David agreements. For Sadat, the overthrow of the Shah, a strong supporter of his peace moves, and Iran's alignment with his most militant Arab critics and opponents, reinforced his isolation. This intensified the pressure on him to demonstrate that he was not signing a separate peace and betraying his Arab "brothers." Not surprisingly, therefore, the negotiations almost broke down. Only President Carter's personal intervention with a trip to Egypt and Israel finally and only at the last moment (as the president was about to return home without a peace treaty and with his personal reputation and America's prestige tarnished) produced the necessary diplomatic breakthroughs and brought peace between these two long-term enemies.

Yet even this treaty is unlikely to bring a stable peace to the area. On the eve of the Israeli–Egyptian peace treaty in March 1979, Prime Minister Begin in a defiant mood told his parliament—and therefore the Arabs—that Israel would never withdraw to its 1967 borders, Jerusalem would remain Israel's "eternal capital," and that there would never be a Palestinian state on the West Bank and Gaza. Thus the prospect for regional peace in the long-run remained somber. For a stable and long-run peace can be created only if the peace process continues and does not end when Israel and Egypt sign a peace treaty. If, on the other hand, Israel, with Egypt now neutralized, shows itself less willing to accommodate the grievances and aspirations of the Palestinians, Jordanians, and Syrians, the peace treaty will be subjected to great strain and Sadat might yet collapse.

As it was, in the wake of the peace treaty, Egypt's fellow Arab states suspended Egypt's membership in the Arab League, established an economic boycott, and most of them broke diplomatic relations with her. The treaty also drove Syria and Iraq together, enraged the PLO, and deepened the chasm between them and the United States, whom they saw as having saddled the area with a peace which ignored its central problem—that of the Palestinians. Finally, the treaty greatly enhanced the anxiety, anger, and fear of the Saudis, who were worried by the possibility of internal unrest caused by Arab radicals (especially Palestinians) and deeply troubled by the spreading Soviet influence from the Horn of Africa to Afghanistan, including the southern tip of the Arabian peninsula, and the collapse of the monarchy in Iran. More and more, the Saudis appear to feel compelled to turn from supporting Sadat to alignment with the Arab states opposed to him—and, in a world oil market tightened by Iran's lower oil production exports, they might also at some point feel compelled to resort to its now even more powerful oil weapon. So America may still lose influence throughout the area and Russia gain it once more as it becomes increasingly clear that Washington cannot bring about a comprehensive and equitable peace. In these circumstances, Israel would again be endangered and the security and economic health of all Western societies—including America's—be placed in great jeopardy. At best, the Israeli–Egyptian peace was fragile and volatile; at worst, it would prove a disaster.

Thus, the Carter administration, having initially rejected Kissinger's step-by-step approach for a comprehensive peace treaty, ended up embracing Kissinger's approach. His idea had been that by resolving easier problems first, a momentum would be built up that would eventually resolve the more difficult problems. Brzezinski's rejection of his predecessor's diplomatic strategy had been based on the grounds that it postponed the critical Palestinian issue too long and that time might not be on Sadat's side. How ironic that his predictions might yet prove correct as the administration, fearful of the immense domestic battle that might occur if it really placed great pressure on Israel to be more conciliatory, returned to the incremental approach, and instead of creating the momentum to resolve the issues of the West Bank and Gaza, the Golan Heights and Jerusalem, had made the urgency of resolving them far greater and the likelihood of so doing much smaller. (The ink on the Israeli–Egyptian peace treaty was hardly dry when Israel announced the formation of new settlements on the West Bank.)

No issue, however, could have illustrated more profoundly the deep involvement of the United States in the world. Sympathy for the plight of Jews since Hitler, admiration for the courage of the new Jewish state amid hostile neighbors, combined with recognition of the strategic and economic importance of the Middle East, pulled the United States into the conflict between Israel and the Arab states and the quarrels among the Arabs themselves on how best to deal with this problem. Inevitably, given the superpower rivalry, American–Soviet competition became inextricably intertwined with the other two conflicts. As the world moved into the last two decades of the century, it became increasingly clear that America was affected, often deeply, by virtually all problems, whatever the origin, wherever they occurred and whether the Russians sought to exploit these issues or not—be it nuclear proliferation, the race problem in South Africa, the stability of monarchical regimes in Iran and Saudi Arabia, or the border conflicts between new states (such as between Ethiopia and Somalia). It appeared that regardless of American preferences to play a lesser role, the United States would remain extensively involved in the state system, for the world would not leave it alone; indeed, sometimes it appeared that the nation was even *more* extensively involved then during the days of the cold war and America's frequently criticized role of global policeman. And many of these problems, as in Southern Africa, the Horn of Africa, or the Persian Gulf area, not only held important consequences for the United States which might lead to commitments far beyond those of the Truman and Eisenhower Doctrines of the 1940s and 1950s, but they could not be easily isolated from the American–Soviet rivalry.

If the two superpowers, then, are no longer locked into a bipolar duel as in the days of the cold war, their interests remained nevertheless opposed on many key issues. Soviet aims can be no less adverse to American interests for falling short of something called "world domination." And just because Third World countries are not necessarily dominoes who will fall, inevitably, one after another, it does not mean that events in faraway places whose origins are essentially indigenous do not affect American interests or may not set off a chain-like effect in other countries. In international politics, no less than in domestic affairs, events tend to be interrelated and have an impact on one another; this is the whole meaning of the word *system.* In this more complex contemporary world, furthermore, one does not have to believe that everything bad happens because Moscow willed it; for changes other than the extension of Soviet influence can occur which will adversely affect American and Western interests. Even when Russia may not gain influence in a particular situation, this does not mean that the United States can afford to lose influence or that such a loss of influence is a matter of little concern. It is one thing to say that during the cold war the United States overreacted; but is the lesson for *détente* to underreact, to define American vital interest in narrow terms, to comfort ourselves with the reassuring thought that Soviet (Cuban) attempts to exploit local problems are bound to fail, thus excusing a lack of American action and involvement which, if is often charged, would only have made matters worse? Is it really helpful to counsel ourselves so constantly of "the limits of American power" and to denounce those advocating a more politically—not necessarily militarily—active policy with the epithets "cold warriors" and "globalists?" The secretary of state is correct when he says that in this more complex world "we cannot dictate events" because the U.S. is not omnipotent. But does this mean that this country cannot or should not exercise its great influence to help shape events? The country may not be omnipotent but neither is it impotent. The continuing First–Second (Soviet-led) World problems, plus First–Third World problems, and the frequent interactions of these two sets of relationships, seem to suggest that the contemporary, more multipolar world can be at least as dangerous as a bipolar one and that America's role will remain extensive and necessitate new commitments, as in the Persian Gulf area. It surely will be ironic if at some point in the not-too-distant future, the United States—haunted by oil shortages, ever-higher energy prices, continued stagflation, slower economic growth, and lowered expectations about standards of living, all symbolized by a collapsing dollar—will look back to the cold war era with nostalgia and view it as less dangerous than the current world, as one in which American interests and values had been more secure.

a selective bibliography

AMERICAN SOCIETY AND STYLE IN FOREIGN POLICY

Almond, Gabriel A. *The American People and Foreign Policy.** New York: Praeger, 1960.
Boorstin, Daniel J. *The Genius of American Politics.** Chicago: Phoenix Books, 1953.
Hartz, Louis. *The Liberal Tradition in America.** New York: Harvest Books, 1955.
Herberg, Will. *Protestant, Catholic, and Jew,** rev. ed. New York: Anchor Books, 1960.
Hofstadter, Richard. *The Paranoid Style in American Politics.** New York: Vintage Books, 1967.
Krasner, Stephen D. *Defending the National Interest.** Princeton, N.J.: Princeton University Press, 1978.
Packenham, Robert A. *Liberal America and the Third World** Princeton, N.J.: Princeton University Press, 1973.
Potter, David M. *The People of Plenty.** Chicago: Phoenix Books, 1954.

AMERICAN FOREIGN POLICY

Alperovitz, Gar. *Atomic Diplomacy: Hiroshima and Potsdam.** New York: Vintage Books, 1967.
Aron, Raymond. *The Imperial Republic.** Cambridge, Mass.: Winthrop Publishers, 1974.

*Asterisked titles are available in paperback editions.

Barnet, Richard. *Roots of War.** New York: Atheneum, 1972.
———. *The Giants.* New York: Simon and Schuster, 1977.
Bell, Coral. *The Diplomacy of Détente.* New York: St. Martin's, 1977.
Bloomfield, Lincoln P. *In Search of American Foreign Policy.** New York: Oxford University Press, 1974.
Draper, Theodore, and others. *Defending America.* New York: Basic Books, 1978.
Fleming, D. F. *The Cold War and Its Origins, 1917–1960,* 2 vols. Garden City, N.Y.: Doubleday, 1961.
Fulbright, J. William. *Old Myths and New Realities.** New York: Vintage Books, 1964.
———. *The Arrogance of Power.** New York: Vintage Books, 1967.
———. *The Crippled Giant.** New York: Vintage Books, 1972.
Gaddis, John L. *The United States and the Origins of the Cold War, 1941–1947.** New York: Columbia University Press, 1972.
———. *Russia, the Soviet Union and the United States.* New York: Wiley, 1978.
Gilbert, Felix. *To the Farewell Address.* Princeton, N.J.: Princeton University Press, 1961.
Halle, Louis J. *The Cold War as History.** New York: Harper & Row, 1967.
Hilsman, Roger. *To Move a Nation.* Garden City, N.Y.: Doubleday, 1967.
Hoffmann, Stanley. *Primacy or World Order.* New York: McGraw-Hill, 1978.
Kennan, George F. *American Diplomacy, 1900–1950.** New York: Mentor Books, 1952.
———. *Russia and the West under Lenin and Stalin.** New York: Mentor Books, 1961.
———. *Memoirs.* Boston: Little, Brown, 1967.
———. *The Clouds of Danger.* Boston: Atlantic/Little, Brown, 1977.
Kolko, Gabriel. *The Roots of American Foreign Policy.* Boston: Beacon Press, 1969.
——— and Joyce Kolko. *The Limits of Power.* New York: Harper & Row, 1972.
May, Ernest R. *Lessons of the Past.** New York: Oxford University Press, 1973.
Morgenthau, Hans. *A New Foreign Policy for the United States.** New York: Praeger, 1969.
Oglesby, Carl, and Richard Schaull. *Containment and Change.* New York: Macmillan, 1967.
Osgood, Robert, et al. *America & the World.** Baltimore, Md.: The Johns Hopkins Press, 1970.
———. *Retreat from Empire?** Baltimore, Md.: The Johns Hopkins Press, 1973.
Steel, Ronald. *Pax Americana.** New York: Viking, 1967.
Szulc, Tad. *The Illusion of Peace.* New York: Viking, 1978.
Williams, William A. *The Tragedy of American Diplomacy,* rev. ed. New York: World, 1962.

AMERICAN MILITARY POLICY

Abel, Elie. *The Missile Crisis.** New York: Bantam Books, 1966.
Blechman, Barry M., and Stephen S. Kaplan. *Force Without War.* Washington, D.C.: Brookings Institution, 1978.
Dinerstein, Herbert. *The Making of a Missile Crisis.* Baltimore, Md.: The Johns Hopkins Press, 1976.
Epstein, William. *The Last Chance.* New York: Free Press, 1976.

George, Alexander L. *The Limits of Coercive Diplomacy.** Boston: Little, Brown, 1971.
——— and Richard Smoke. *Deterrence in American Foreign Policy.** New York: Columbia University Press, 1974.
Gompert, David, Michael Mandelbaum, Richard Garwin, and John Barton. *Nuclear Weapons and World Politics.* New York: McGraw-Hill (for the Council of Foreign Relations/1980s Project), 1977.
Gray, Colin. *The Soviet-American Arms Race.* Lexington, Mass.: Lexington Books, 1976.
Horelick, Arnold L. and Myron Rush. *Strategic Power and Soviet Foreign Policy.* Chicago: University of Chicago Press, 1966.
Kissinger, Henry A. *The Necessity for Choice.** New York: Anchor Books, 1961.
———. *Nuclear Weapons and Foreign Policy.** New York: Harper & Brothers, 1957.
———. *The Troubled Partnership.** New York: Anchor Books, 1966.
Pranger, Robert, and Roger Labrie, eds. *Nuclear Strategy and National Security.* Washington, D.C.: American Enterprise Institute, 1977.
Thayer, Charles W. *Guerrilla.** New York: New American Library, 1963.
Whetten, Lawrence, ed. *The Political Implications of Soviet Military Power.* New York: Crane, Russak, 1977.
Wolf, Joseph. *The Growing Dimensions of Security.* Washington, D.C.: Atlantic Council, 1977.

AMERICAN POLICY IN POSTWAR EUROPE

Calleo, David P. *The Atlantic Fantasy.* Baltimore, Md.: The Johns Hopkins Press, 1970.
———. *Europe's Future.** New York: Norton, 1967.
Davison, W. Phillips. *The Berlin Blockade.* Princeton, N.J.: Princeton University Press, 1958.
De Porte, A. W. *Europe between the Superpowers.* New Haven: Yale University Press, 1979.
Feld, Werner, and John Wildger. *Domestic Political Realities and European Unification.* Boulder, Colo.: Westview Press, 1977.
Hoffmann, Stanley. *Gulliver's Troubles or the Setting of American Foreign Policy.** New York: McGraw-Hill, 1968.
Holborn, Hajo. *The Political Collapse of Europe.* New York: Knopf, 1951.
Jones, Joseph. *The Fifteen Weeks.* New York: Viking, 1955.
Kleiman, Robert. *Atlantic Crisis.** New York: Norton, 1964.
Kriegel, Annie. *Euro-Communism.* Stanford, Conn.: Hoover Institute, 1978.
Mally, Gerhard. *Interdependence.* Lexington, Mass.: Lexington Books, 1976.
Mander, John. *Berlin, Hostage for the West.** Baltimore, Md.: Penguin Books, 1962.
Newhouse, John, ed. *U.S. Troops in Europe.** Washington, D.C.: The Brookings Institution, 1971.
Pipes, Richard, ed. *Soviet Strategy in Europe.* New York: Crane, Russak, 1976.
Ranney, Austin, and Giovanni, Sartori, eds. *Euro Communism.* Washington, D.C.: American Enterprise Institute, 1978.
Willis, Geoffrey. *The Permanent Alliance.* Leiden, Netherlands: Sythoff, 1977.
Speier, Hans. *Divided Berlin.* New York: Praeger, 1961.
Steel, Ronald. *The End of Alliance.** New York: Delta Books, 1966.

AMERICAN POLICY IN ASIA

Barnett, A. Doak. *China Policy.** Washington, D.C.: Brookings Institution, 1977.
———. *China and the Major Powers in East Asia.** Washington, D.C.: Brookings Institution, 1977.
Clough, Ralph N. *East Asia and U.S. Security.** Washington, D.C.: Brookings Institution, 1975.
Clubb, O. Edmund. *China and Russia.** New York: Columbia University Press, 1971.
Cohen, Warren I. *America's Response to China.** New York: Wiley, 1971.
Dulles, Foster R. *American Foreign Policy Toward Communist China.** New York: Crowell, 1972.
Fall, Bernard B. *The Two Viet-Nams,* 2d rev. ed. New York: Praeger, 1967.
Feis, Herbert. *China Tangle.** Princeton, N.J.: Princeton University Press, 1953.
Gurtov, Melvin. *The First Vietnam Crisis.** New York: Columbia University Press, 1967.
Halberstram, David. *The Best and the Brightest.** New York: Random House, 1969.
Hammer, Ellen J. *The Struggle for Indochina, 1940–1955.** Stanford, Calif.: Stanford University Press, 1966.
Hellmann, Donald C. *Japan and East Asia.** New York: Praeger, 1972.
Hinton, Harold C. *Three and a Half Powers.** Bloomington, Ind.: Indiana University Press, 1975.
Hoopes, Townsend. *The Limits of Intervention.** New York: McKay, 1969.
Lake, Anthony, ed. *The Vietnam Legacy.* New York: New York University Press, 1976.
Lewy, Guenter. *America in Vietnam.* New York: Oxford University Press, 1978.
Meisner, Maurice. *Mao's China.* New York: Free Press, 1977.
Oberdorfer, Don. *Tet.* New York: Doubleday, 1971.
Oksenberg, Michel, and Robert Oxnam, eds. *Dragon and Eagle.* New York: Basic Books, 1978.
———. *The Pentagon Papers.** New York: Bantam Books, 1971.
Sutter, Robert. *Chinese Foreign Policy After the Cultural Revolution.* Boulder, Colo.: Westview Press, 1978.
Spanier, John W. *The Truman–MacArthur Controversy and the Korean War,** rev. ed. New York: Norton, 1965.
Tsou, Tang. *America's Failure in China, 1941–50,** 2 vols. Chicago: Phoenix Books, 1963.
Thompson, Sir Robert. *No Exit from Vietnam.* New York: McKay, 1969.

MIDDLE EAST

Doran, Charles. *Myth, Oil and Politics.* New York: Free Press, 1977.
Golan, Galia. *Yom Kippur and After.* New York: Cambridge University Press, 1977.
Golan, Matti. *The Secret Conversations of Henry Kissinger.** New York: Quadrangle/ The New York Times Book Co., 1976.
Quandt, William. *Decade of Decisions.* Berkeley, Calif.: University of California Press, 1977.
Reich, Bernard. *Quest for Peace.* New Brunswick, N.J.: Transaction Books, 1977.

Sadat, Anwar. *In Search of Identity.* New York: Harper & Row, 1978.
Safran, Nadav. *Israel.* Cambridge, Mass.: Harvard University Press, 1978.
Sheehan, Edward. *The Arabs, Israelis and Kissinger.* New York: Reader's Digest Press, 1976.

AFRICA AND LATIN AMERICA

El-Khawas, Mohamed, and Barry Cohen, eds. *The Kissinger Strategy for Southern Africa.* Westport, Conn.: Lawrence Hill, 1976.
La Feber, Walter. *The Panama Canal.** New York: Oxford University Press, 1978.
Lake, Anthony. *The "Tar Baby" Option.* New York: Columbia University Press, 1976.
Lemarchand, René, ed. *American Policy in Southern Africa.* Washington, D.C.: University Press of America, 1978.
Rangel, Carlos. *The Latin Americans.* New York: Harcourt, 1977.
Sigmund, Paul. *The Overthrow of Allende and the Politics of Chile.* Pittsburgh: University of Pittsburgh, 1977.

THE NEW INTERNATIONAL POLITICS

Atlantic Council Working Group on the U.S. and the Developing Countries. *The United States and the Developing Countries.* Boulder, Colo.: Westview Press, 1977.
Bhagwati, Jagdish, ed. *The New International Economic Order.* Cambridge, Mass.: The M.I.T. Press, 1977.
Blake, David, and Robert Walters. *The Politics of Economic Relations.** Englewood Cliffs, N.J.: Prentice-Hall, 1976.
Brown, Harrison. *The Human Future Revisited.* New York: Norton, 1978.
Fishlow, Albert, Carlos Diaz-Alejandro, Richard Fagen, and Roger Hansen. *Rich and Poor Nations in the World Economy.* New York: McGraw-Hill (for the Council of Foreign Relations/1980s Project), 1978.
Keohane, Robert, and Joseph Nye. *Power and Interdependence.** Boston: Little, Brown, 1977.
Lewis, Arthur. *The Evolution of the International Economic Order.** Princeton, N.J.: Princeton University Press, 1978.
Morse, Edward. *Modernization and the Transformation of International Relations.* New York: Free Press, 1976.
Rothstein, Robert. *The Weak in the World of the Strong.* New York: Columbia University Press, 1977.
Spero, Joan. *The Politics of International Economic Relations.** New York: St. Martin's, 1977.
Tucker, Robert. *Inequality of Nations.* New York: Basic Books, 1977.
Vernon, Raymond, ed. *The Oil Crisis.** New York: Norton, 1976.
Wriggins, Howard, and Gunnar Adler-Karlsson. *Reducing Global Inequities.* New York: McGraw-Hill (for the Council of Foreign Relations/1980s Project), 1978.

MEMOIRS AND BIOGRAPHIES OF AMERICAN STATESMEN AND ADMINISTRATIONS

Acheson, Dean. *Present at the Creation.* New York: Norton, 1969.
Bundy, McGeorge, ed. *The Pattern of Responsibility.* Boston: Houghton Mifflin, 1952.
Byrnes, James F. *Speaking Frankly.* New York: Harper & Brothers, 1947.
Donovan, Robert J. *Eisenhower: The Inside Story.* New York: Harper & Brothers, 1956.
Eisenhower, Dwight D. *Mandate for Change.** New York: New American Library, 1965.
———. *Waging Peace.* New York: Doubleday, 1965.
Ferrell, Robert H. *George C. Marshall.* New York: Cooper Square Publishers, 1966.
Gerson, Louis. *John Foster Dulles.* New York: Cooper Square Publishers, 1967.
Guhin, Michael. *John Foster Dulles.* New York: Columbia University Press, 1972.
Harriman, W. Averell. *Special Envoy to Churchill and Stalin, 1941–1946.* New York: Random House, 1975.
Hoopes, Townsend. *The Devil and John Foster Dulles.** Boston: Atlantic/Little, Brown, 1975.
Johnson, Lyndon B. *The Vantage Point.** New York: Popular Library, 1971.
Kalb, Marvin, and Bernard Kalb. *Kissinger.** Boston: Little, Brown, 1974.
Kearns, Doris. *Lyndon Johnson and the American Dream.** New York: Harper & Row, 1976.
Kennedy, Robert S. *Thirteen Days.** New York: Norton, 1971.
Nixon, Richard. *RN.* New York: Grosset & Dunlap, 1978.
Parmet, Herbert S. *Eisenhower and the American Crusades.* New York: Macmillan, 1972.
Schlesinger, Arthur M., Jr. *A Thousand Days.** New York: Crest Books, 1967.
Smith, Gaddis. *Dean Acheson.* New York: Cooper Square Publishers, 1972.
Sorensen, Theodore C. *Kennedy.** New York: Bantam Books, 1966.
Stoessinger, John. *Henry Kissinger.** New York: Norton, 1976.
Truman, Harry S. *Memoirs,** 2 vols. New York: New American Library, 1965.

index